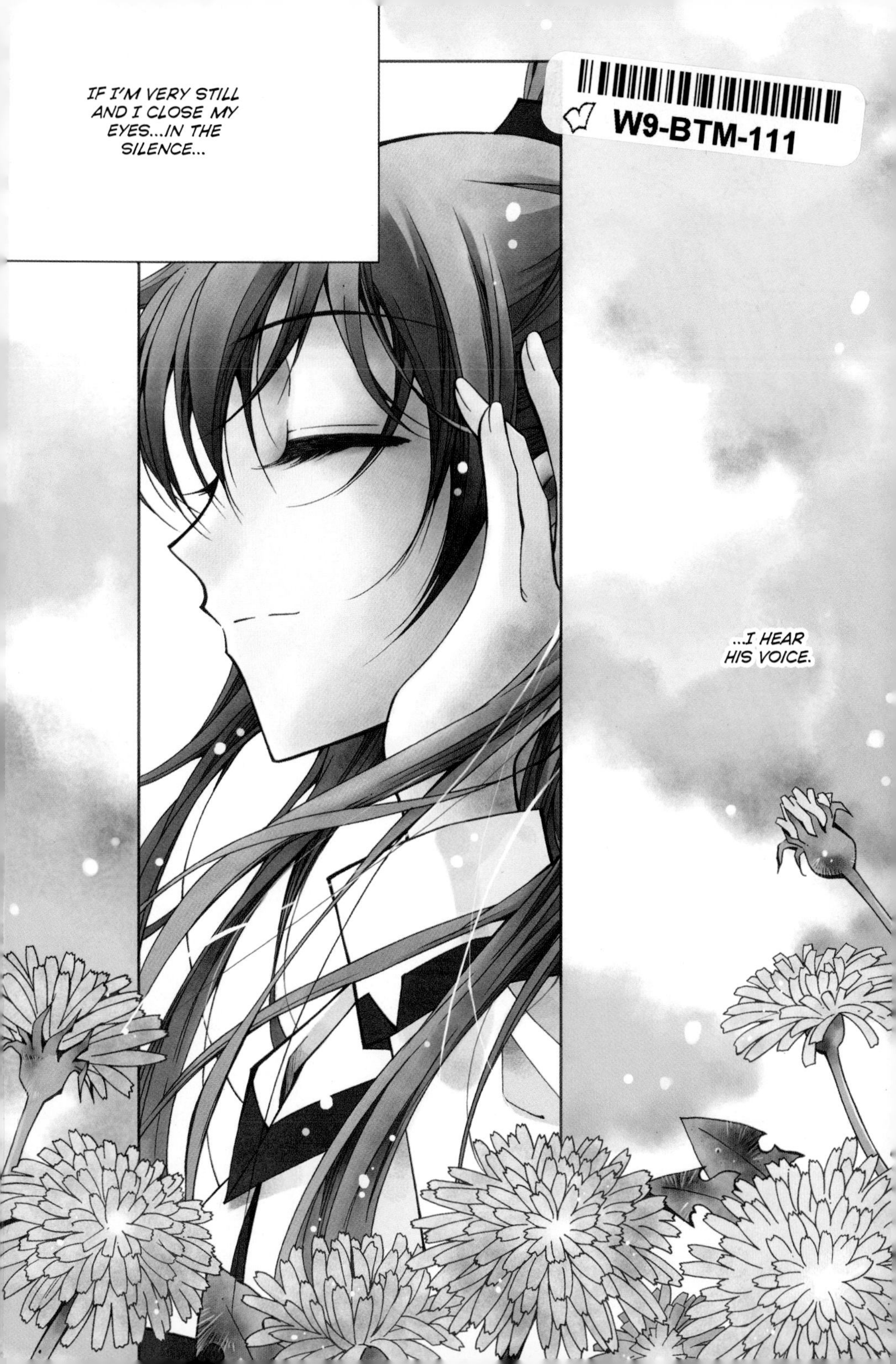
IF I'M VERY STILL AND I CLOSE MY EYES...IN THE SILENCE...
...I HEAR HIS VOICE.

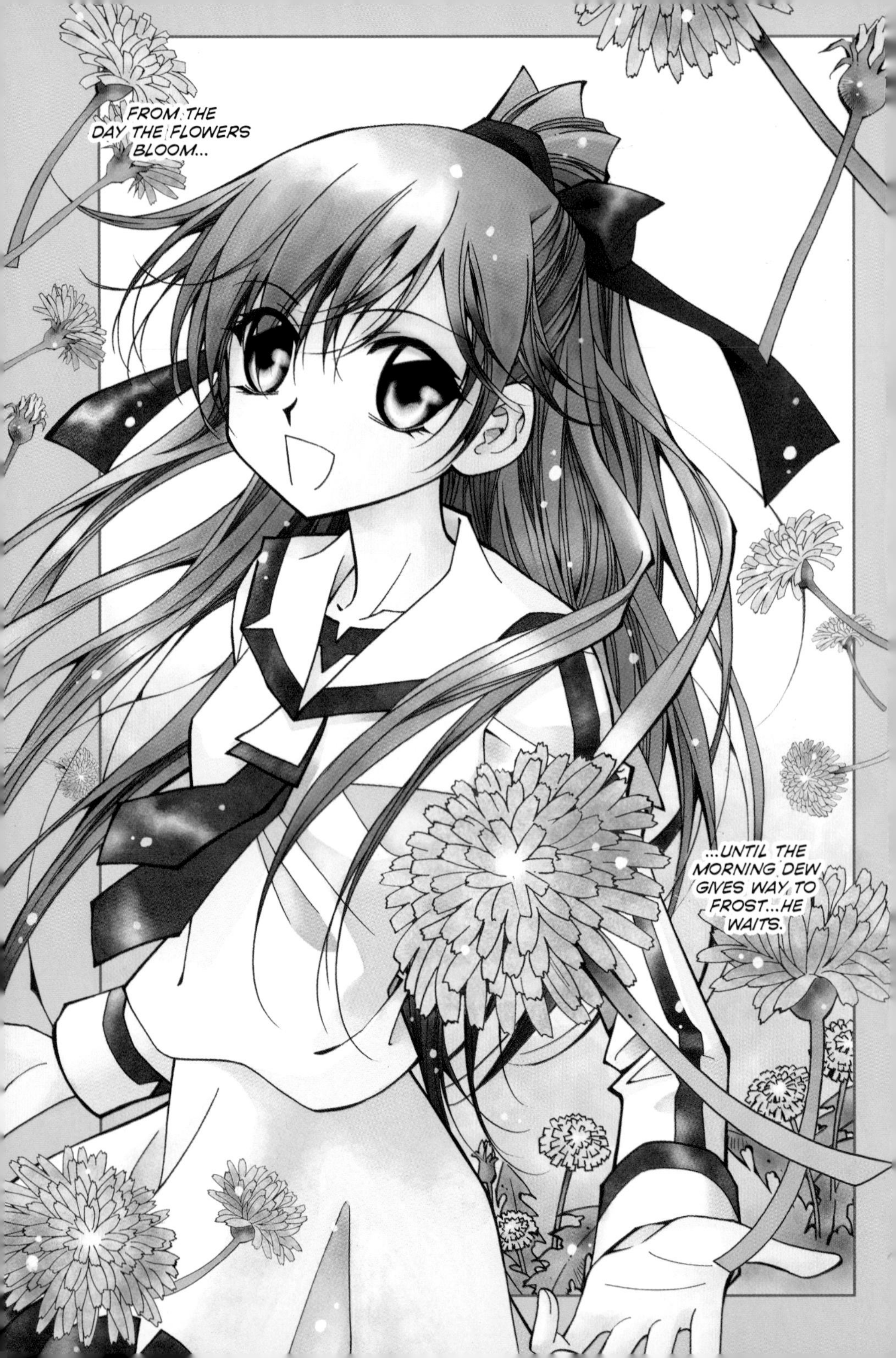
FROM THE DAY THE FLOWERS BLOOM...
...UNTIL THE MORNING DEW GIVES WAY TO FROST...HE WAITS.

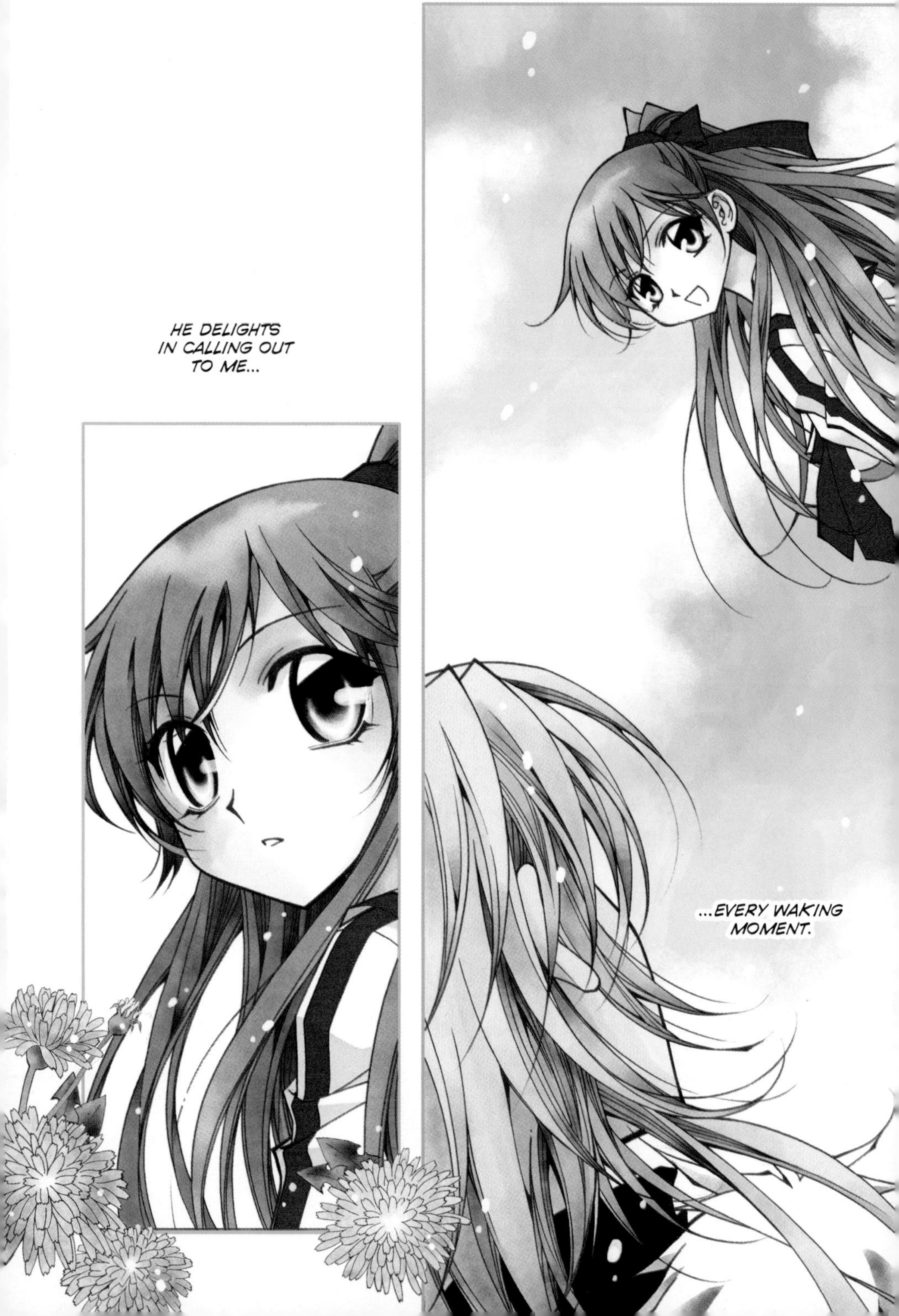
HE DELIGHTS IN CALLING OUT TO ME...
...EVERY WAKING MOMENT.

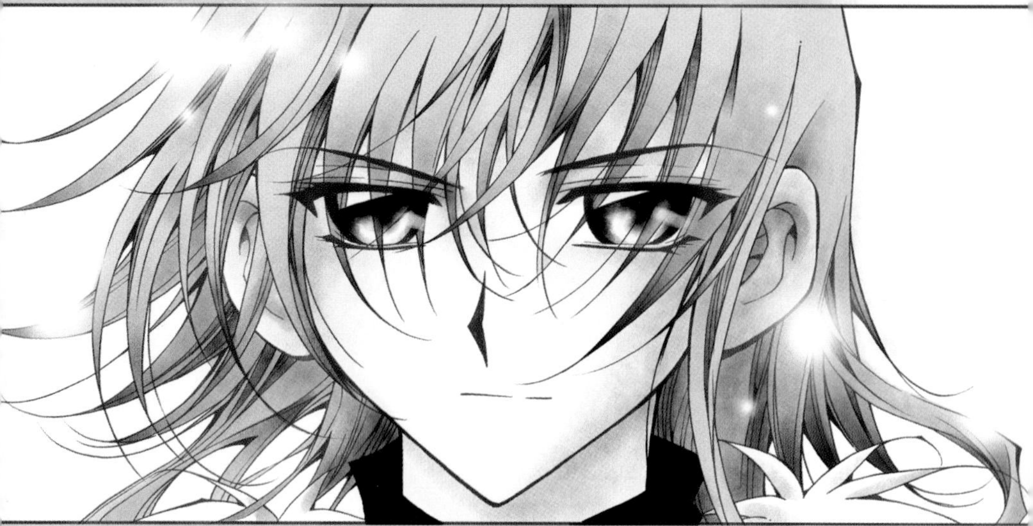

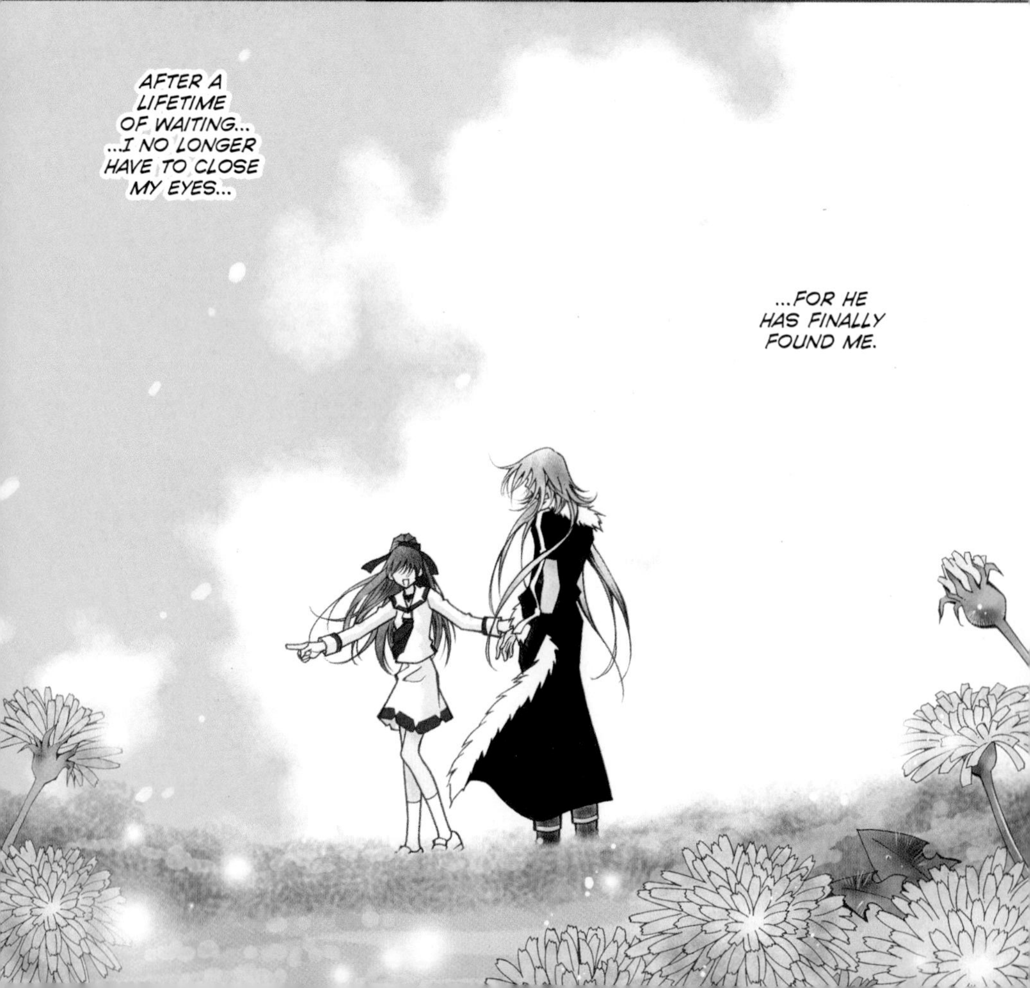
AFTER A LIFETIME OF WAITING...
...I NO LONGER HAVE TO CLOSE MY EYES...
...FOR HE HAS FINALLY FOUND ME.

Vol. 2

Kara · Woo SooJung

Yen
Press

CONTENTS

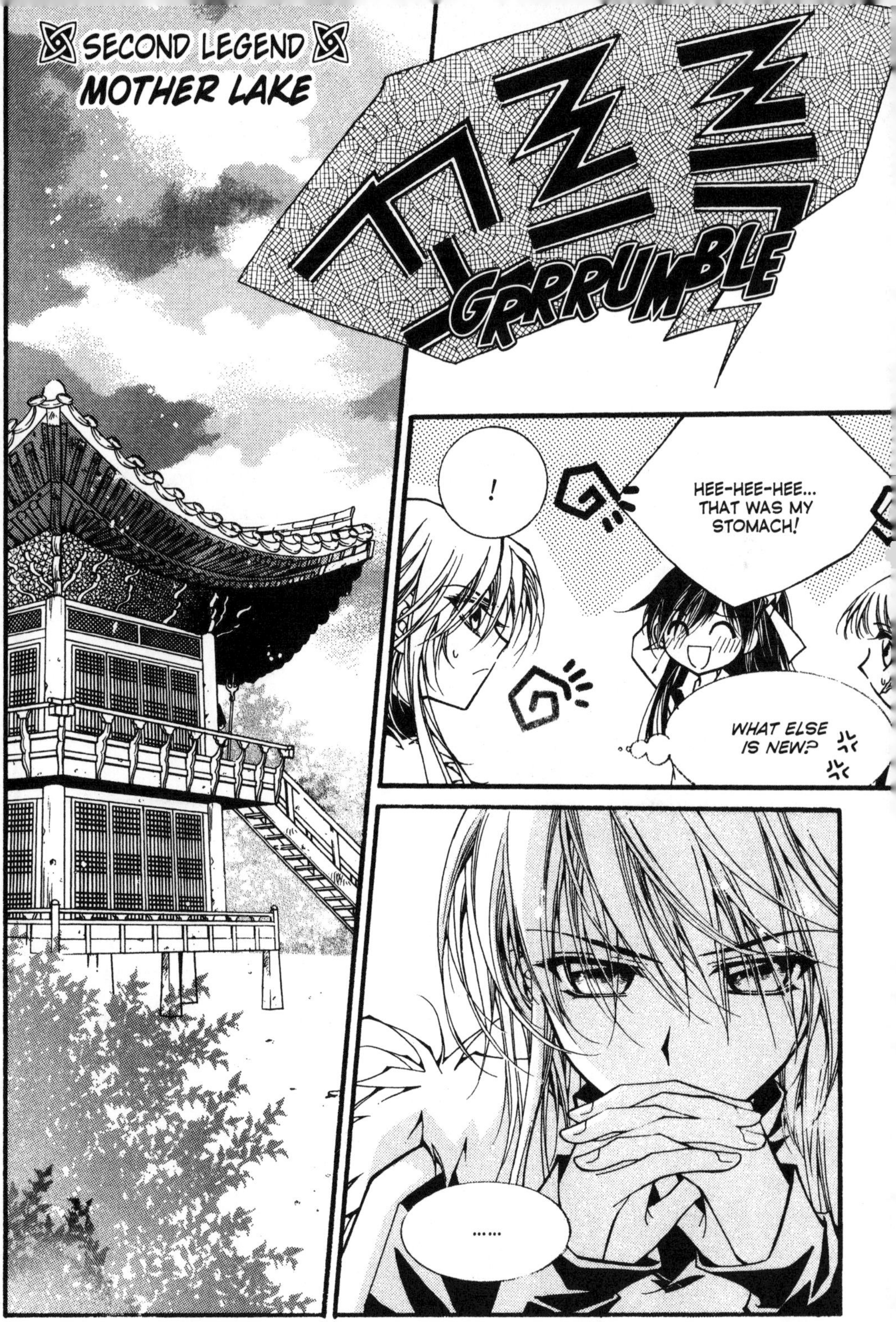
SECOND LEGEND
MOTHER LAKE
GRRRUMBLE
!
HEE-HEE-HEE... THAT WAS MY STOMACH!
WHAT ELSE IS NEW?
......

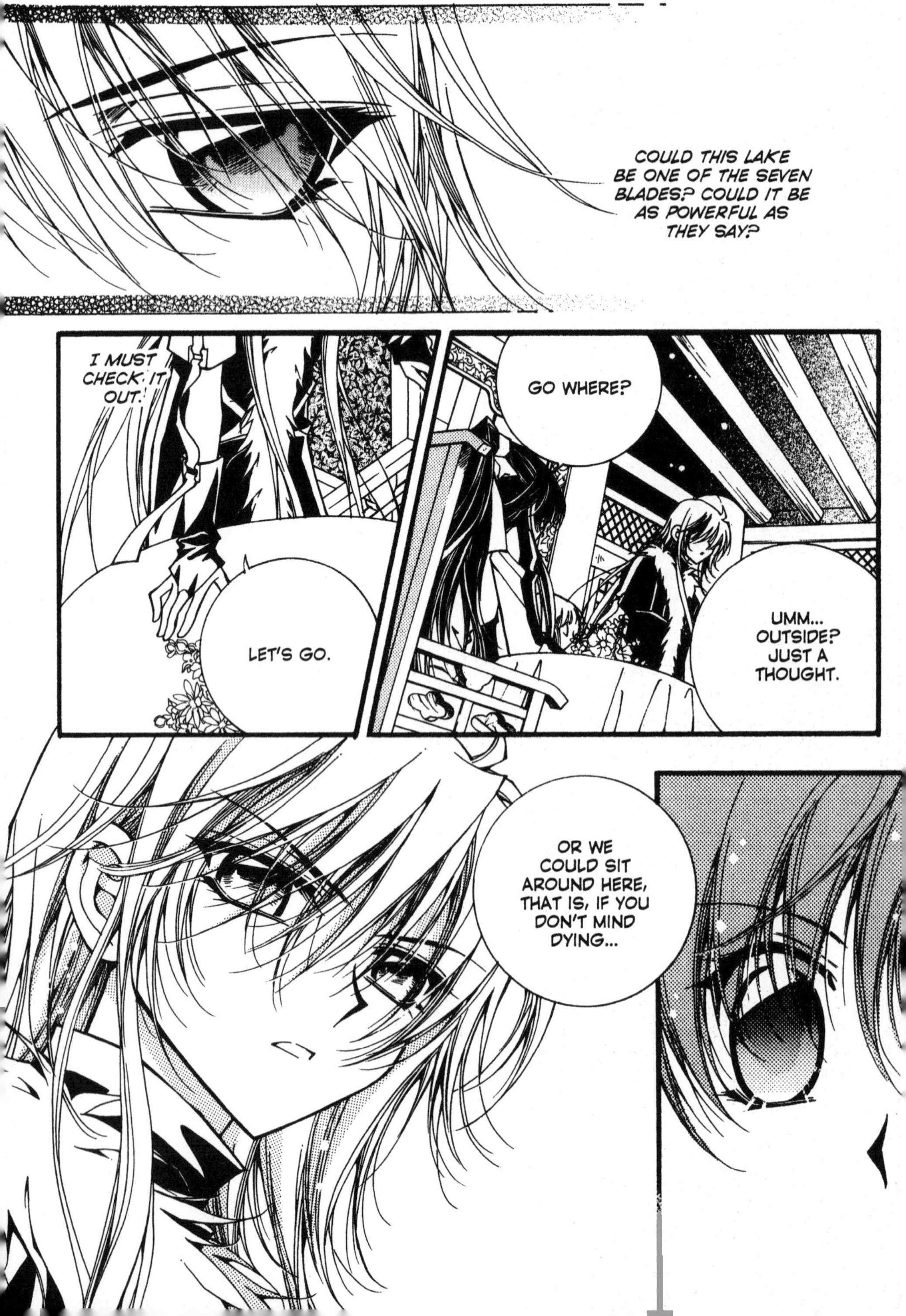
COULD THIS LAKE BE ONE OF THE SEVEN BLADES? COULD IT BE AS POWERFUL AS THEY SAY?
I MUST CHECK IT OUT.
LET'S GO.
GO WHERE?
UMM... OUTSIDE? JUST A THOUGHT.
OR WE COULD SIT AROUND HERE, THAT IS, IF YOU DON'T MIND DYING...

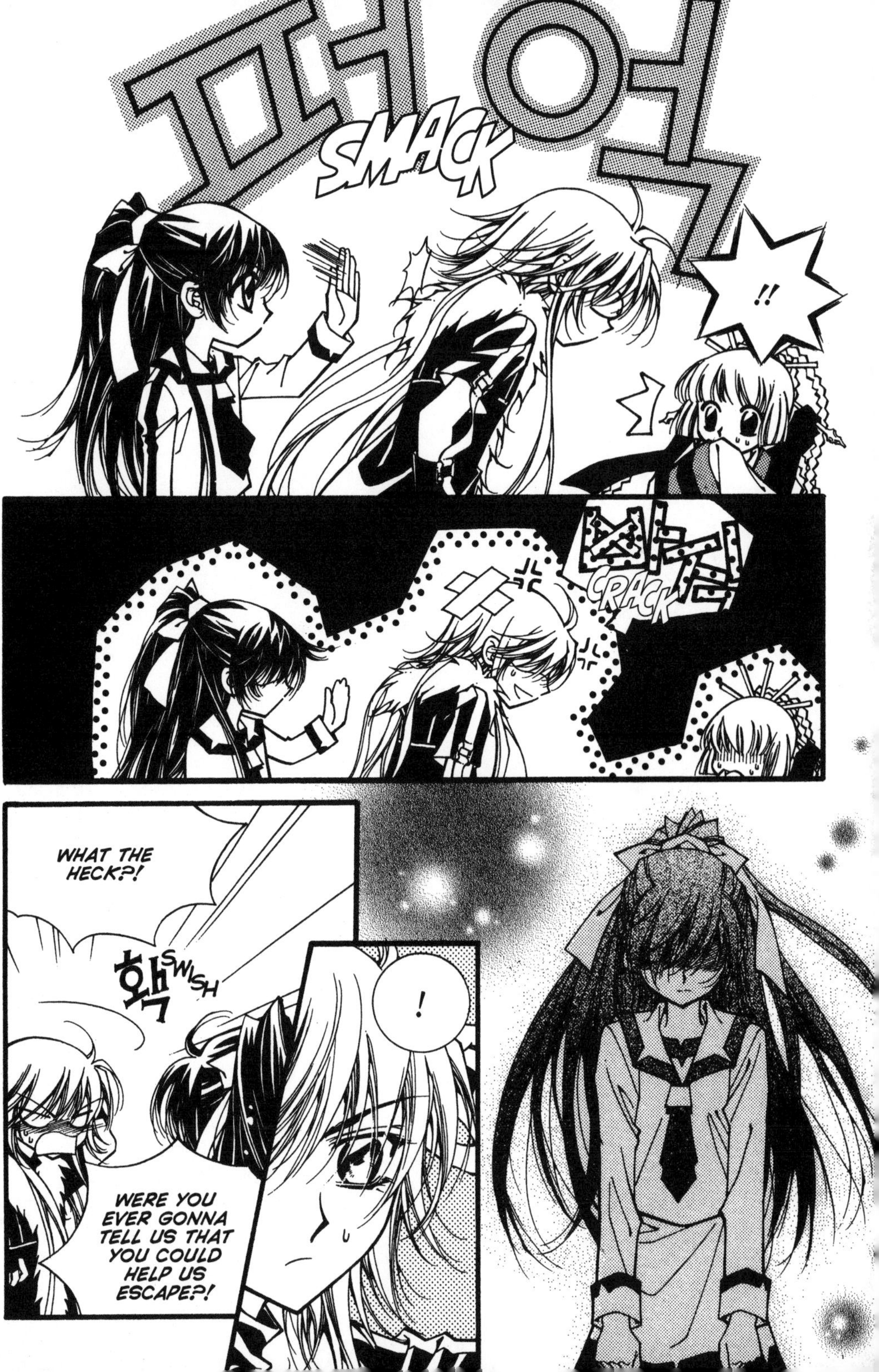
SMACK
!!
CRACK
WHAT THE HECK?!
SWISH
!
WERE YOU EVER GONNA TELL US THAT YOU COULD HELP US ESCAPE?!

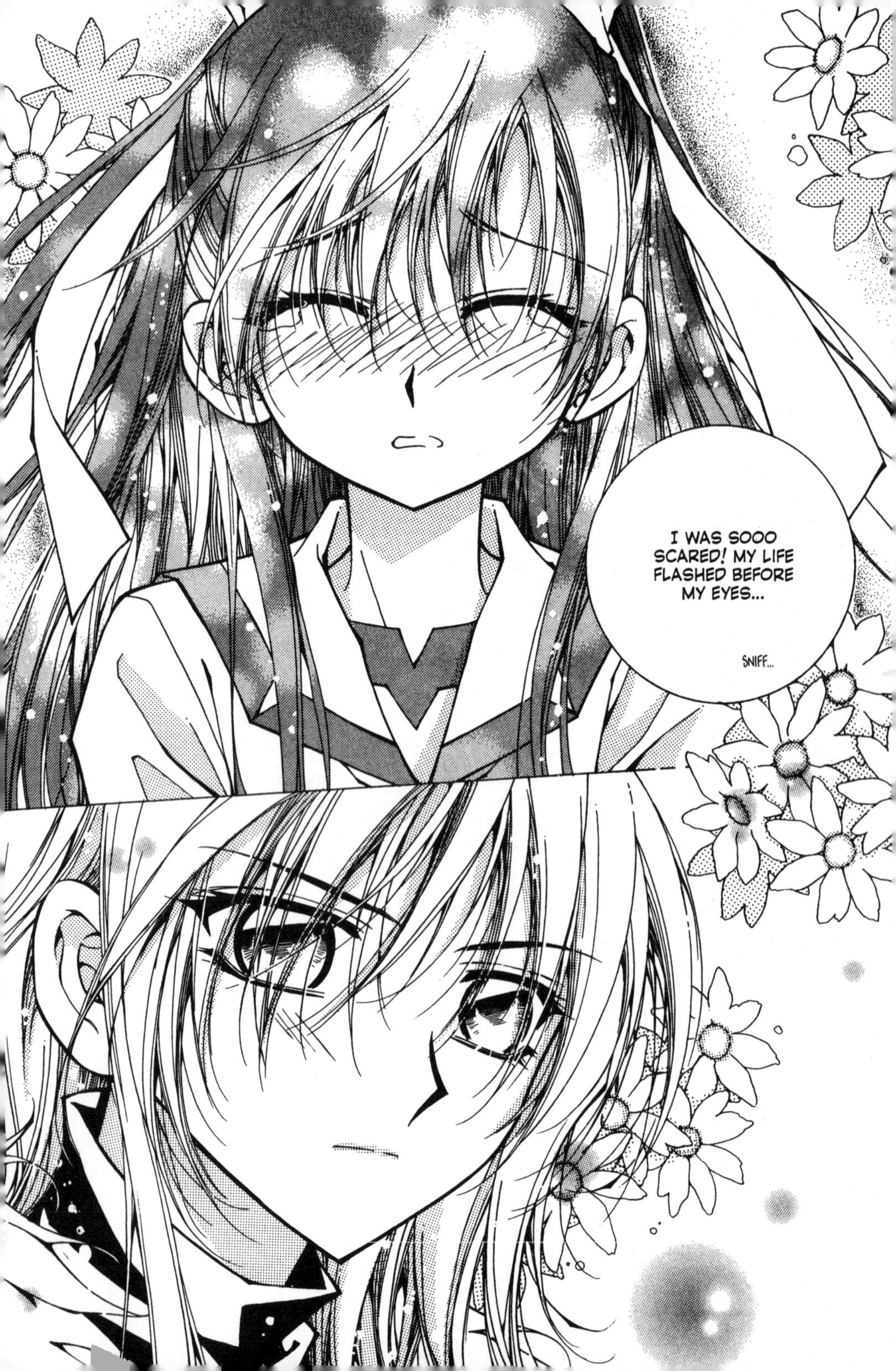
I WAS SOOO SCARED! MY LIFE FLASHED BEFORE MY EYES...
SNIFF...

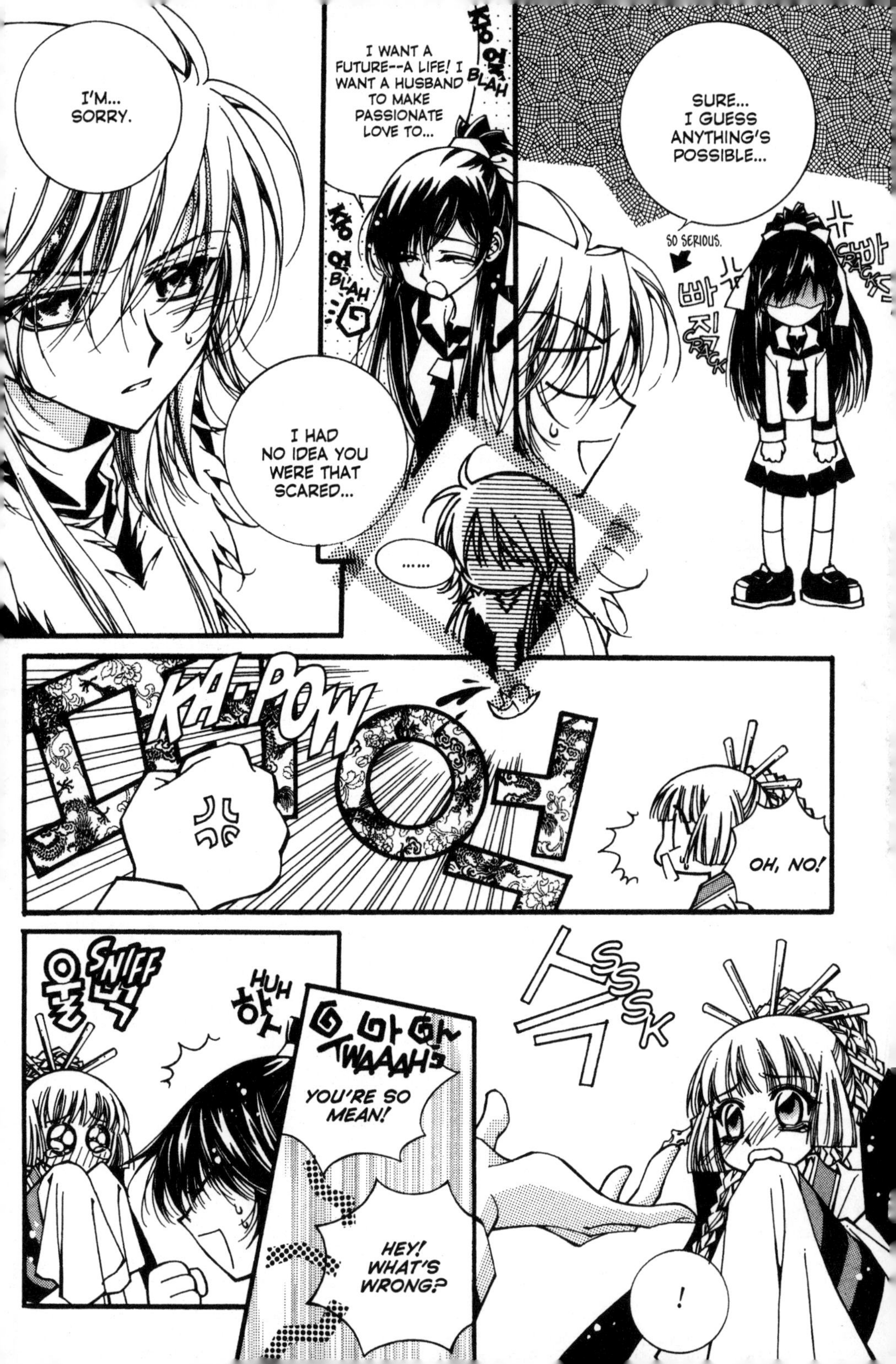

I'M... SORRY.
I WANT A FUTURE--A LIFE! I WANT A HUSBAND TO MAKE PASSIONATE LOVE TO...
BLAH
BLAH
I HAD NO IDEA YOU WERE THAT SCARED...
......
SURE... I GUESS ANYTHING'S POSSIBLE...
SO SERIOUS.
빠직
CRACK
CRACK
KA-POW
OH, NO!
SNIFF
HUH
WAAAH
YOU'RE SO MEAN!
HEY! WHAT'S WRONG?
SSSK
!

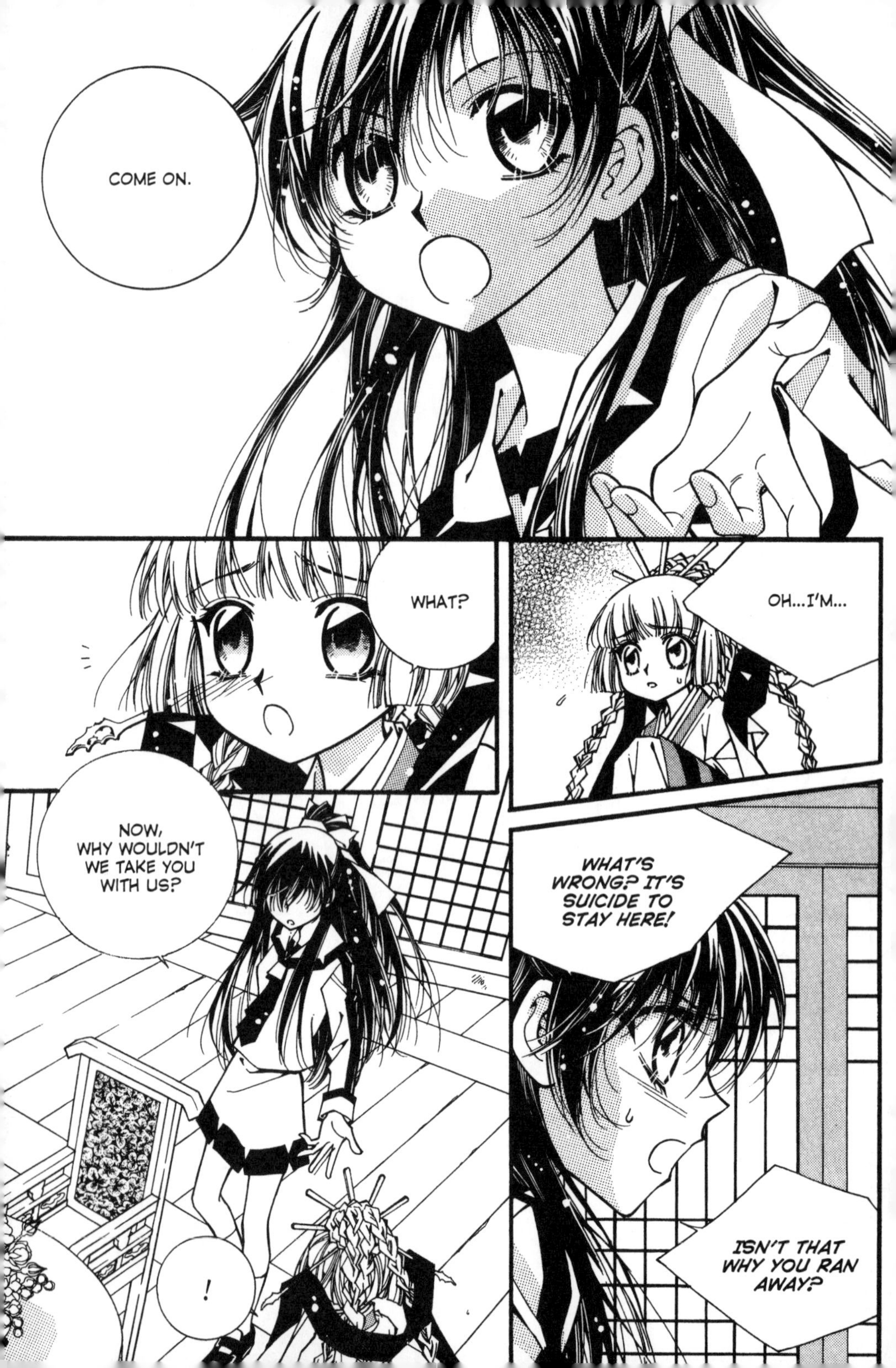
COME ON.
WHAT?
OH...I'M...
NOW, WHY WOULDN'T WE TAKE YOU WITH US?
!
WHAT'S WRONG? IT'S SUICIDE TO STAY HERE!
ISN'T THAT WHY YOU RAN AWAY?

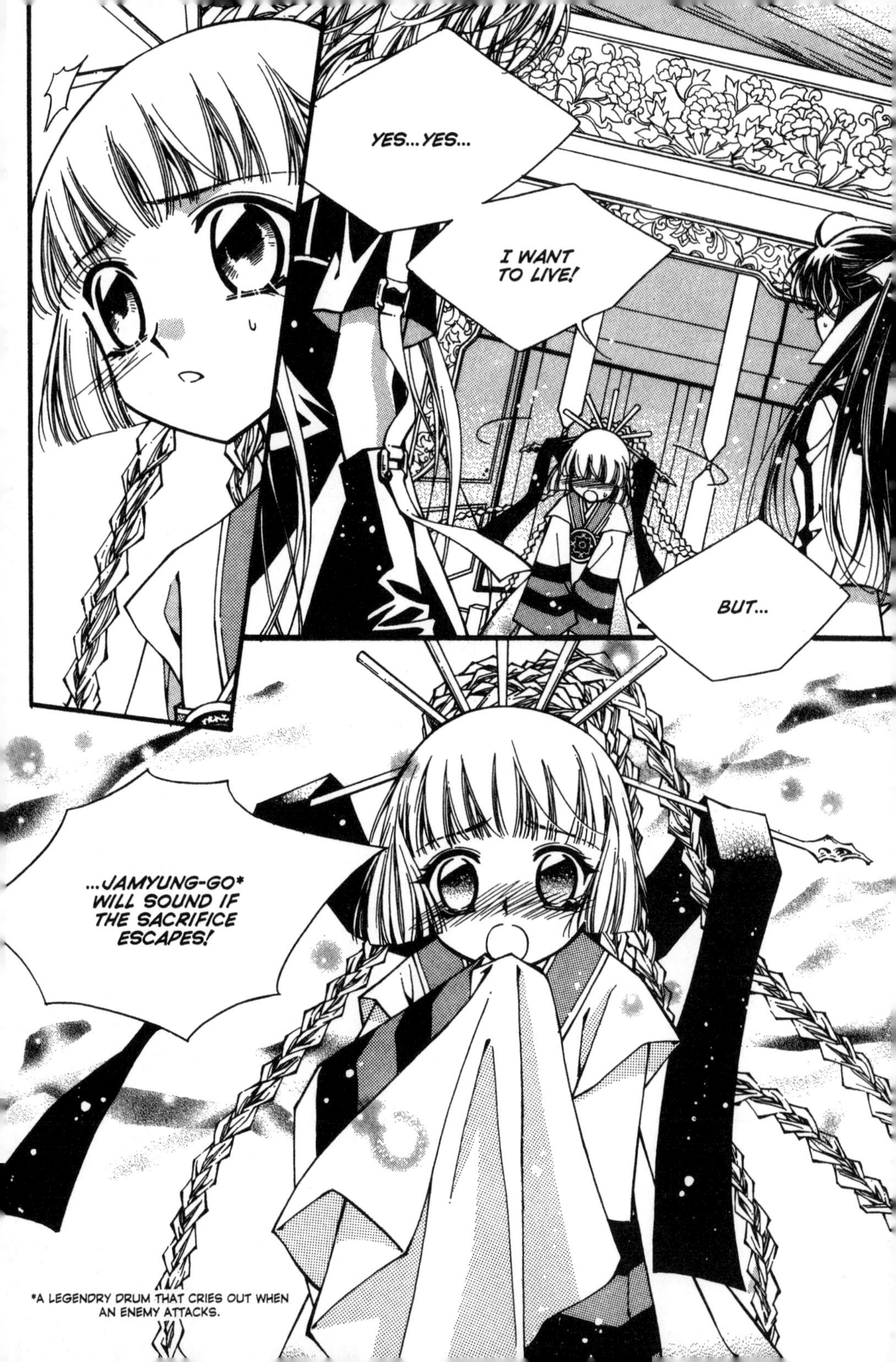
YES...YES...
I WANT TO LIVE!
BUT...
...JAMYUNG-GO* WILL SOUND IF THE SACRIFICE ESCAPES!
*A LEGENDRY DRUM THAT CRIES OUT WHEN AN ENEMY ATTACKS.

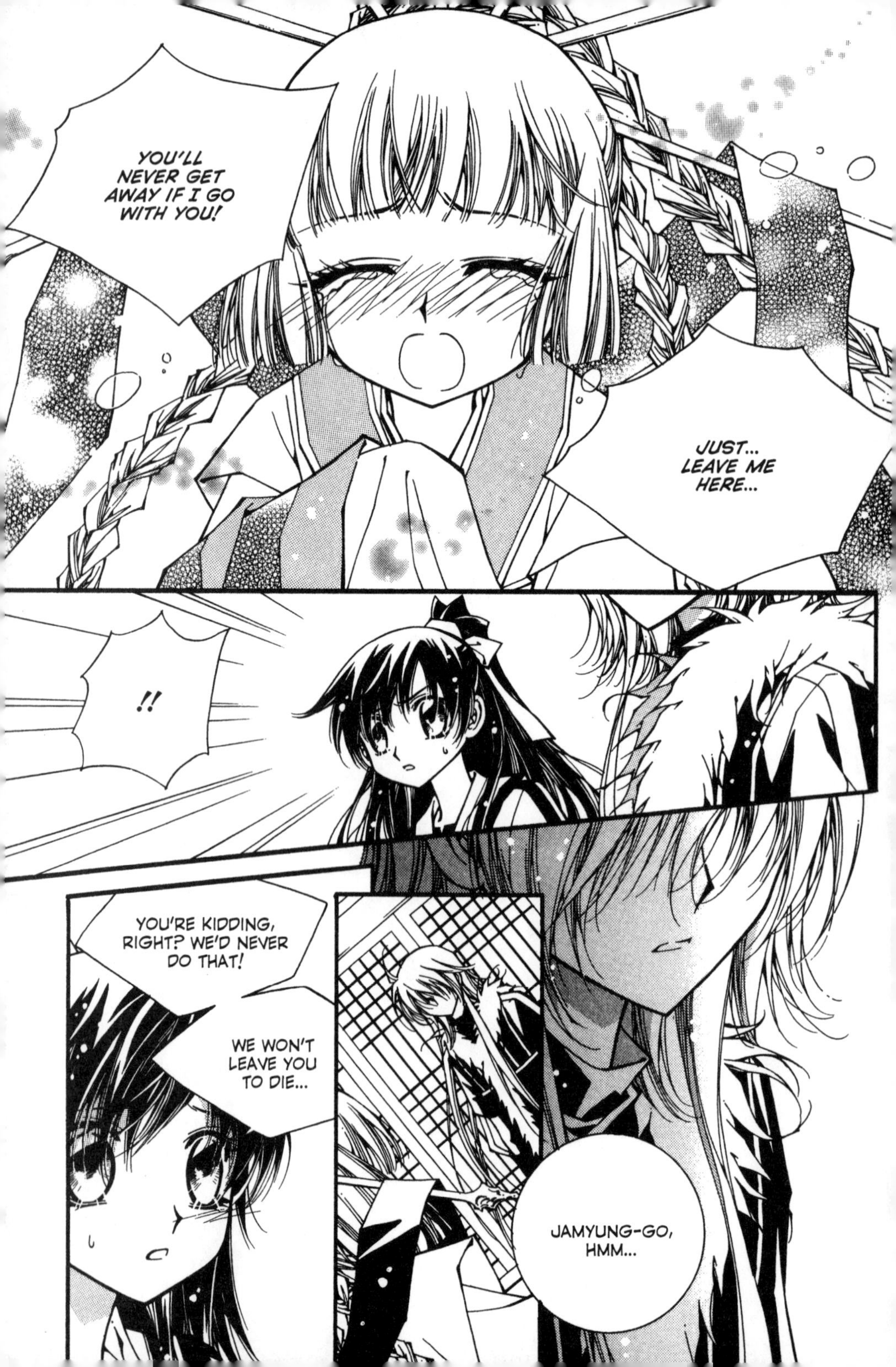
YOU'LL NEVER GET AWAY IF I GO WITH YOU!
JUST... LEAVE ME HERE...
!!
YOU'RE KIDDING, RIGHT? WE'D NEVER DO THAT!
WE WON'T LEAVE YOU TO DIE...
JAMYUNG-GO, HMM...

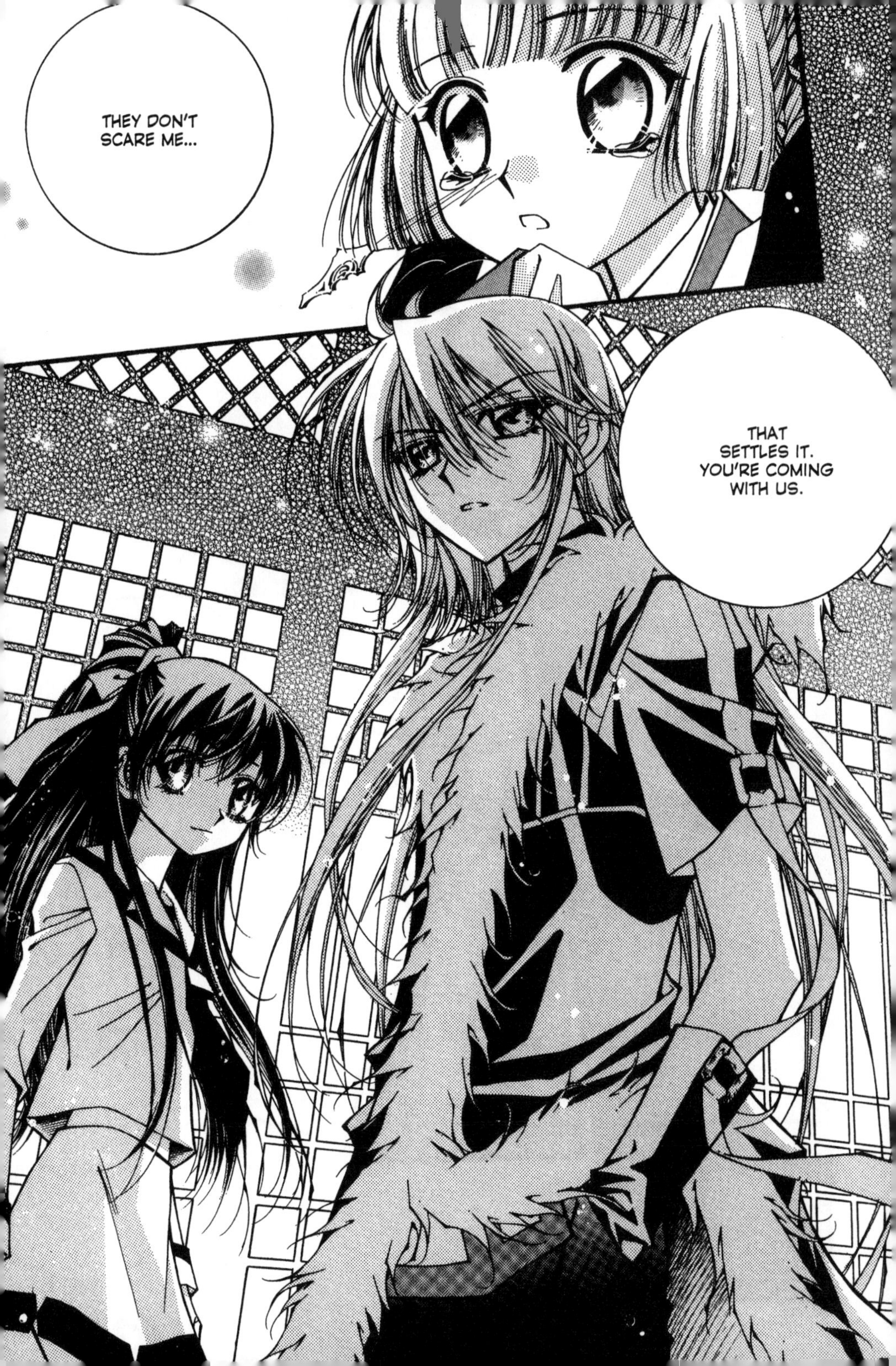
THEY DON'T SCARE ME...
THAT SETTLES IT. YOU'RE COMING WITH US.

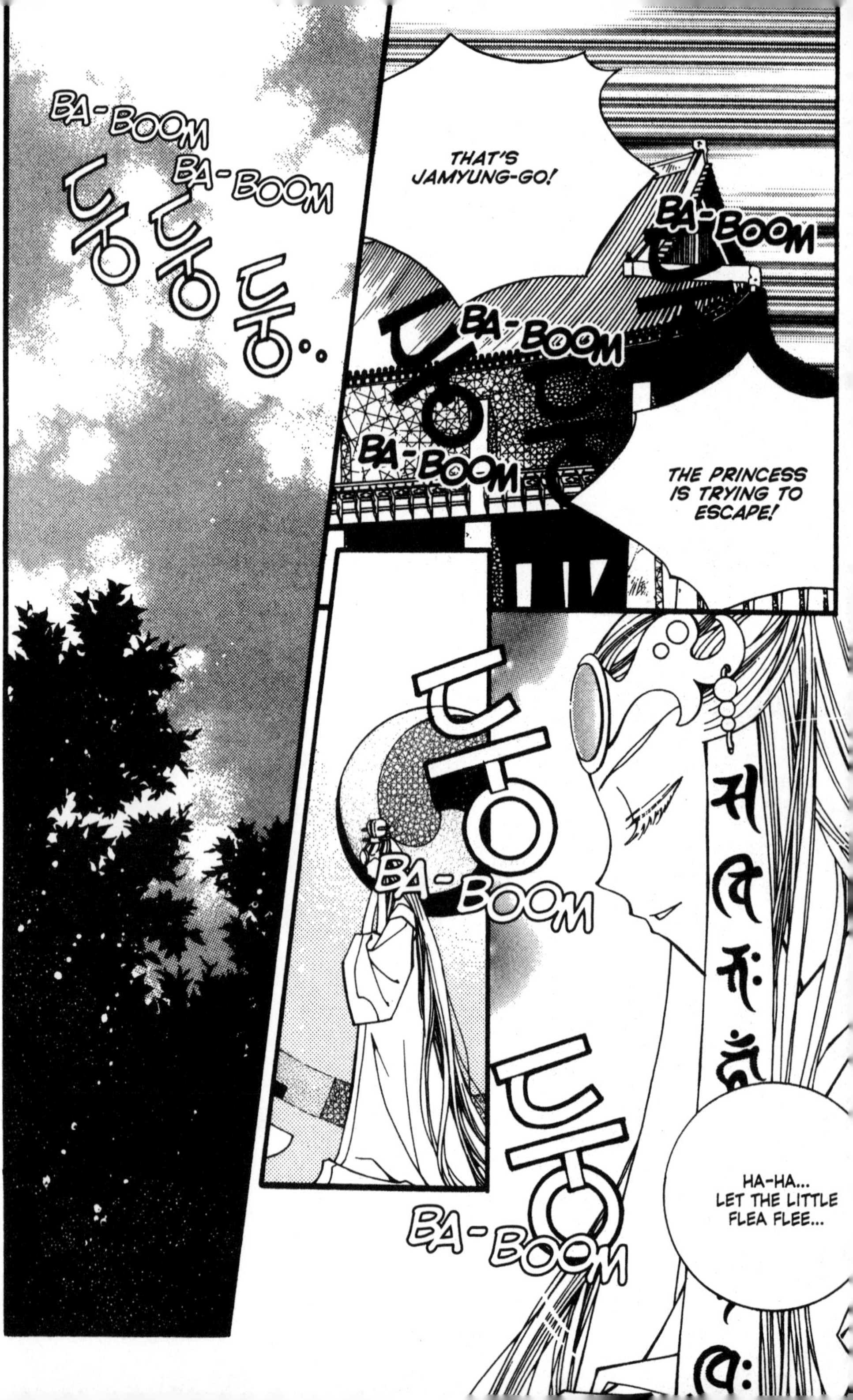
BA-BOOM
BA-BOOM
둥둥둥..
THAT'S JAMYUNG-GO!
BA-BOOM
BA-BOOM
BA-BOOM
THE PRINCESS IS TRYING TO ESCAPE!
BA-BOOM
BA-BOOM
HA-HA... LET THE LITTLE FLEA FLEE...

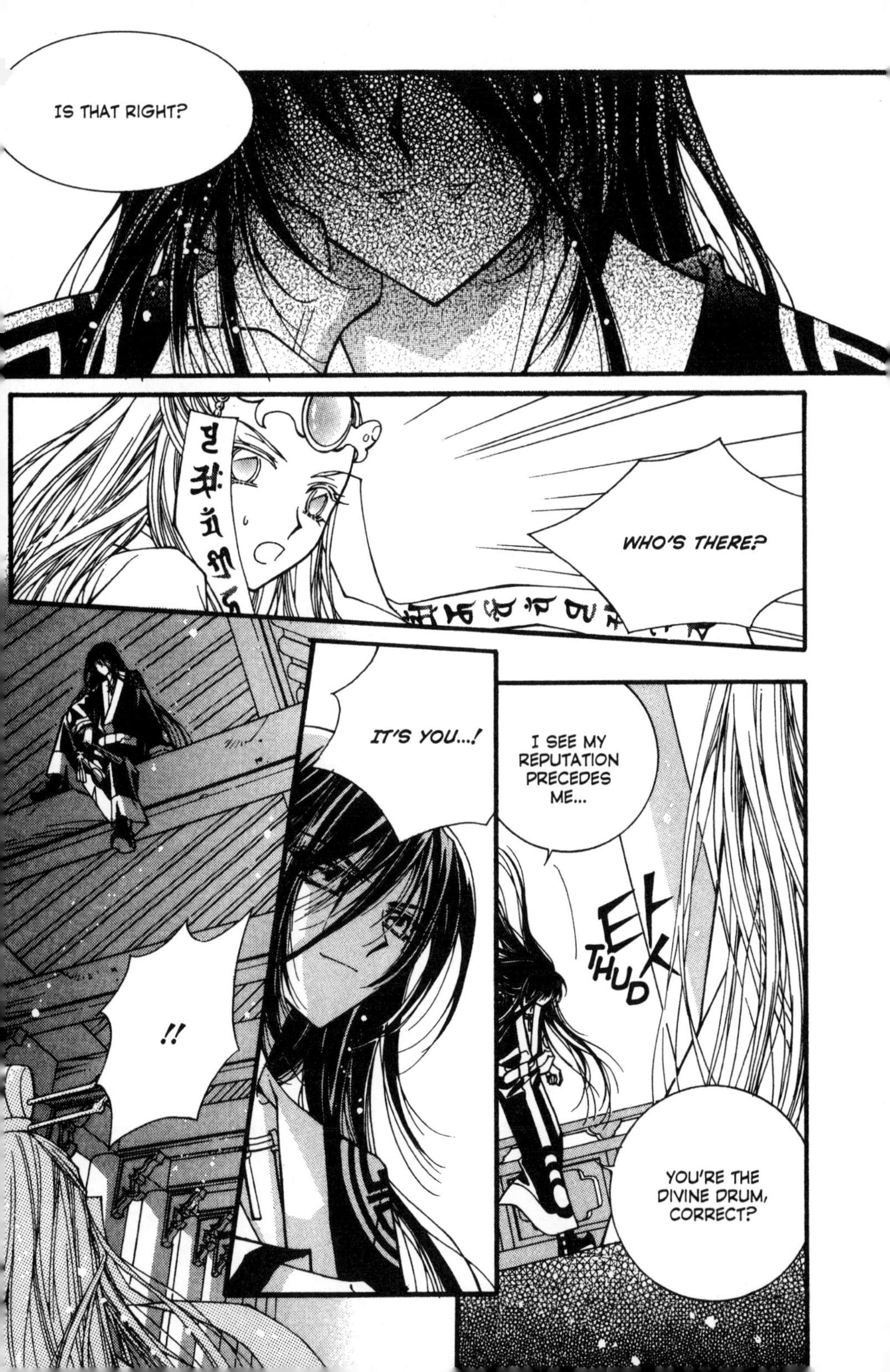
IS THAT RIGHT?
WHO'S THERE?
!!
IT'S YOU...!
I SEE MY REPUTATION PRECEDES ME...
THUD
YOU'RE THE DIVINE DRUM, CORRECT?

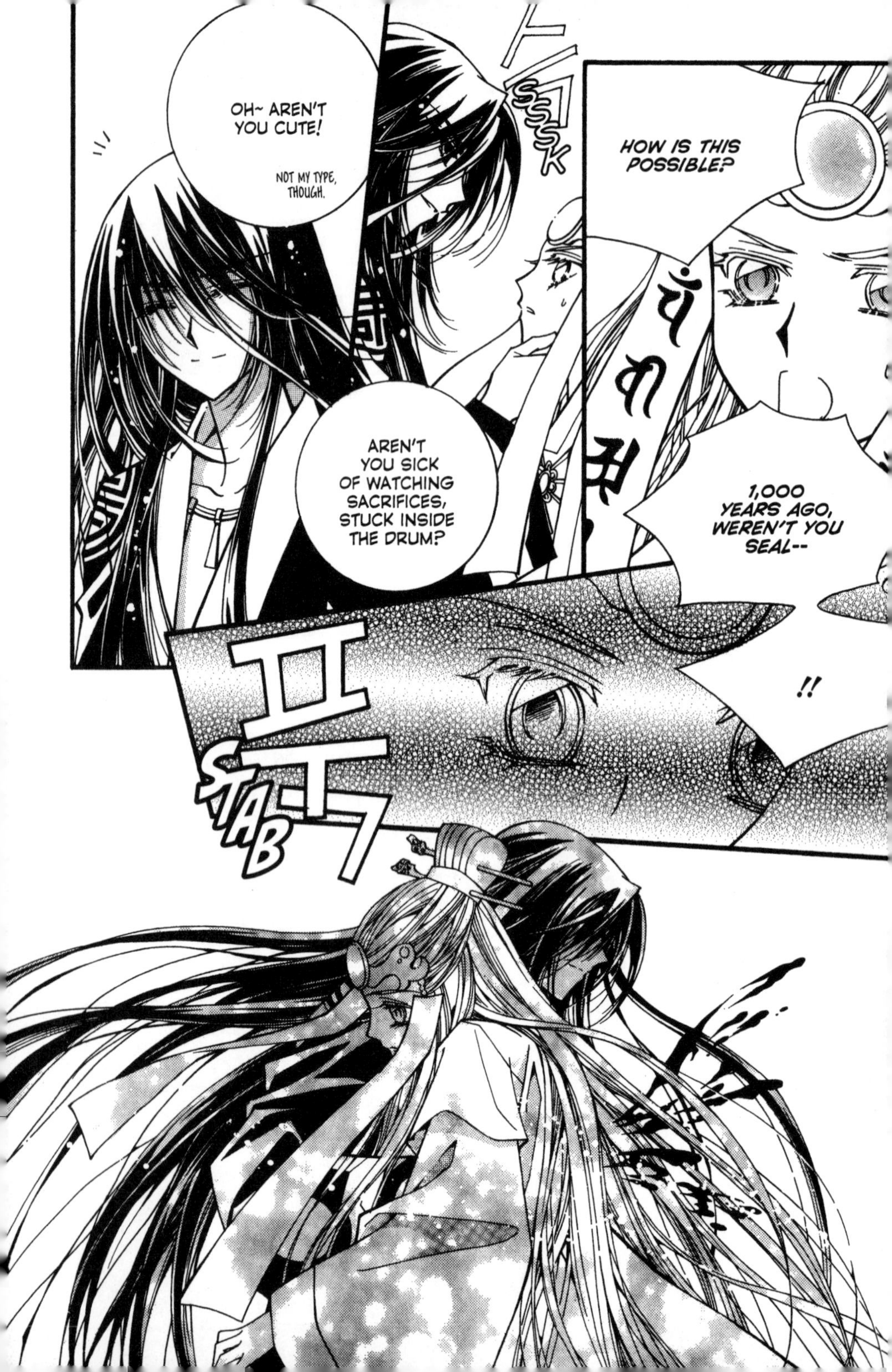
OH~ AREN'T YOU CUTE!
NOT MY TYPE, THOUGH.
SSSK
AREN'T YOU SICK OF WATCHING SACRIFICES, STUCK INSIDE THE DRUM?
HOW IS THIS POSSIBLE?
1,000 YEARS AGO, WEREN'T YOU SEAL--
!!
STAB

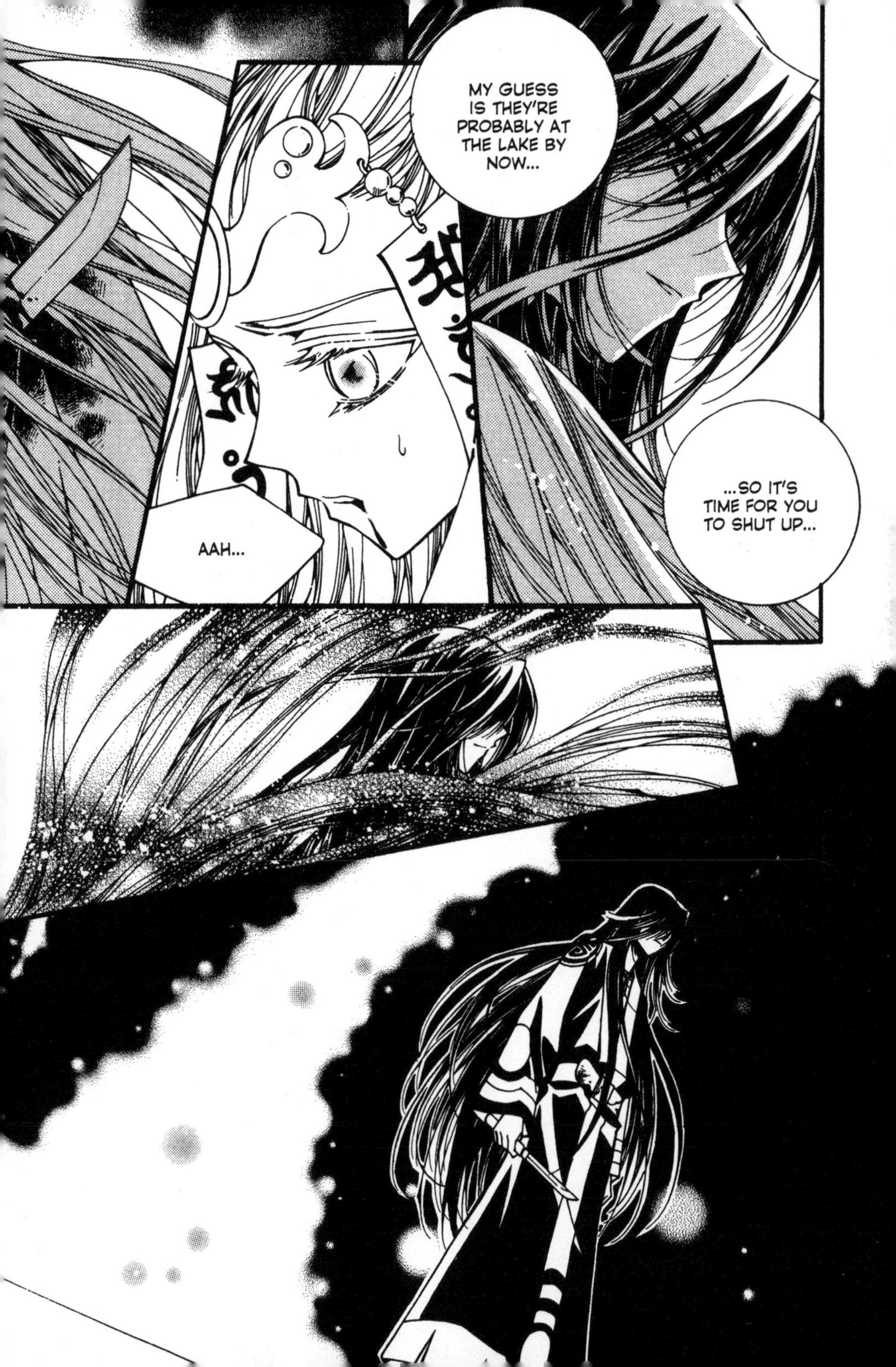
MY GUESS IS THEY'RE PROBABLY AT THE LAKE BY NOW...
AAH...
...SO IT'S TIME FOR YOU TO SHUT UP...

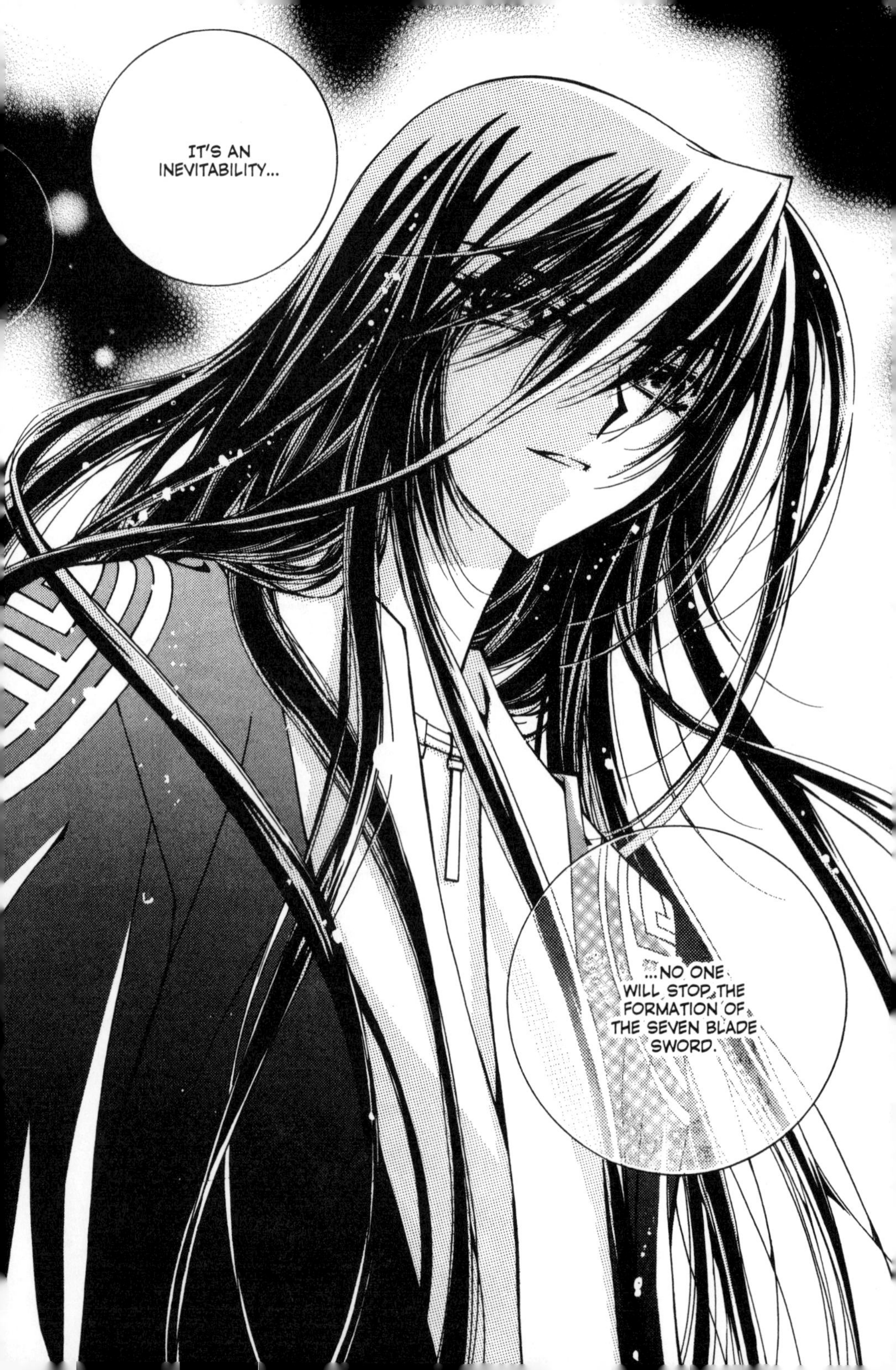
IT'S AN INEVITABILITY...
...NO ONE WILL STOP THE FORMATION OF THE SEVEN BLADE SWORD.

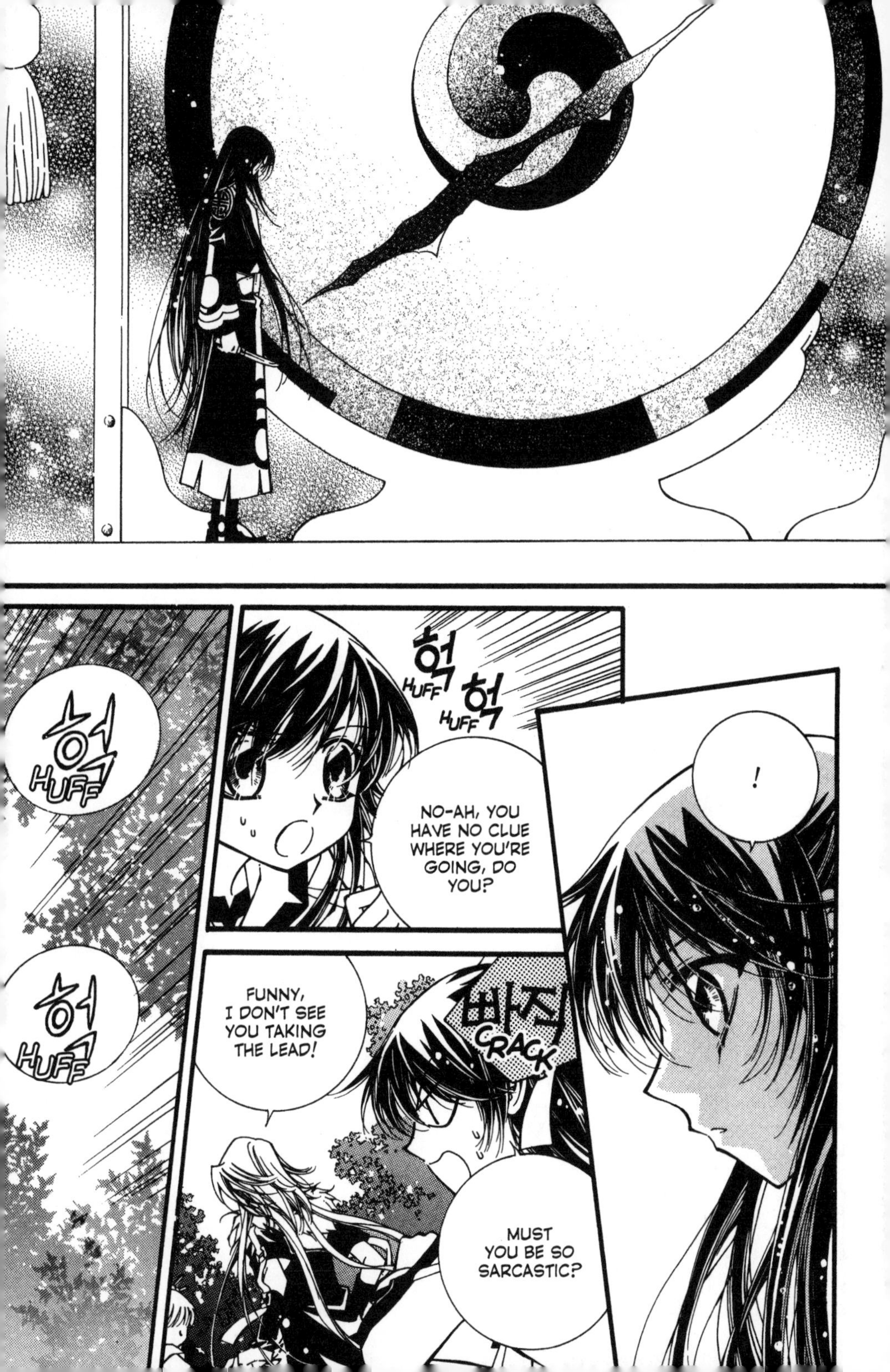

헉
HUFF
헉
HUFF
헉
HUFF
헉
HUFF
NO-AH, YOU HAVE NO CLUE WHERE YOU'RE GOING, DO YOU?
FUNNY, I DON'T SEE YOU TAKING THE LEAD!
빠직
CRACK
MUST YOU BE SO SARCASTIC?
!

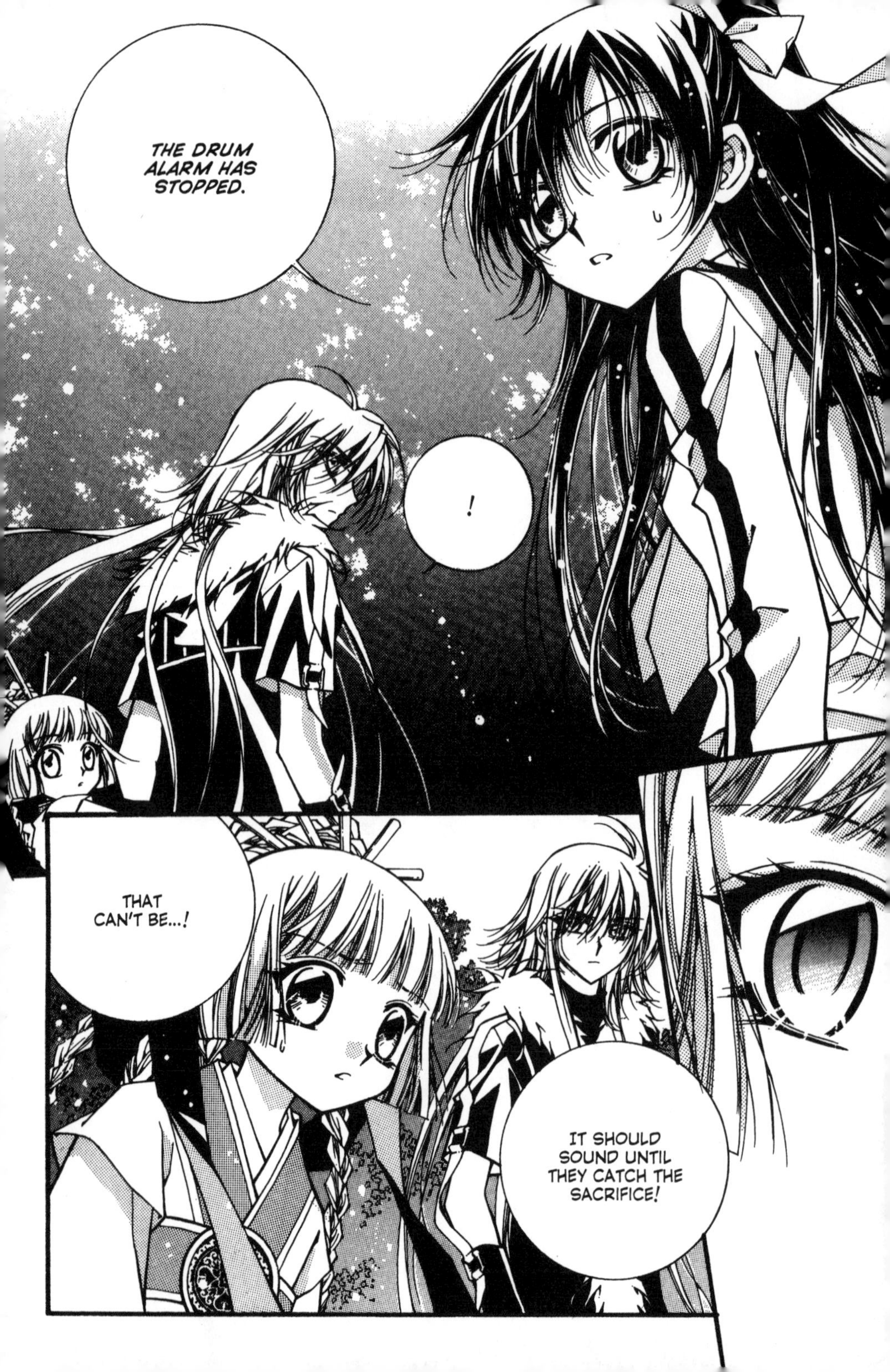
THE DRUM ALARM HAS STOPPED.
!
THAT CAN'T BE...!
IT SHOULD SOUND UNTIL THEY CATCH THE SACRIFICE!

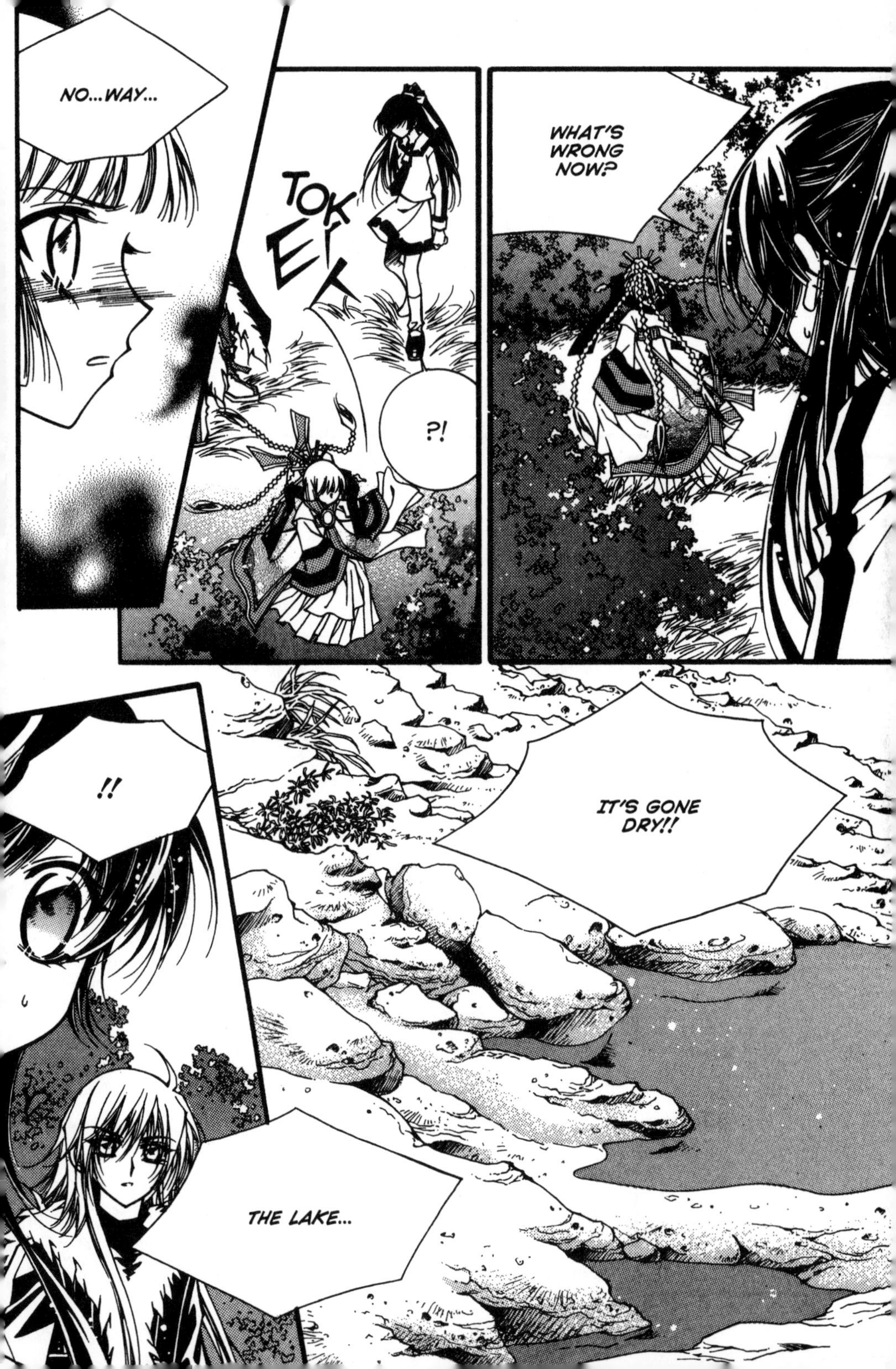
NO...WAY...
TOK
TOK
?!
WHAT'S WRONG NOW?
!!
IT'S GONE DRY!!
THE LAKE...

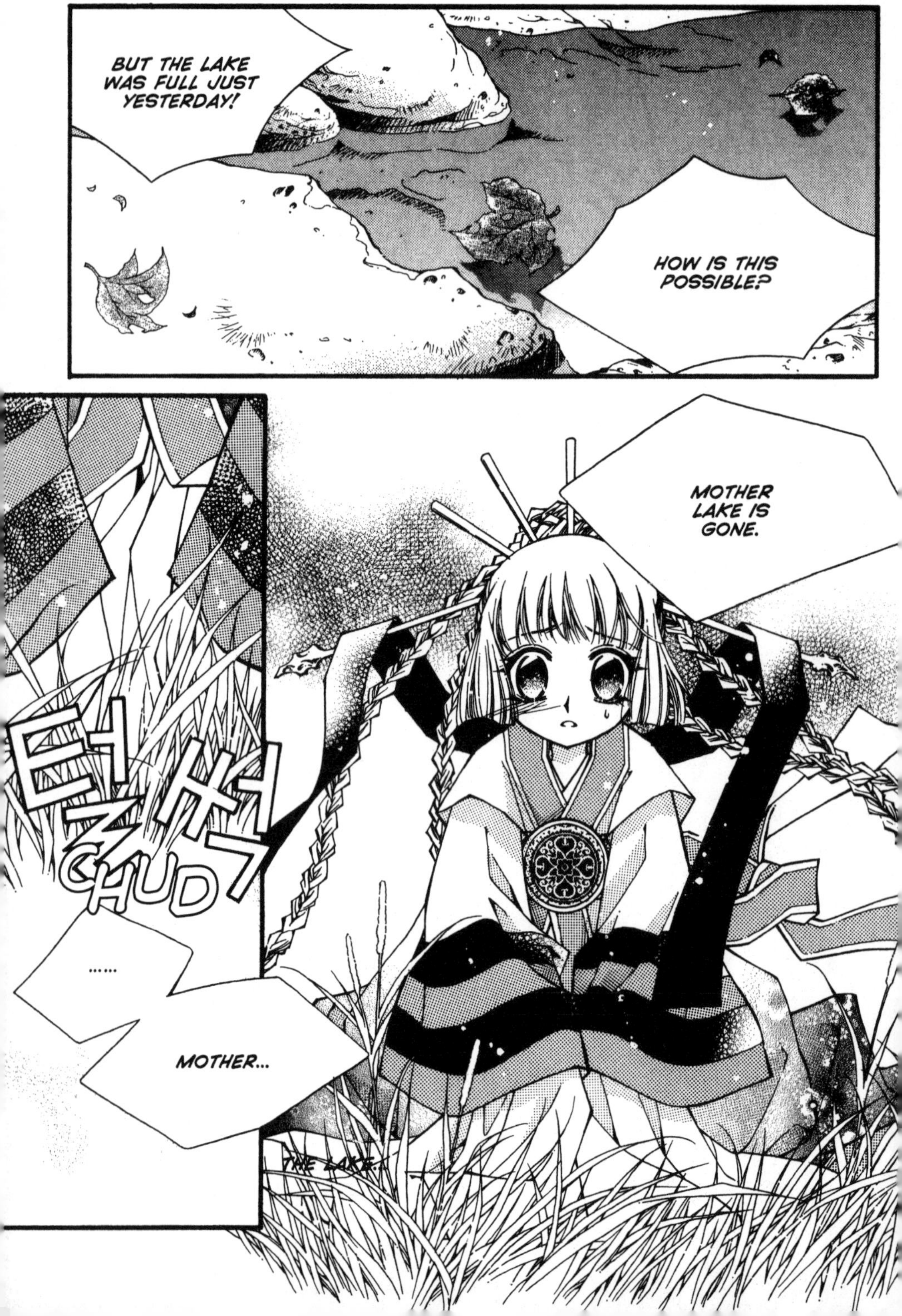
BUT THE LAKE WAS FULL JUST YESTERDAY!
HOW IS THIS POSSIBLE?
CHUD
......
MOTHER...
MOTHER LAKE IS GONE.
THE LAKE...

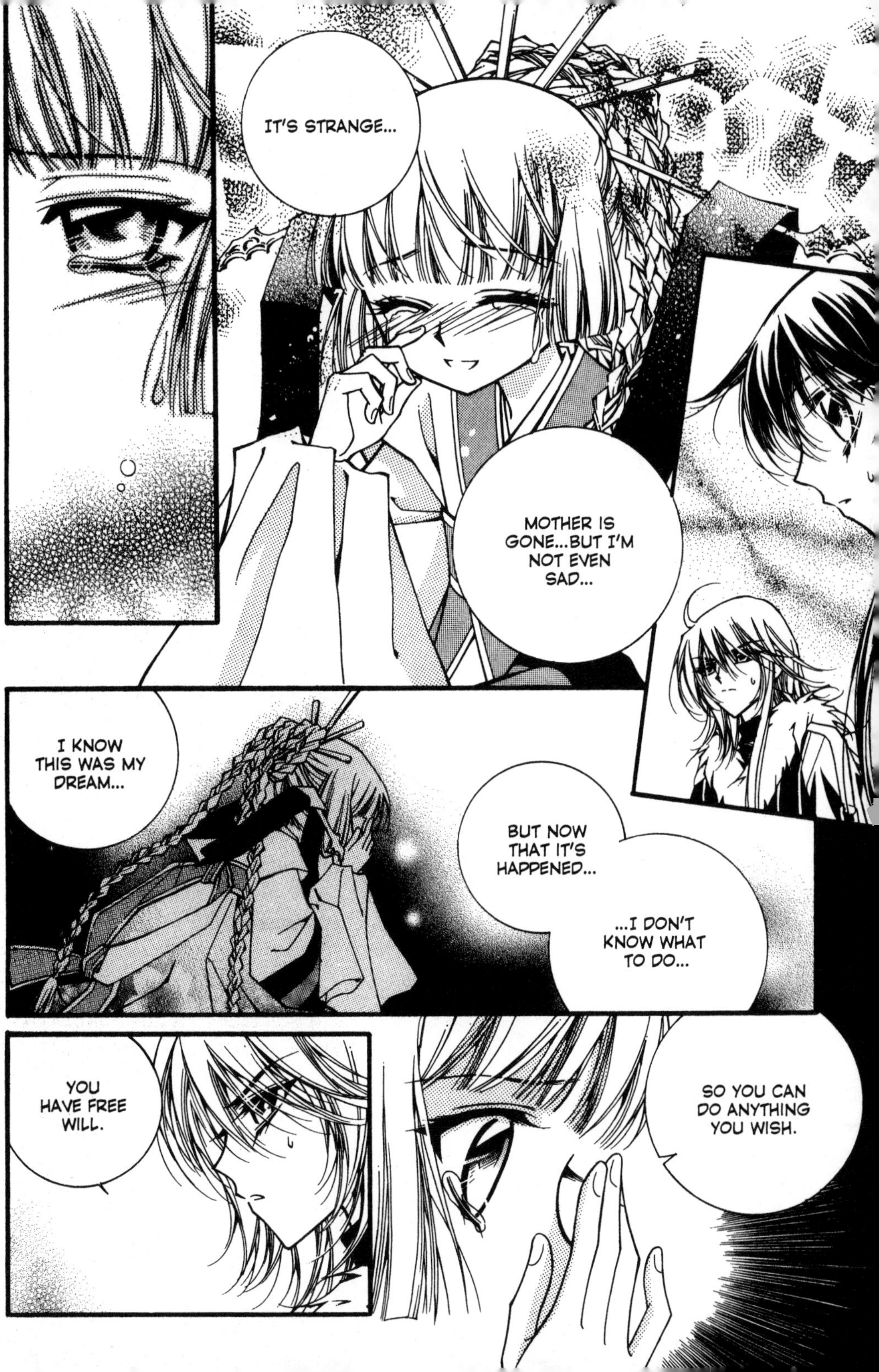
IT'S STRANGE...
MOTHER IS GONE...BUT I'M NOT EVEN SAD...
I KNOW THIS WAS MY DREAM...
BUT NOW THAT IT'S HAPPENED...
...I DON'T KNOW WHAT TO DO...
YOU HAVE FREE WILL.
SO YOU CAN DO ANYTHING YOU WISH.

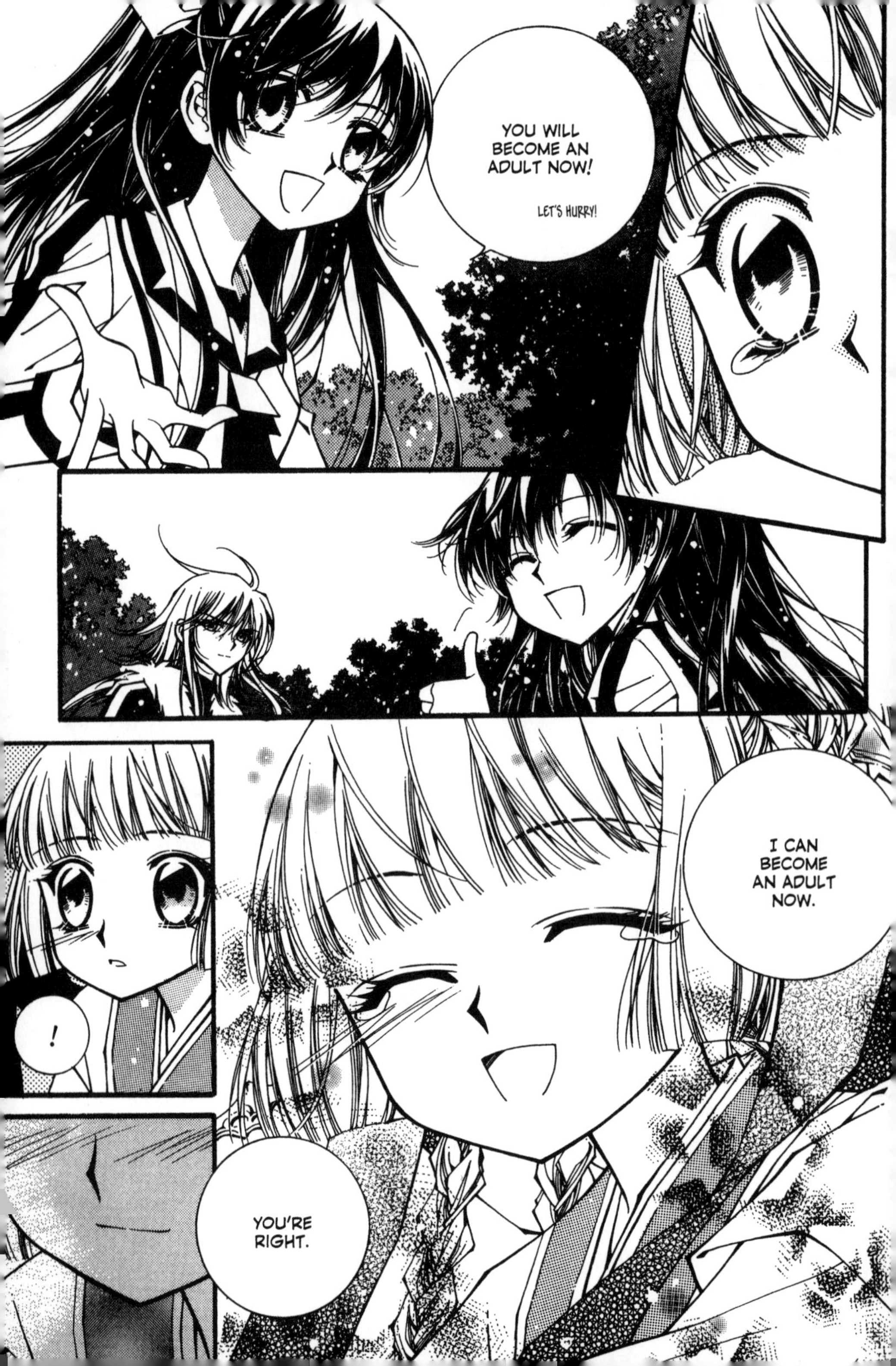
YOU WILL BECOME AN ADULT NOW!
LET'S HURRY!
!
YOU'RE RIGHT.
I CAN BECOME AN ADULT NOW.

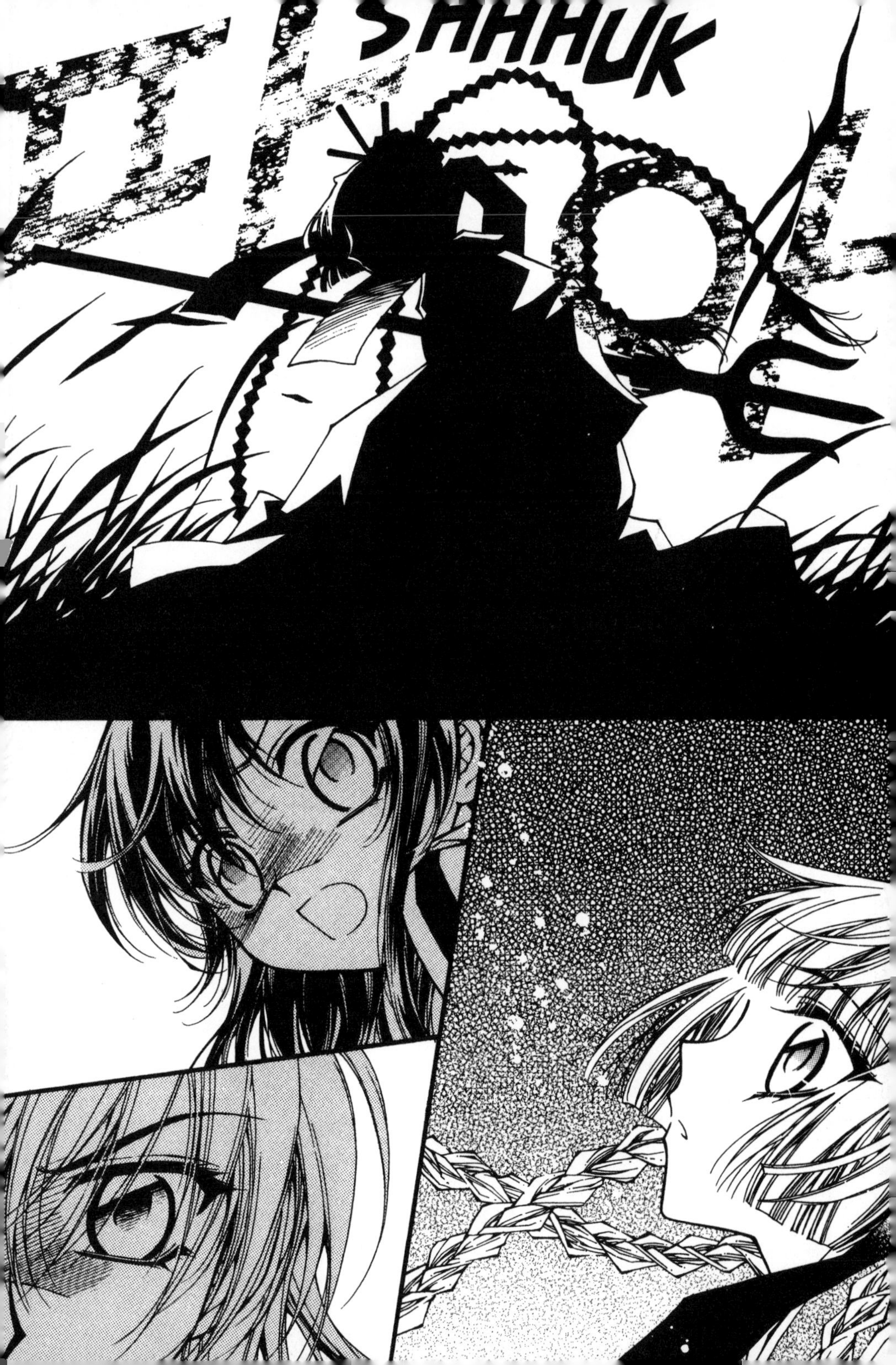
SHHHUK

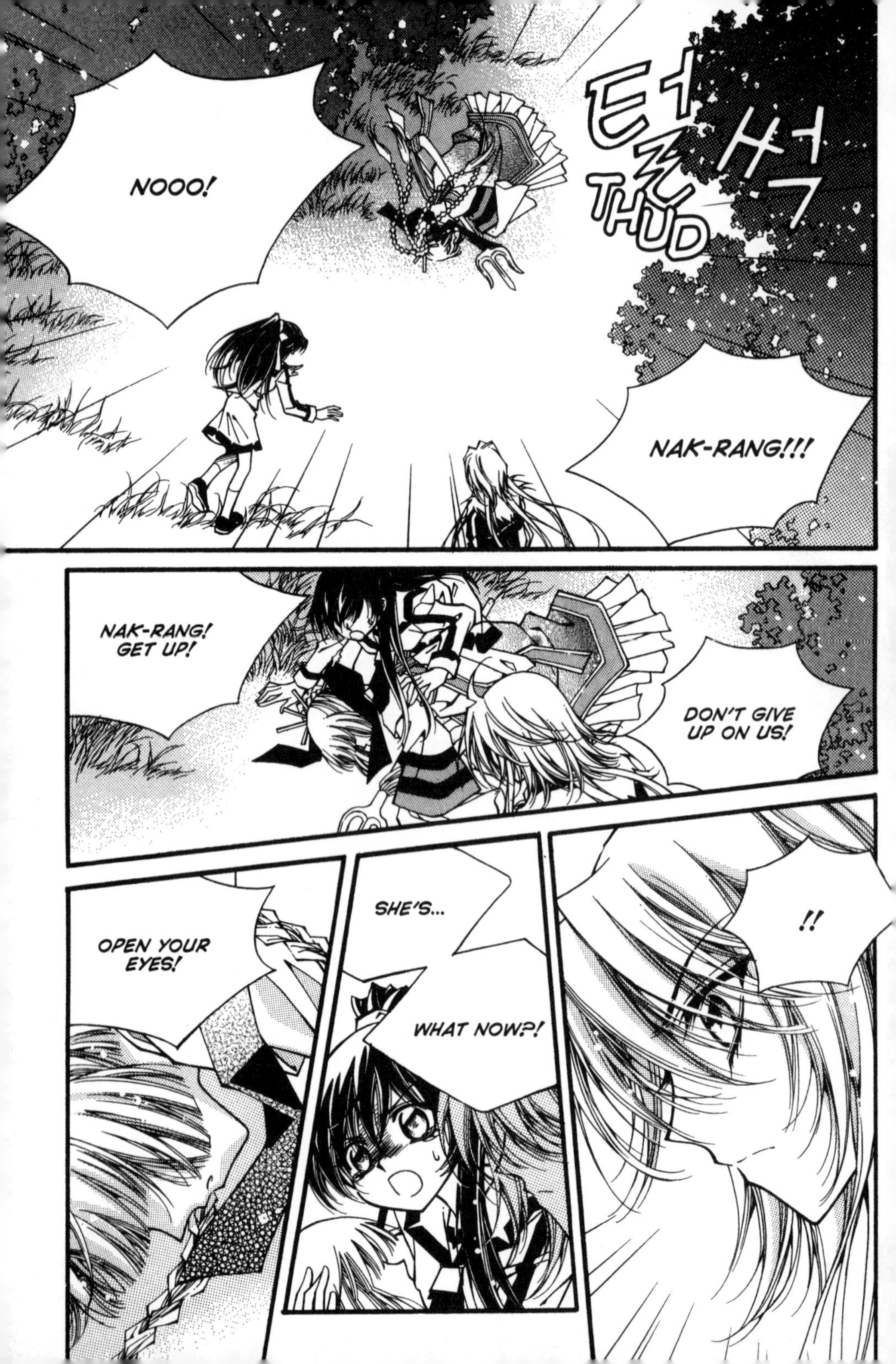
NOOO!
THUD
NAK-RANG!!!
NAK-RANG! GET UP!
DON'T GIVE UP ON US!
OPEN YOUR EYES!
SHE'S...
WHAT NOW?!
!!

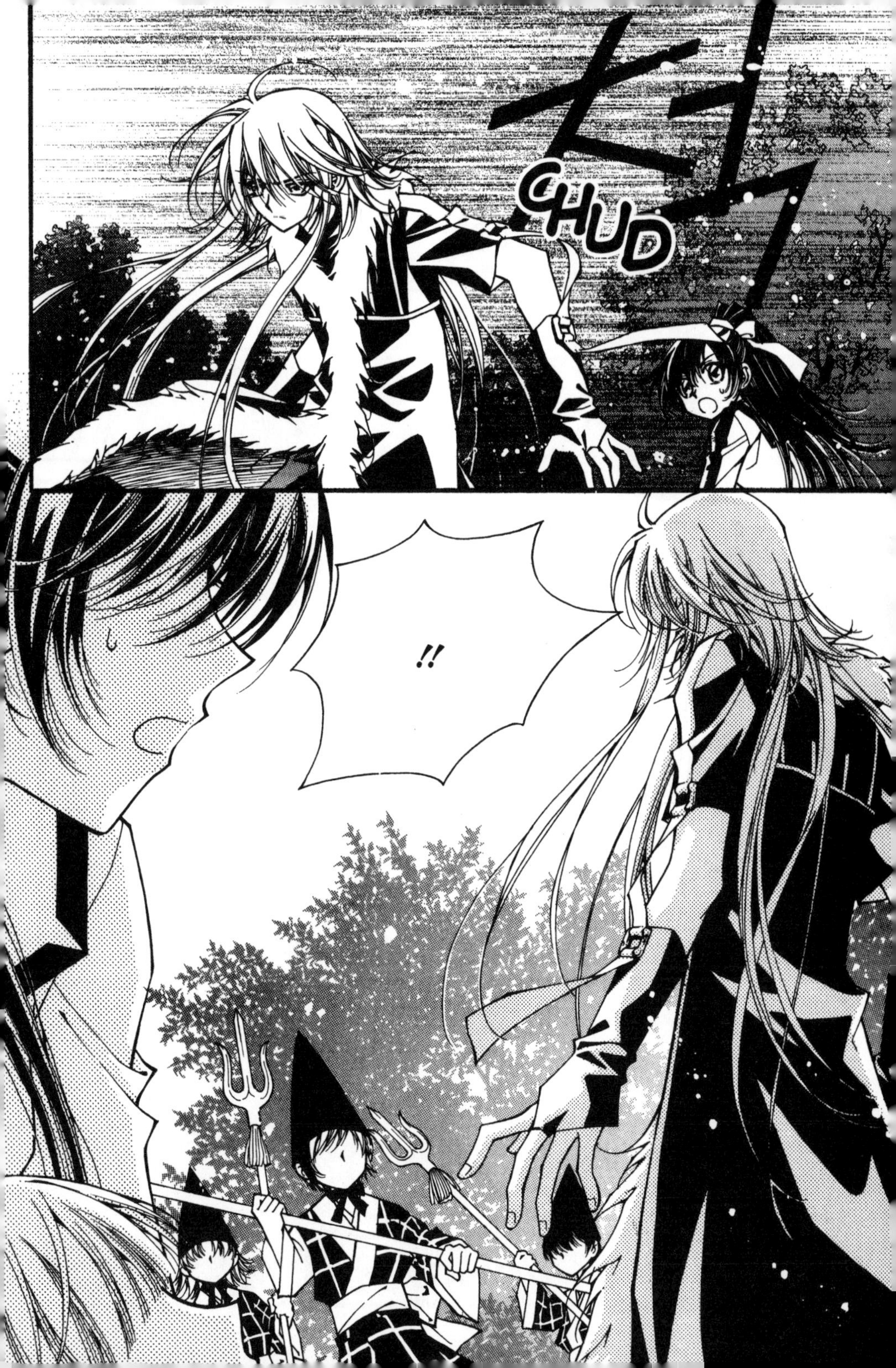
CHUD
!!

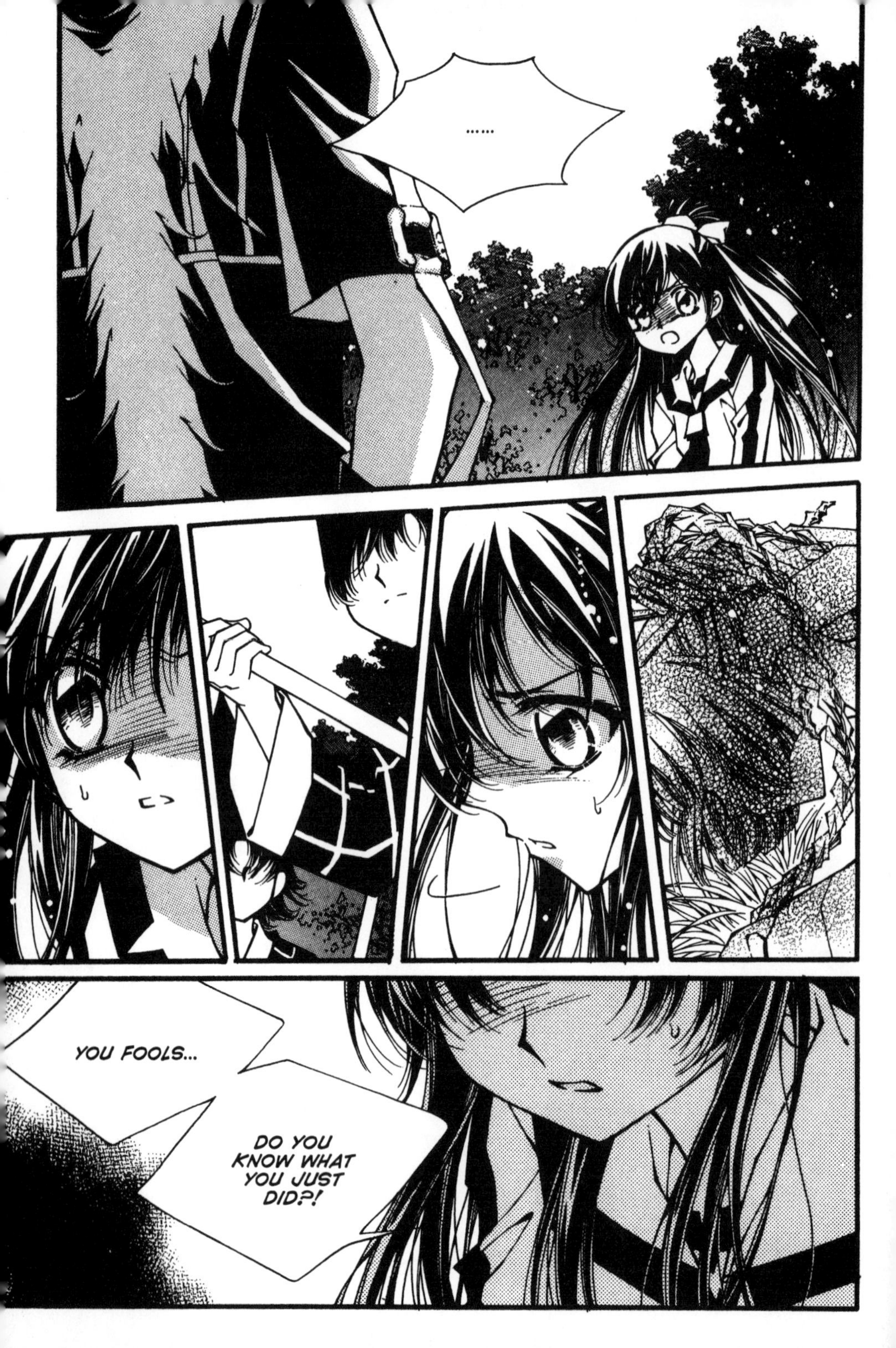
......
YOU FOOLS...
DO YOU KNOW WHAT YOU JUST DID?!

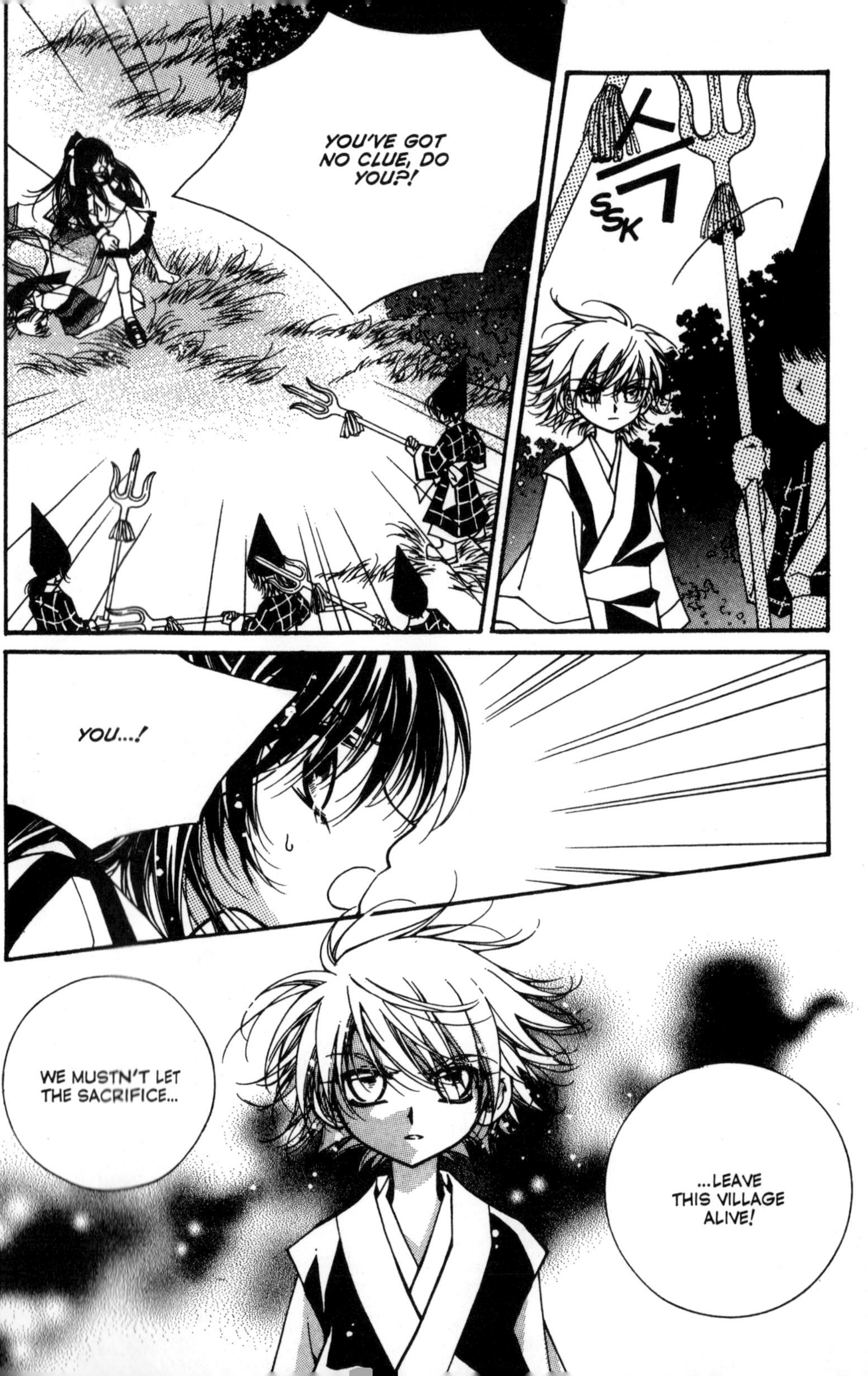
YOU'VE GOT NO CLUE, DO YOU?!
SSK
YOU...!
WE MUSTN'T LET THE SACRIFICE...
...LEAVE THIS VILLAGE ALIVE!

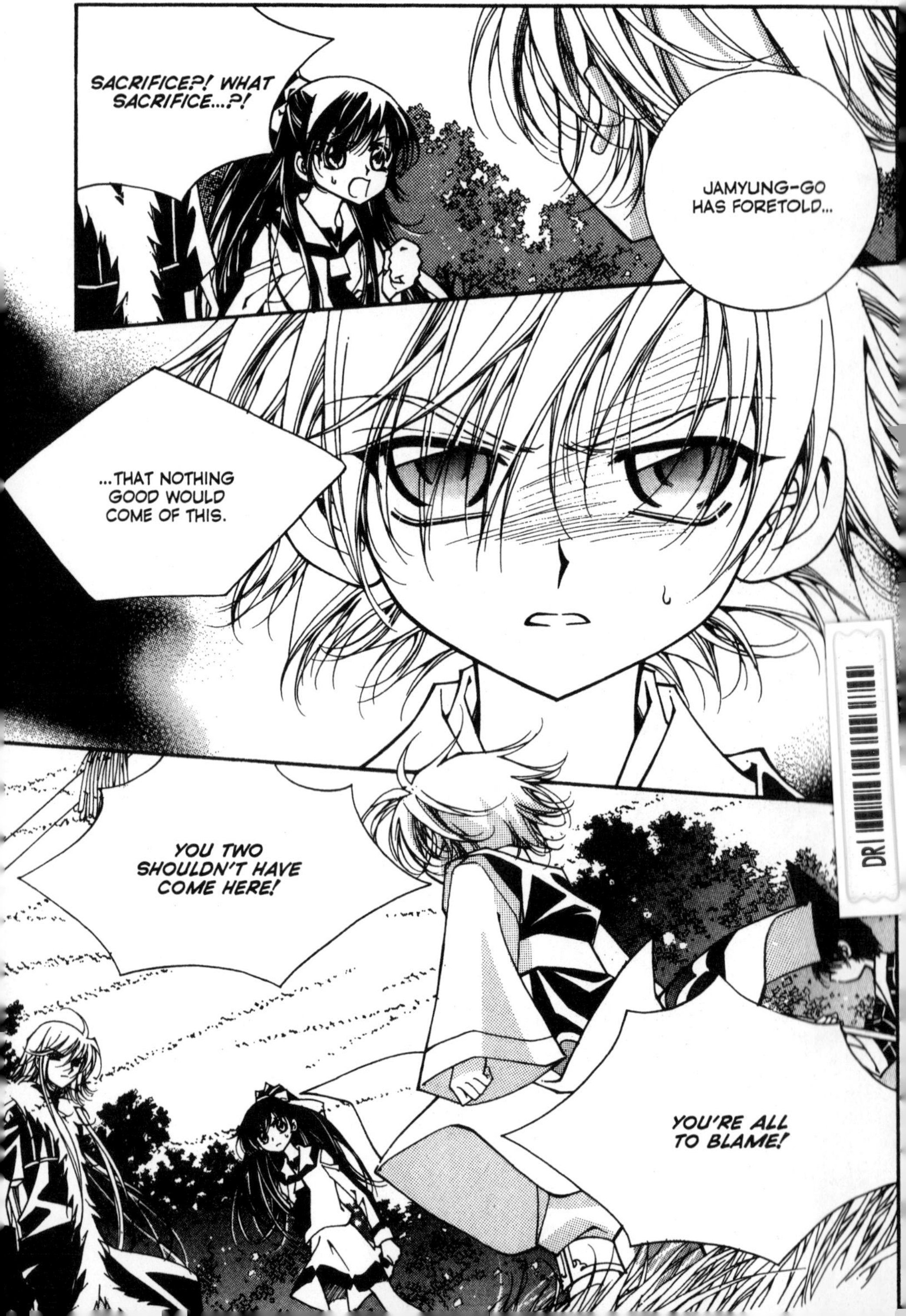
SACRIFICE?! WHAT SACRIFICE...?!
JAMYUNG-GO HAS FORETOLD...
...THAT NOTHING GOOD WOULD COME OF THIS.
YOU TWO SHOULDN'T HAVE COME HERE!
YOU'RE ALL TO BLAME!

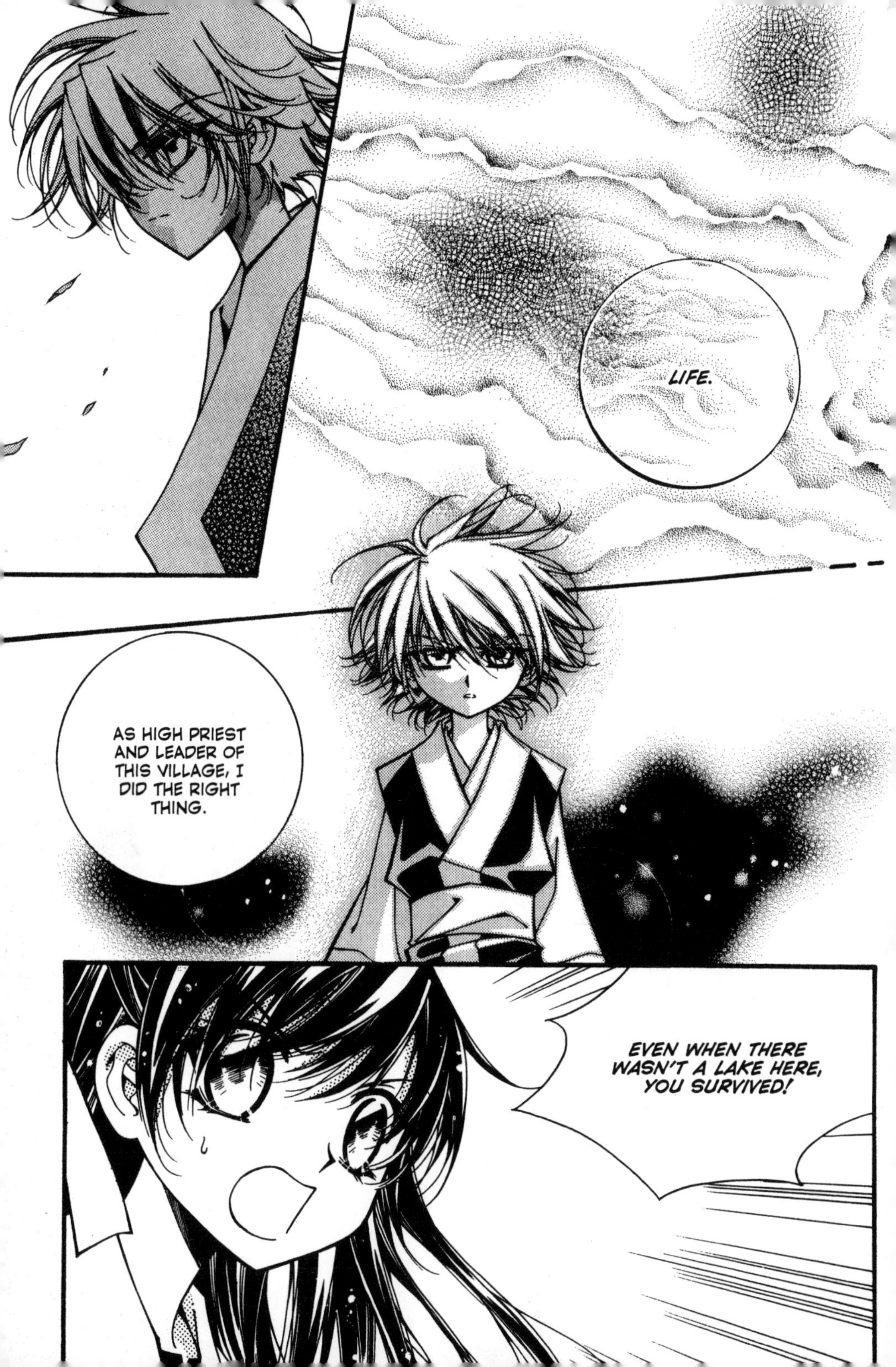
LIFE.
AS HIGH PRIEST AND LEADER OF THIS VILLAGE, I DID THE RIGHT THING.
EVEN WHEN THERE WASN'T A LAKE HERE, YOU SURVIVED!

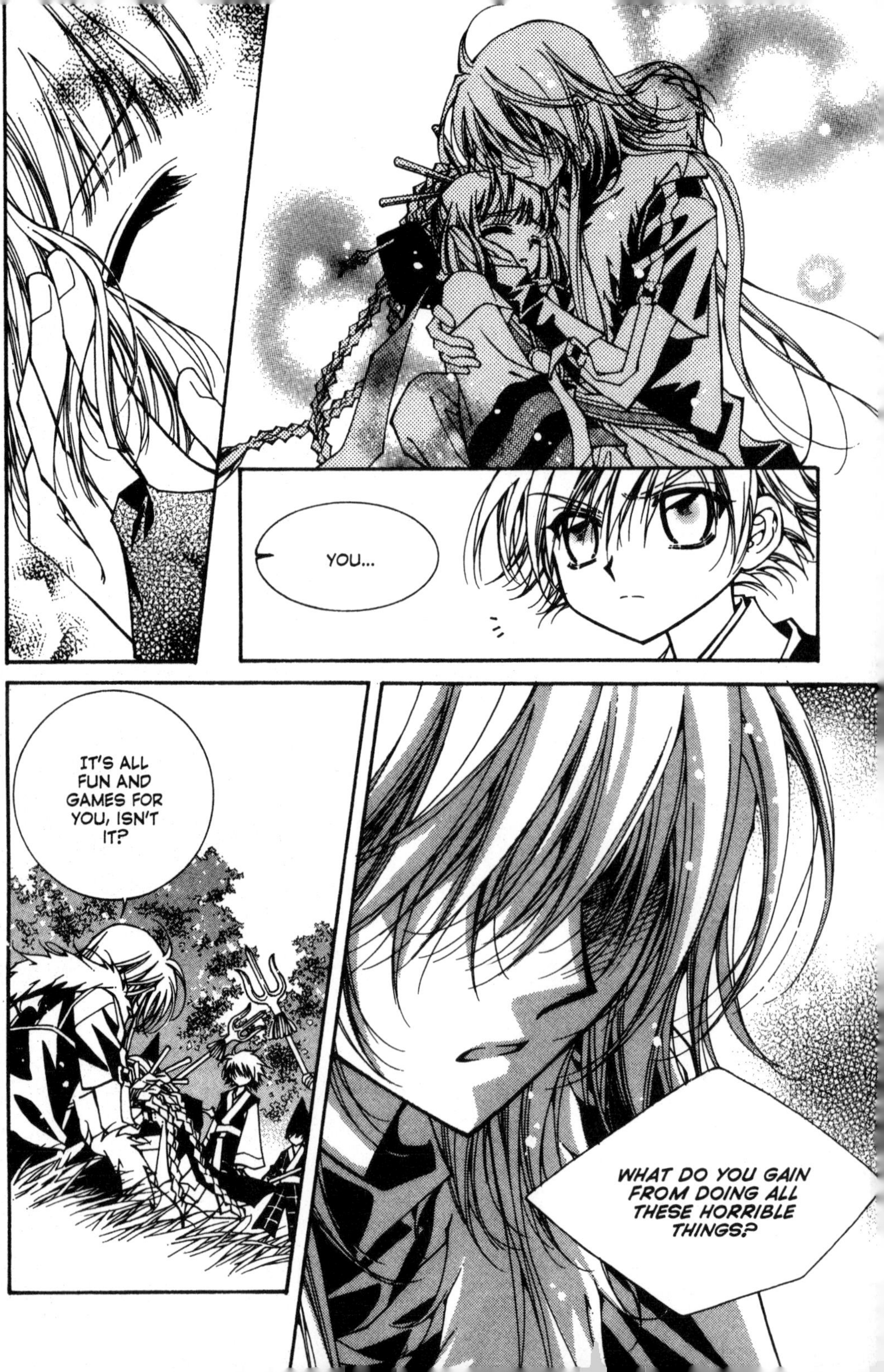
YOU...
IT'S ALL FUN AND GAMES FOR YOU, ISN'T IT?
WHAT DO YOU GAIN FROM DOING ALL THESE HORRIBLE THINGS?

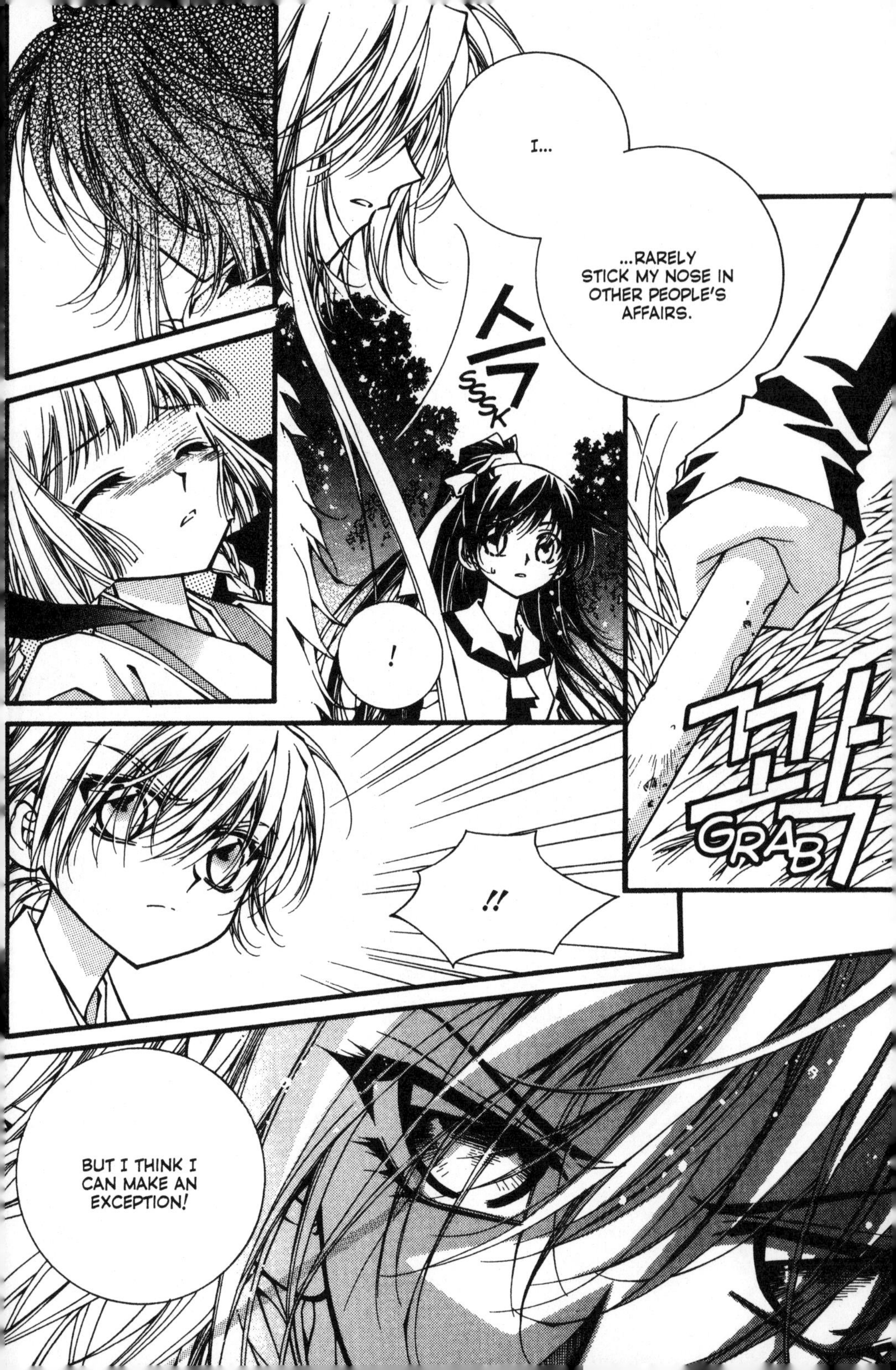
I...
...RARELY STICK MY NOSE IN OTHER PEOPLE'S AFFAIRS.
SSSK
!
GRAB
!!
BUT I THINK I CAN MAKE AN EXCEPTION!

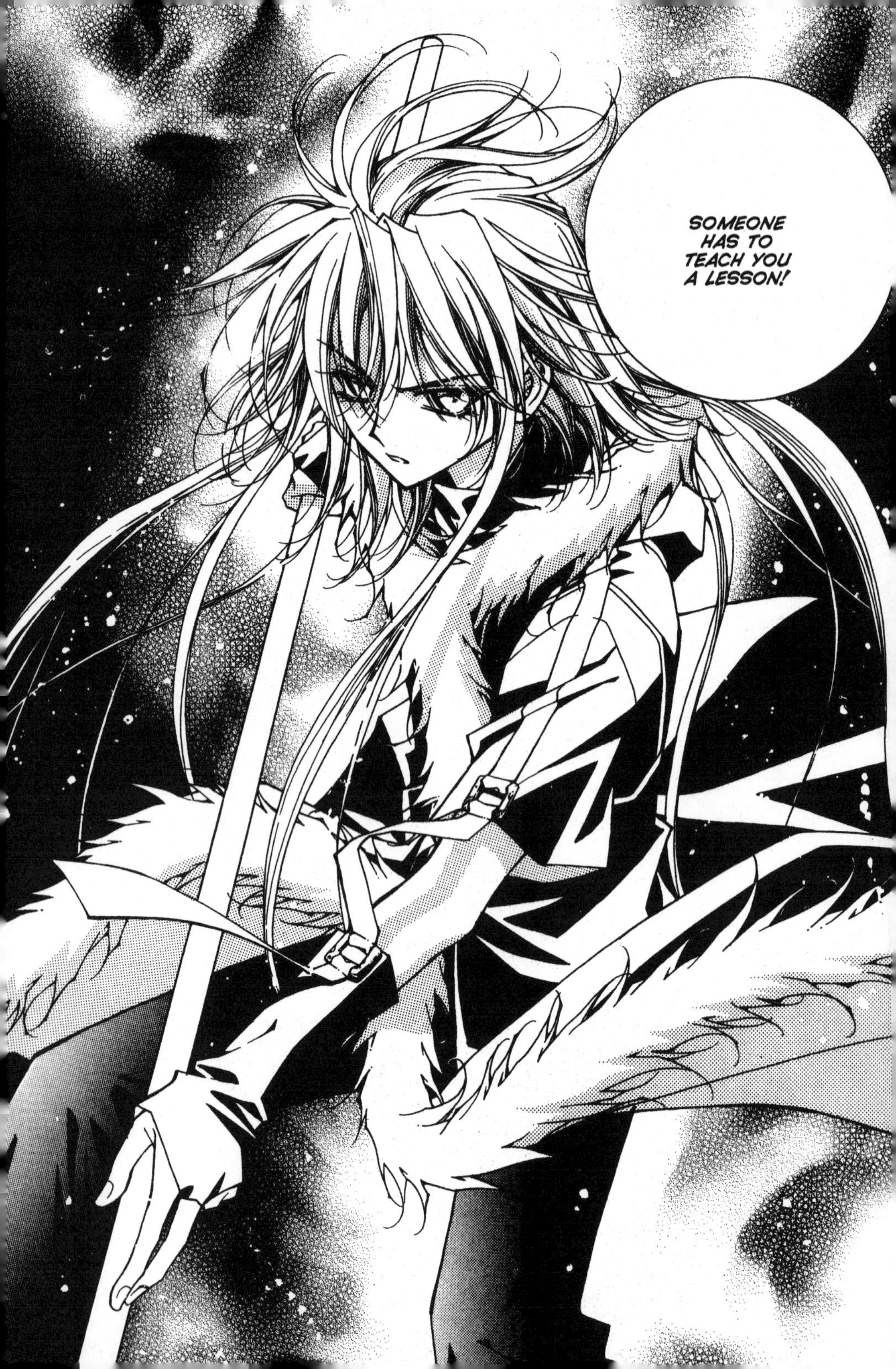
SOMEONE HAS TO TEACH YOU A LESSON!

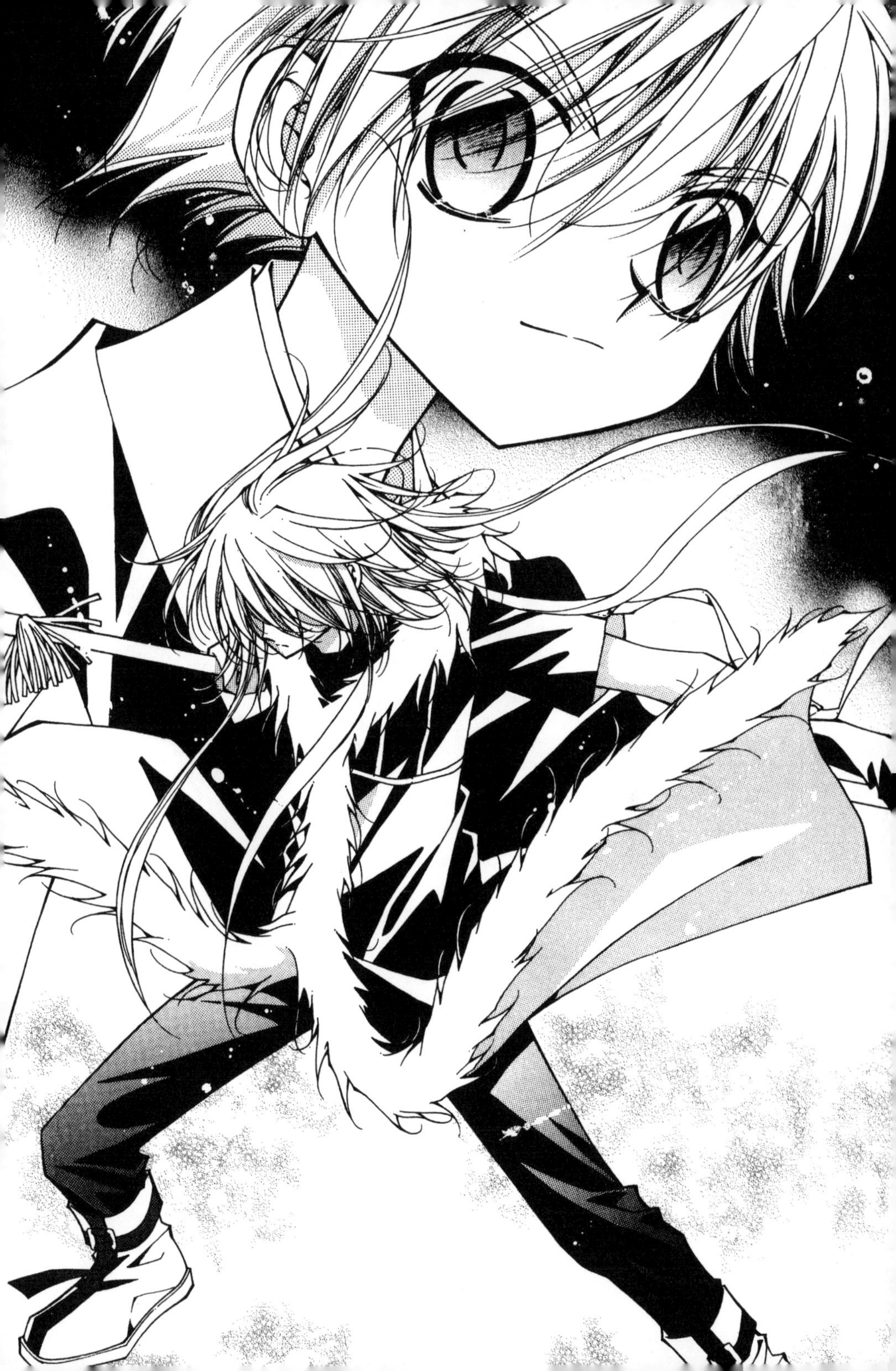

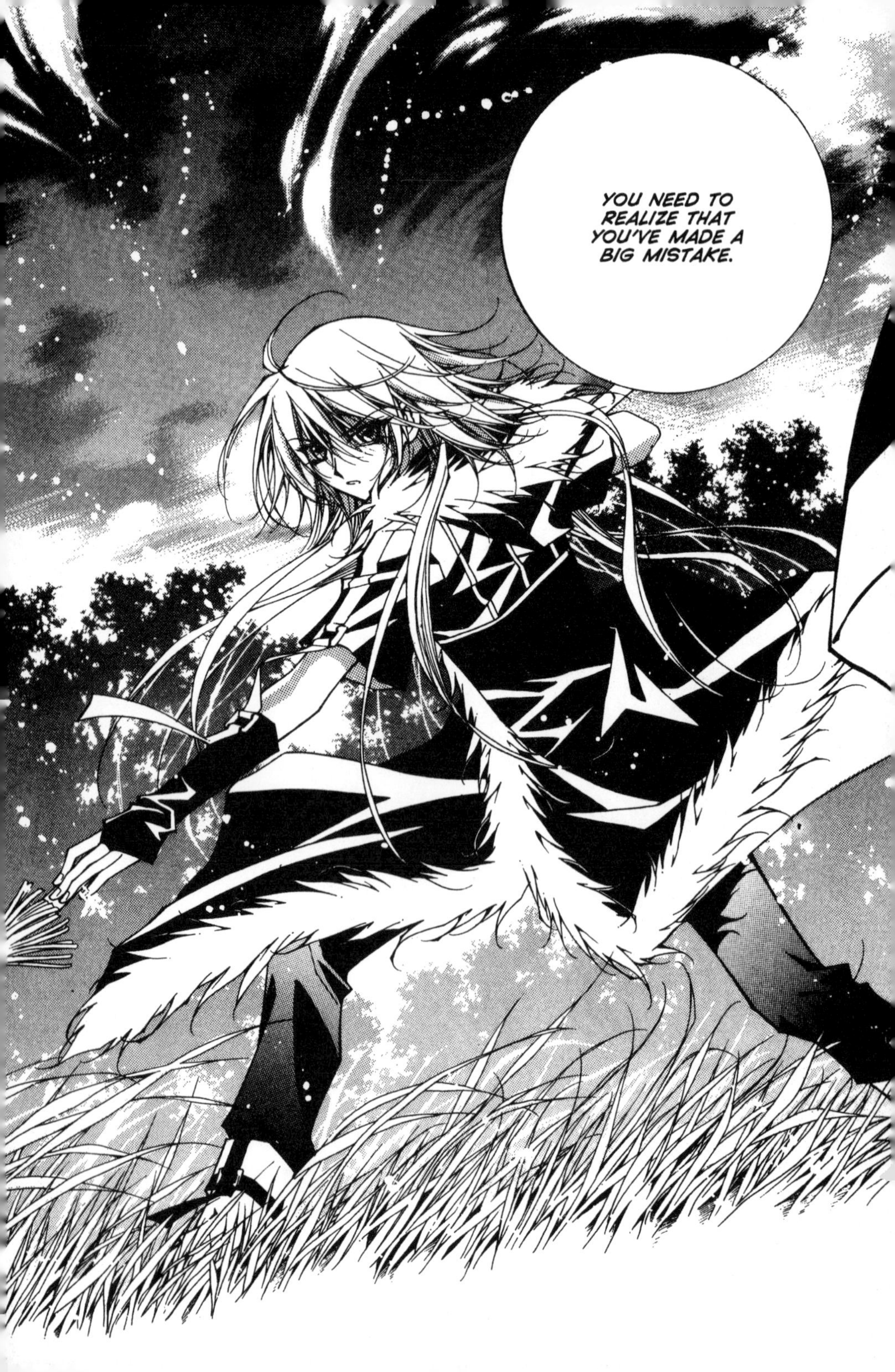
YOU NEED TO REALIZE THAT YOU'VE MADE A BIG MISTAKE.

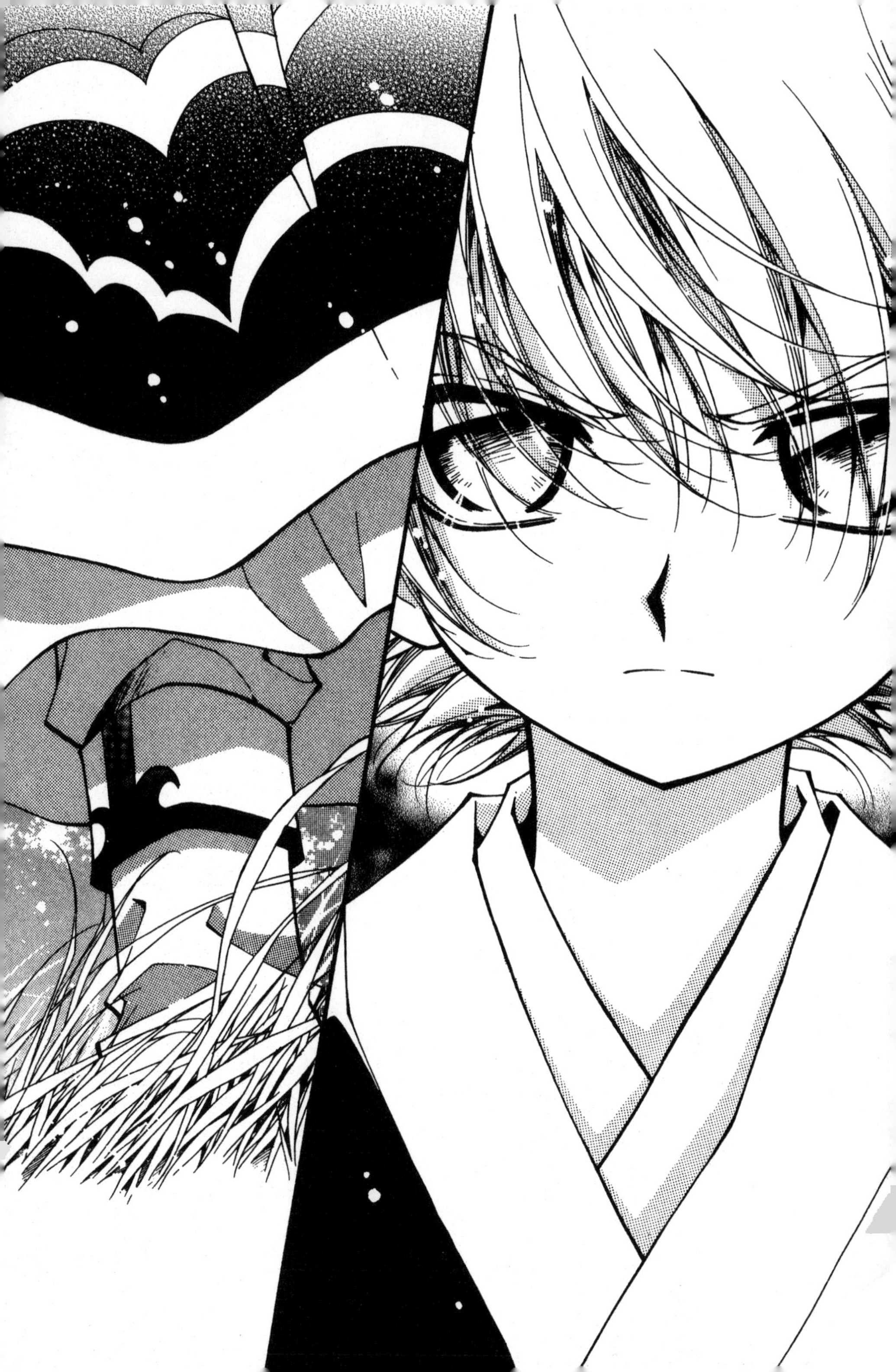

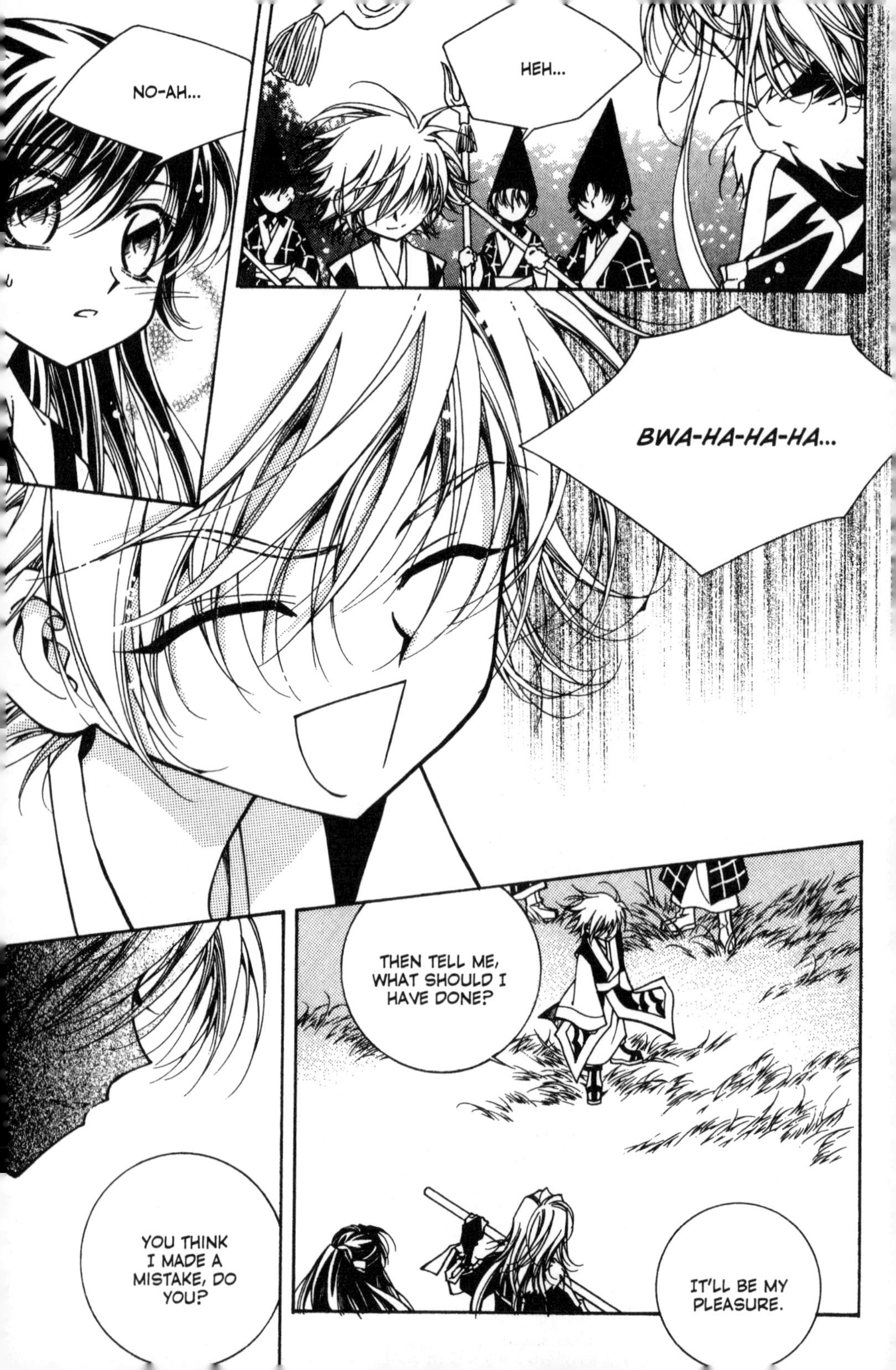
NO-AH...
HEH...
BWA-HA-HA-HA...
YOU THINK I MADE A MISTAKE, DO YOU?
THEN TELL ME, WHAT SHOULD I HAVE DONE?
IT'LL BE MY PLEASURE.

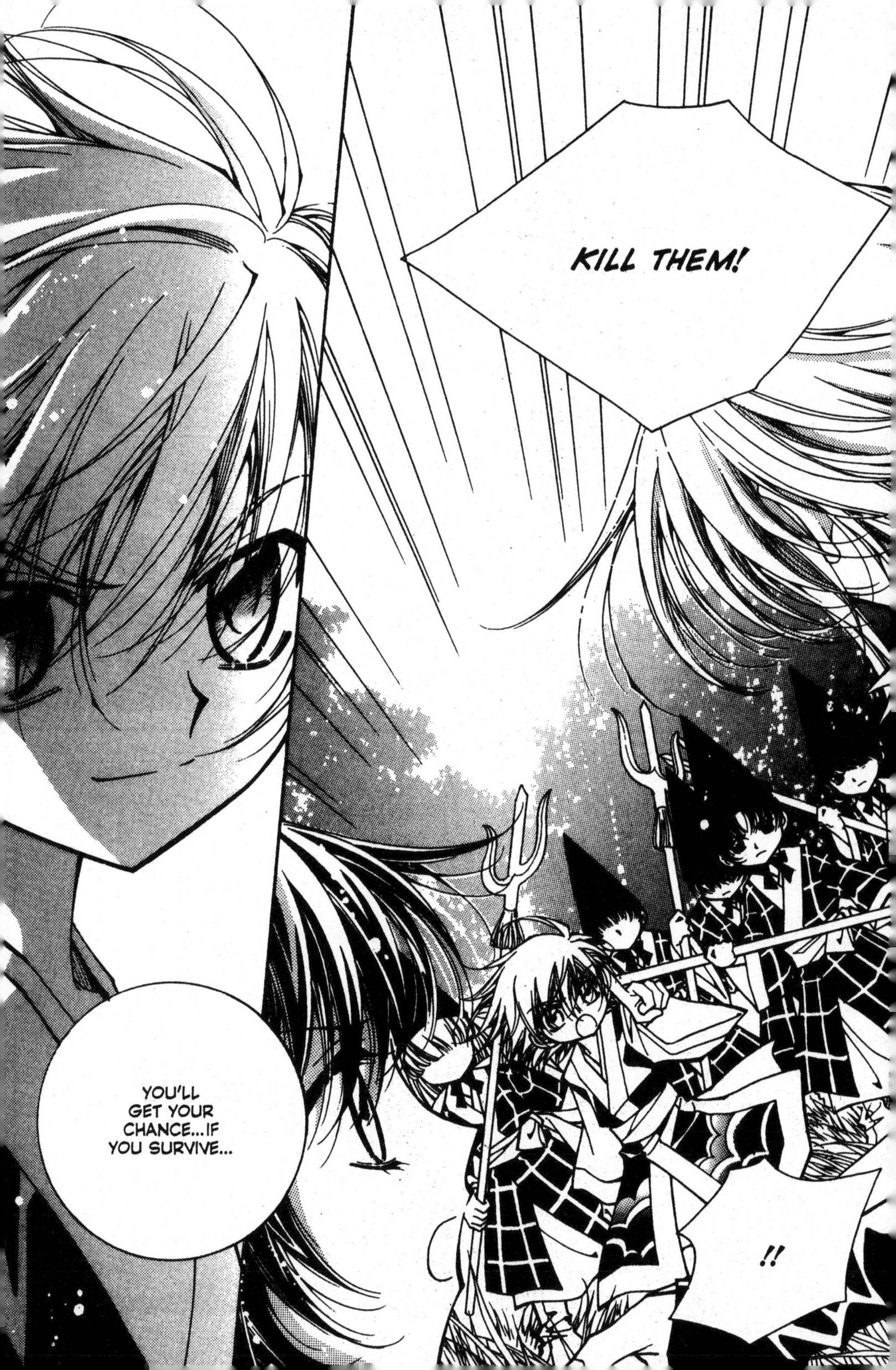
YOU'LL GET YOUR CHANCE...IF YOU SURVIVE...
KILL THEM!
!!

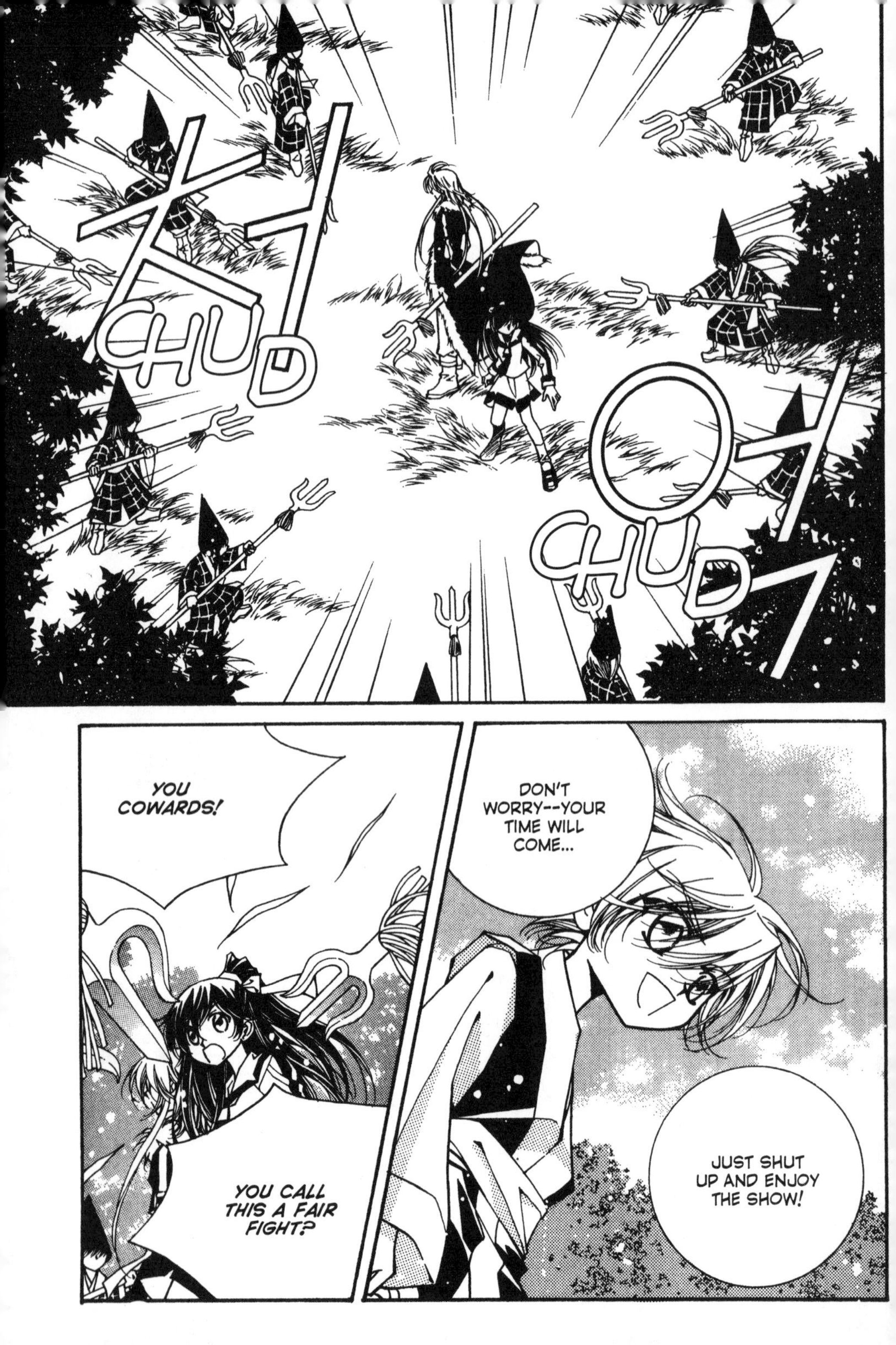
CHUD
CHUD
YOU COWARDS!
YOU CALL THIS A FAIR FIGHT?
DON'T WORRY--YOUR TIME WILL COME...
JUST SHUT UP AND ENJOY THE SHOW!

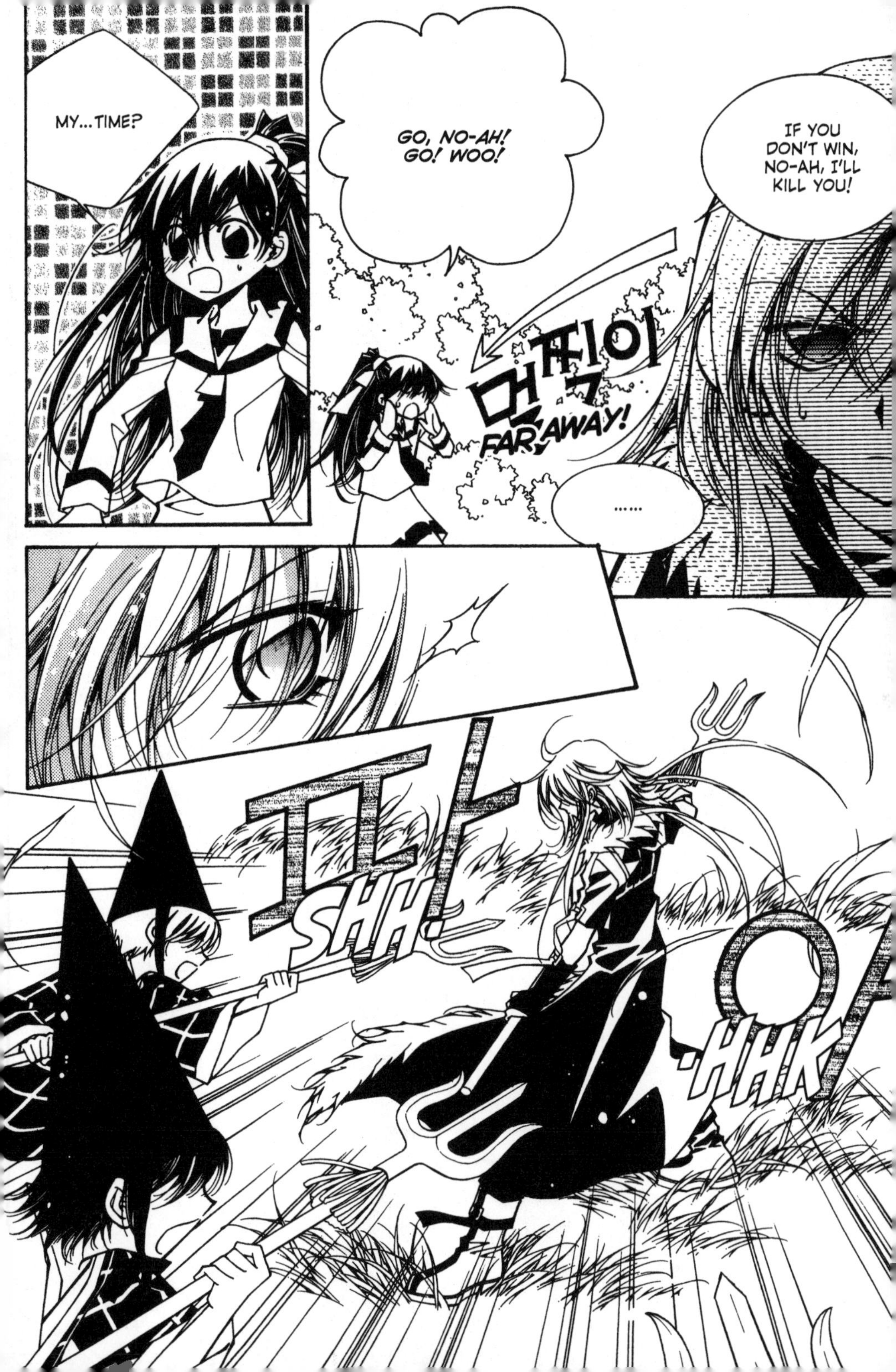
MY...TIME?
GO, NO-AH!
GO! WOO!
IF YOU DON'T WIN, NO-AH, I'LL KILL YOU!
머어어어 뜨이이
FAR AWAY!
......
피~ㅅ
SHH!
으~ㄱ
HHK!

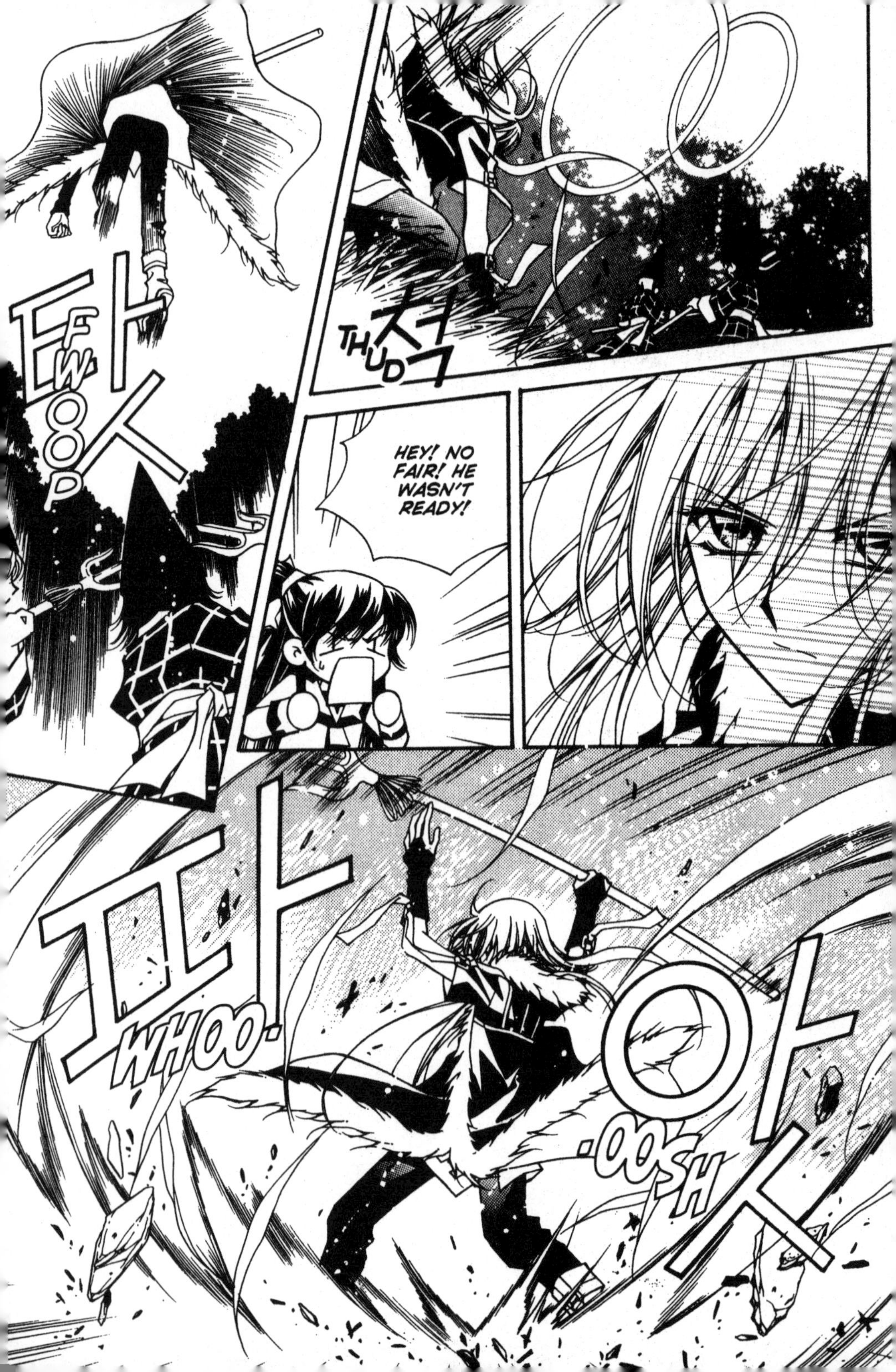
FWOOP
척
THUD
HEY! NO FAIR! HE WASN'T READY!
WHOO-
-OOSH

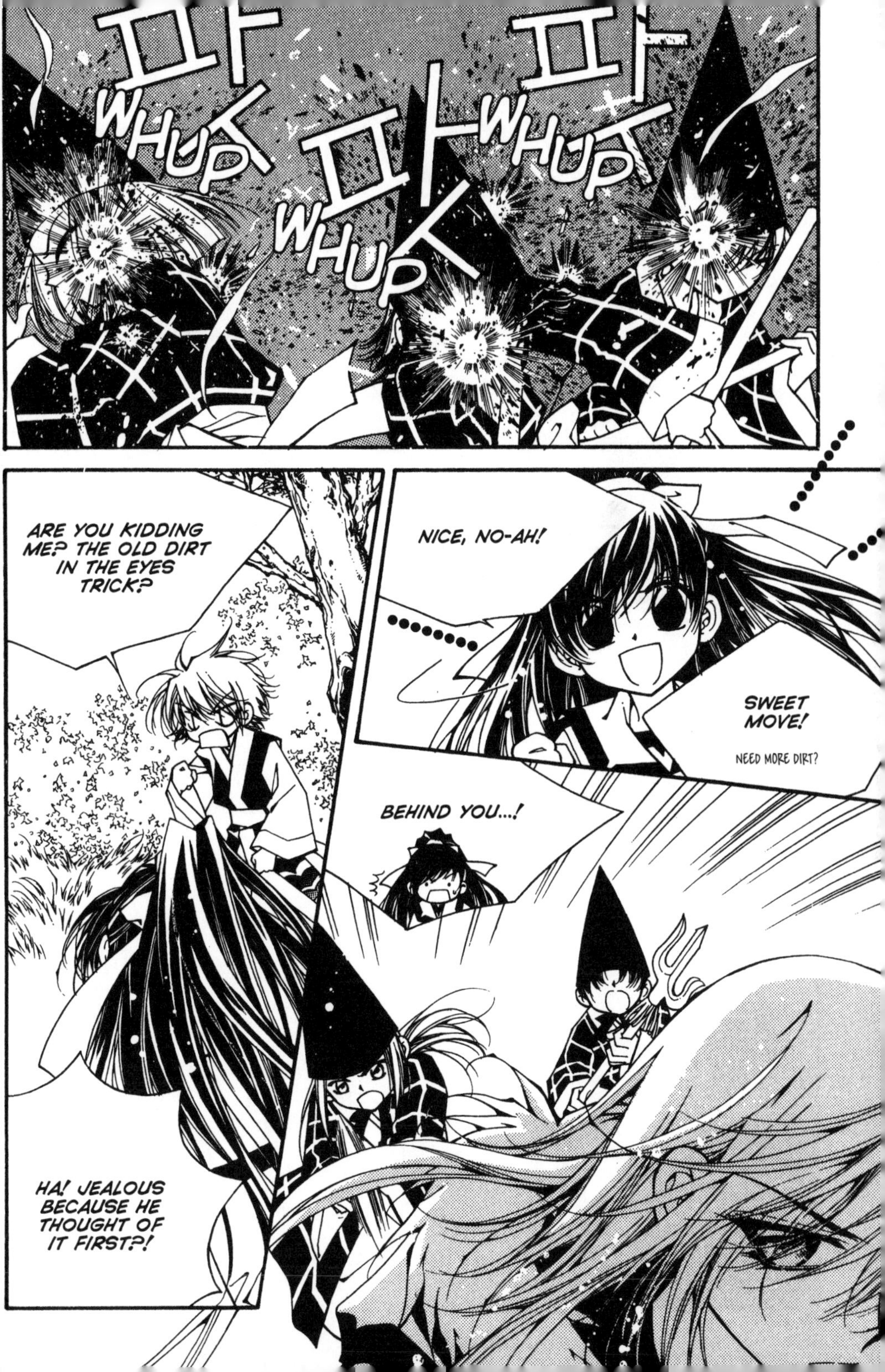

파 WHUP
파 WHUP
파 WHUP
ARE YOU KIDDING ME? THE OLD DIRT IN THE EYES TRICK?
HA! JEALOUS BECAUSE HE THOUGHT OF IT FIRST?!
NICE, NO-AH!
....
SWEET MOVE!
NEED MORE DIRT?
....
BEHIND YOU...!

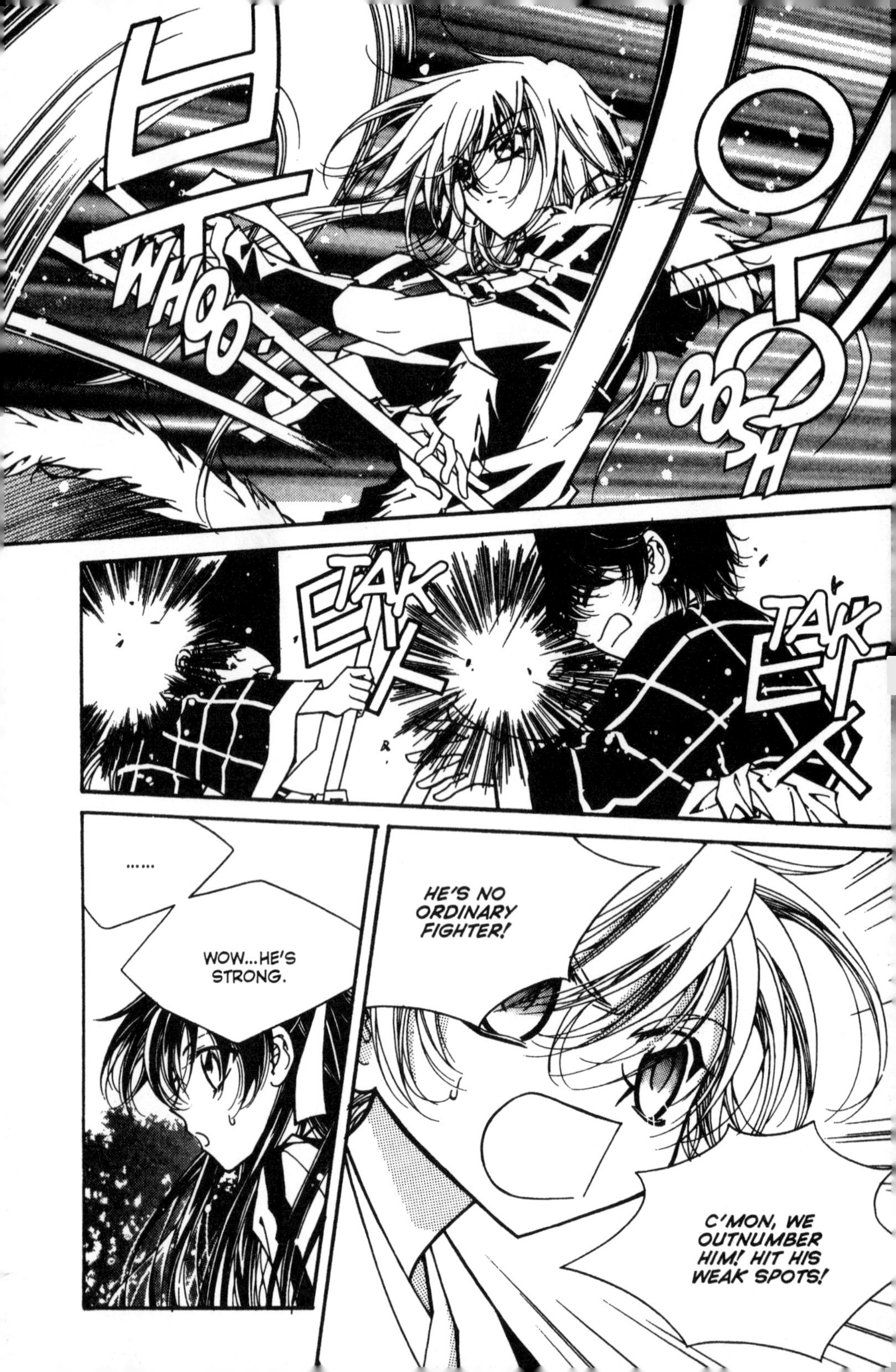
WHOO-
-OOSH
TAK
TAK
......
WOW...HE'S STRONG.
HE'S NO ORDINARY FIGHTER!
C'MON, WE OUTNUMBER HIM! HIT HIS WEAK SPOTS!

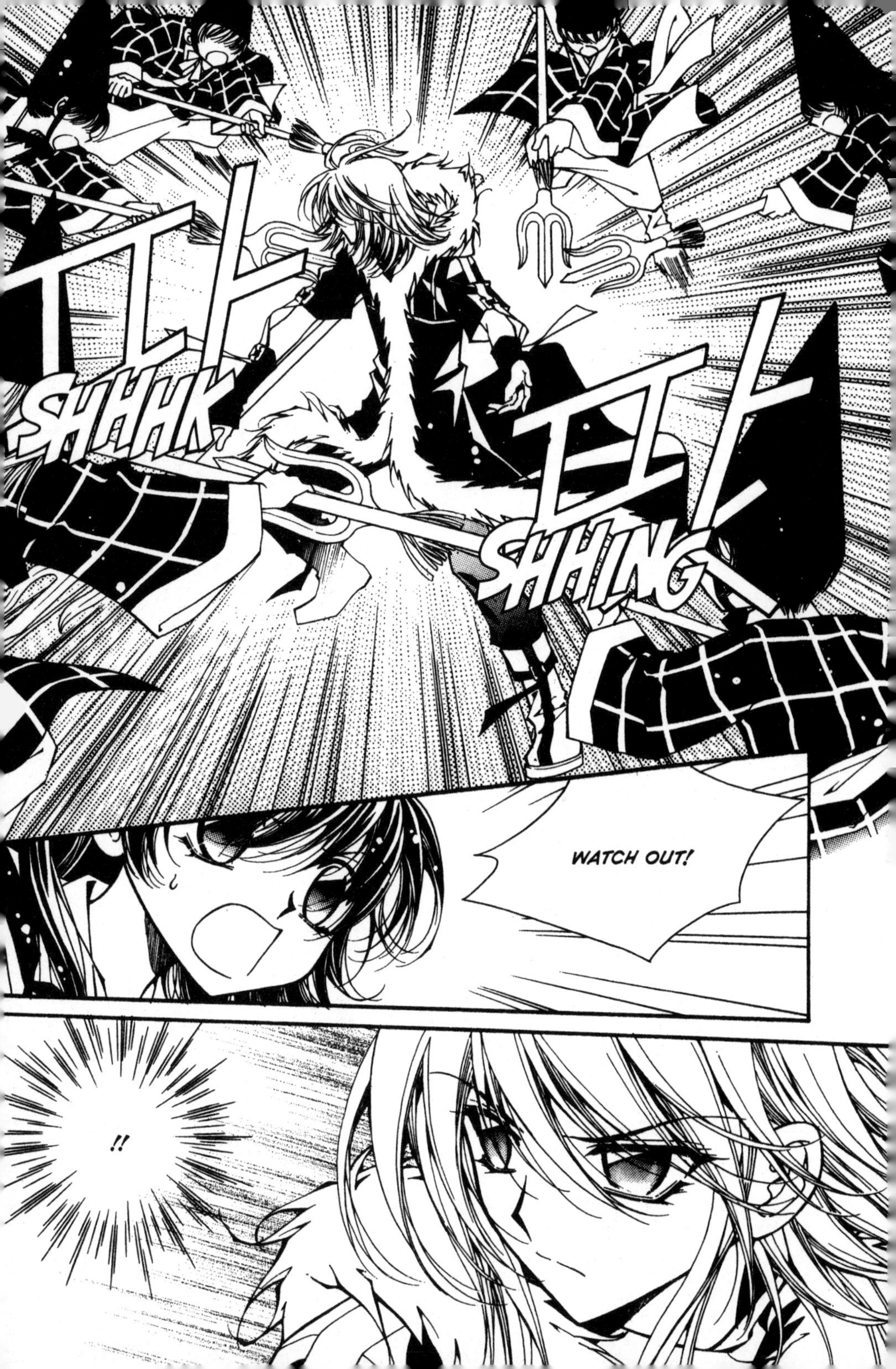
SHHHK
SHHING
WATCH OUT!
!!

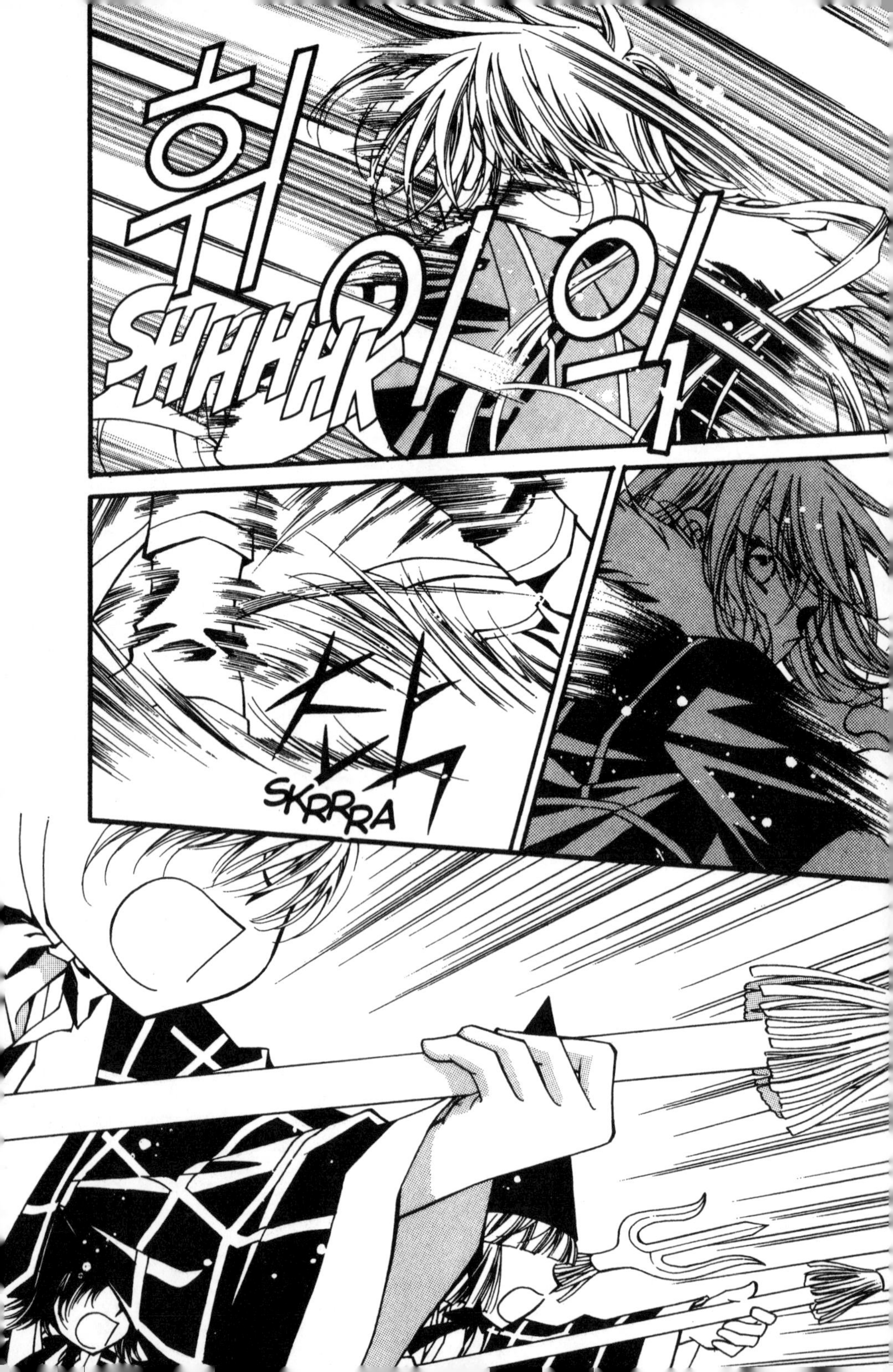
SHHHHK
SKRRRA

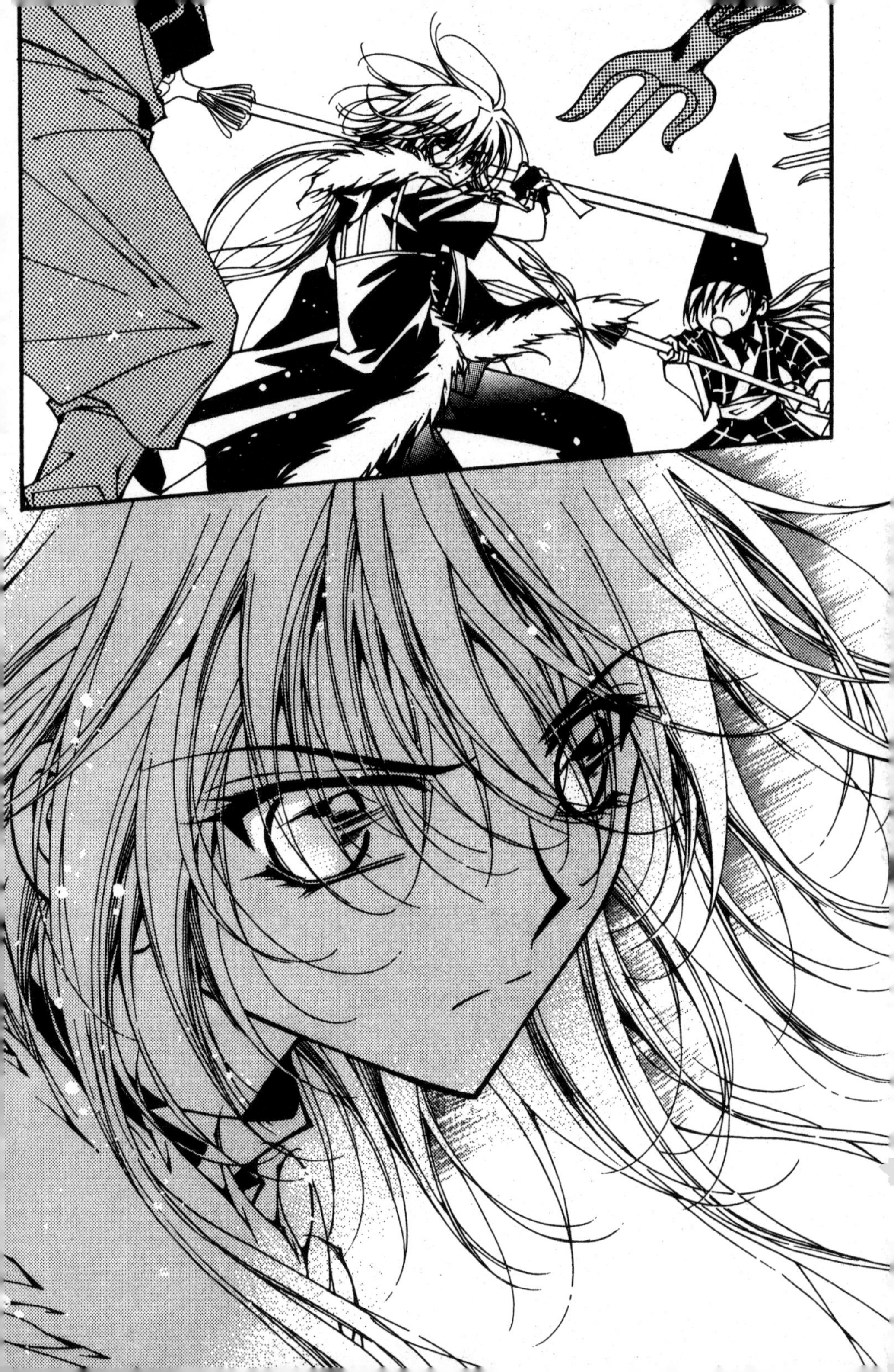

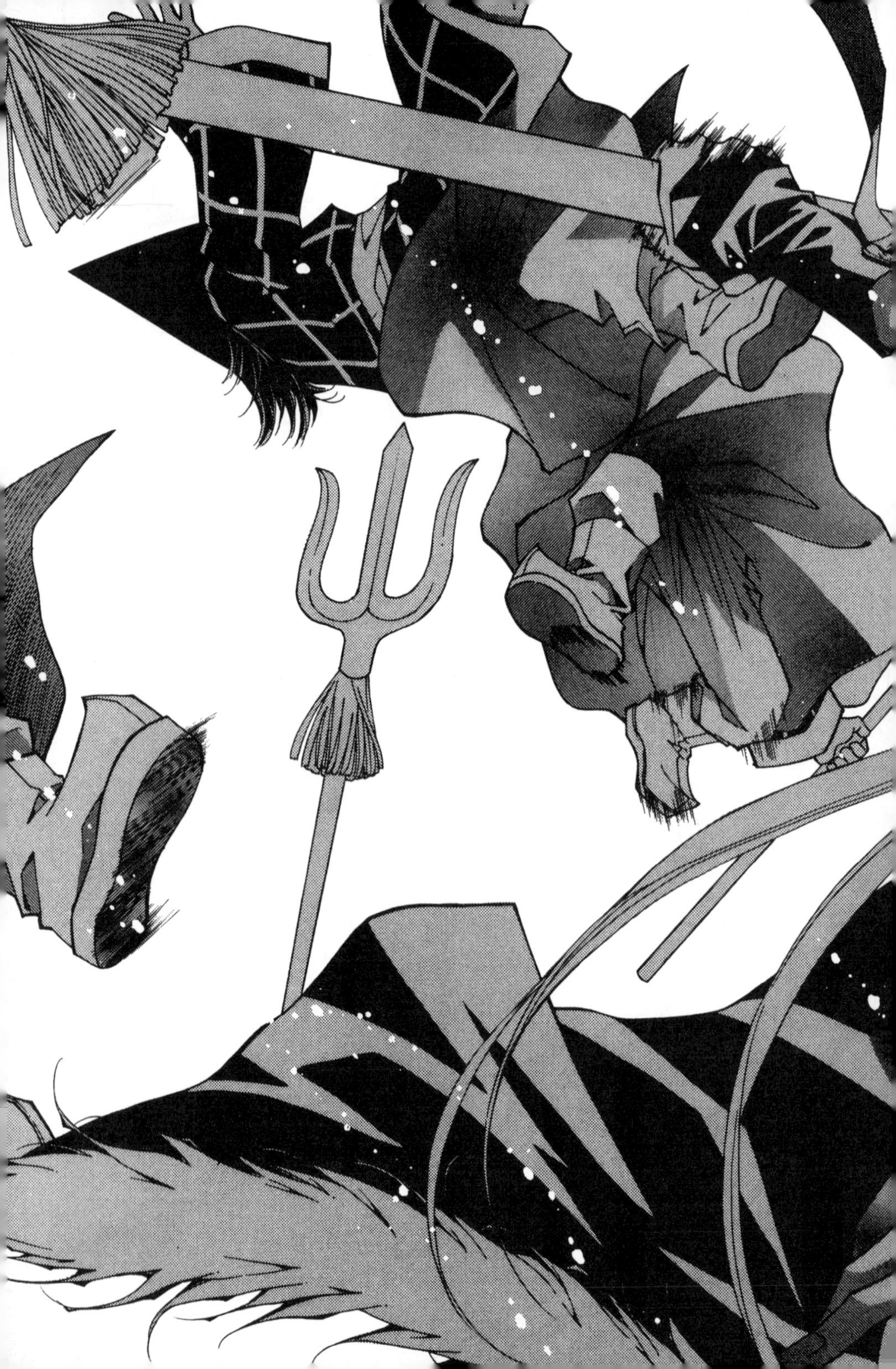

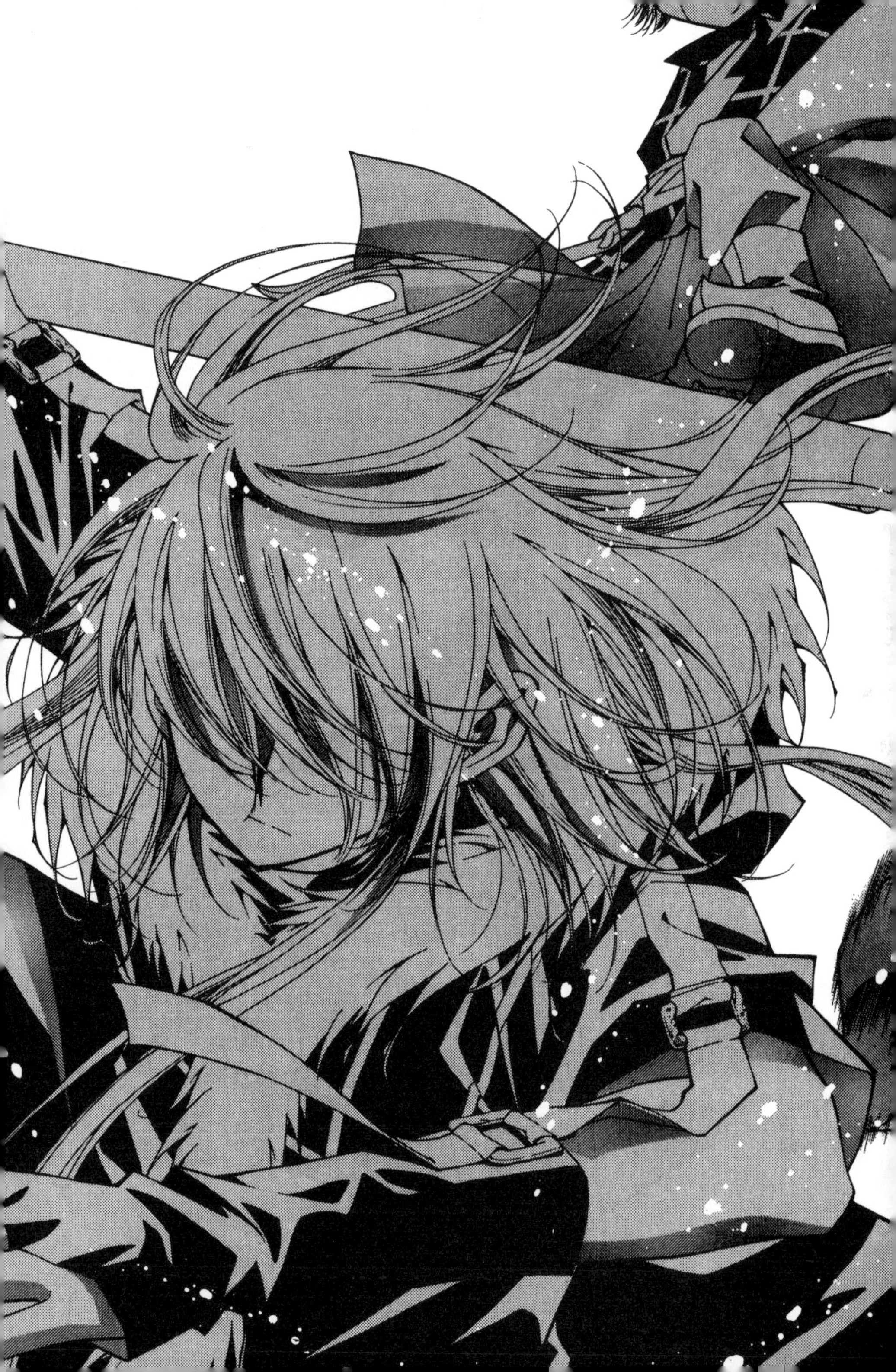

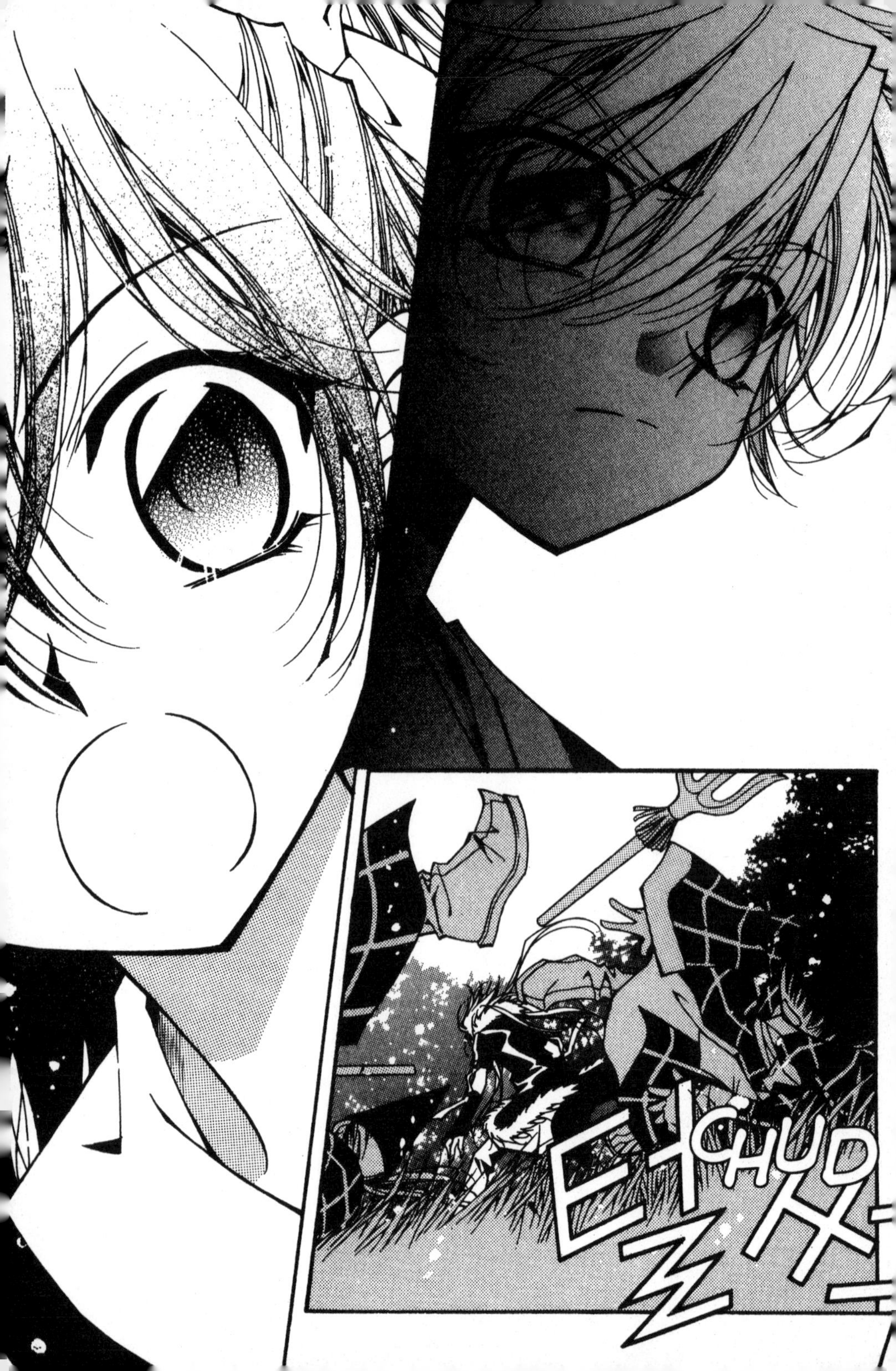
CHUD

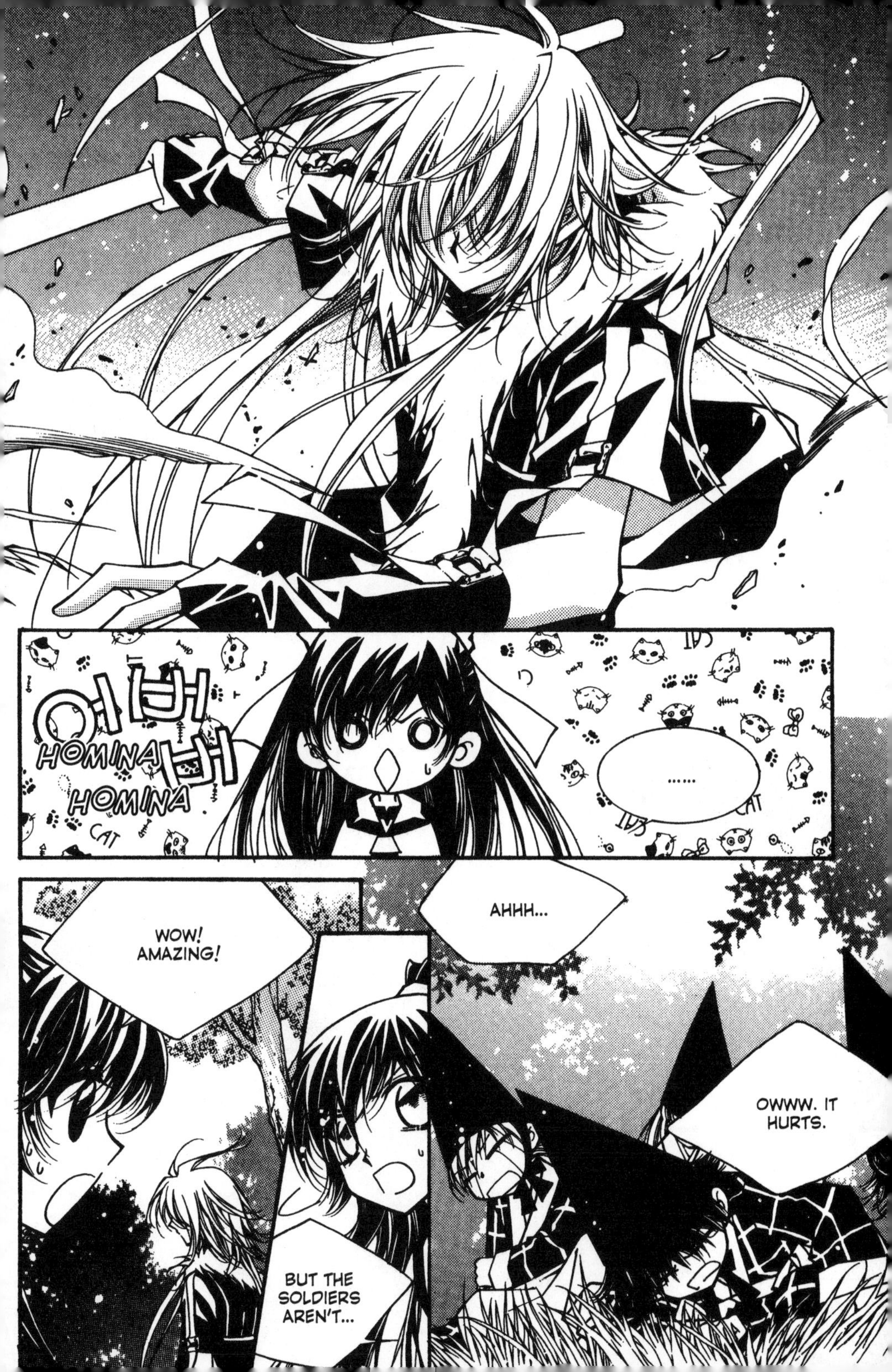
HOMINA
HOMINA
......
WOW! AMAZING!
BUT THE SOLDIERS AREN'T...
AHHH...
OWWW. IT HURTS.

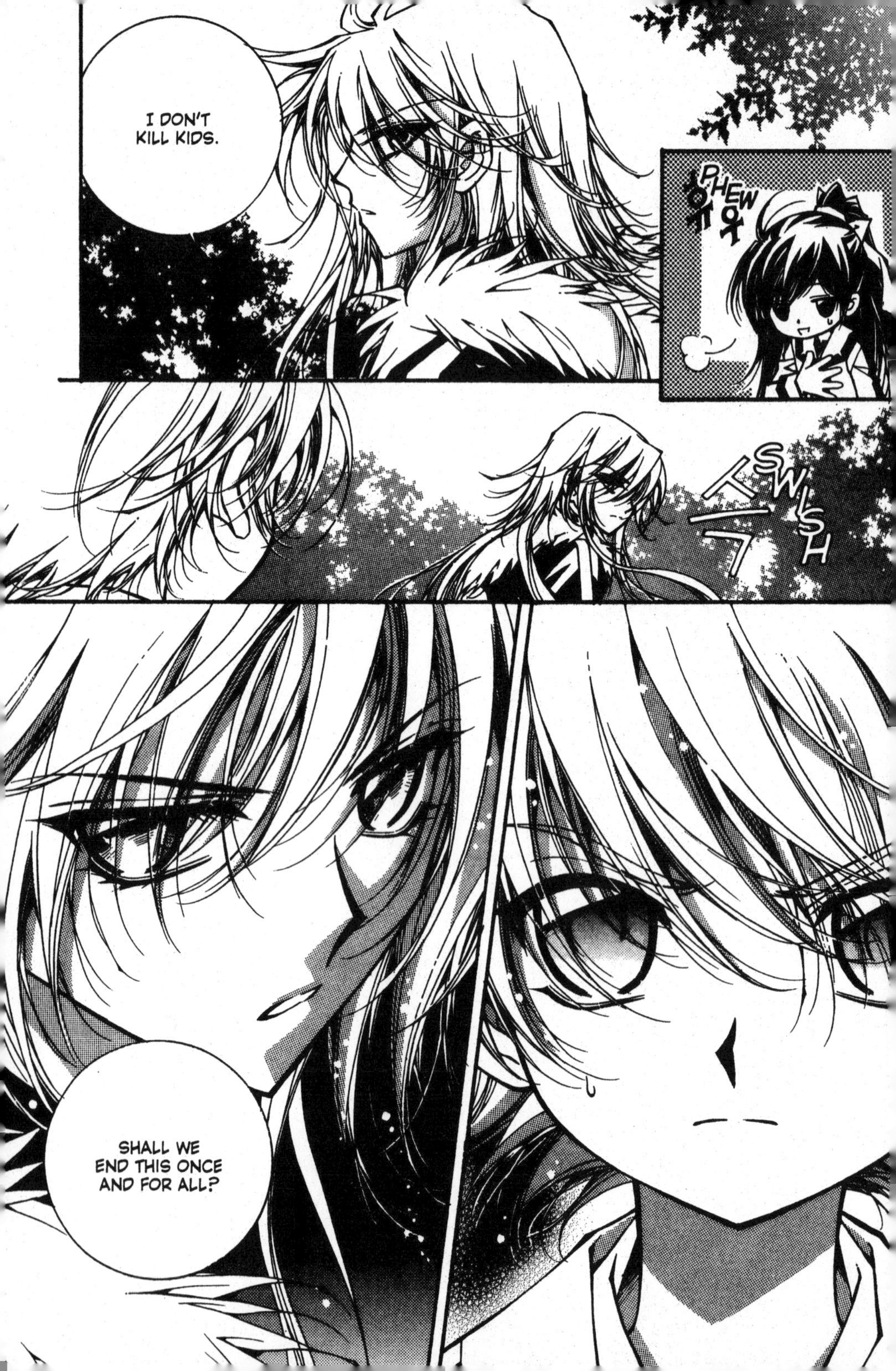
I DON'T KILL KIDS.
PHEW
SWISH
SHALL WE END THIS ONCE AND FOR ALL?

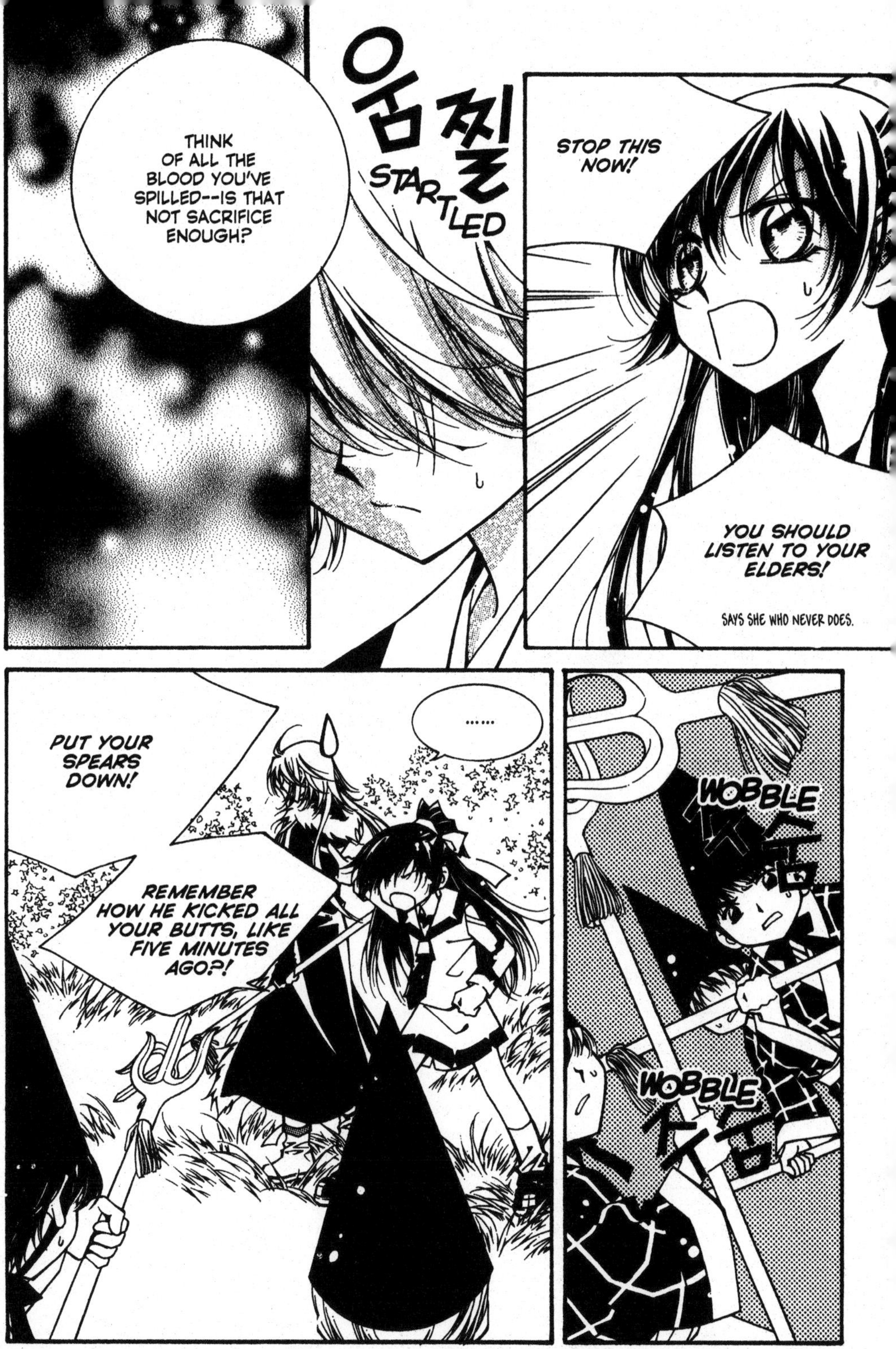
THINK OF ALL THE BLOOD YOU'VE SPILLED--IS THAT NOT SACRIFICE ENOUGH?
움찔
STARTLED
STOP THIS NOW!
YOU SHOULD LISTEN TO YOUR ELDERS!
SAYS SHE WHO NEVER DOES.
PUT YOUR SPEARS DOWN!
REMEMBER HOW HE KICKED ALL YOUR BUTTS, LIKE FIVE MINUTES AGO?!
......
WOBBLE
WOBBLE

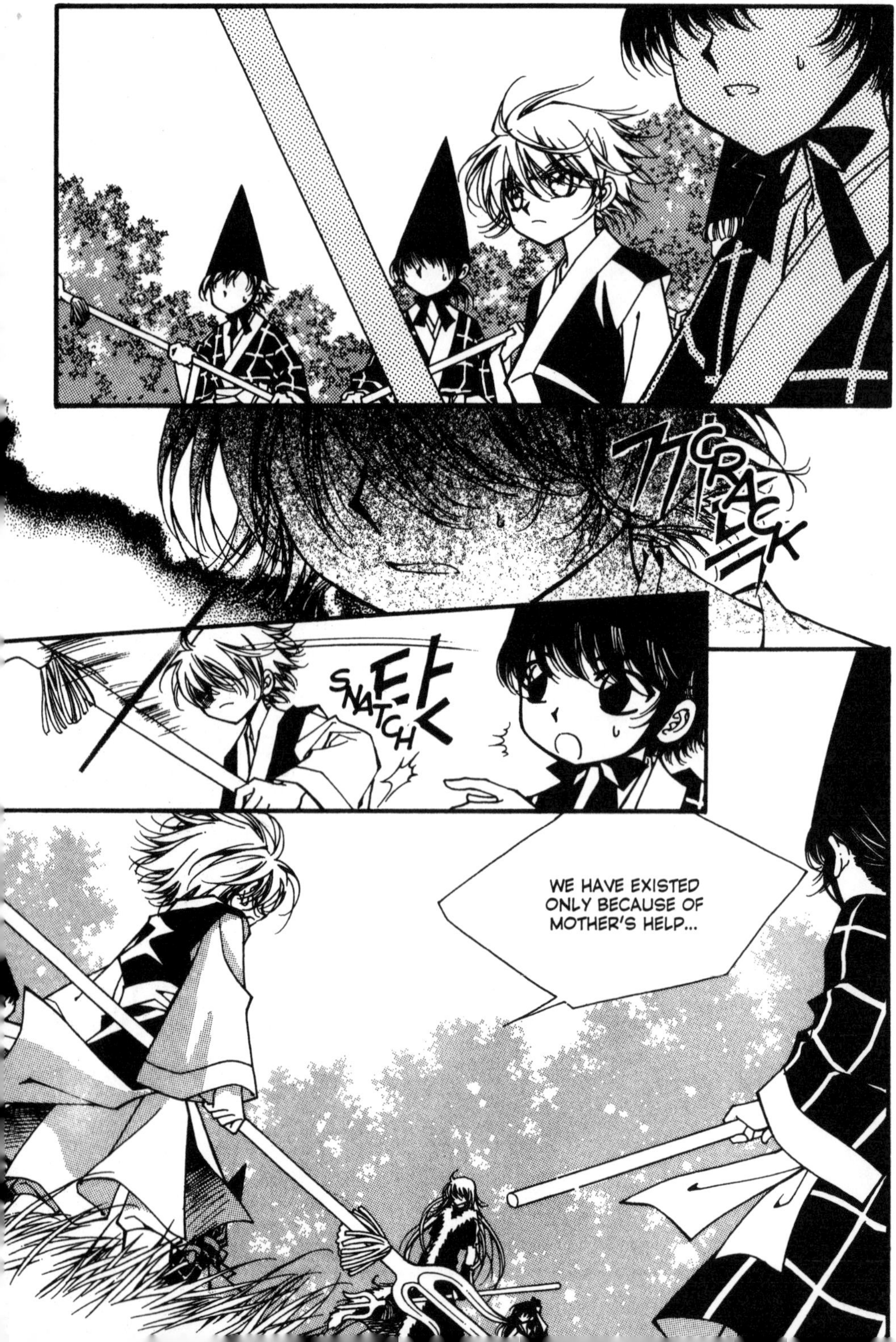
CRACK
SNATCH
WE HAVE EXISTED ONLY BECAUSE OF MOTHER'S HELP...

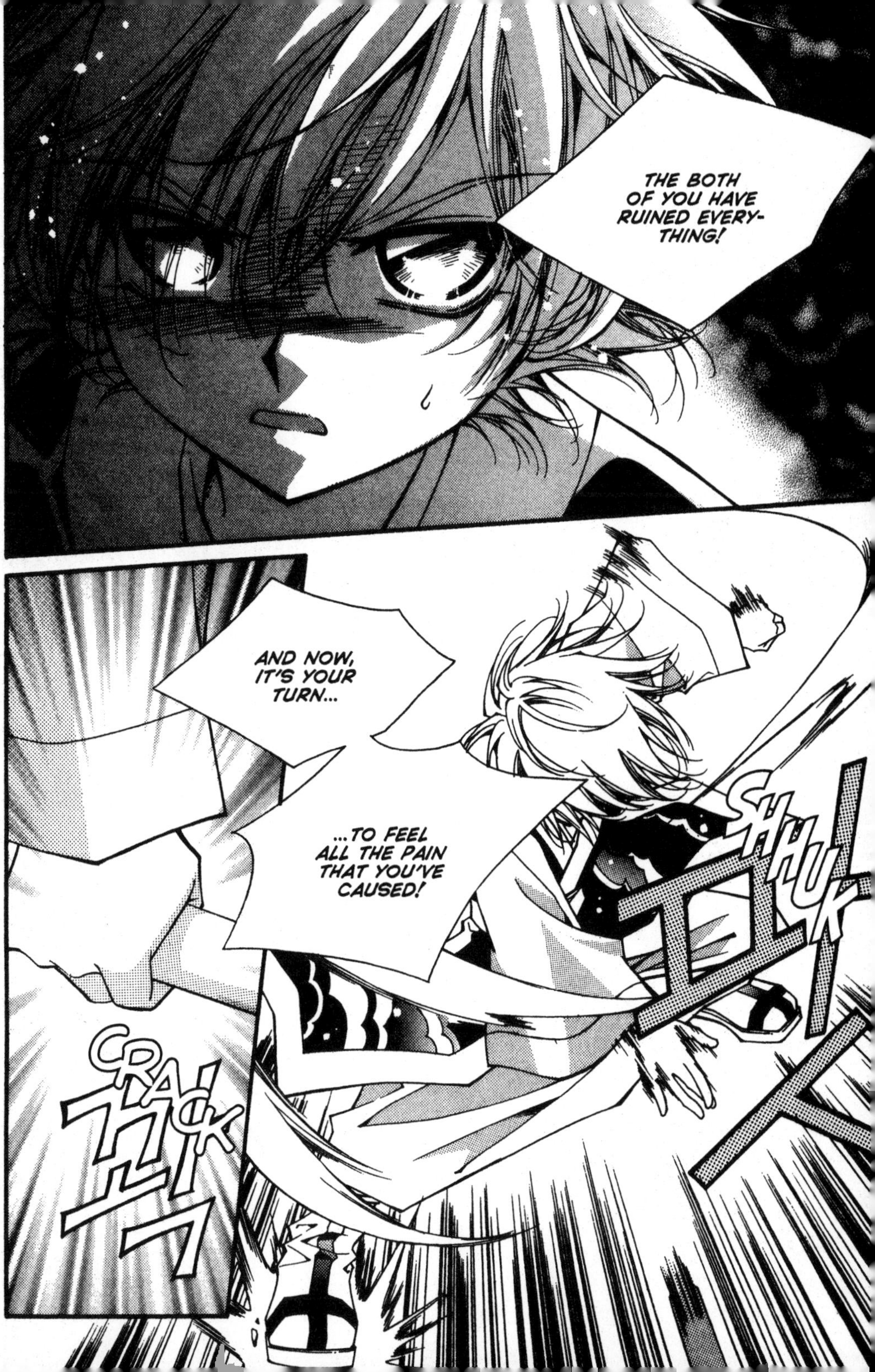
THE BOTH OF YOU HAVE RUINED EVERY-THING!
AND NOW, IT'S YOUR TURN...
...TO FEEL ALL THE PAIN THAT YOU'VE CAUSED!
SHHUK
CRACK

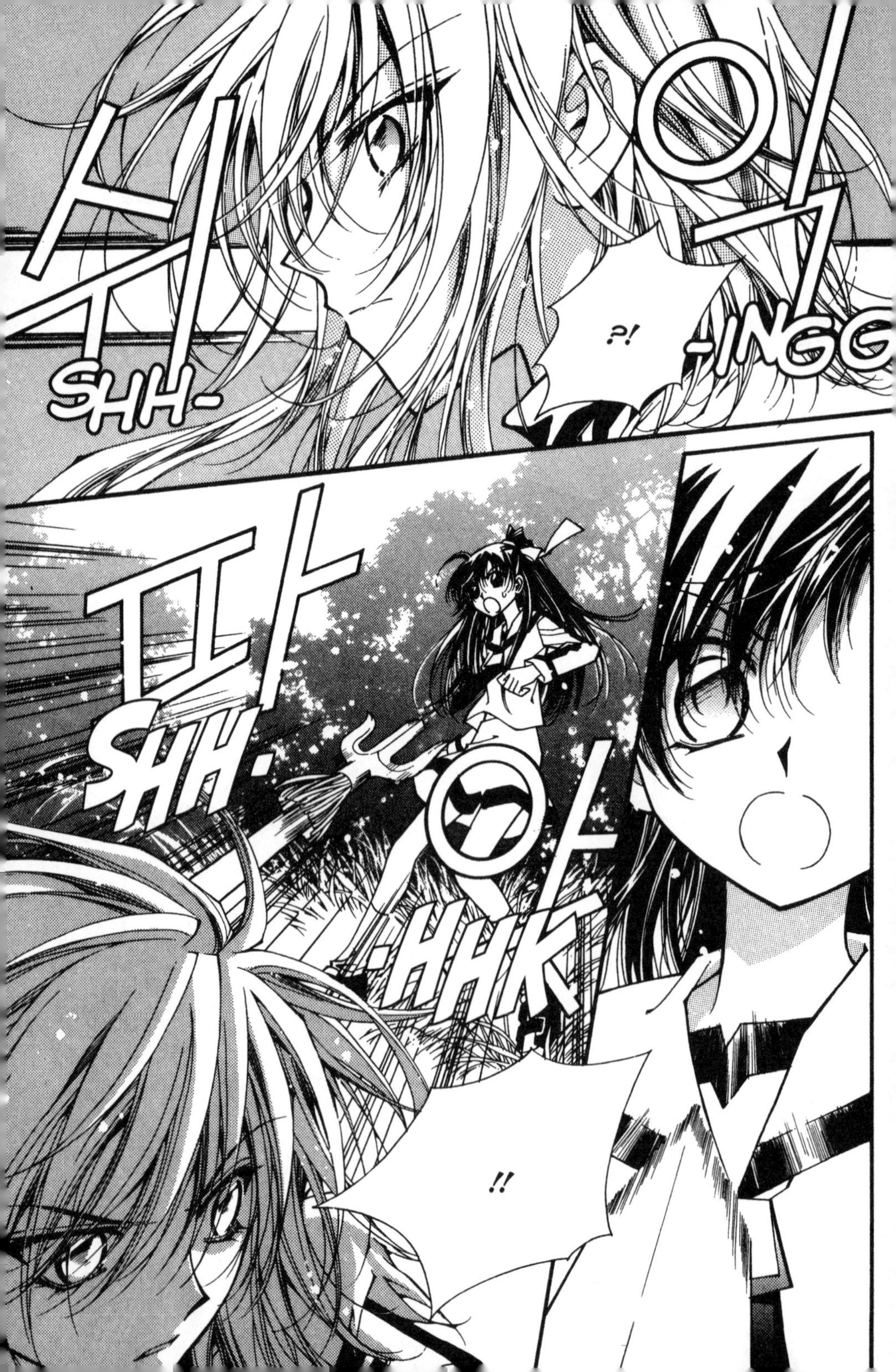
SHH-
?!
-INGG
SHH-
-HHK
!!

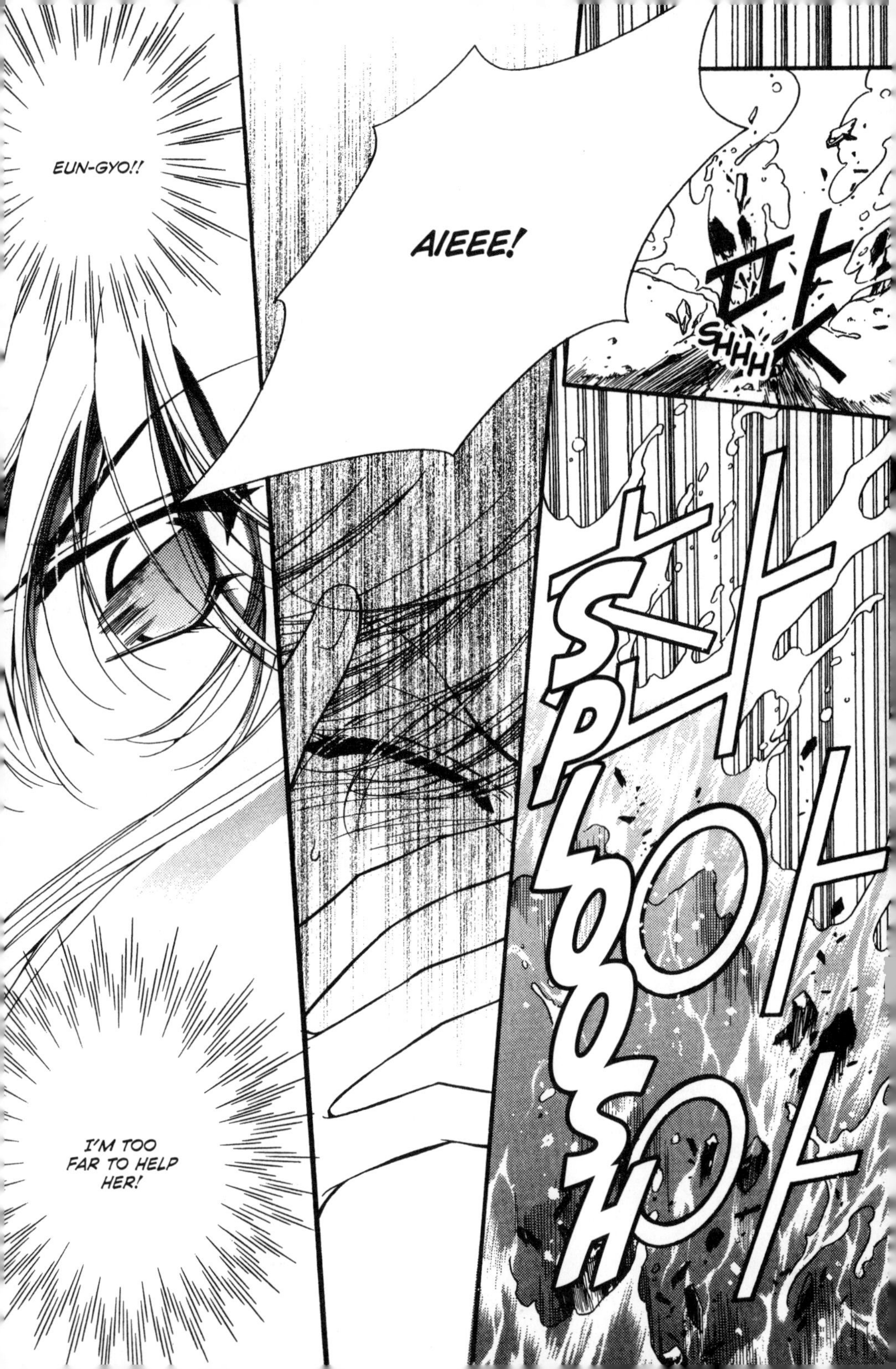
EUN-GYO!!
I'M TOO FAR TO HELP HER!
AIEEE!
SHHHH
SPLOOOSH

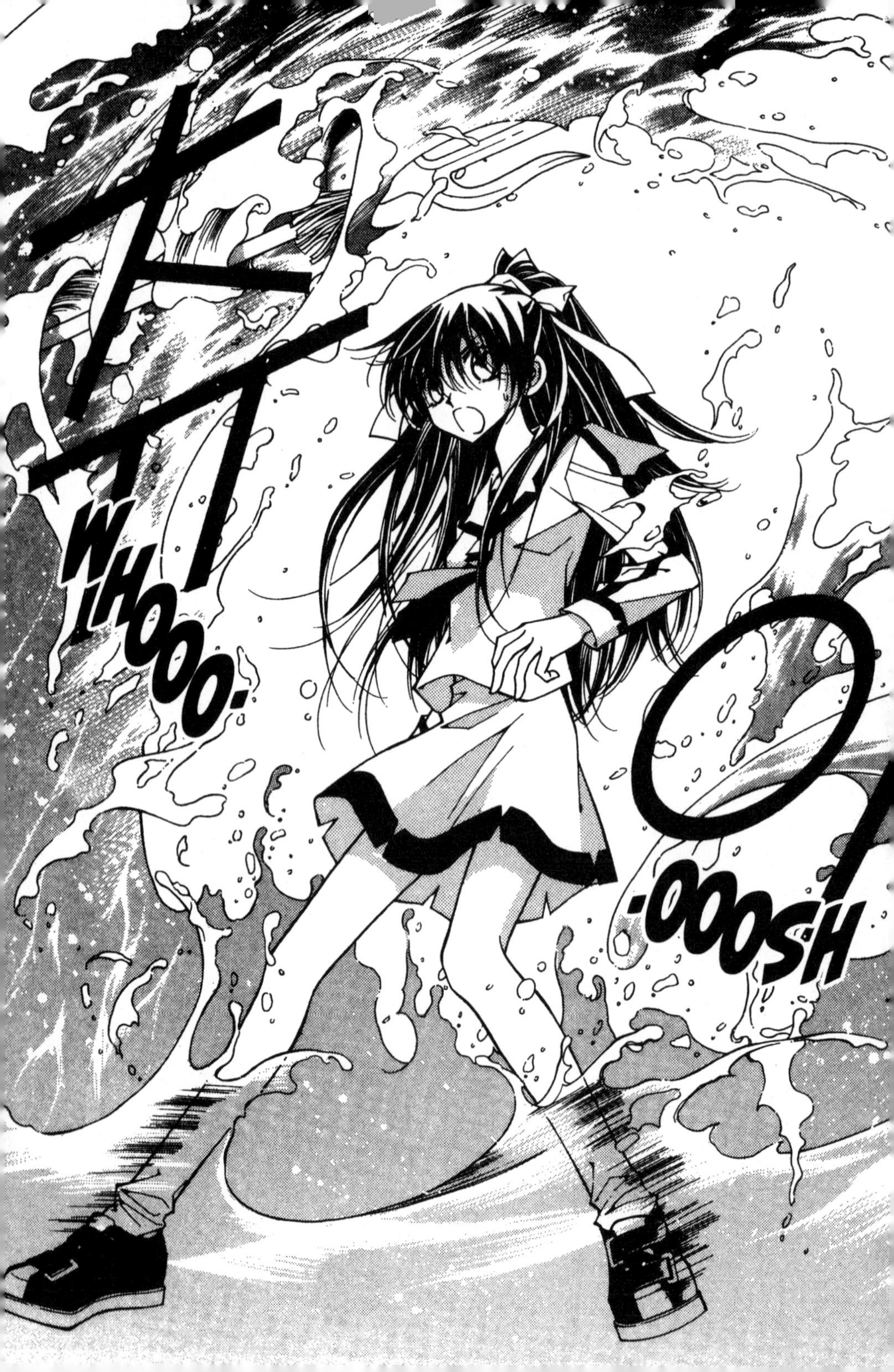
WHOOO-
-OOOSH

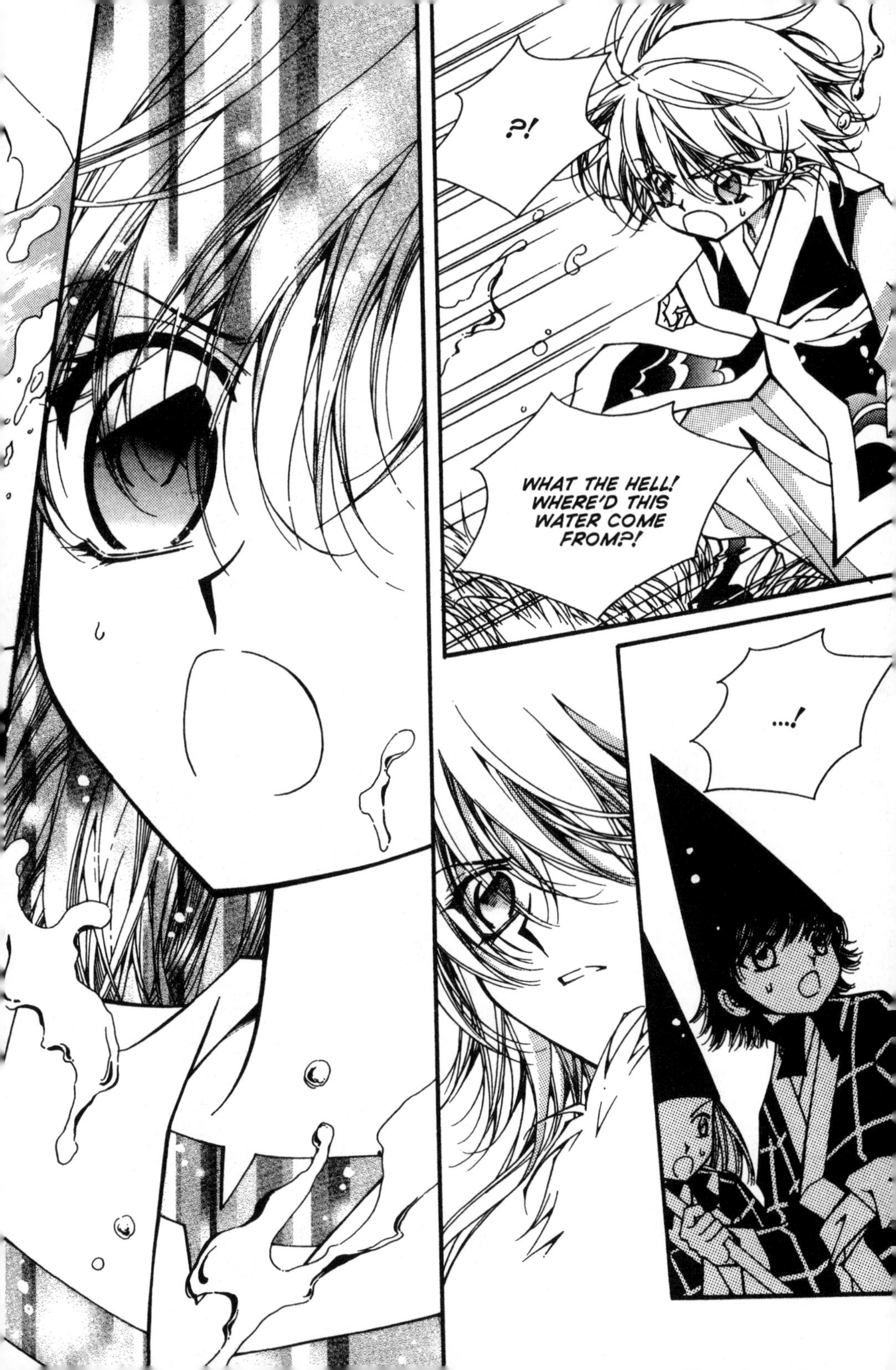
?!
WHAT THE HELL! WHERE'D THIS WATER COME FROM?!
...!

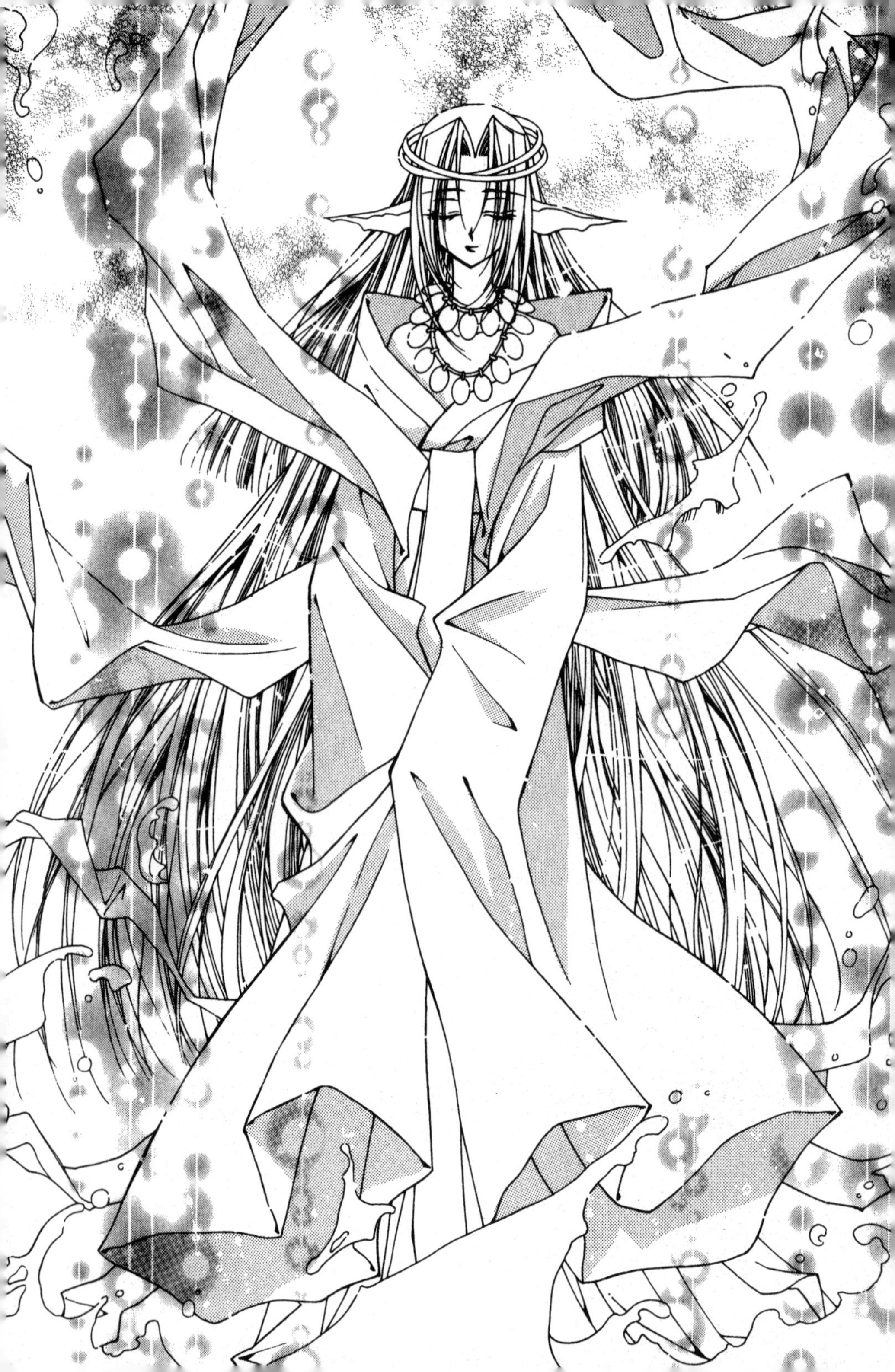

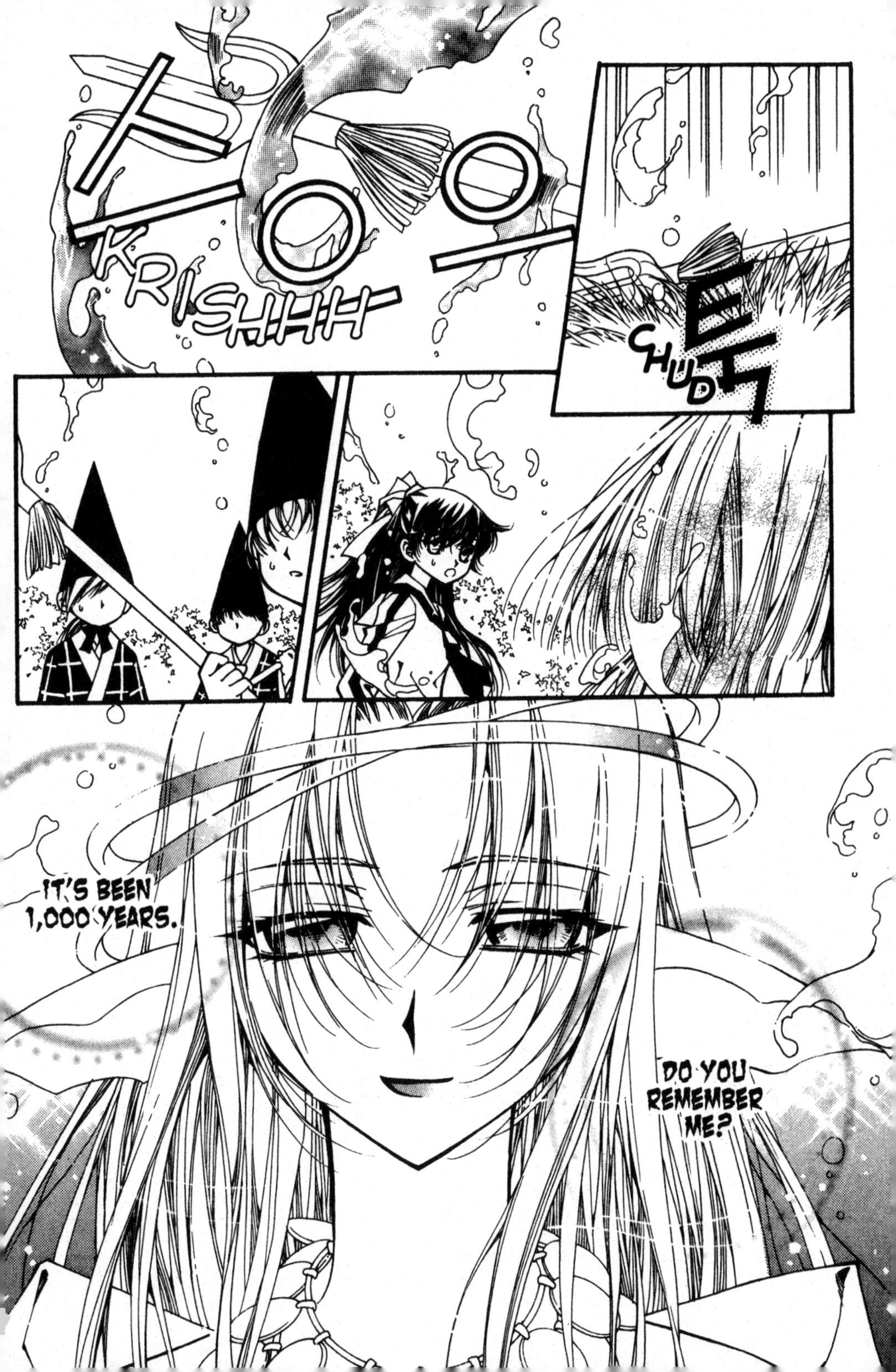
KRISHHH
CHUD
IT'S BEEN 1,000 YEARS.
DO YOU REMEMBER ME?

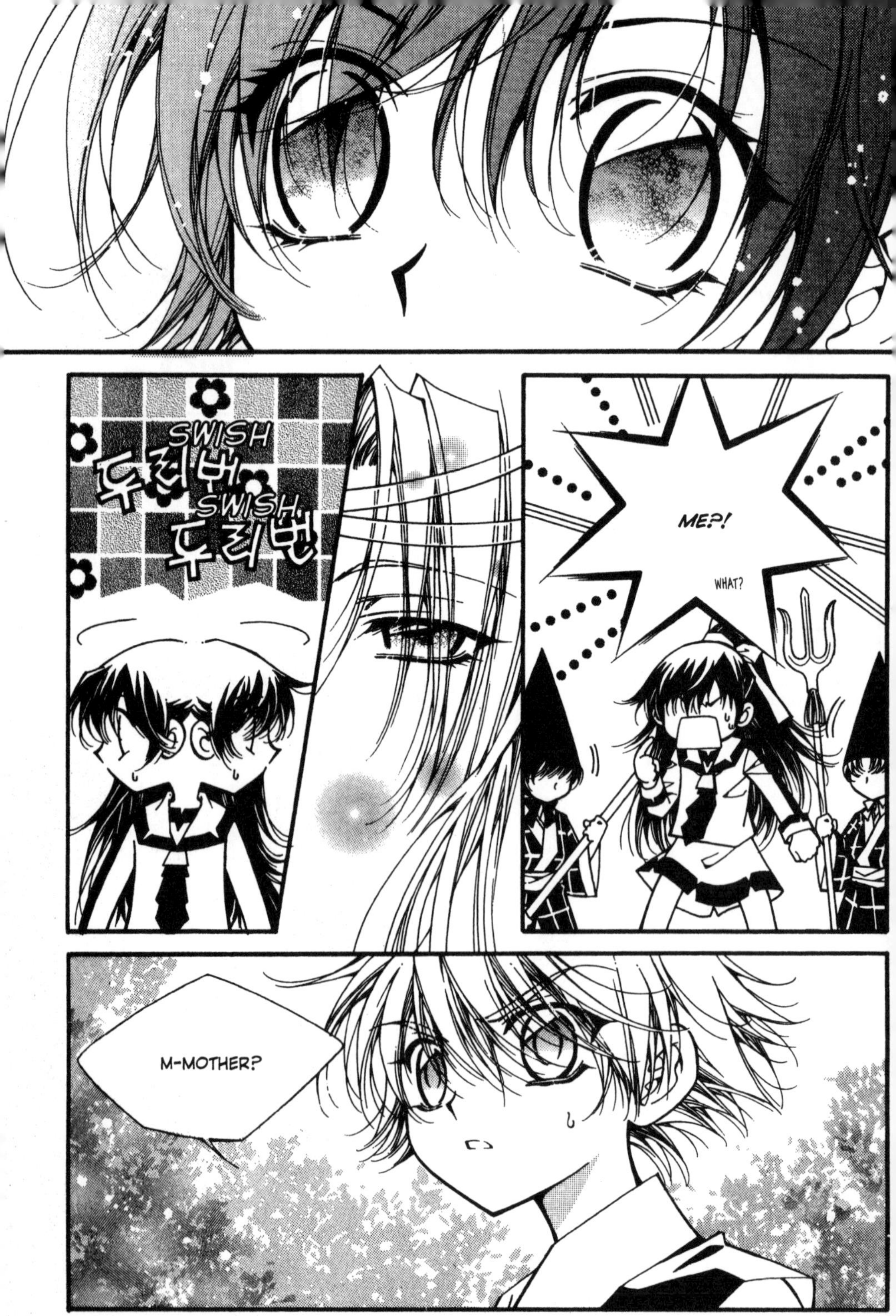
SWISH
두리번
SWISH
두리번
ME?!
WHAT?
M-MOTHER?

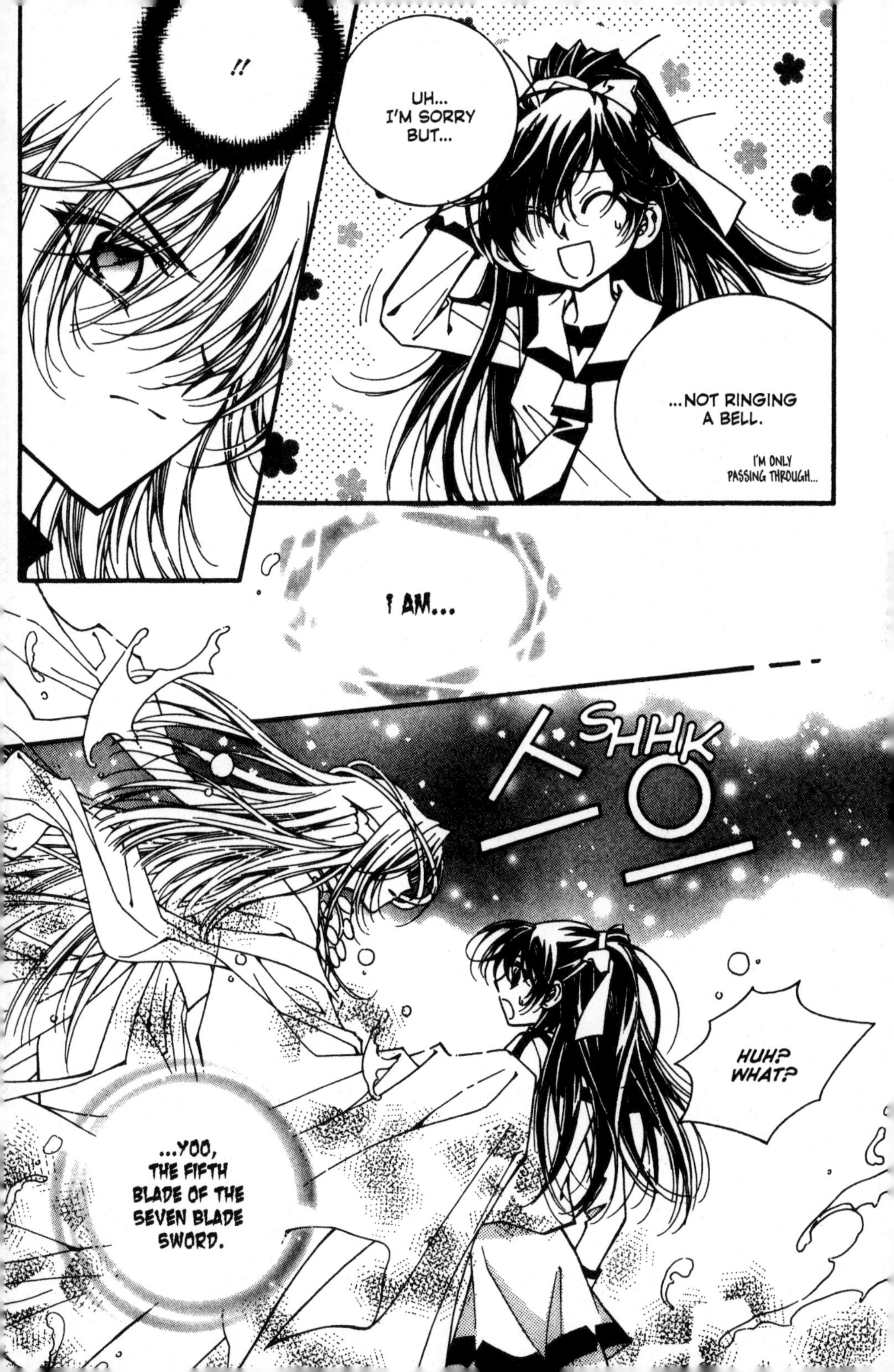
!!
UH... I'M SORRY BUT...
...NOT RINGING A BELL.
I'M ONLY PASSING THROUGH...
I AM...
SHHK
...YOO, THE FIFTH BLADE OF THE SEVEN BLADE SWORD.
HUH? WHAT?

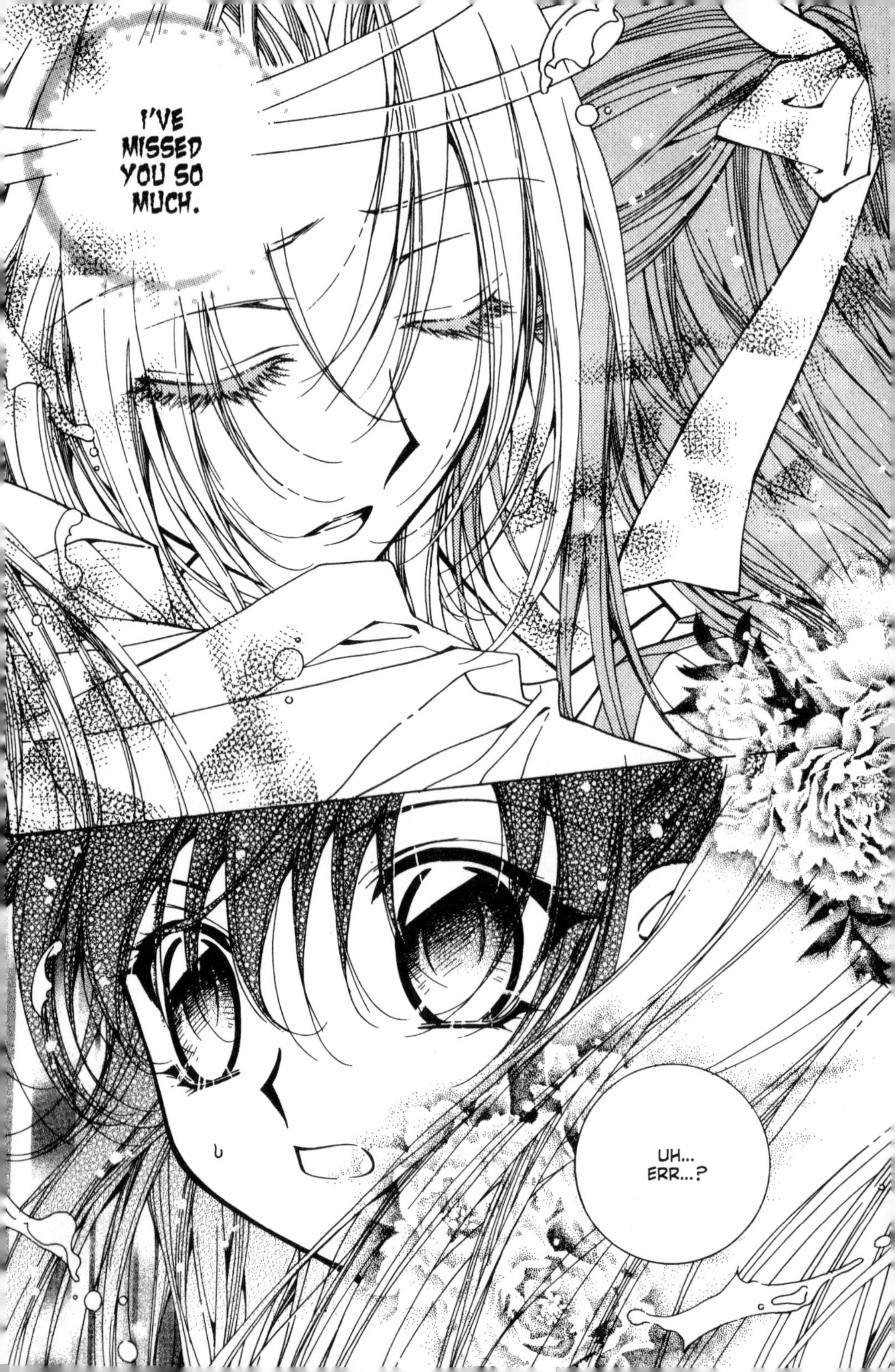
I'VE MISSED YOU SO MUCH.
UH... ERR...?

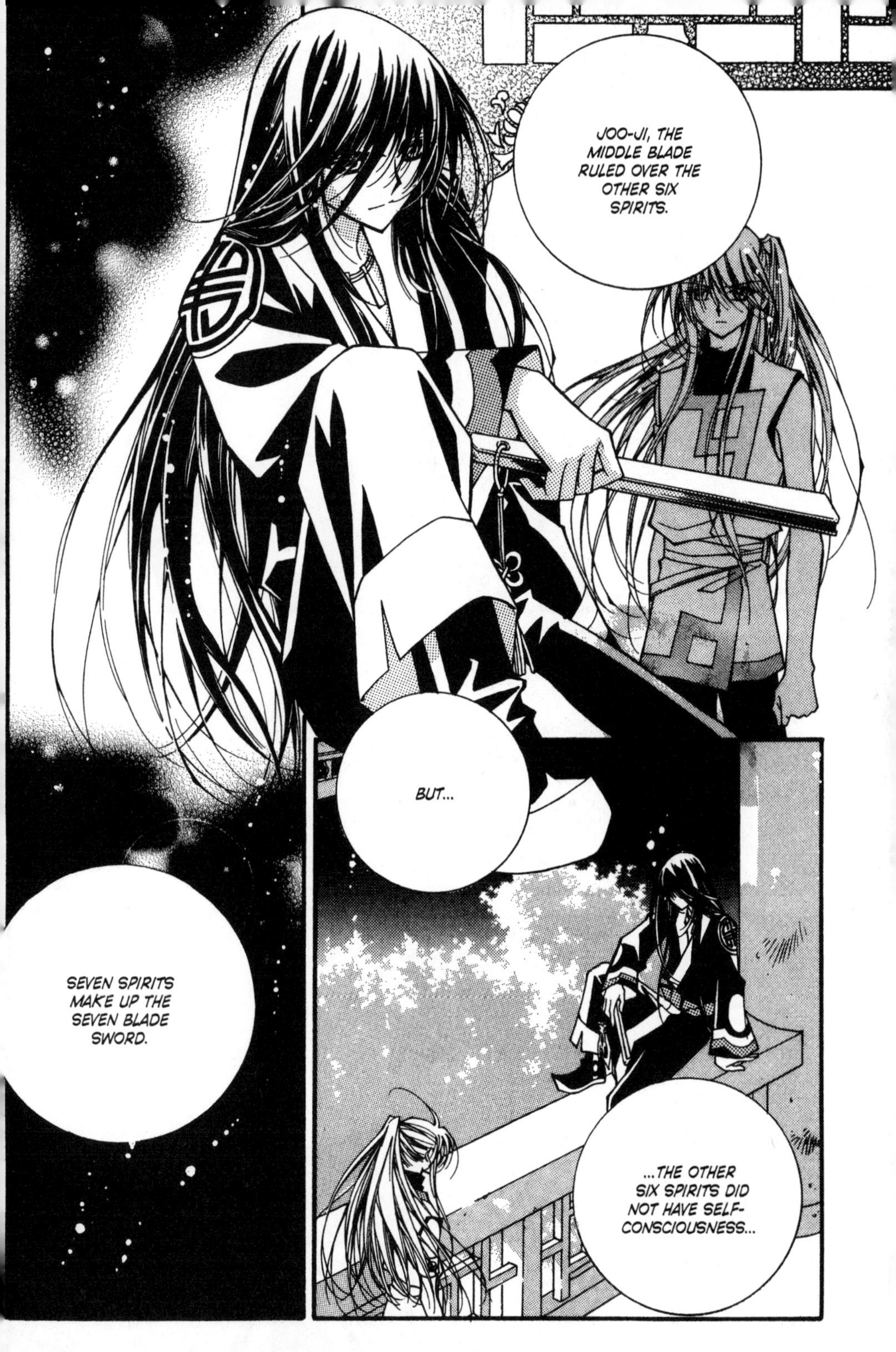

SEVEN SPIRITS MAKE UP THE SEVEN BLADE SWORD.
JOO-JI, THE MIDDLE BLADE RULED OVER THE OTHER SIX SPIRITS.
BUT...
...THE OTHER SIX SPIRITS DID NOT HAVE SELF-CONSCIOUSNESS...

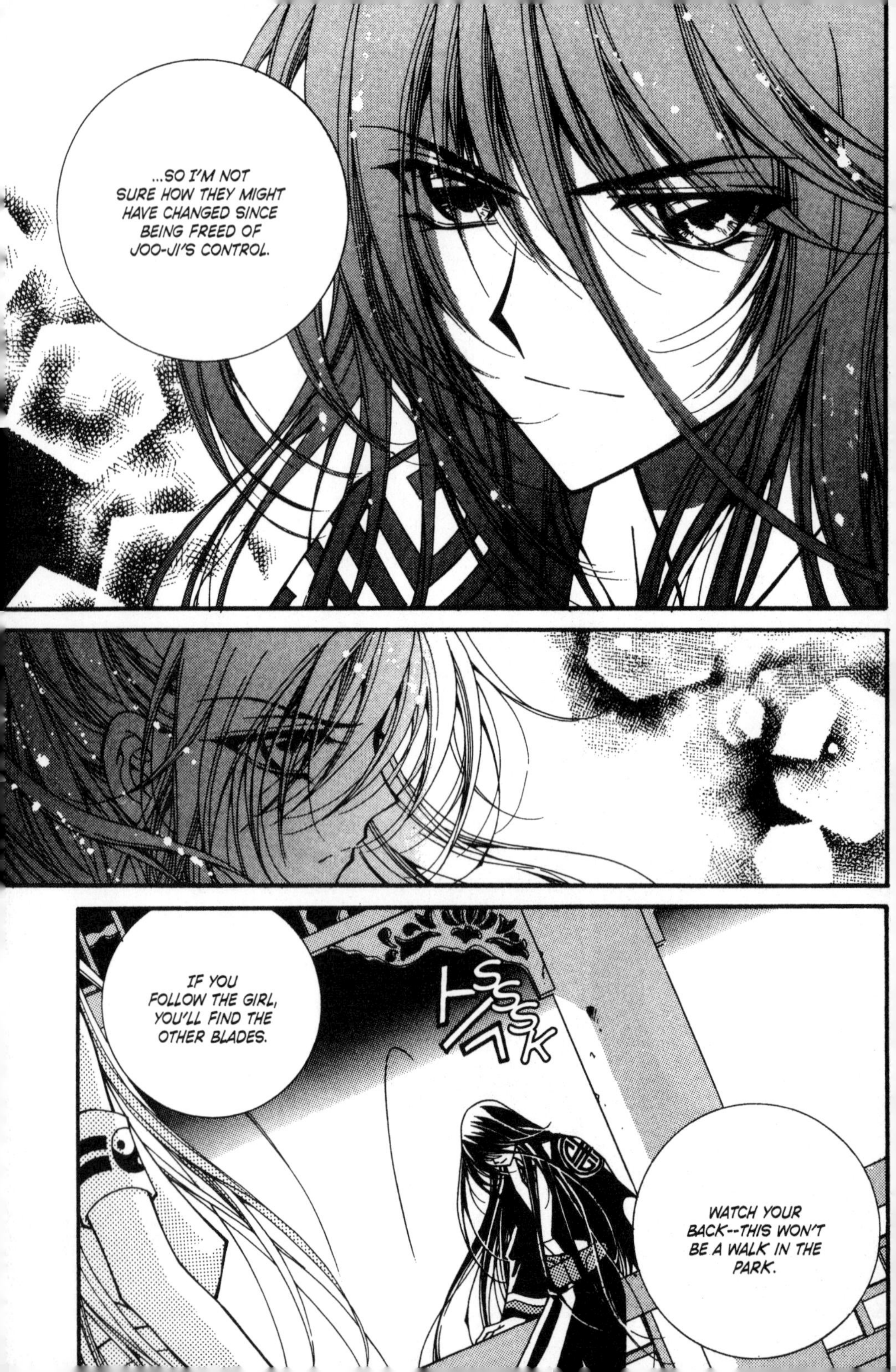
...SO I'M NOT SURE HOW THEY MIGHT HAVE CHANGED SINCE BEING FREED OF JOO-JI'S CONTROL.
IF YOU FOLLOW THE GIRL, YOU'LL FIND THE OTHER BLADES.
SSSK
WATCH YOUR BACK--THIS WON'T BE A WALK IN THE PARK.

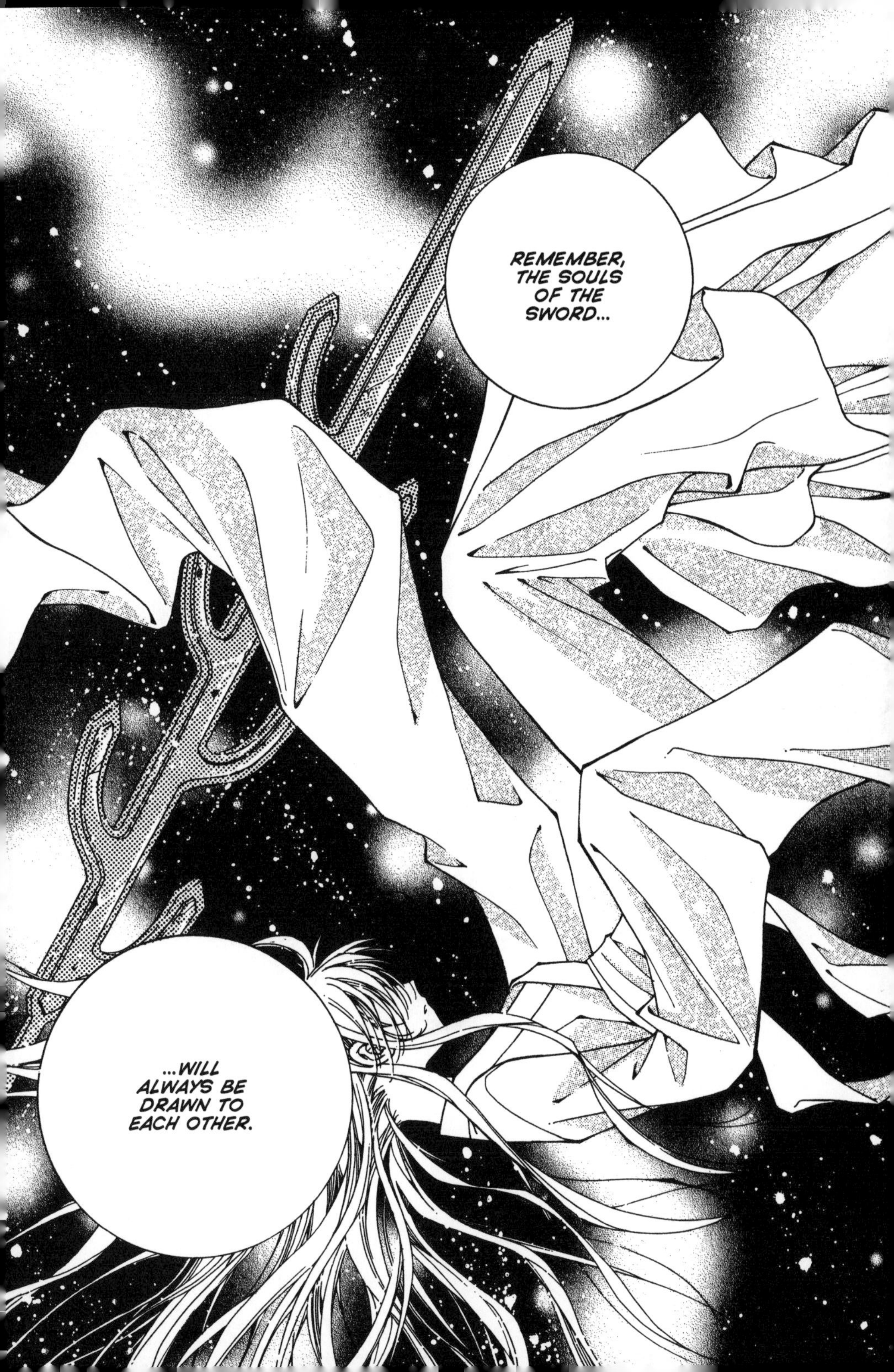
REMEMBER, THE SOULS OF THE SWORD...
...WILL ALWAYS BE DRAWN TO EACH OTHER.

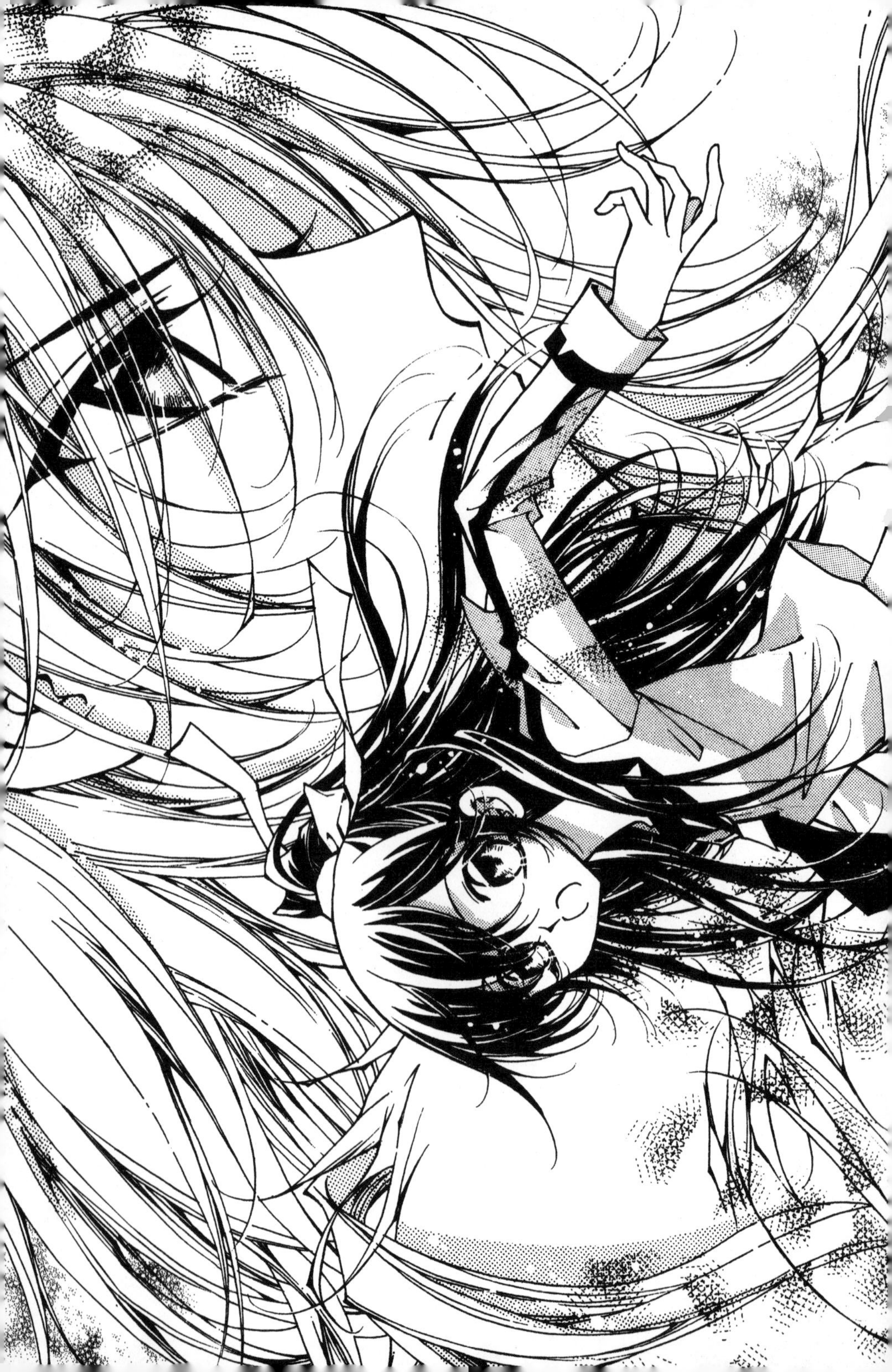

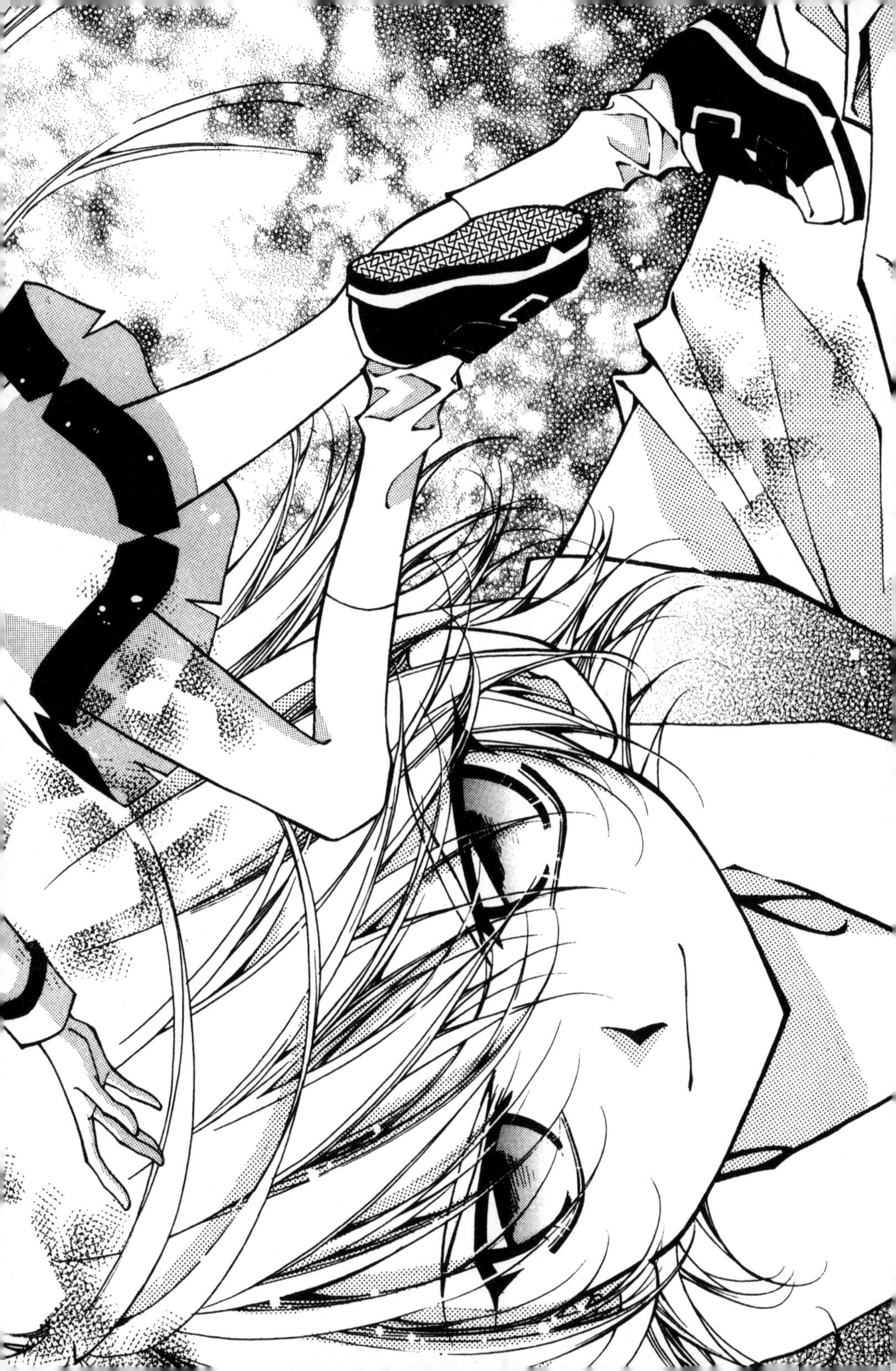

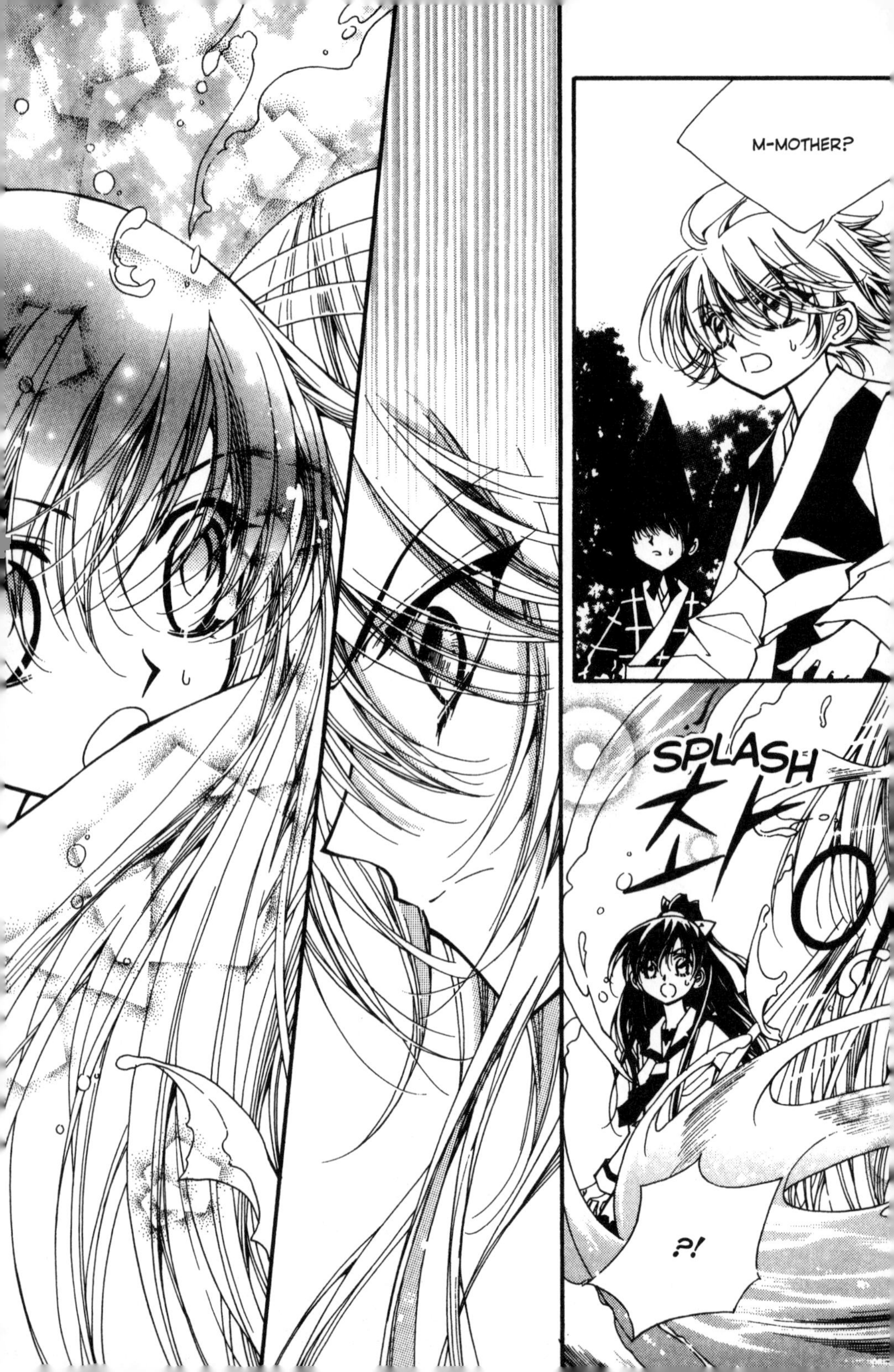
M-MOTHER?
SPLASH
촤
?!

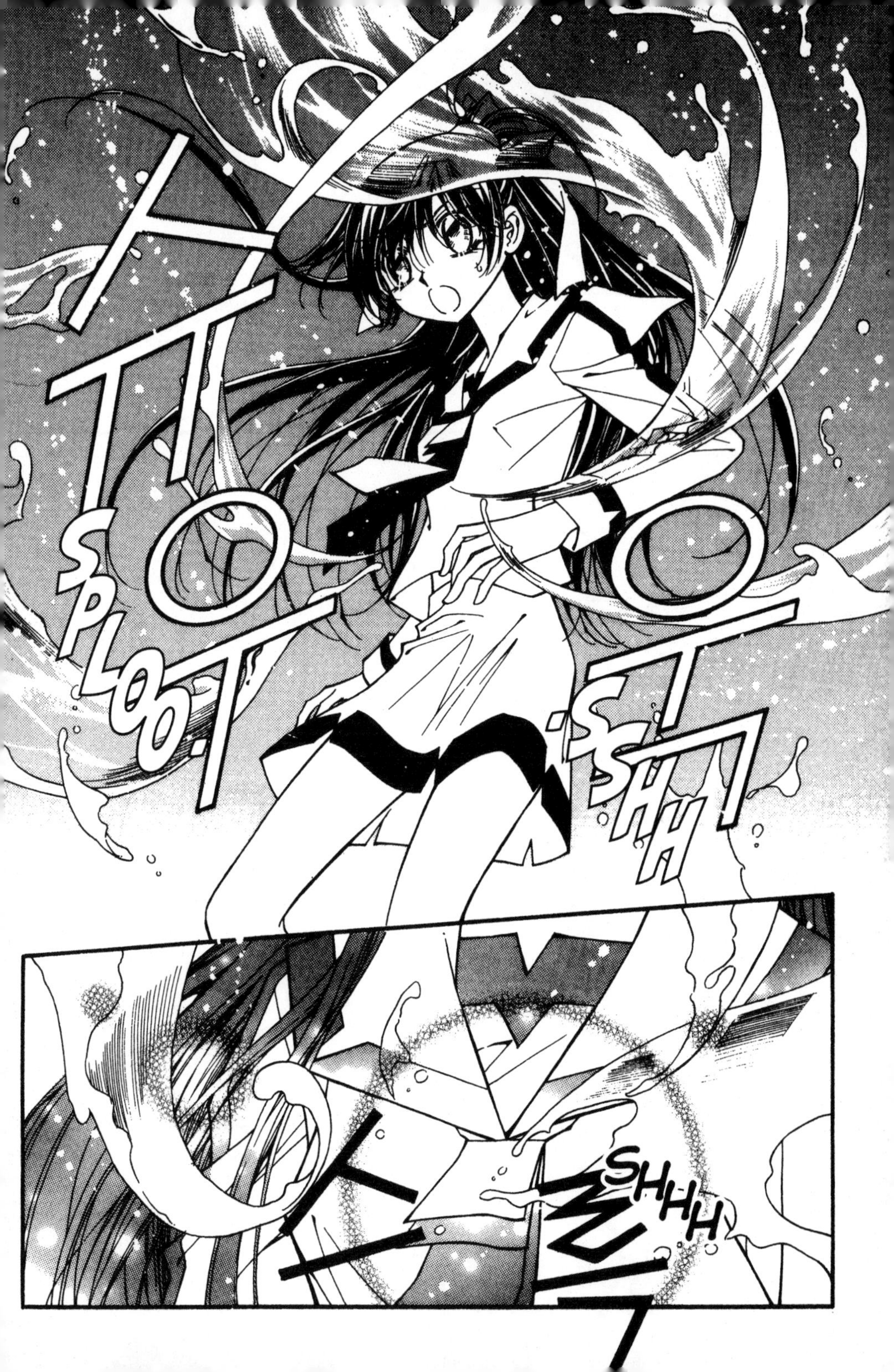
SPLOOT
SSHH
SHHHH

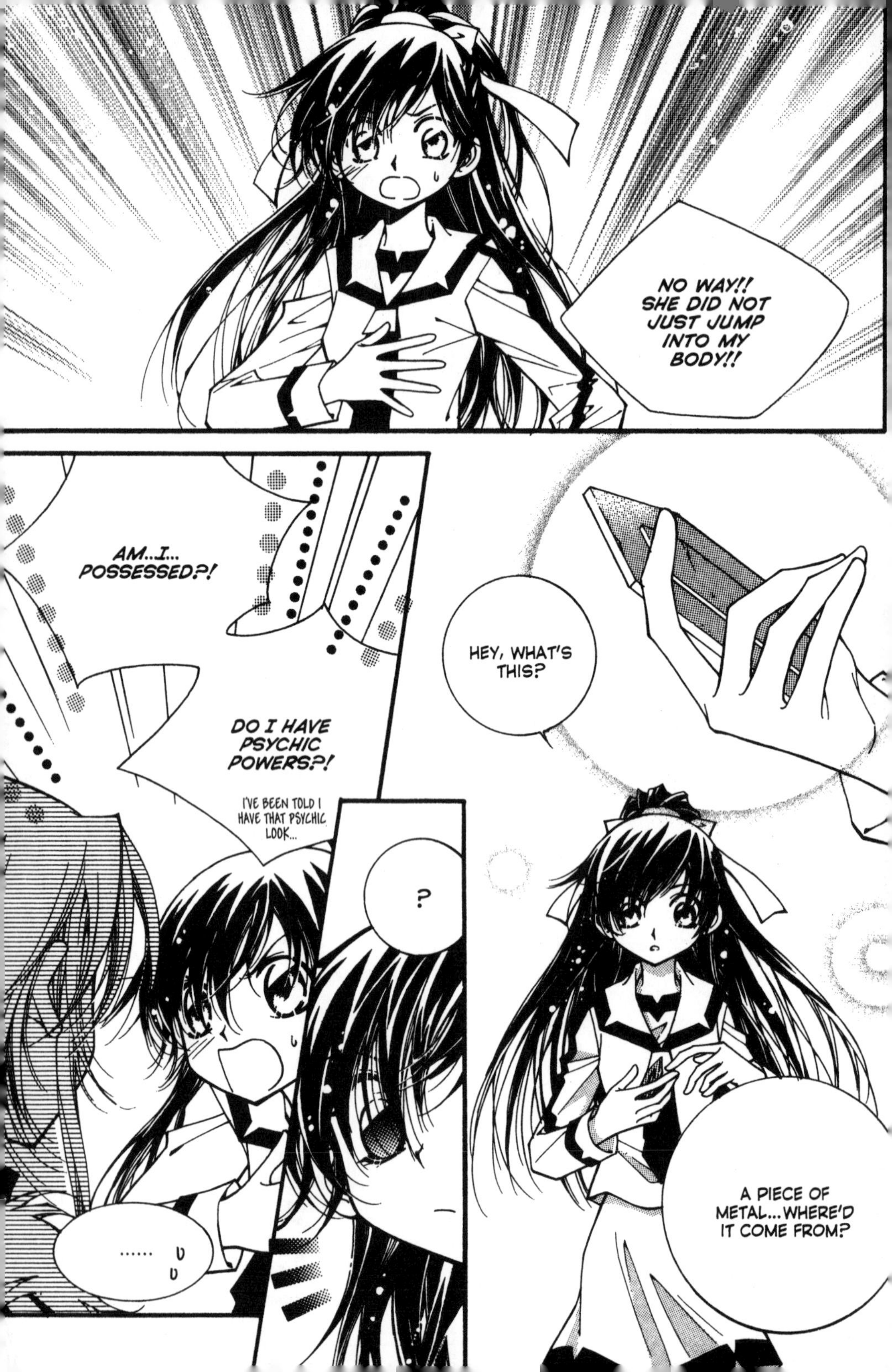
NO WAY!! SHE DID NOT JUST JUMP INTO MY BODY!!
AM...I... POSSESSED?!
DO I HAVE PSYCHIC POWERS?!
I'VE BEEN TOLD I HAVE THAT PSYCHIC LOOK...
?
......
HEY, WHAT'S THIS?
A PIECE OF METAL...WHERE'D IT COME FROM?

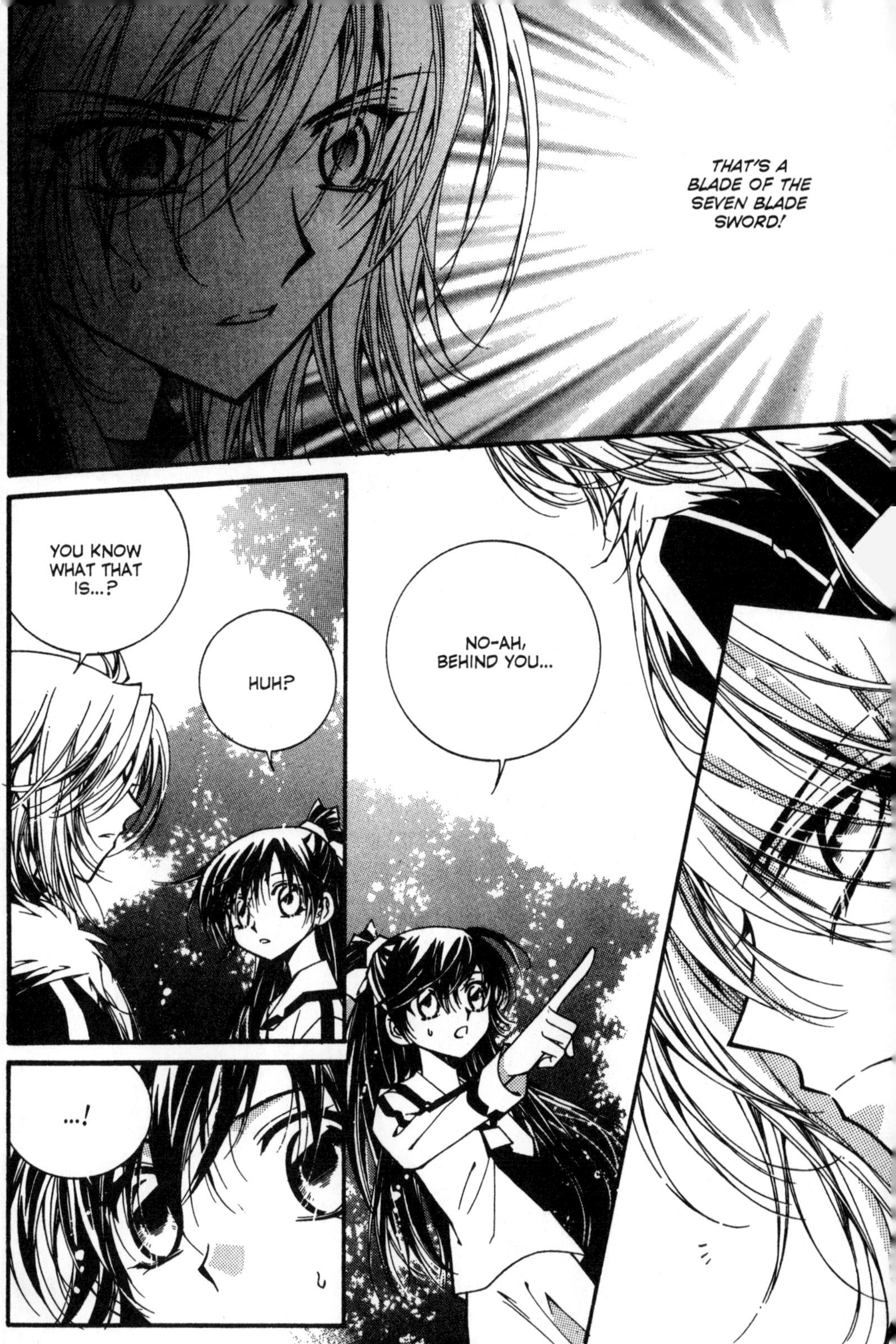
THAT'S A BLADE OF THE SEVEN BLADE SWORD!
YOU KNOW WHAT THAT IS...?
HUH?
NO-AH, BEHIND YOU...
...!

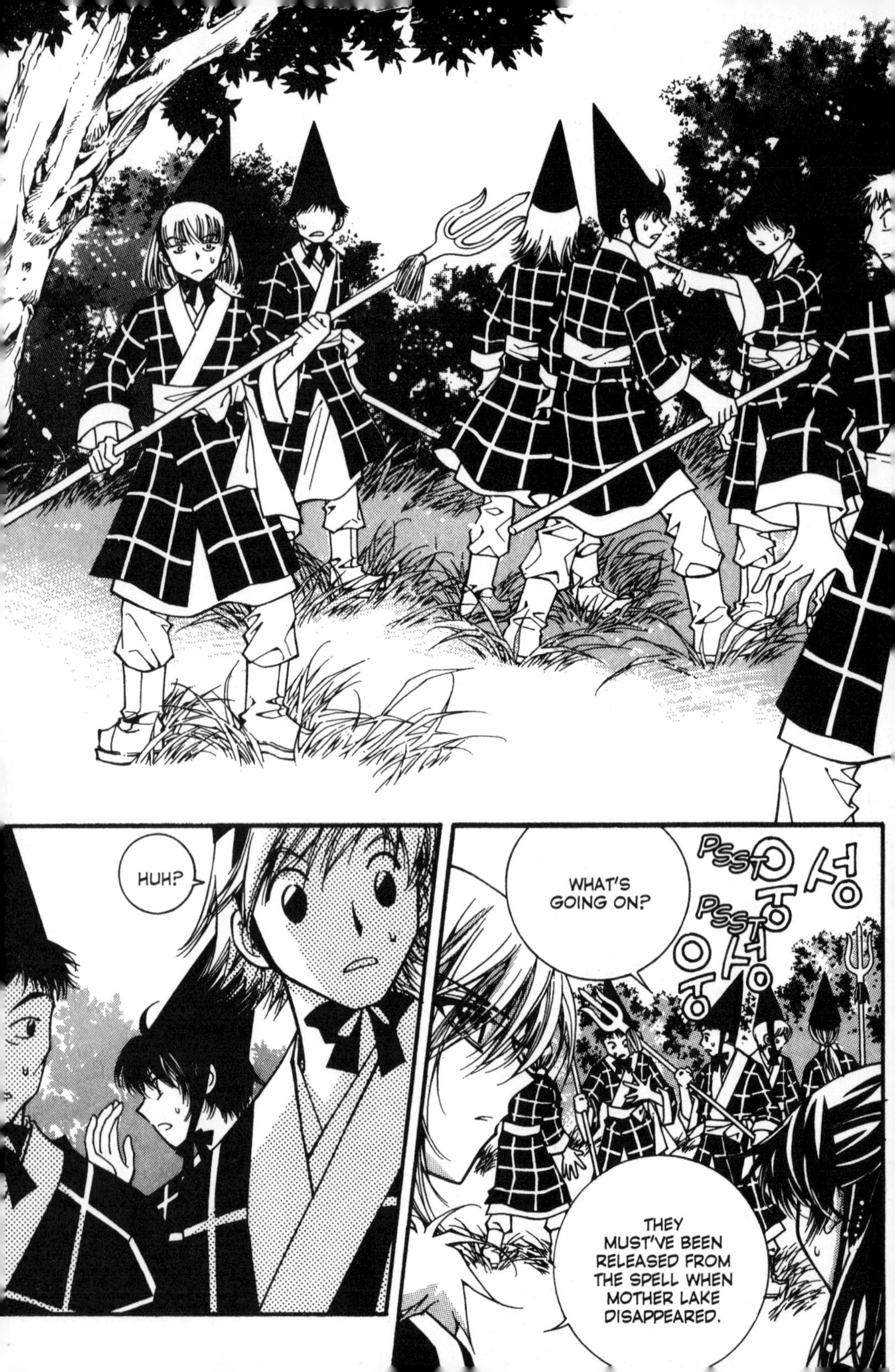
HUH?
WHAT'S GOING ON?
PSST PSST
THEY MUST'VE BEEN RELEASED FROM THE SPELL WHEN MOTHER LAKE DISAPPEARED.

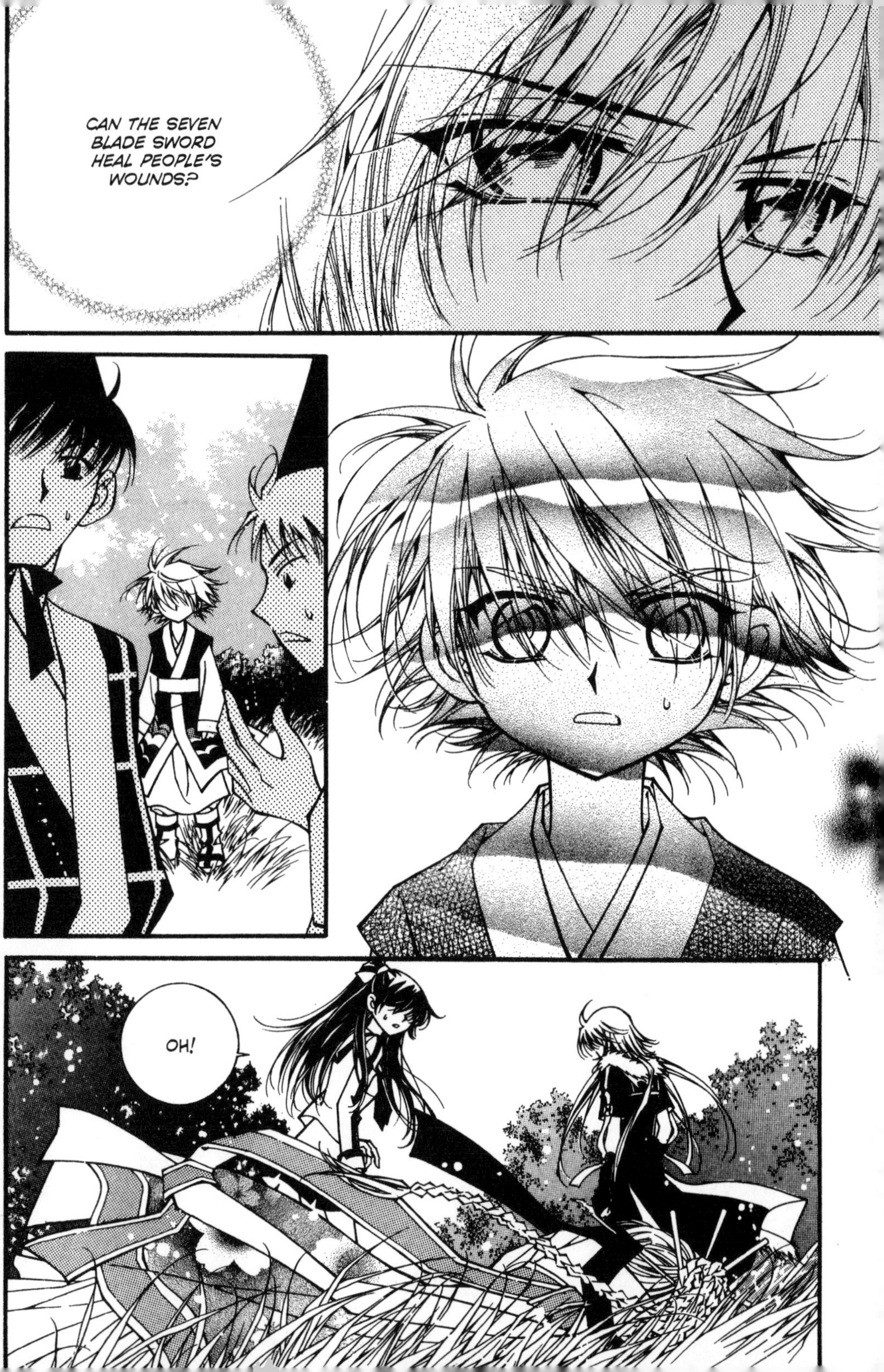
CAN THE SEVEN BLADE SWORD HEAL PEOPLE'S WOUNDS?
OH!

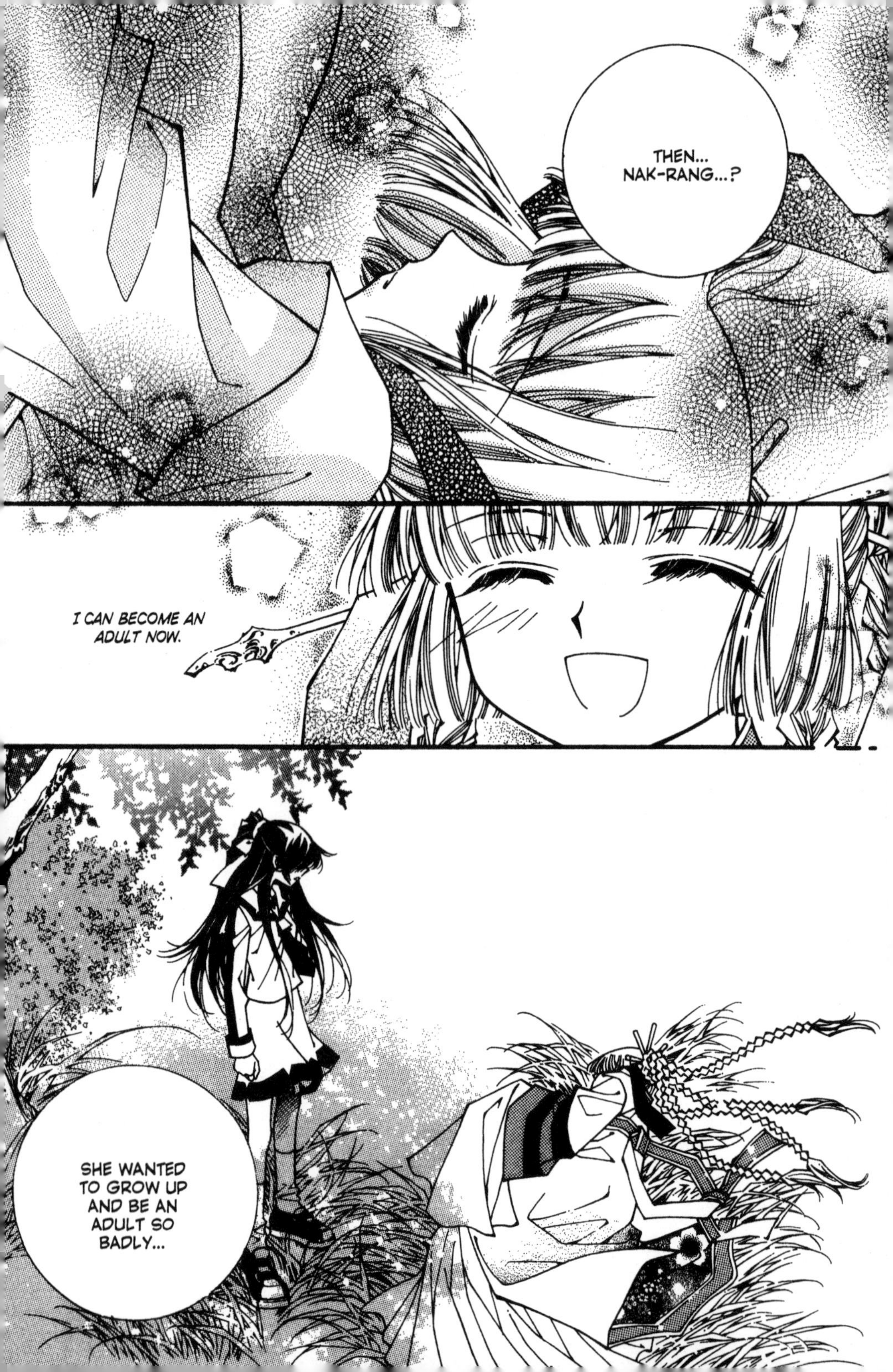
THEN... NAK-RANG...?
I CAN BECOME AN ADULT NOW.
SHE WANTED TO GROW UP AND BE AN ADULT SO BADLY...

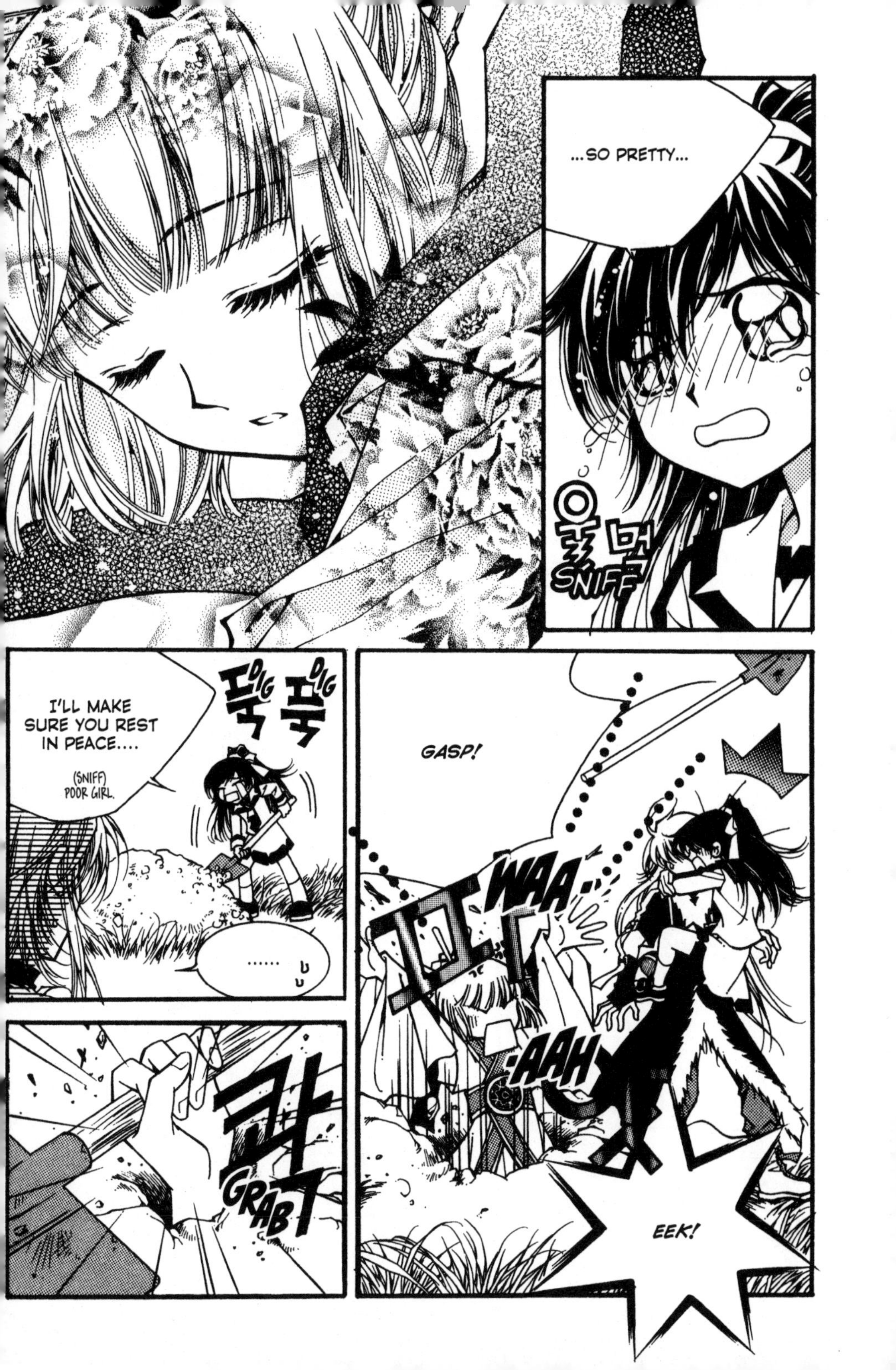
...SO PRETTY...
SNIFF
I'LL MAKE SURE YOU REST IN PEACE....
(SNIFF) POOR GIRL.
푹 푹
DIG DIG
......
콱
GRAB
GASP!
WAA-AAH
EEK!

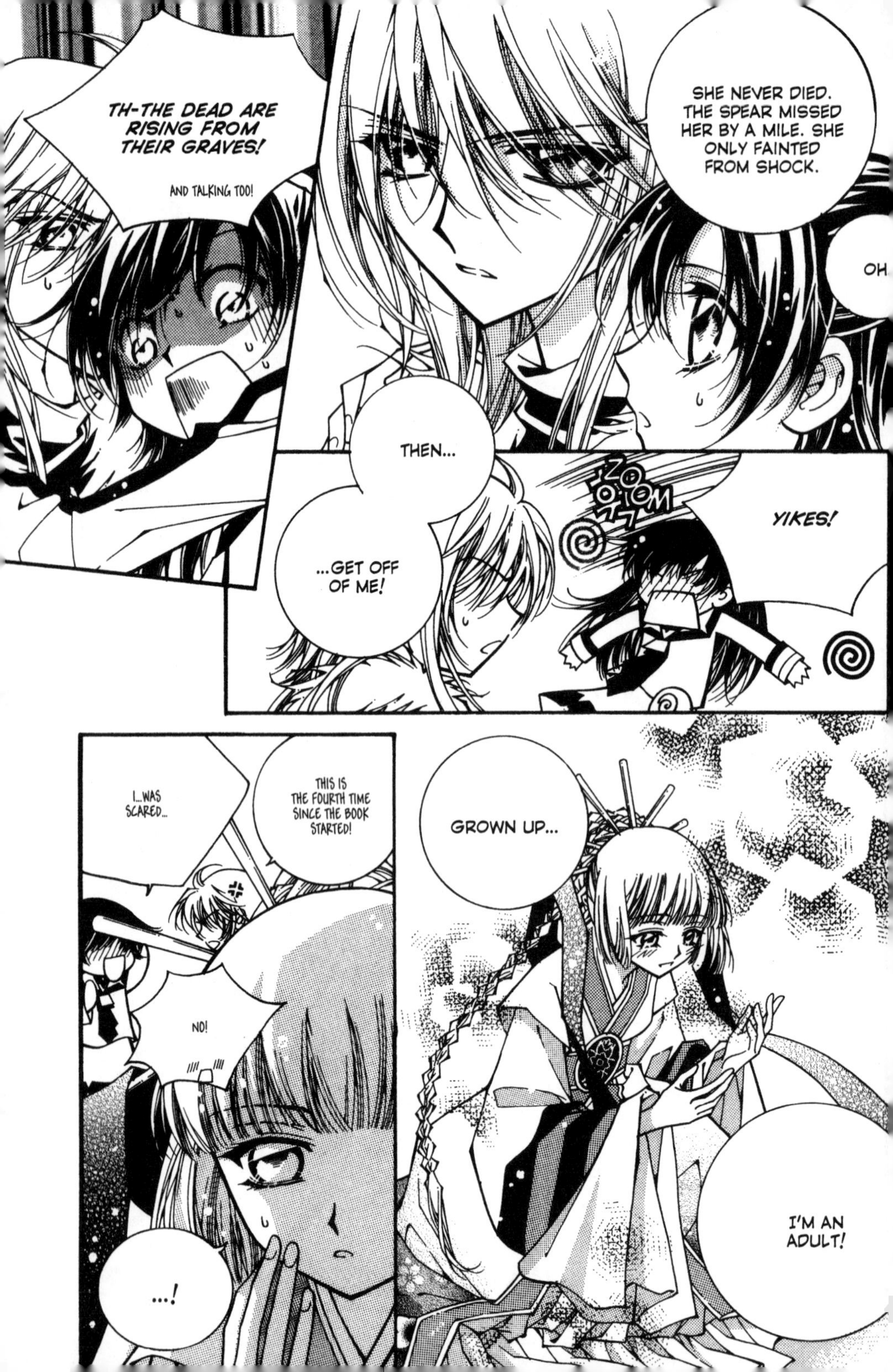
TH-THE DEAD ARE RISING FROM THEIR GRAVES!
AND TALKING TOO!
SHE NEVER DIED. THE SPEAR MISSED HER BY A MILE. SHE ONLY FAINTED FROM SHOCK.
OH
THEN...
...GET OFF OF ME!
ZOOM
YIKES!
I...WAS SCARED...
THIS IS THE FOURTH TIME SINCE THE BOOK STARTED!
NO!
...!
GROWN UP...
I'M AN ADULT!

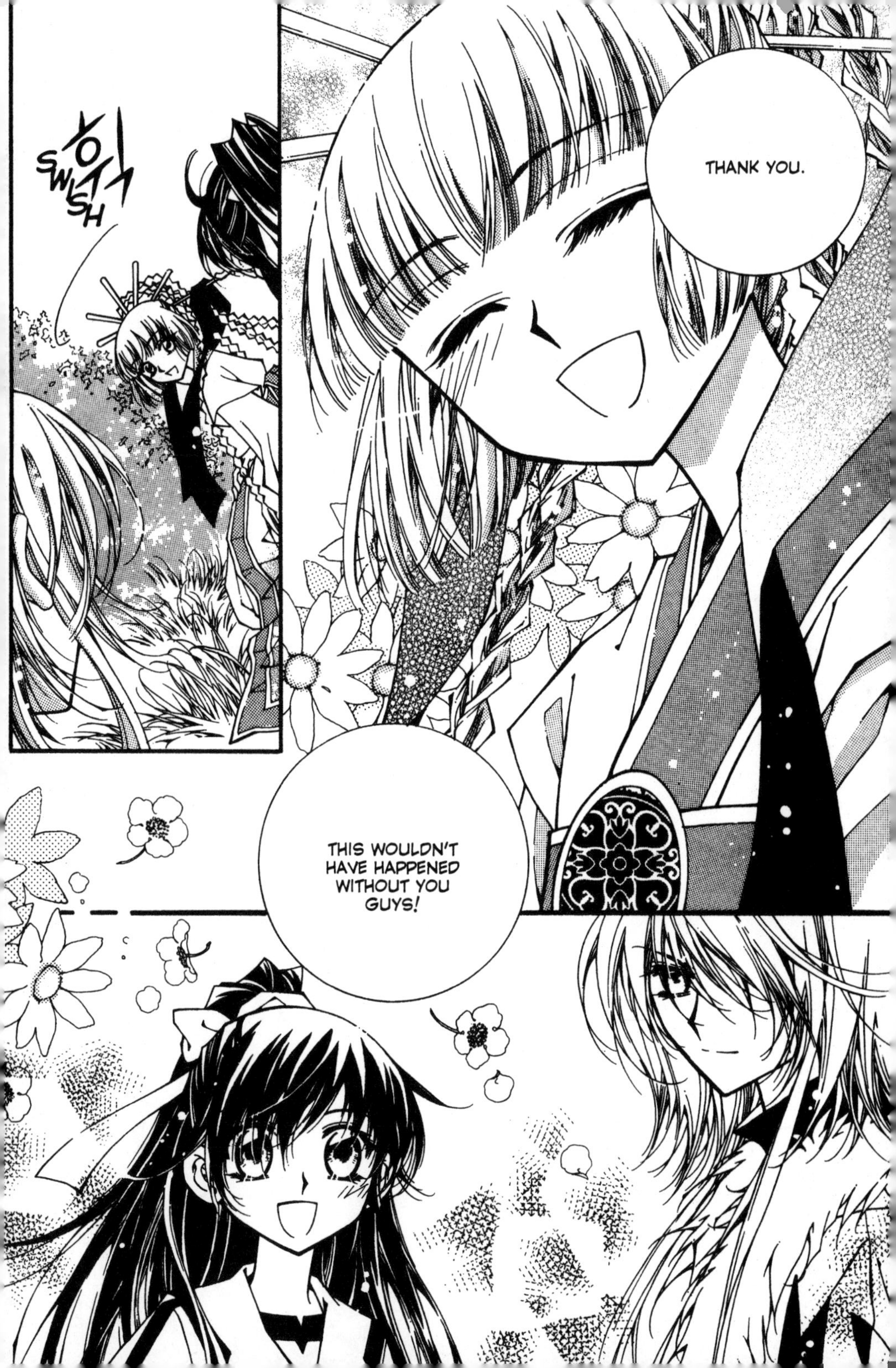
THANK YOU.
SWISH
THIS WOULDN'T HAVE HAPPENED WITHOUT YOU GUYS!

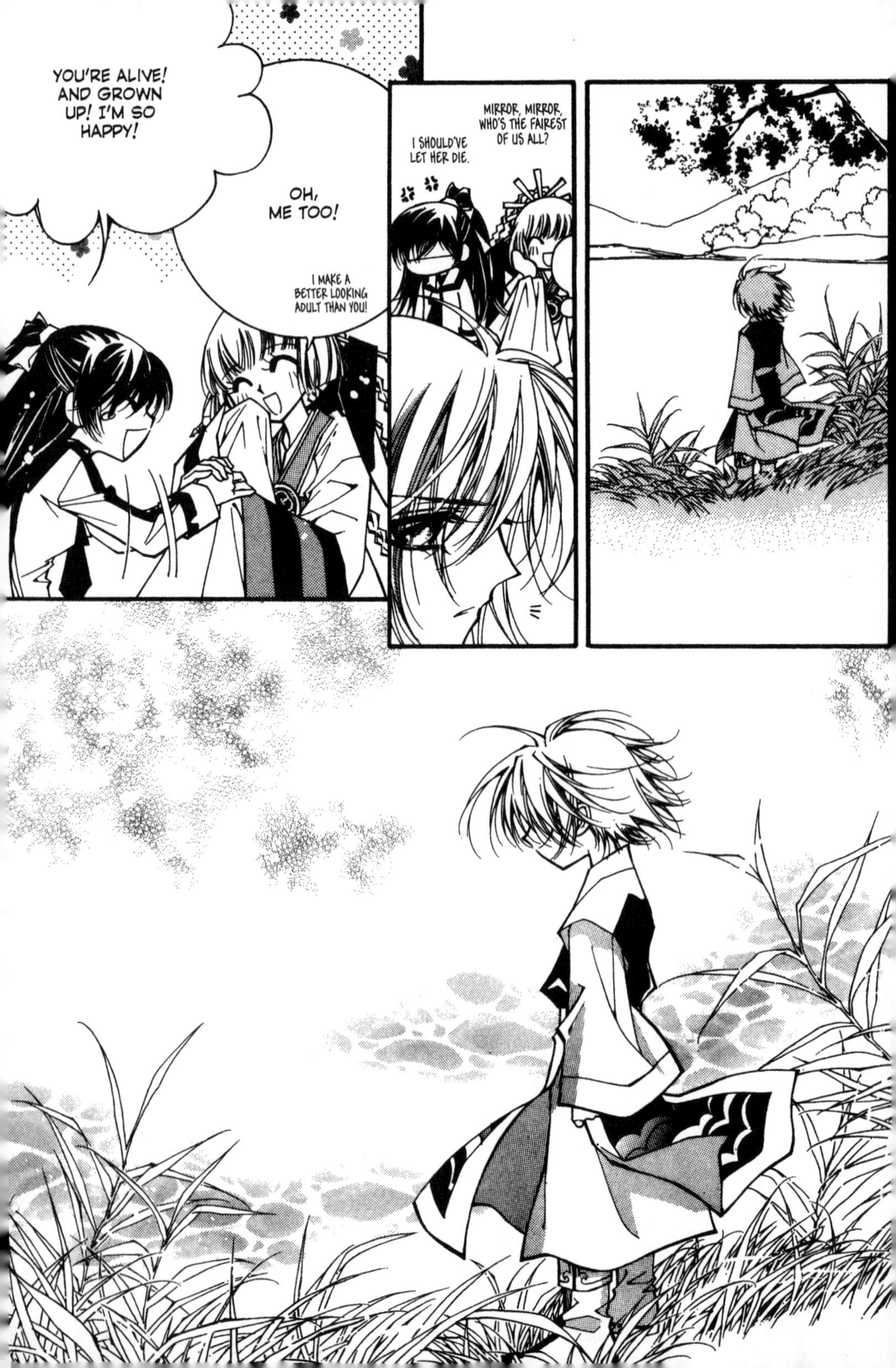
YOU'RE ALIVE! AND GROWN UP! I'M SO HAPPY!
OH, ME TOO!
I MAKE A BETTER LOOKING ADULT THAN YOU!
MIRROR, MIRROR, WHO'S THE FAIREST OF US ALL?
I SHOULD'VE LET HER DIE.

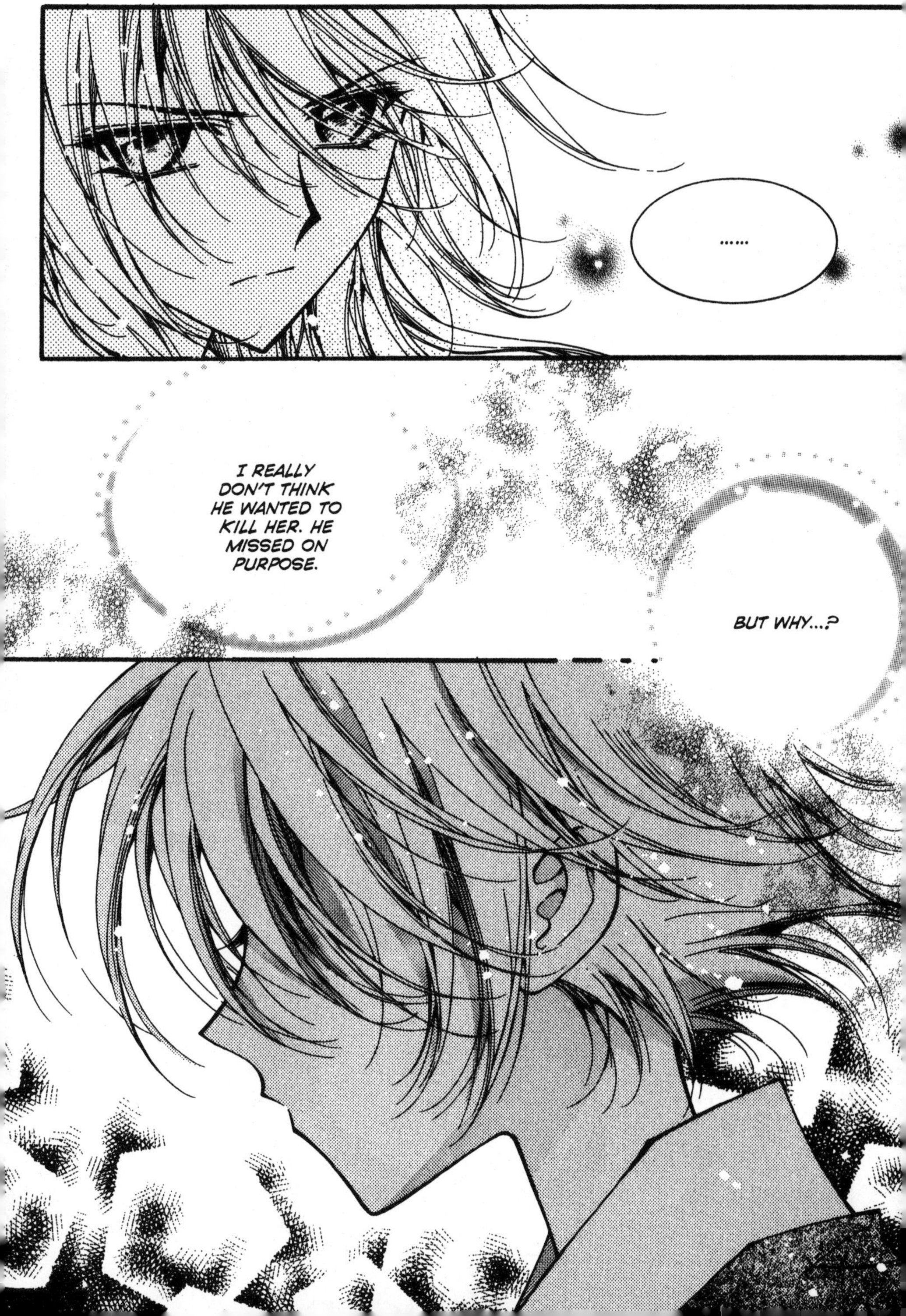
......
I REALLY DON'T THINK HE WANTED TO KILL HER. HE MISSED ON PURPOSE.
BUT WHY...?

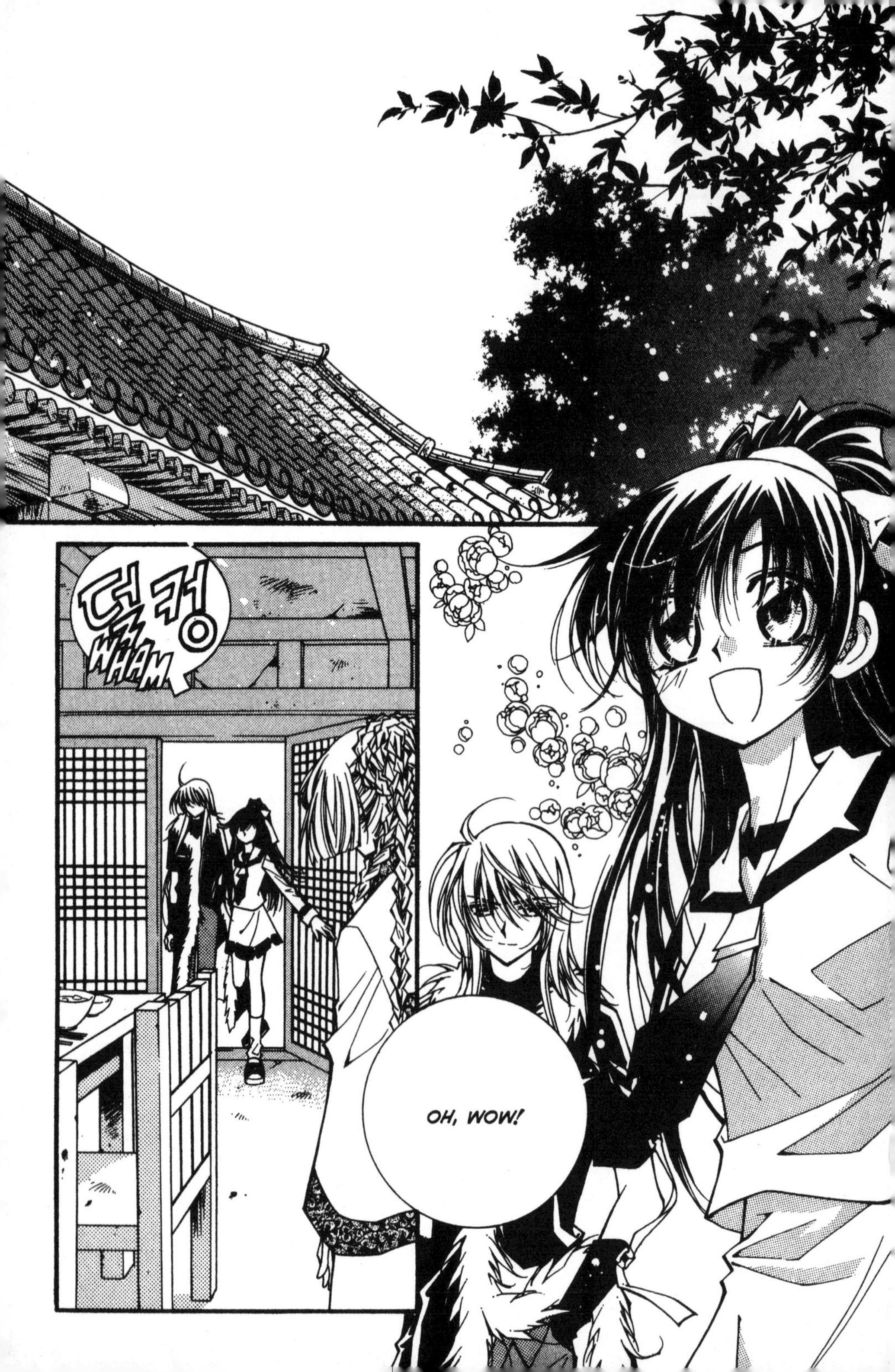
덜컹
WHAM
OH, WOW!

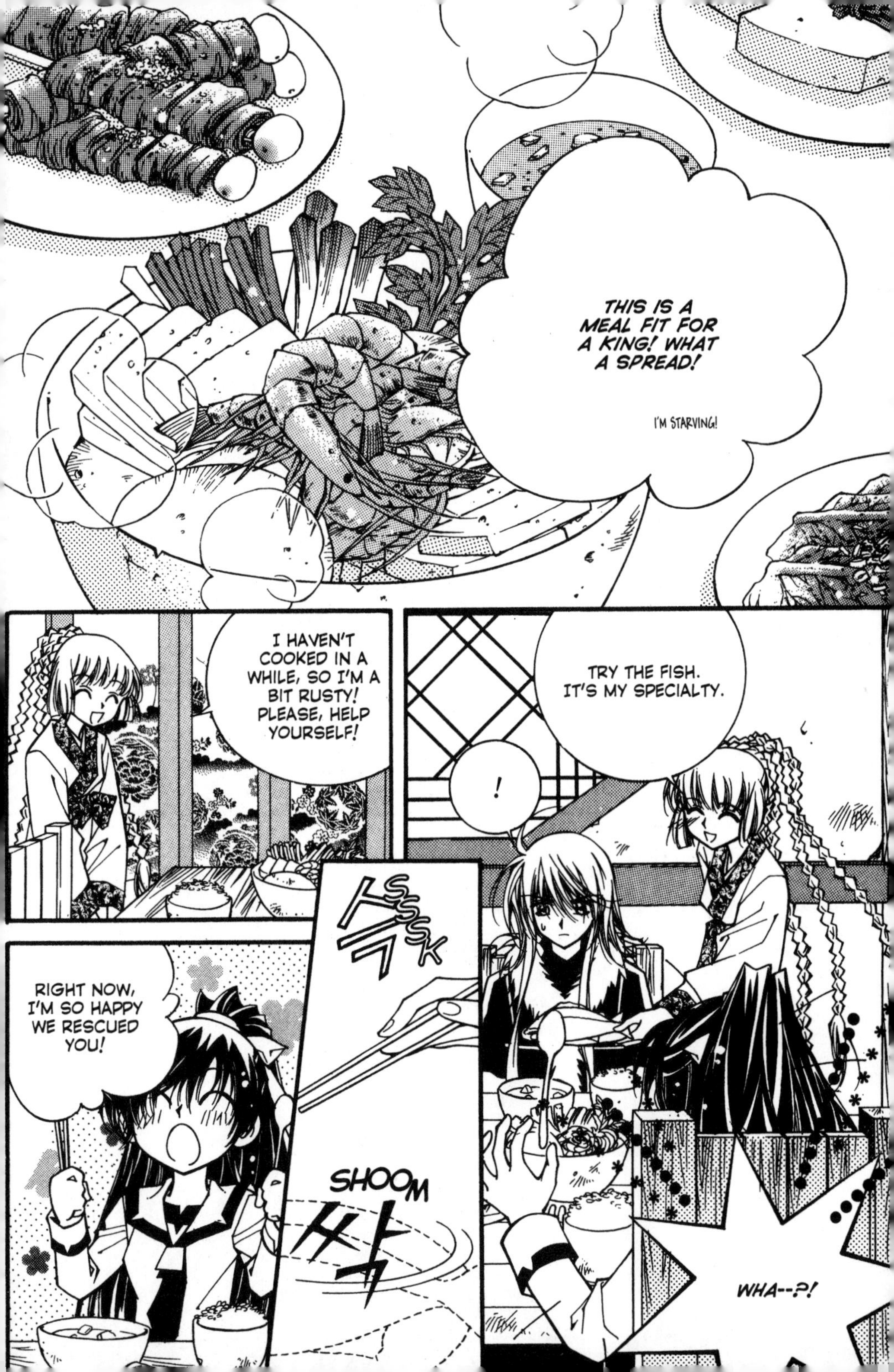

THIS IS A MEAL FIT FOR A KING! WHAT A SPREAD!
I'M STARVING!
I HAVEN'T COOKED IN A WHILE, SO I'M A BIT RUSTY! PLEASE, HELP YOURSELF!
RIGHT NOW, I'M SO HAPPY WE RESCUED YOU!
SSSSK
SHOOM
TRY THE FISH. IT'S MY SPECIALTY.
!
WHA--?!

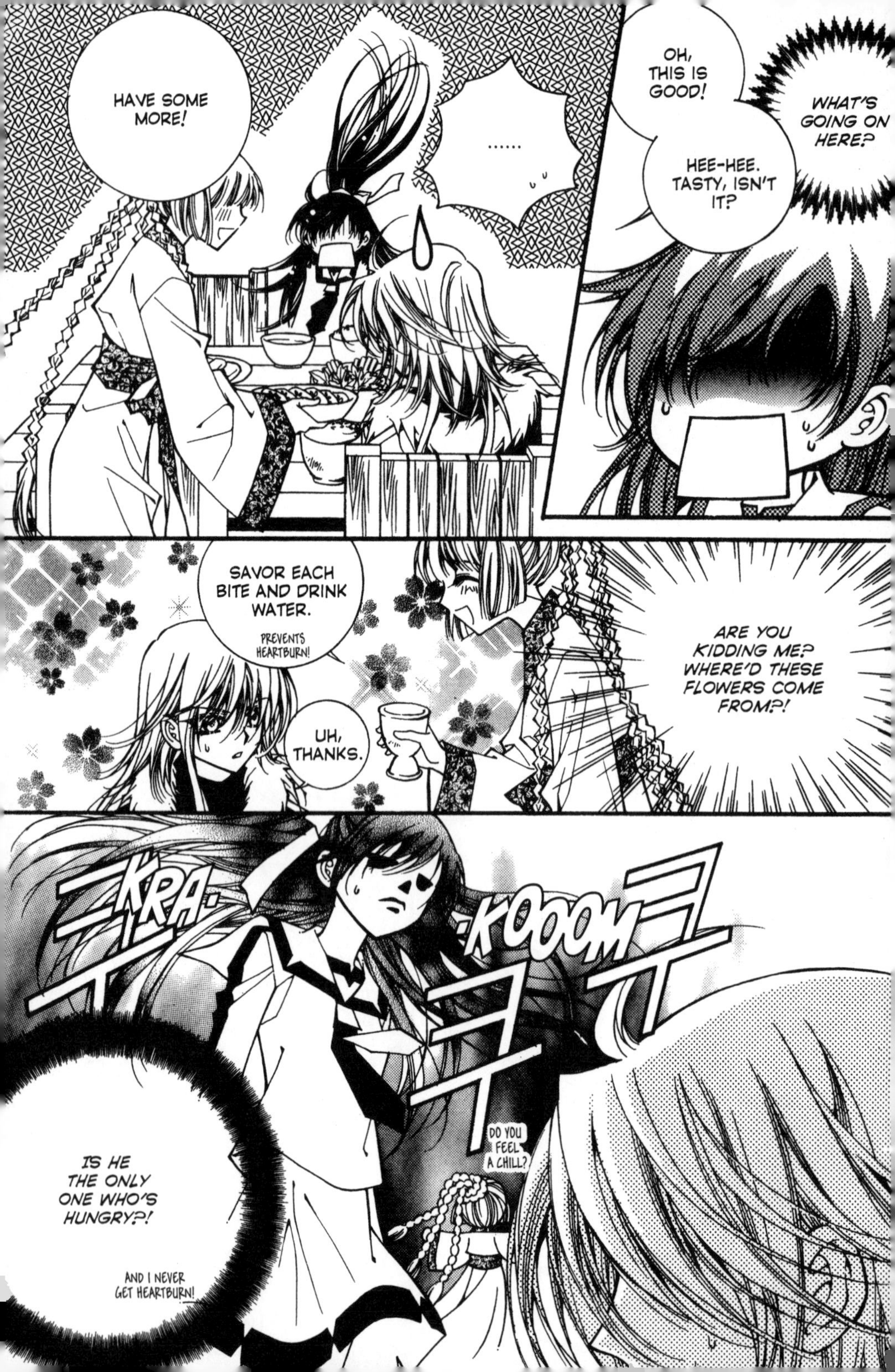
HAVE SOME MORE!
......
OH, THIS IS GOOD!
HEE-HEE. TASTY, ISN'T IT?
WHAT'S GOING ON HERE?
SAVOR EACH BITE AND DRINK WATER.
PREVENTS HEARTBURN!
UH, THANKS.
ARE YOU KIDDING ME? WHERE'D THESE FLOWERS COME FROM?!
KRA-
KOOOM
DO YOU FEEL A CHILL?
IS HE THE ONLY ONE WHO'S HUNGRY?!
AND I NEVER GET HEARTBURN!

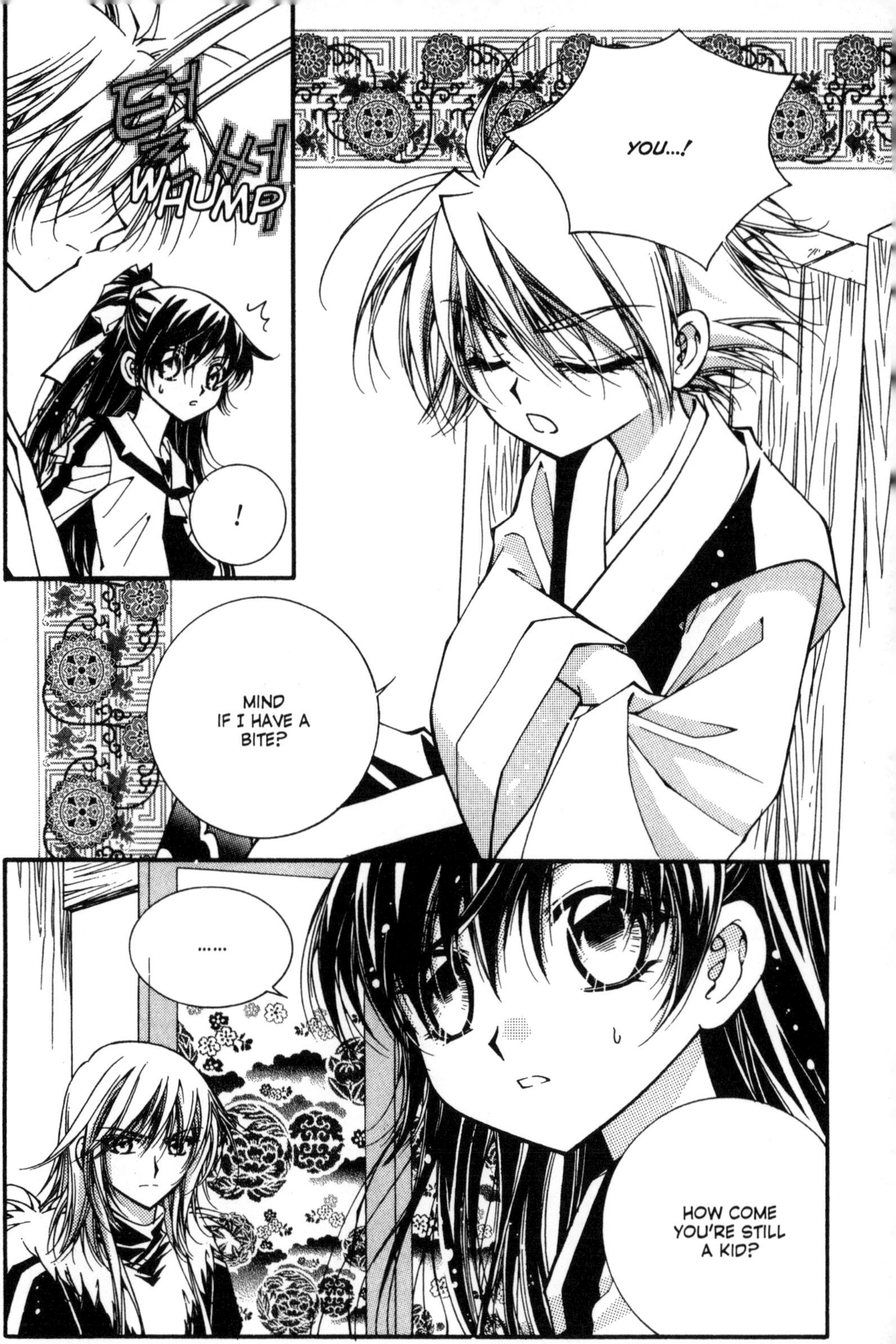
WHUMP
!
YOU...!
MIND IF I HAVE A BITE?
......
HOW COME YOU'RE STILL A KID?

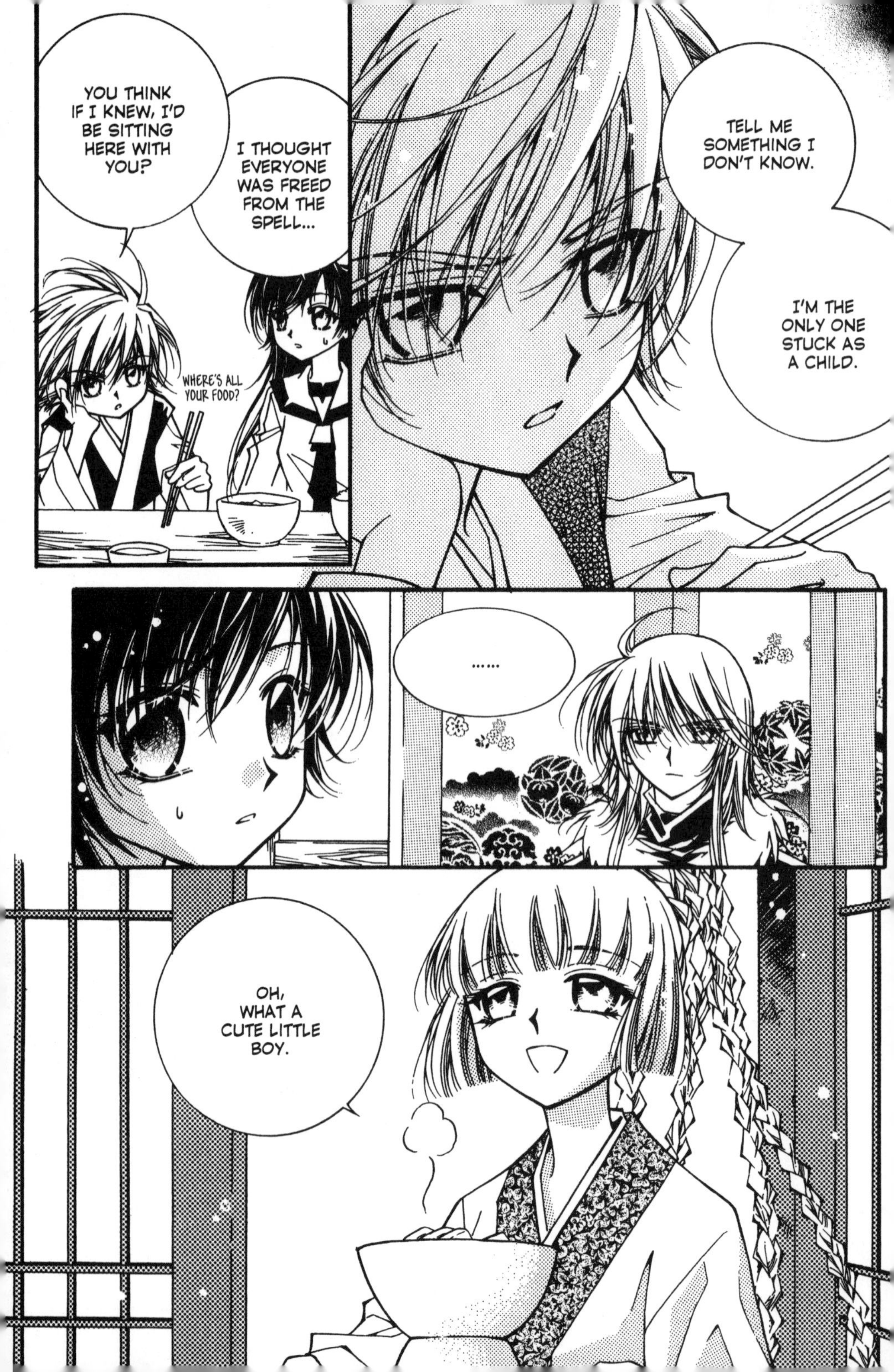
YOU THINK IF I KNEW, I'D BE SITTING HERE WITH YOU?
I THOUGHT EVERYONE WAS FREED FROM THE SPELL...
WHERE'S ALL YOUR FOOD?
TELL ME SOMETHING I DON'T KNOW.
I'M THE ONLY ONE STUCK AS A CHILD.
......
OH, WHAT A CUTE LITTLE BOY.

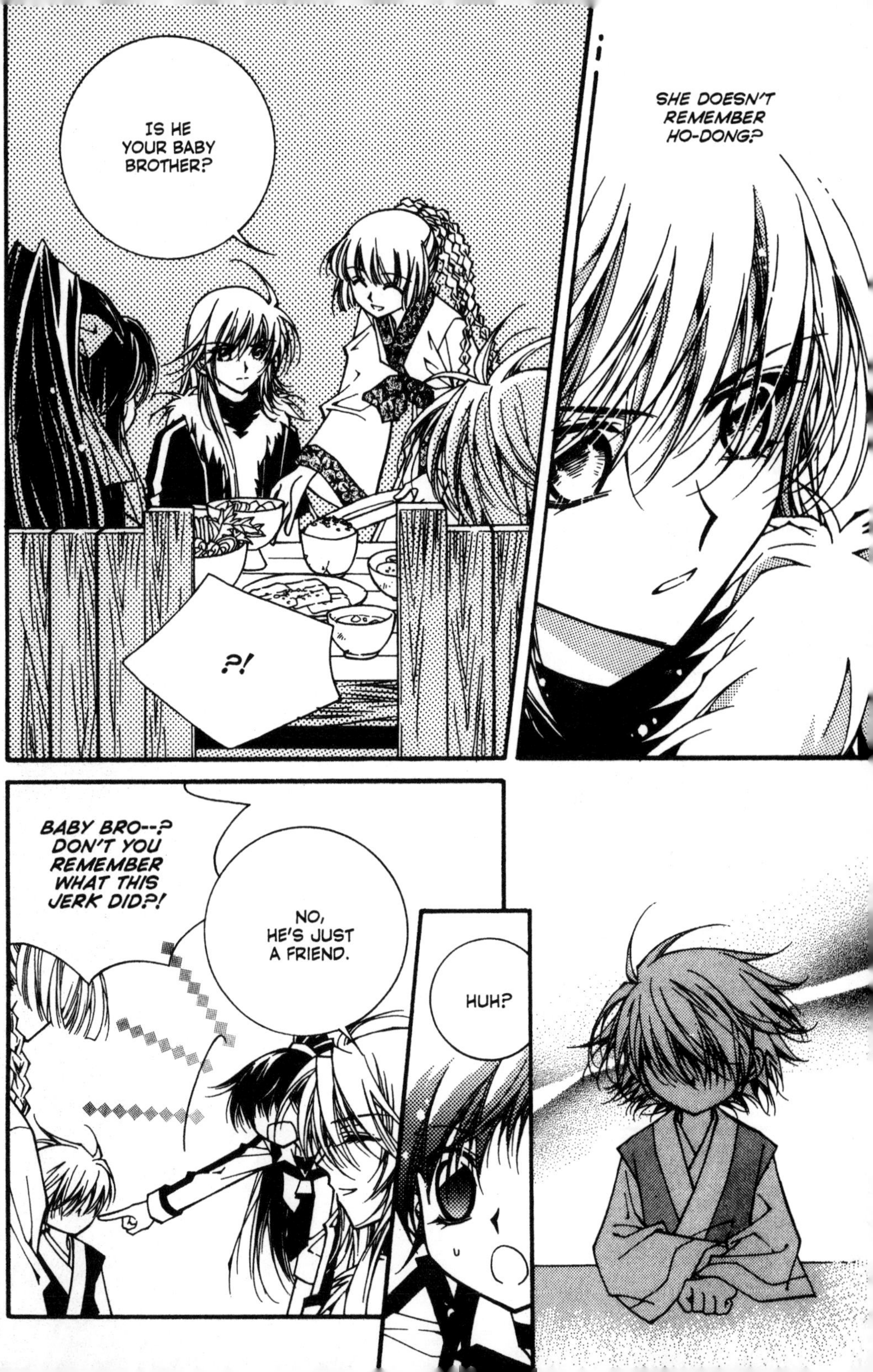
IS HE YOUR BABY BROTHER?
?!
SHE DOESN'T REMEMBER HO-DONG?
BABY BRO--? DON'T YOU REMEMBER WHAT THIS JERK DID?!
NO, HE'S JUST A FRIEND.
HUH?

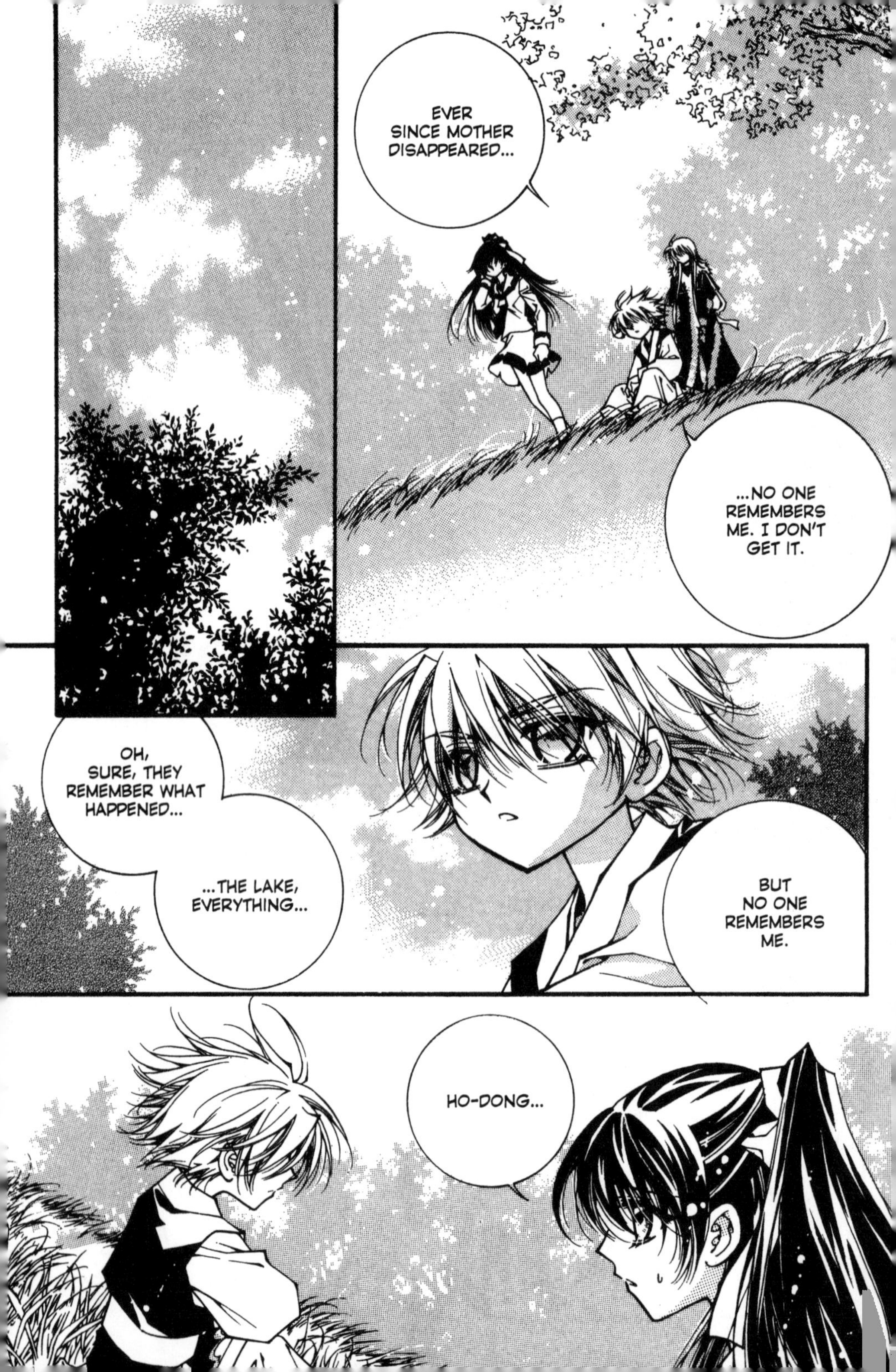
EVER SINCE MOTHER DISAPPEARED...
...NO ONE REMEMBERS ME. I DON'T GET IT.
OH, SURE, THEY REMEMBER WHAT HAPPENED...
...THE LAKE, EVERYTHING...
BUT NO ONE REMEMBERS ME.
HO-DONG...

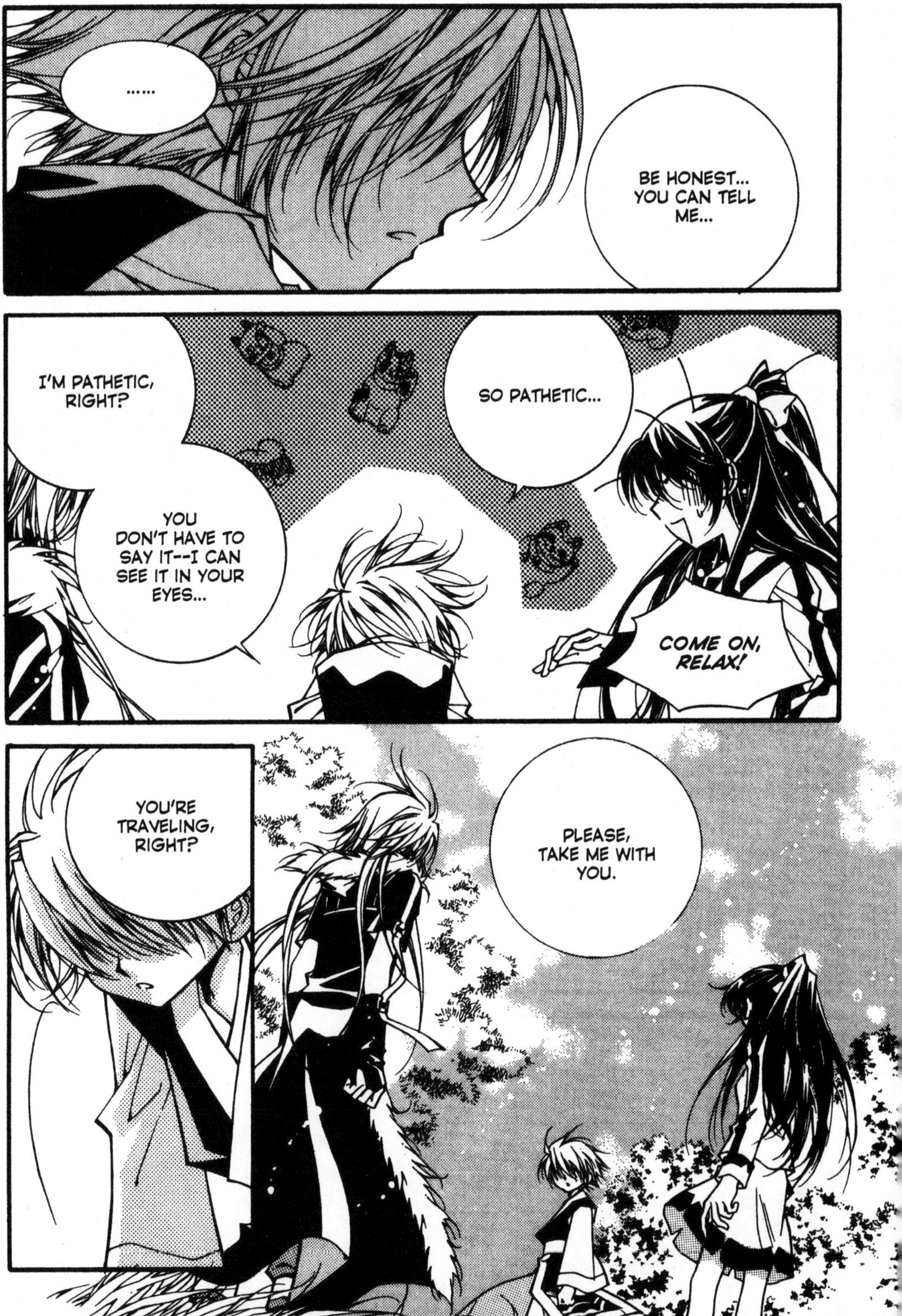
......
BE HONEST... YOU CAN TELL ME...
I'M PATHETIC, RIGHT?
YOU DON'T HAVE TO SAY IT--I CAN SEE IT IN YOUR EYES...
SO PATHETIC...
COME ON, RELAX!
YOU'RE TRAVELING, RIGHT?
PLEASE, TAKE ME WITH YOU.

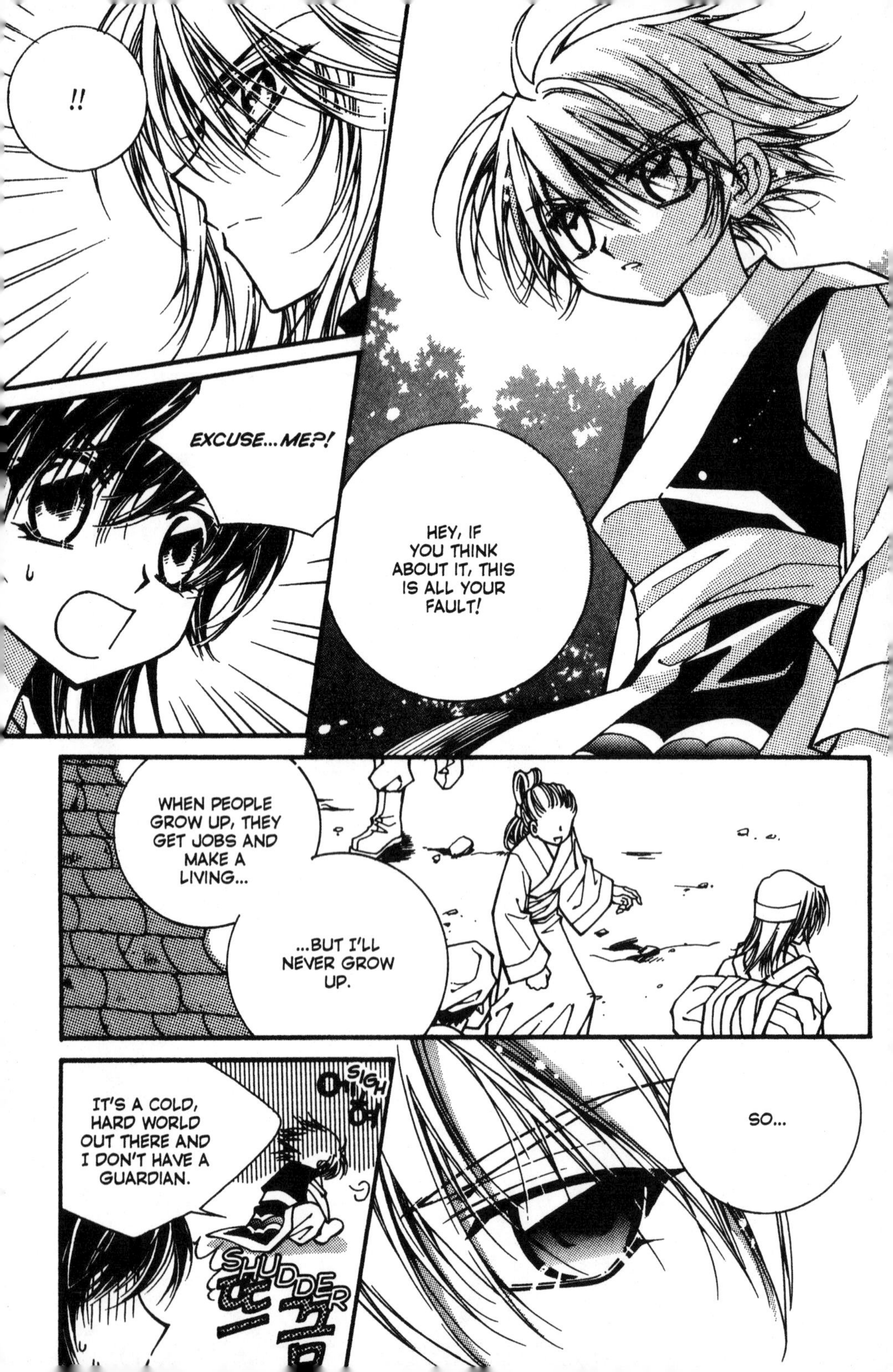
!!
EXCUSE...ME?!
HEY, IF YOU THINK ABOUT IT, THIS IS ALL YOUR FAULT!
WHEN PEOPLE GROW UP, THEY GET JOBS AND MAKE A LIVING...
...BUT I'LL NEVER GROW UP.
IT'S A COLD, HARD WORLD OUT THERE AND I DON'T HAVE A GUARDIAN.
SIGH
SHUDDER
SO...

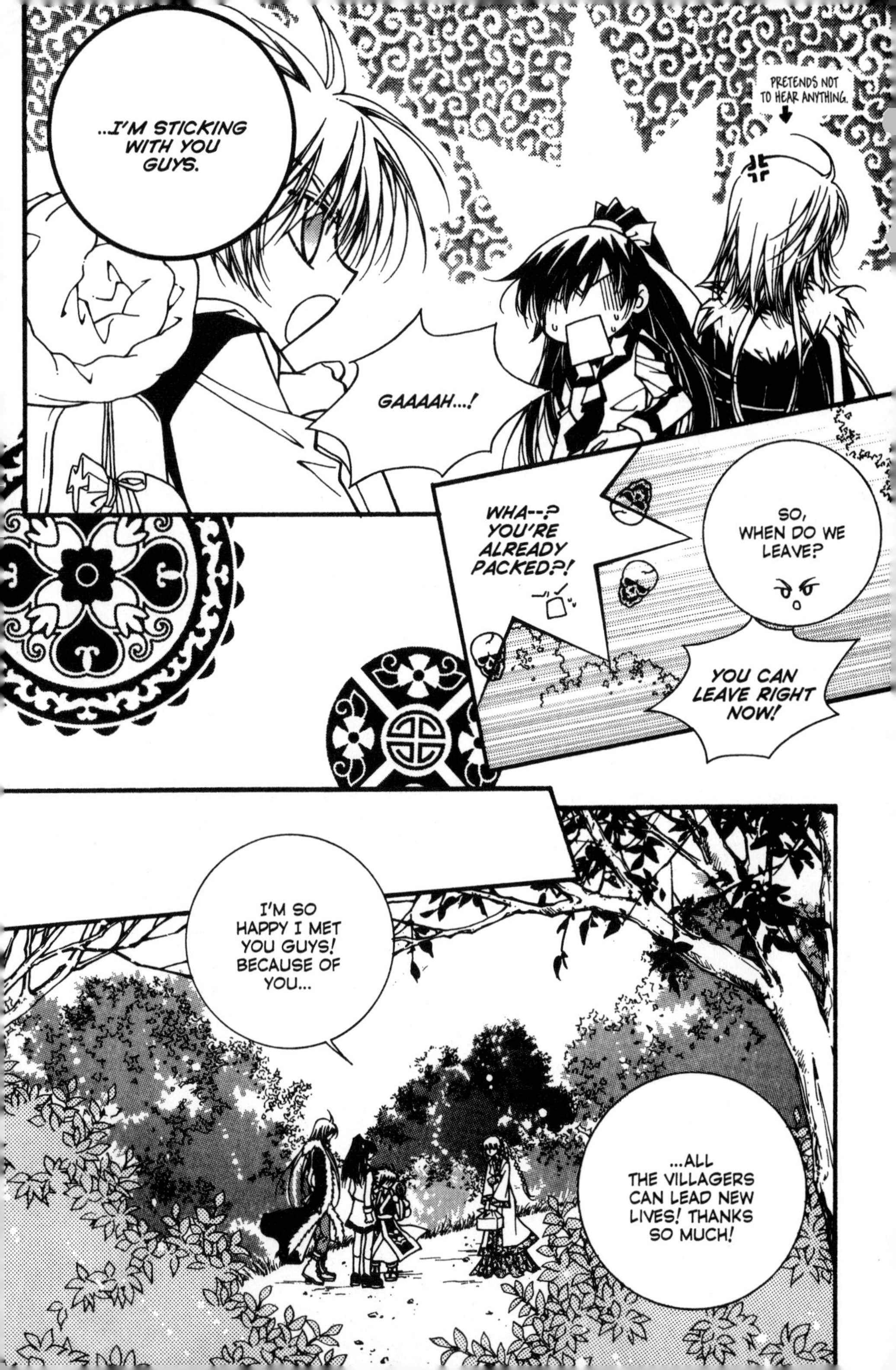
...I'M STICKING WITH YOU GUYS.
GAAAAH...!
PRETENDS NOT TO HEAR ANYTHING.
WHA--? YOU'RE ALREADY PACKED?!
SO, WHEN DO WE LEAVE?
YOU CAN LEAVE RIGHT NOW!
I'M SO HAPPY I MET YOU GUYS! BECAUSE OF YOU...
...ALL THE VILLAGERS CAN LEAD NEW LIVES! THANKS SO MUCH!

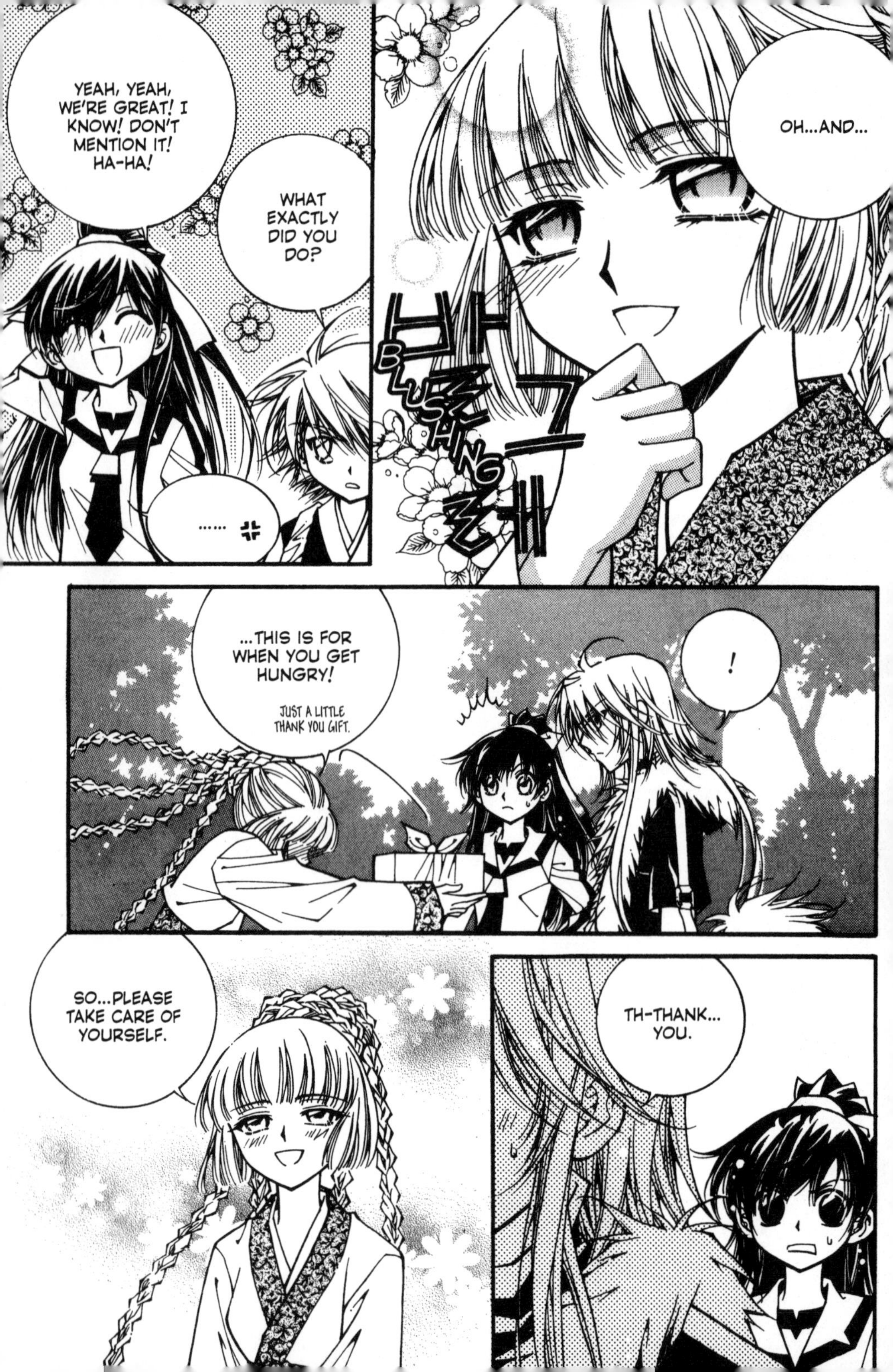
YEAH, YEAH, WE'RE GREAT! I KNOW! DON'T MENTION IT! HA-HA!
WHAT EXACTLY DID YOU DO?
......
OH...AND...
BLUSHING
...THIS IS FOR WHEN YOU GET HUNGRY!
JUST A LITTLE THANK YOU GIFT.
!
SO...PLEASE TAKE CARE OF YOURSELF.
TH-THANK... YOU.

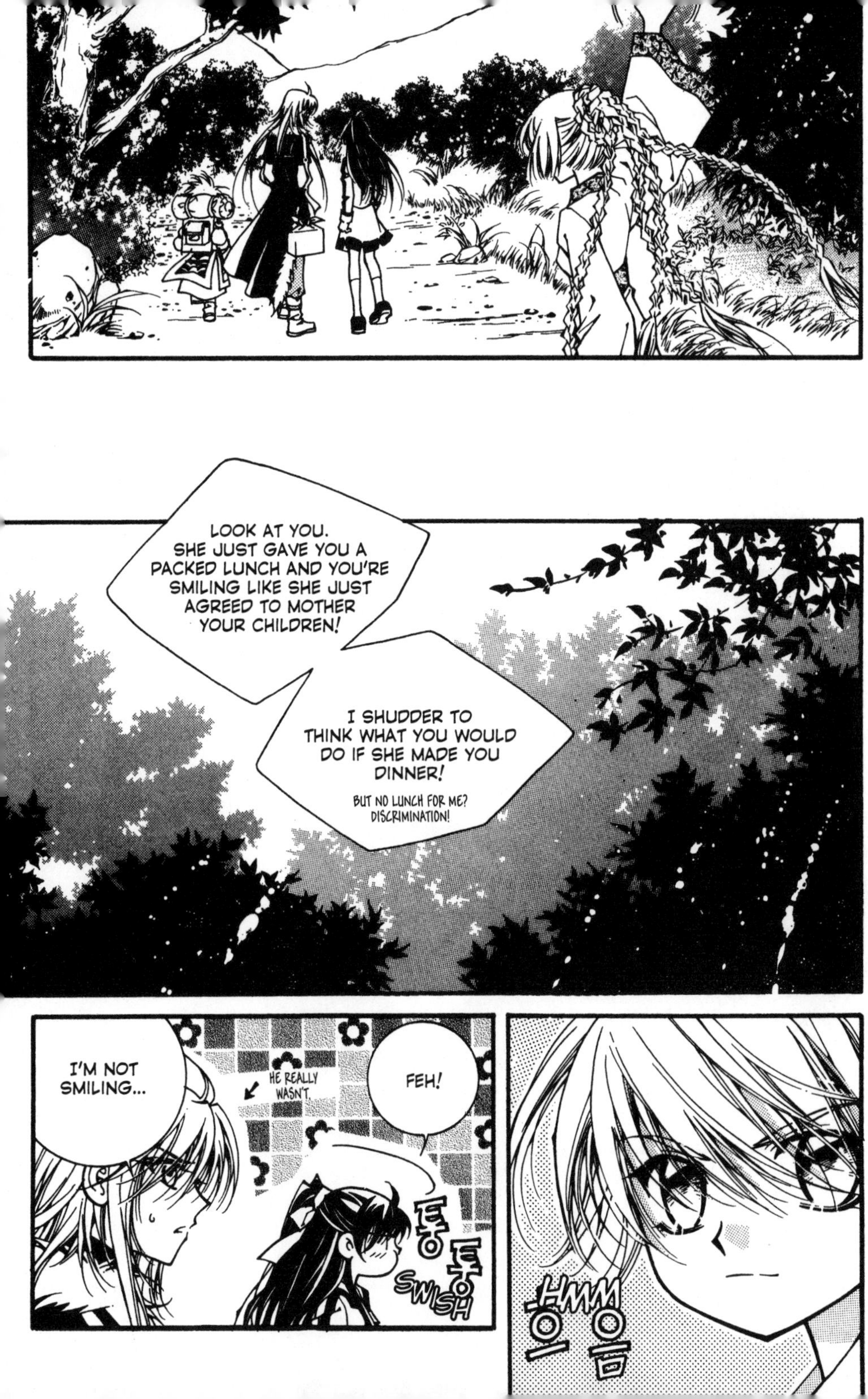
LOOK AT YOU. SHE JUST GAVE YOU A PACKED LUNCH AND YOU'RE SMILING LIKE SHE JUST AGREED TO MOTHER YOUR CHILDREN!
I SHUDDER TO THINK WHAT YOU WOULD DO IF SHE MADE YOU DINNER!
BUT NO LUNCH FOR ME? DISCRIMINATION!
I'M NOT SMILING...
HE REALLY WASN'T.
FEH!
SWISH
HMM

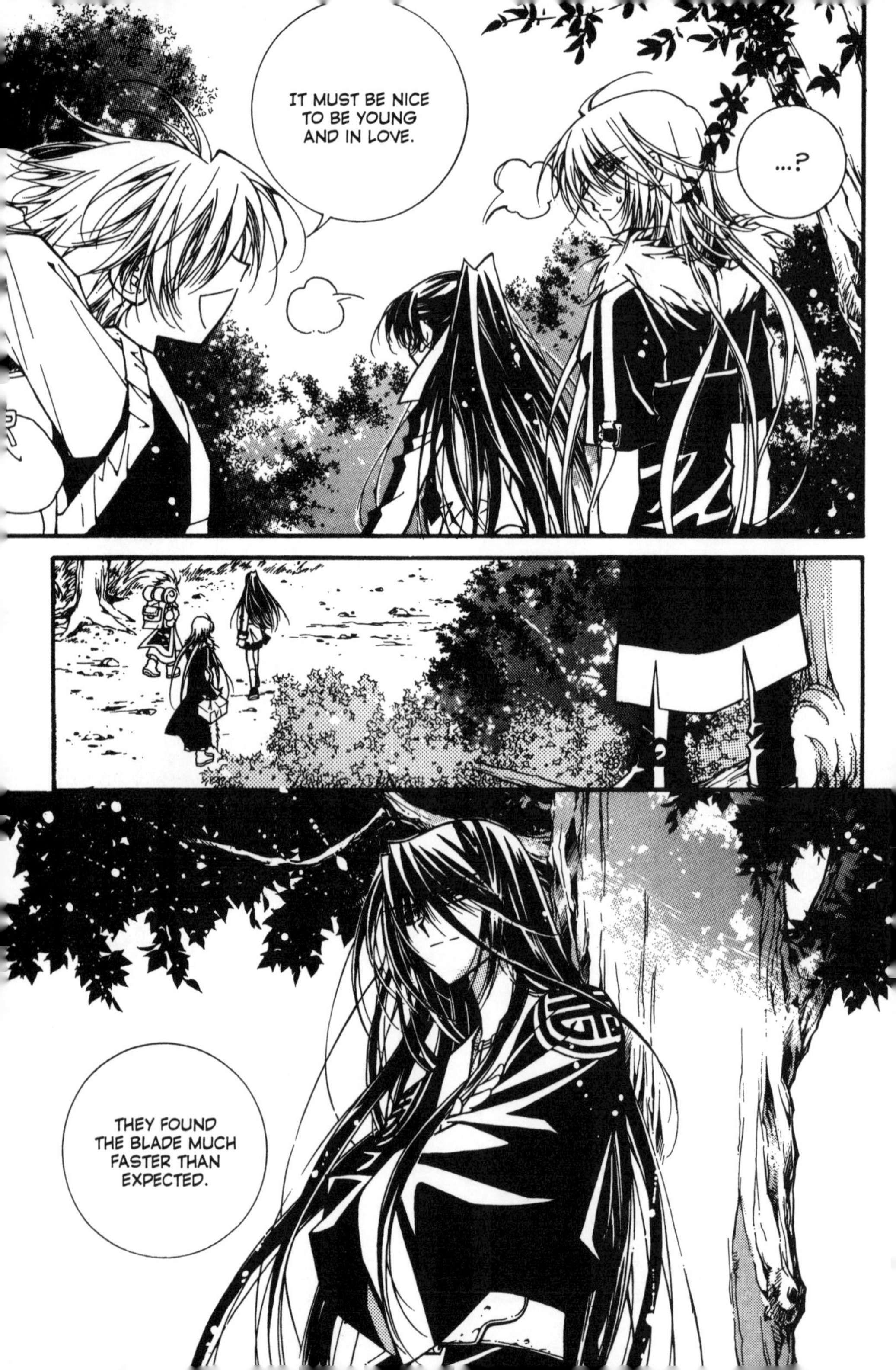
IT MUST BE NICE TO BE YOUNG AND IN LOVE.
...?
THEY FOUND THE BLADE MUCH FASTER THAN EXPECTED.

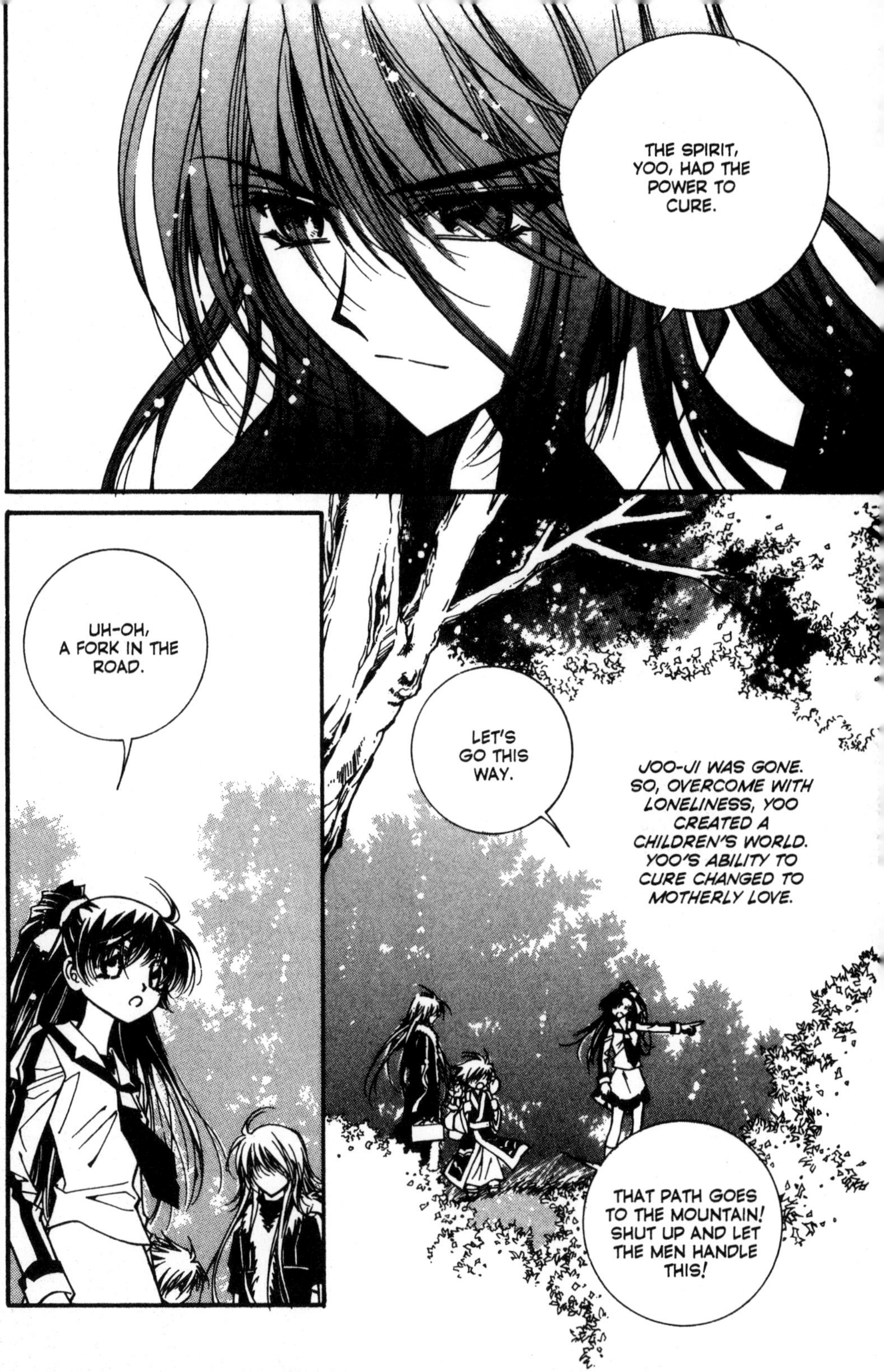
THE SPIRIT, YOO, HAD THE POWER TO CURE.
UH-OH, A FORK IN THE ROAD.
LET'S GO THIS WAY.
JOO-JI WAS GONE. SO, OVERCOME WITH LONELINESS, YOO CREATED A CHILDREN'S WORLD. YOO'S ABILITY TO CURE CHANGED TO MOTHERLY LOVE.
THAT PATH GOES TO THE MOUNTAIN! SHUT UP AND LET THE MEN HANDLE THIS!

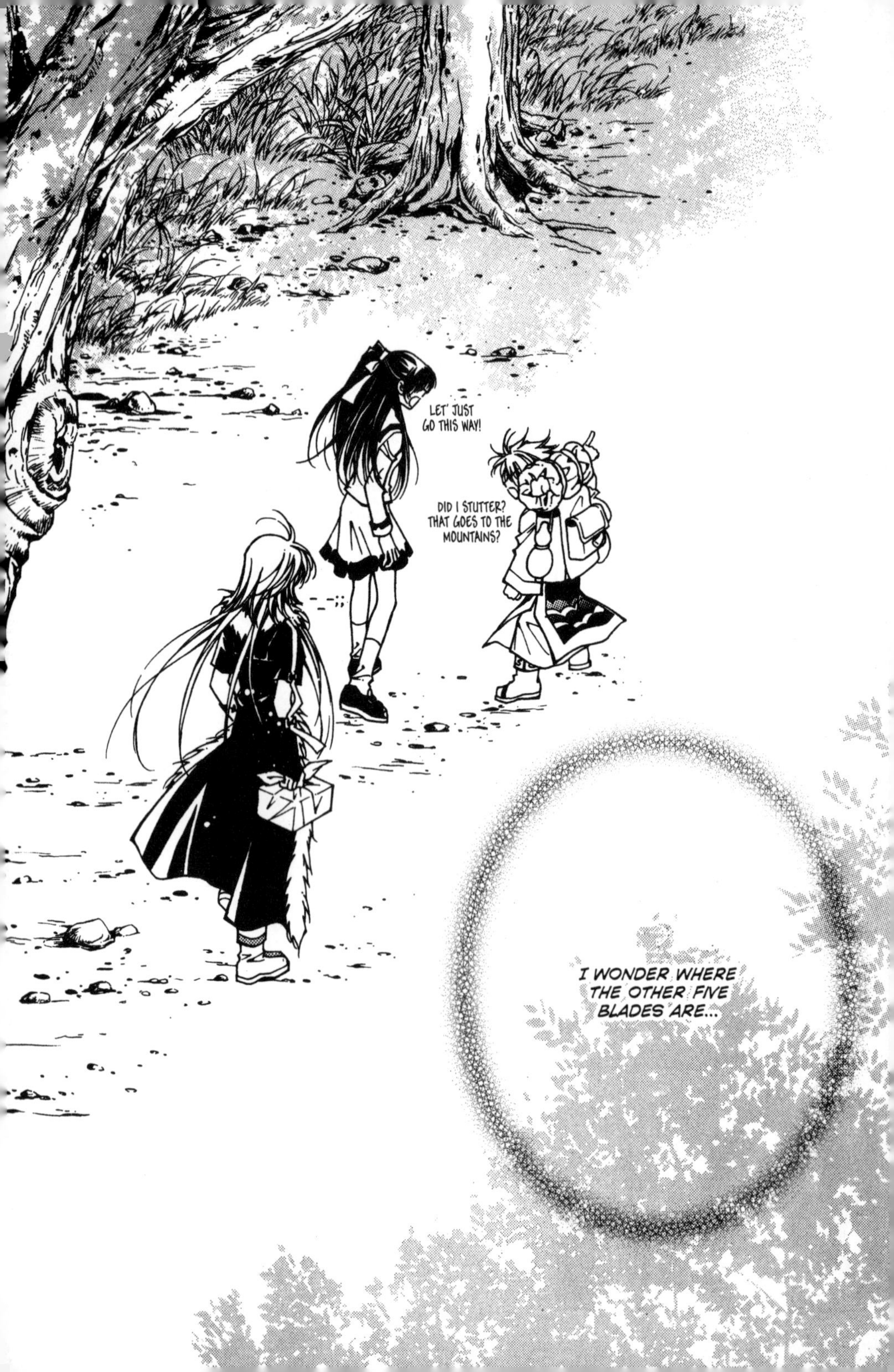
LET' JUST GO THIS WAY!
DID I STUTTER? THAT GOES TO THE MOUNTAINS?
I WONDER WHERE THE OTHER FIVE BLADES ARE...

AS I INTERPRET IT ~ BY ROMANTIC IMPERTINENT

<PRINCESS NAK-RANG AND PRINCE HO-DONG>

THE STORY OF PRINCESS NAK-RANG AND PRINCE HO-DONG WAS CRAFTED BY MOTHER LAKE. AS YOU KNOW, IT IS A SAD LOVE STORY. BUT THERE ISN'T EVEN A LITTLE BIT OF ROMANCE IN THIS BOOK... -_-;;

HERE IS A SUMMARY OF THE ORIGINAL STORY:

PRINCE HO-DONG OF GOGURYO MARRIED PRINCESS NAK-RANG OF THE NAK-RANG KINGDOM. THEY LOVED EACH OTHER BUT OF COURSE THERE WAS A PROBLEM--IT IS A LOVE STORY, AFTER ALL!

HO-DONG'S FATHER, KING DAE-MOO-SHIN, WANTED TO CONQUER NAK-RANG KINGDOM. BUT NAK-RANG HAD THIS MYSTERIOUS DRUM, THE "JAMYUNG-GO," WHICH AUTOMATICALLY STARTED DRUMMING WHEN THE KINGDOM WAS UNDER ATTACK. KING DAE-MOO-SHIN CONTROLLED HO-DONG, AND IN TURN HO-DONG MANIPULATED THE PRINCESS. SHE TORE THE "JAMYUNG-GO" INTO PIECES BECAUSE HER HUSBAND TOLD HER TO. THE PRINCESS'S FATHER, KING CHOI-LEE, GOT ANGRY AND KILLED HER. HO-DONG BECAME DEPRESSED AFTER HIS WIFE'S DEATH. HE ENDED HIS HORRIBLE LIFE BECAUSE OF A CONSPIRACY OF HIS FATHER AND HIS MYSTERIOUS STEPMOTHER. IT'S SAD, ISN'T IT?

THE MORAL I DISCOVERED WHILE RESEARCHING THIS WAS...NOTHING.

I THOUGHT IF THEY WERE JUST A BIT WISER, PRINCESS NAK-RANG COULD'VE HAD A HAPPY LIFE WITH PRINCE HO-DONG INSTEAD OF DYING TRAGICALLY. I'M ALMOST THIRTY, SO IS IT NAIVE TO THINK THAT A LOVE STORY HAS TO HAVE THE HAPPY ENDING?

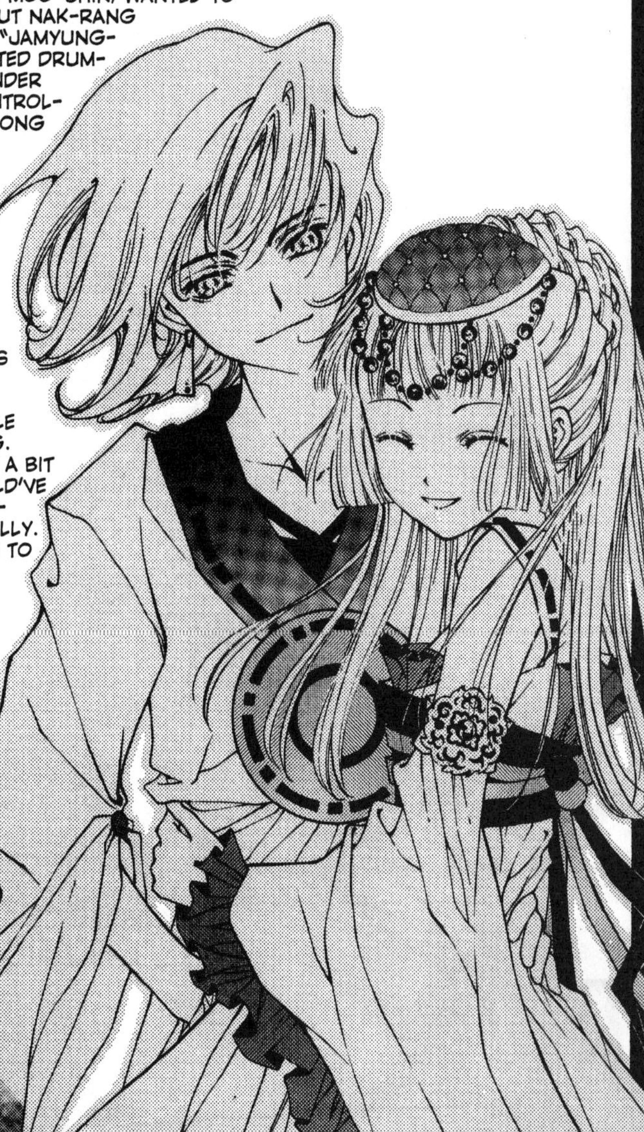

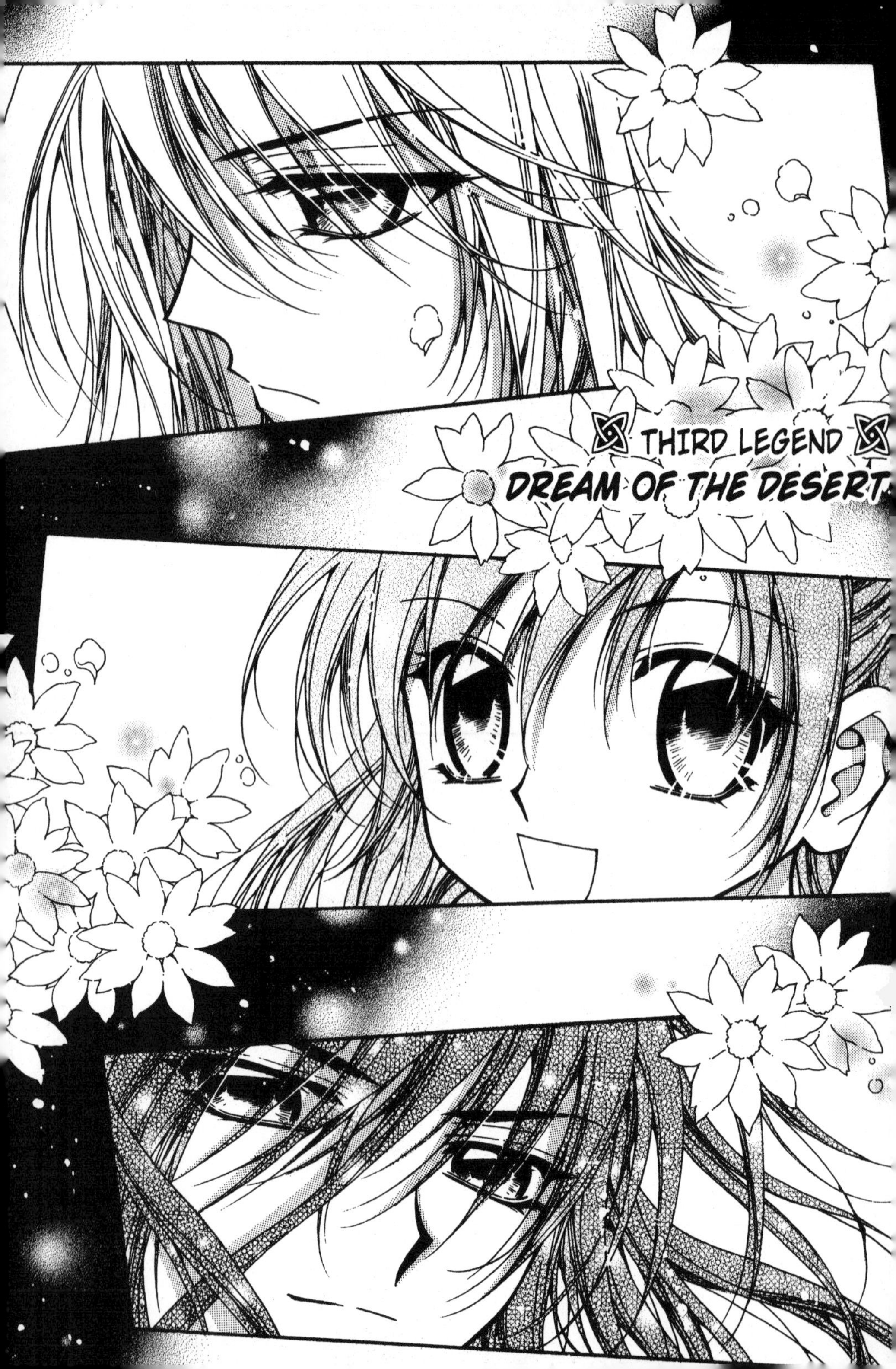
THIRD LEGEND
DREAM OF THE DESERT

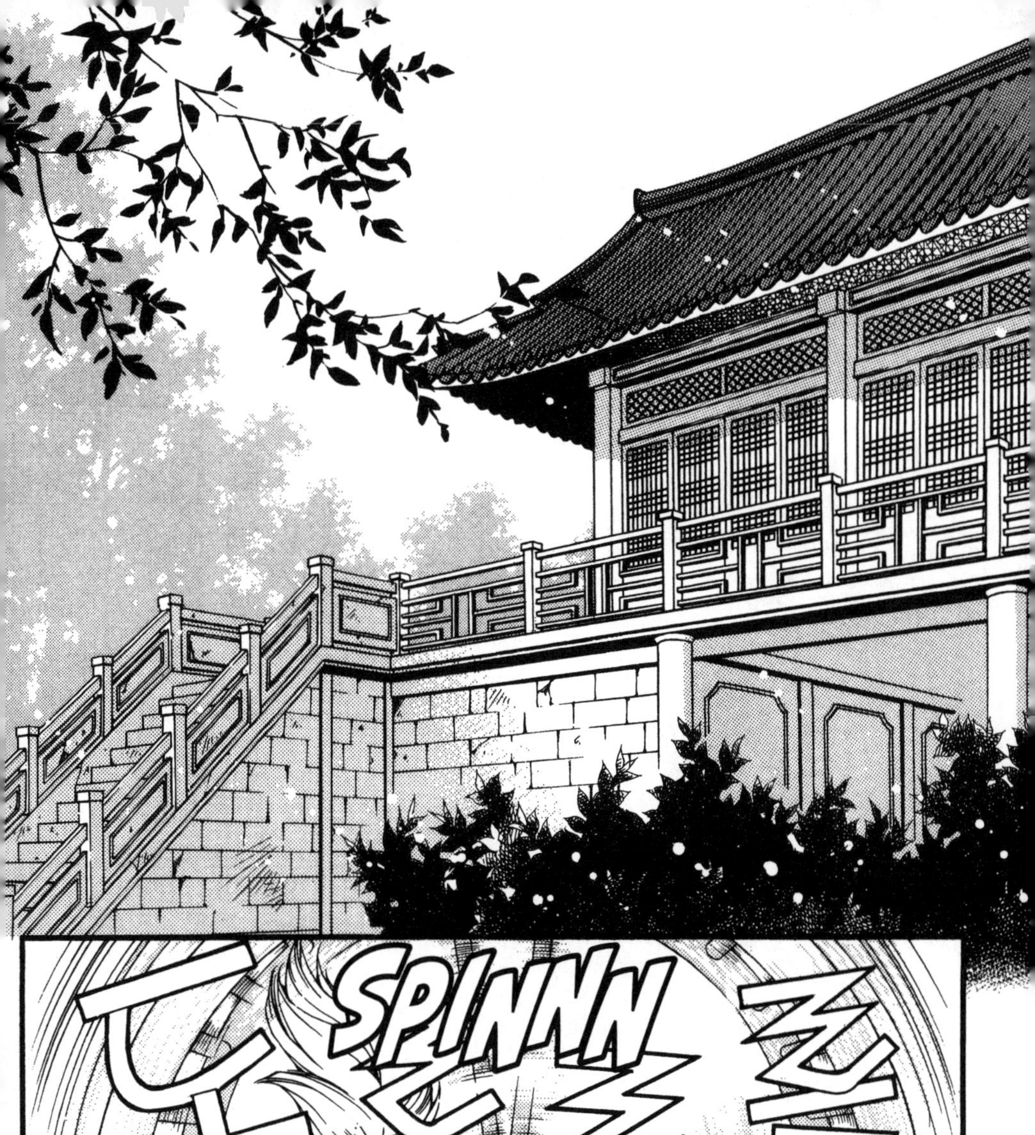

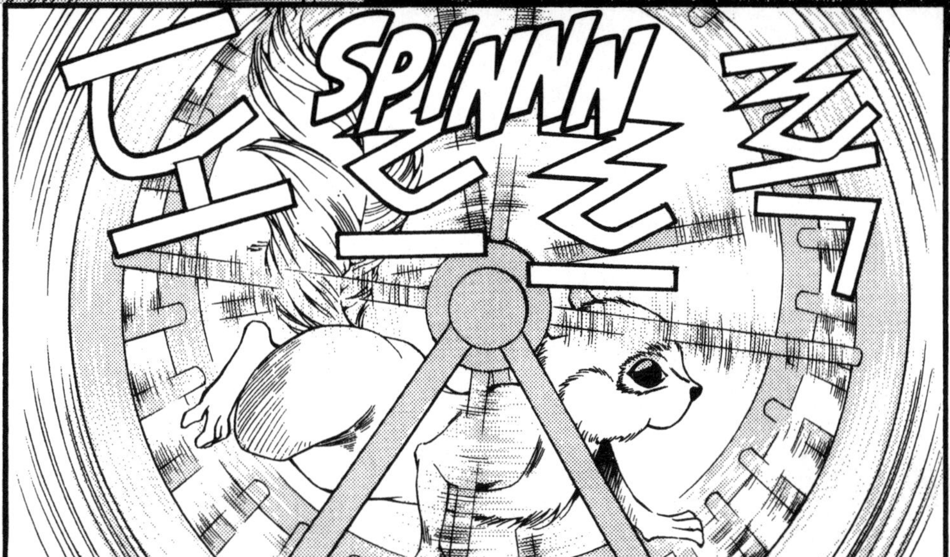
SPINNN

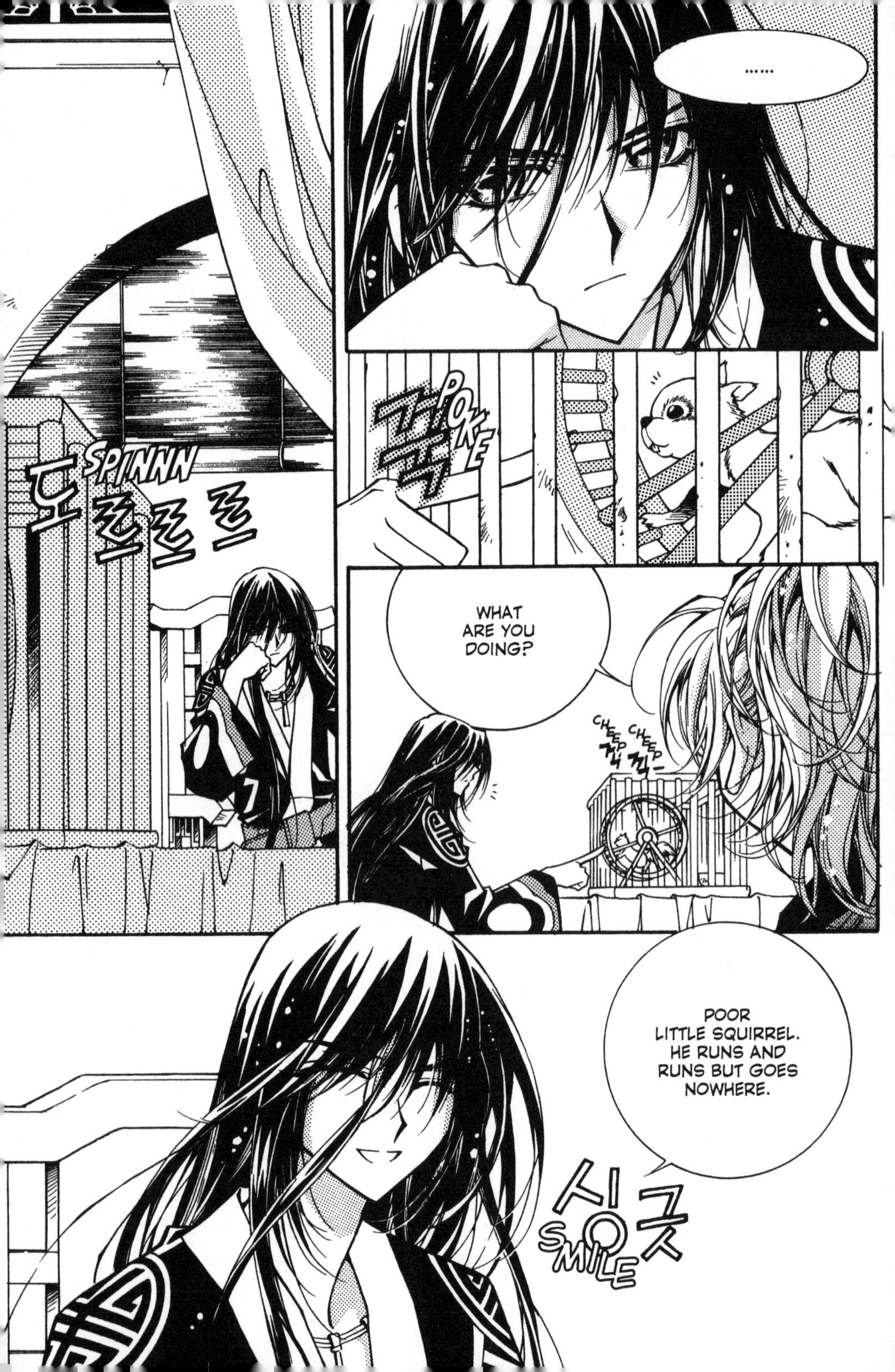
SPINNN
......
POKE
WHAT ARE YOU DOING?
CHEEP CHEEP
찍 찍
POOR LITTLE SQUIRREL. HE RUNS AND RUNS BUT GOES NOWHERE.
싱긋
SMILE

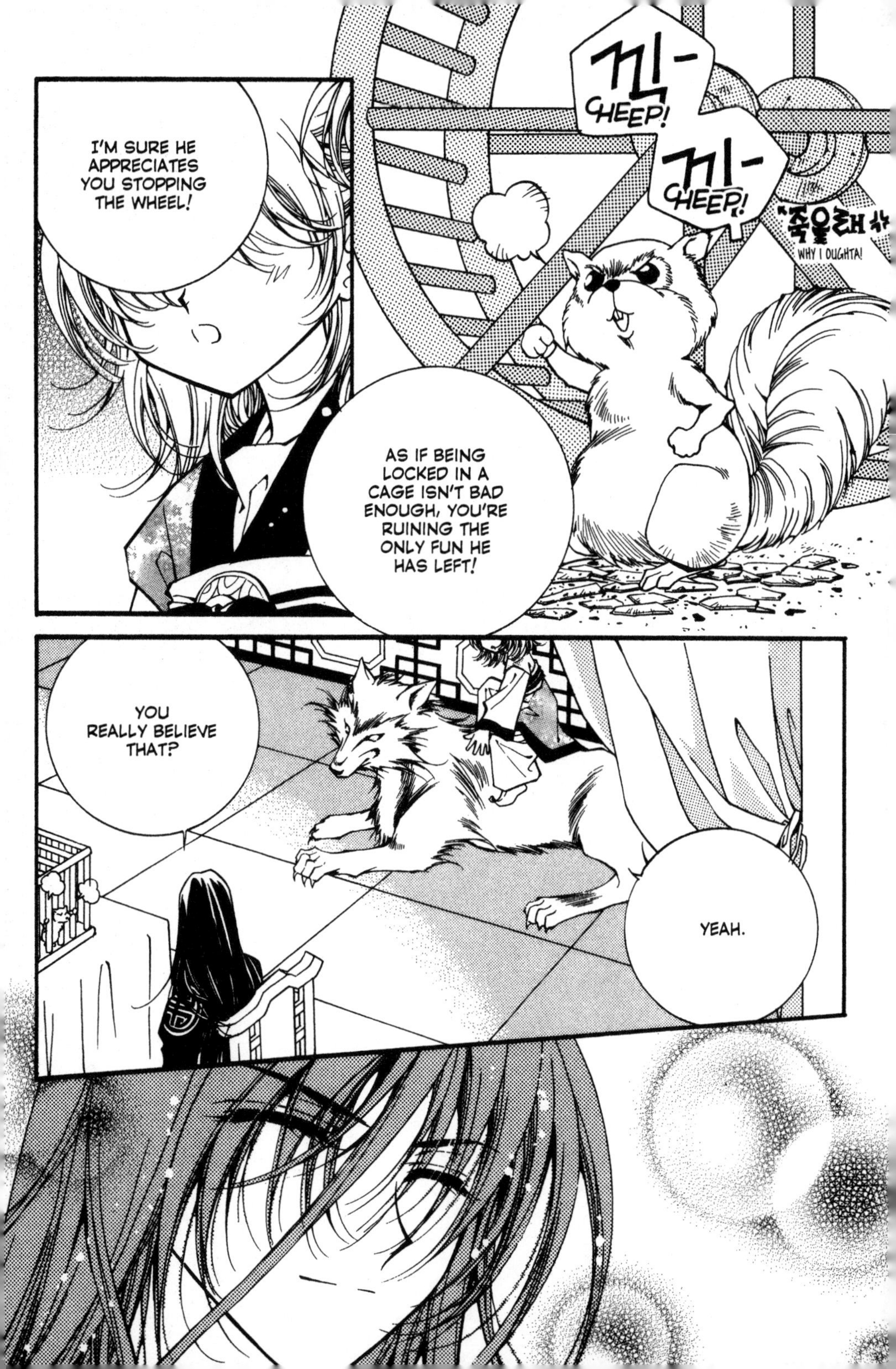
I'M SURE HE APPRECIATES YOU STOPPING THE WHEEL!
끼-
CHEEP!
끼-
CHEEP!
WHY I OUGHTA!
AS IF BEING LOCKED IN A CAGE ISN'T BAD ENOUGH, YOU'RE RUINING THE ONLY FUN HE HAS LEFT!
YOU REALLY BELIEVE THAT?
YEAH.

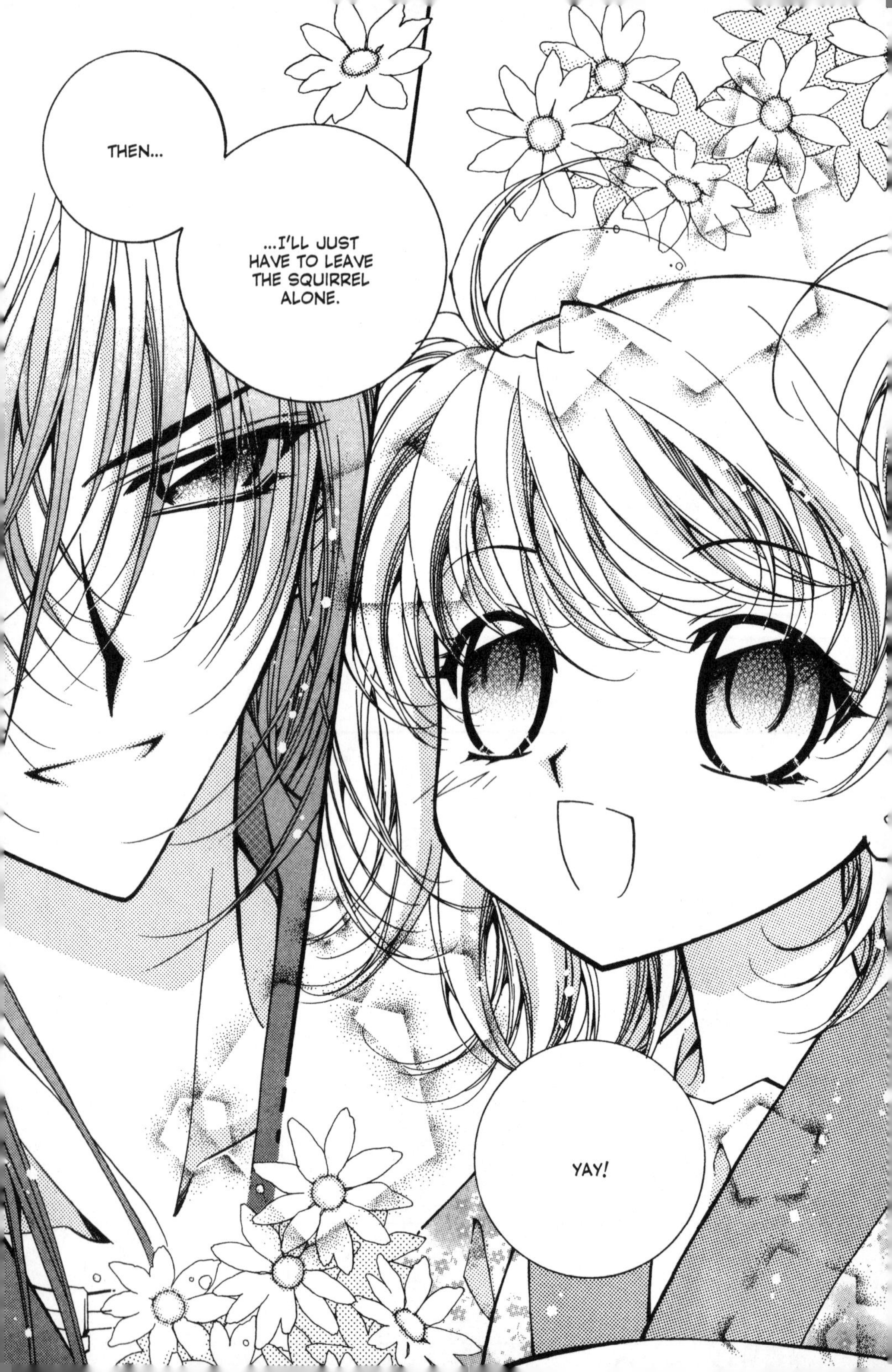
THEN...
...I'LL JUST HAVE TO LEAVE THE SQUIRREL ALONE.
YAY!

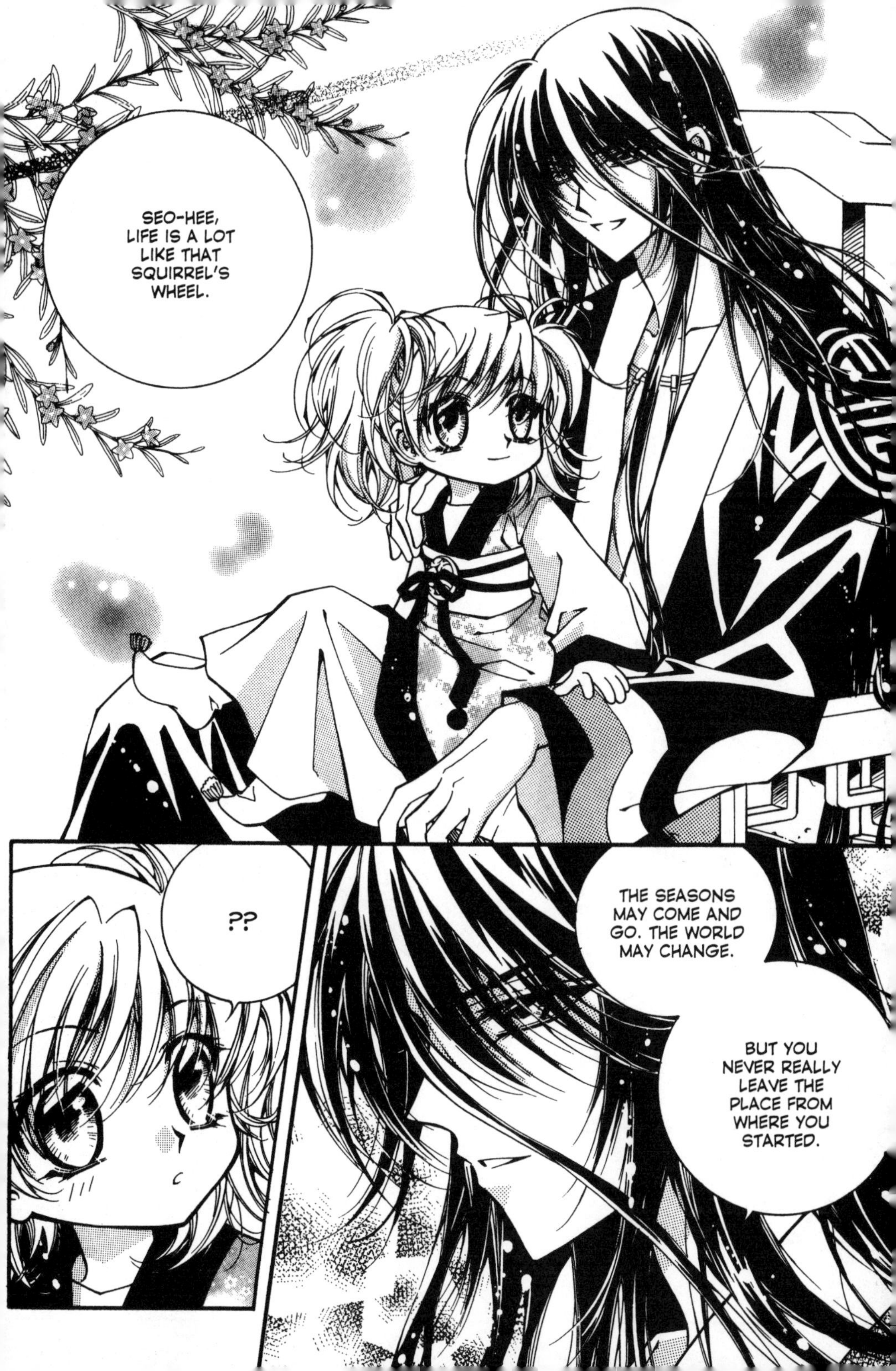
SEO-HEE, LIFE IS A LOT LIKE THAT SQUIRREL'S WHEEL.
??
THE SEASONS MAY COME AND GO. THE WORLD MAY CHANGE.
BUT YOU NEVER REALLY LEAVE THE PLACE FROM WHERE YOU STARTED.

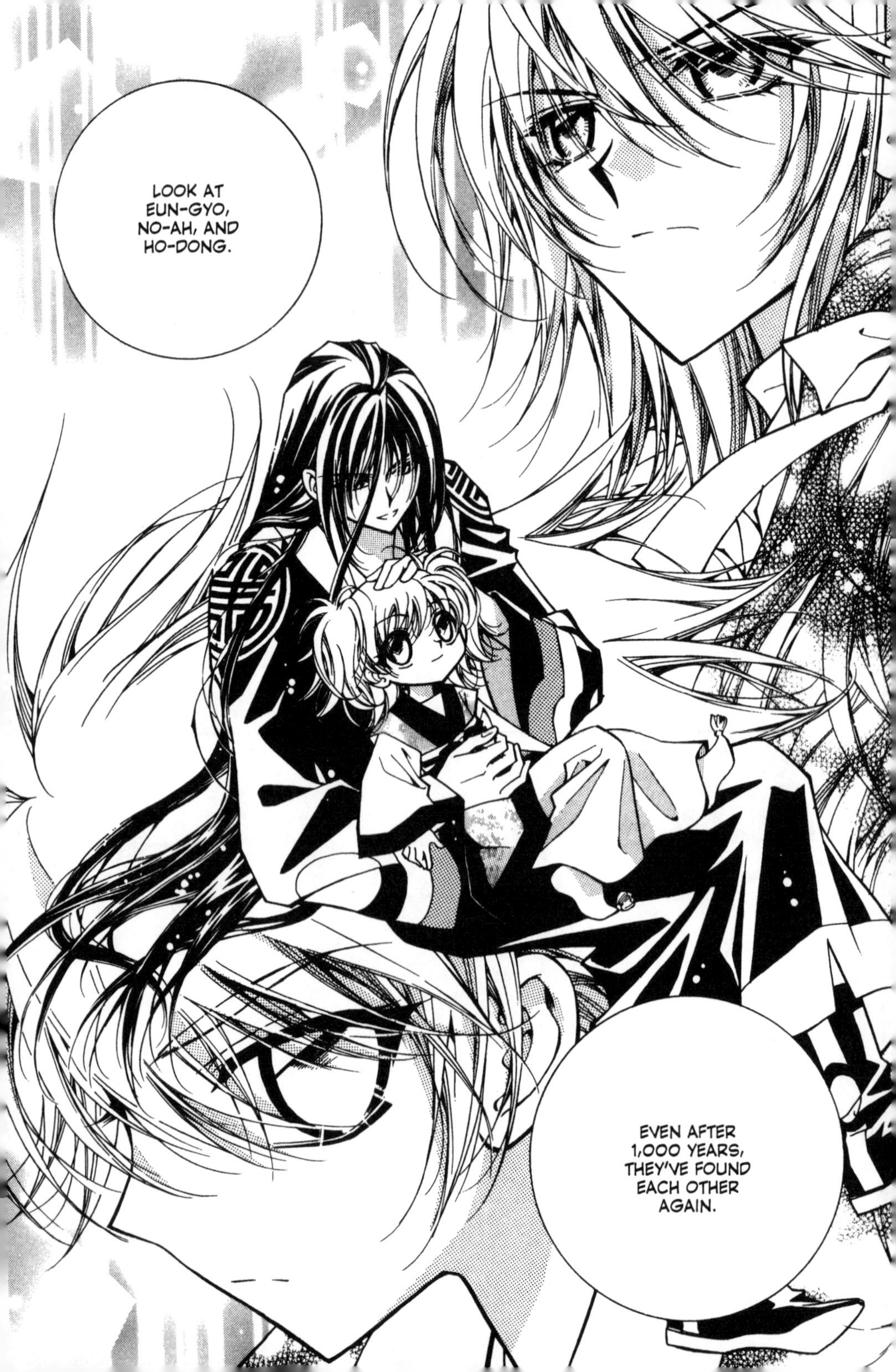
LOOK AT EUN-GYO, NO-AH, AND HO-DONG.
EVEN AFTER 1,000 YEARS, THEY'VE FOUND EACH OTHER AGAIN.

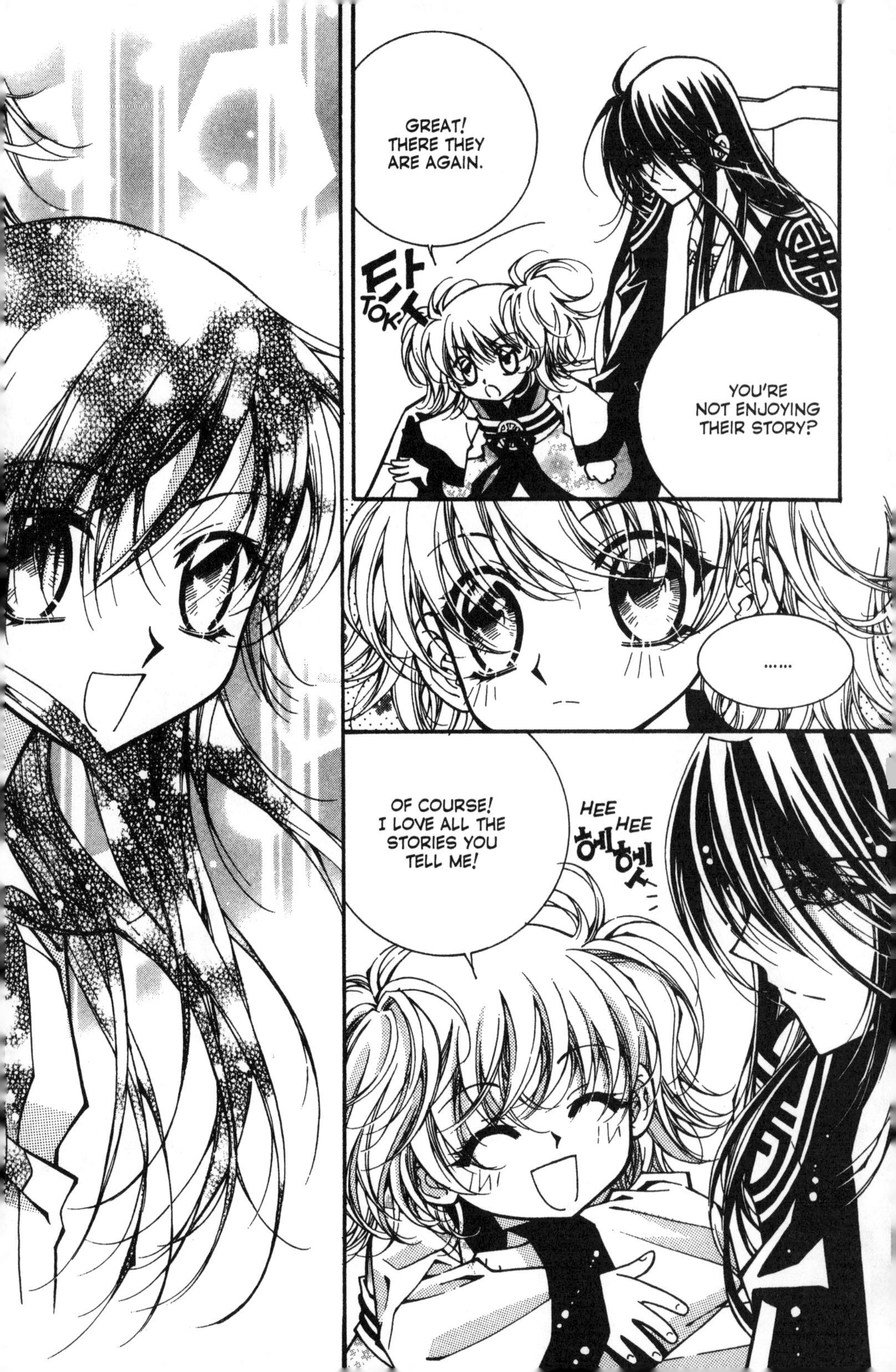
GREAT! THERE THEY ARE AGAIN.
탁
TOK
YOU'RE NOT ENJOYING THEIR STORY?
......
OF COURSE! I LOVE ALL THE STORIES YOU TELL ME!
HEE HEE
헤헷

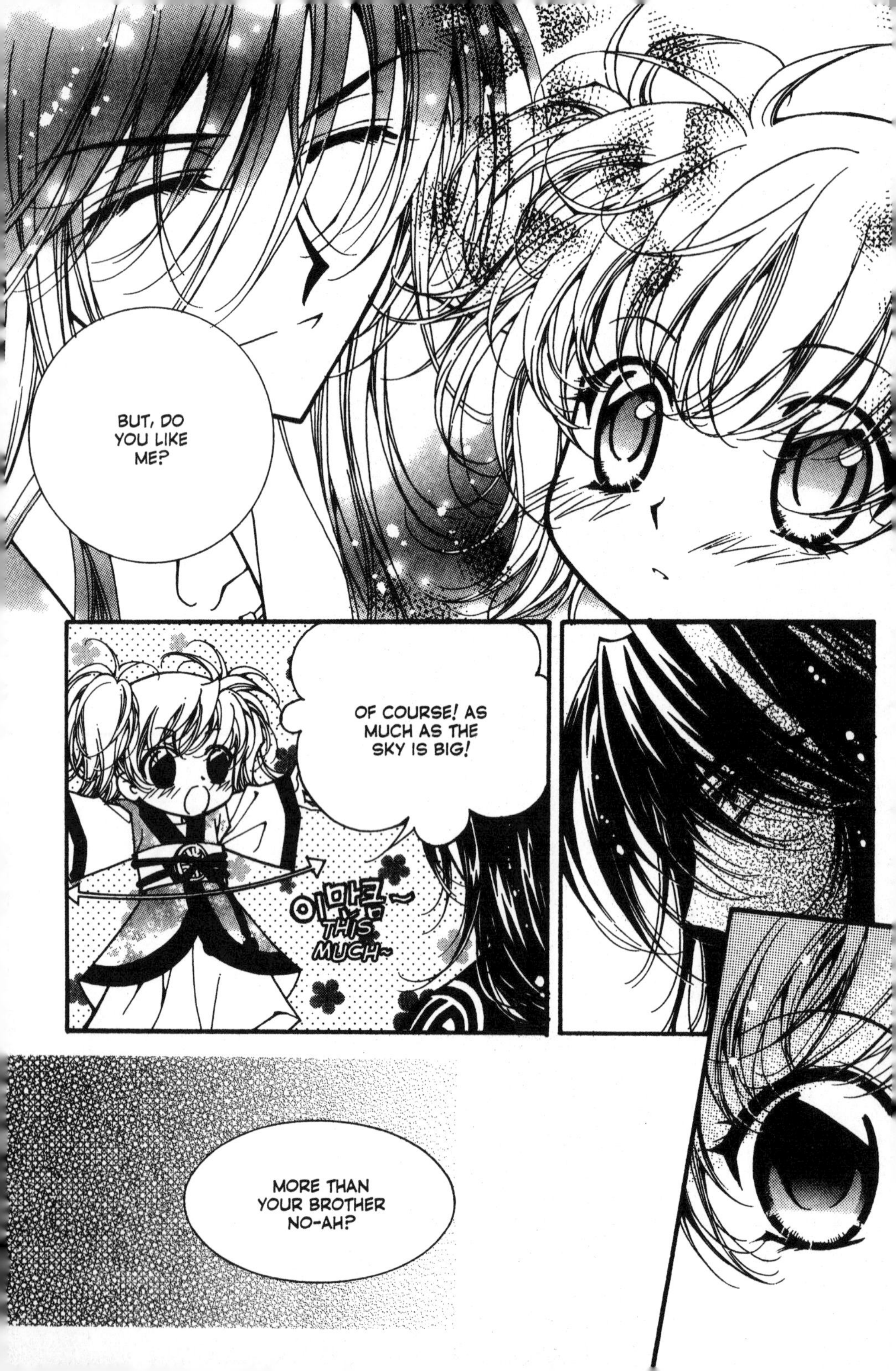
BUT, DO YOU LIKE ME?
OF COURSE! AS MUCH AS THE SKY IS BIG!
이만큼~
THIS MUCH~
MORE THAN YOUR BROTHER NO-AH?

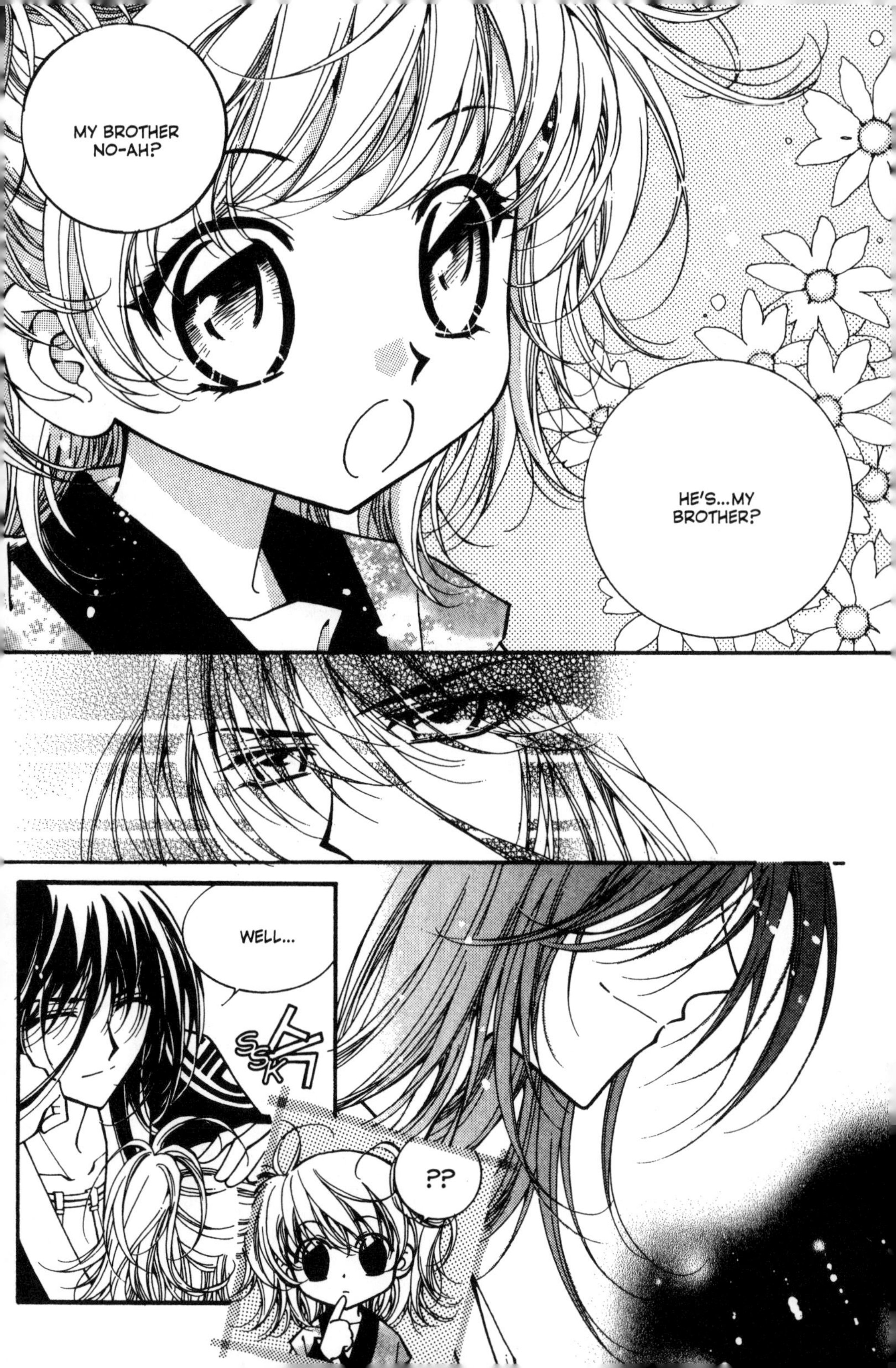
MY BROTHER NO-AH?
HE'S...MY BROTHER?
WELL...
SSK
??

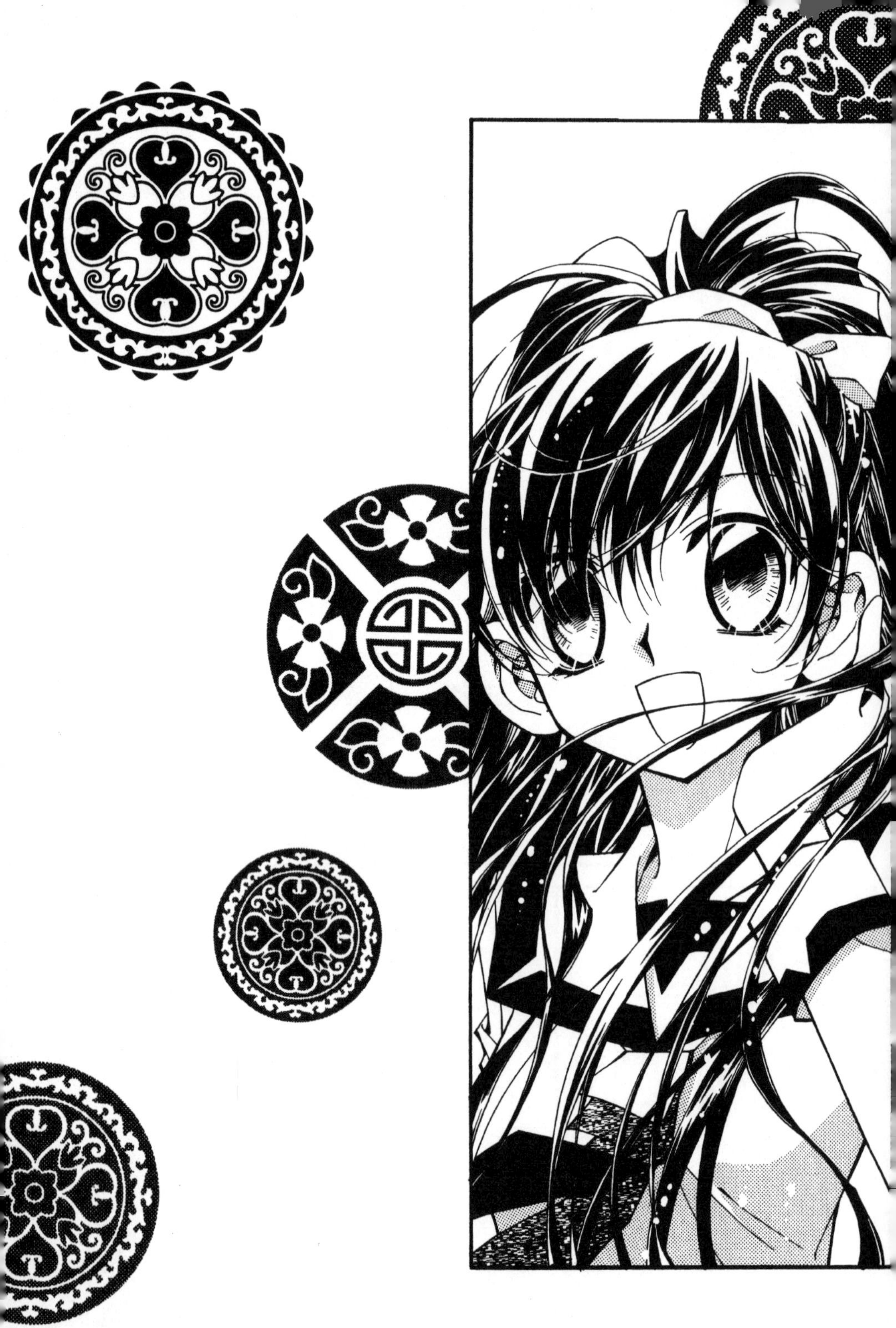

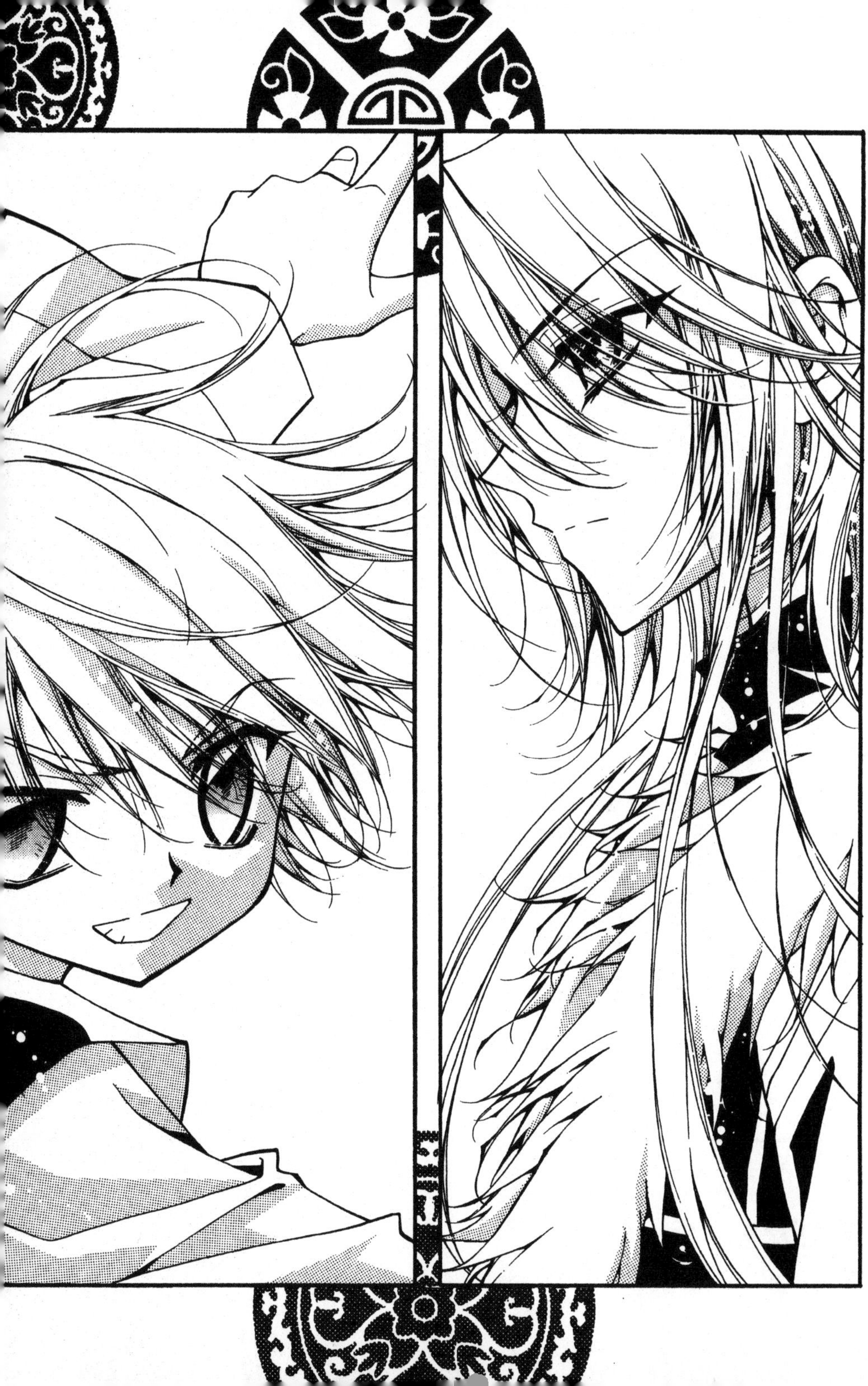

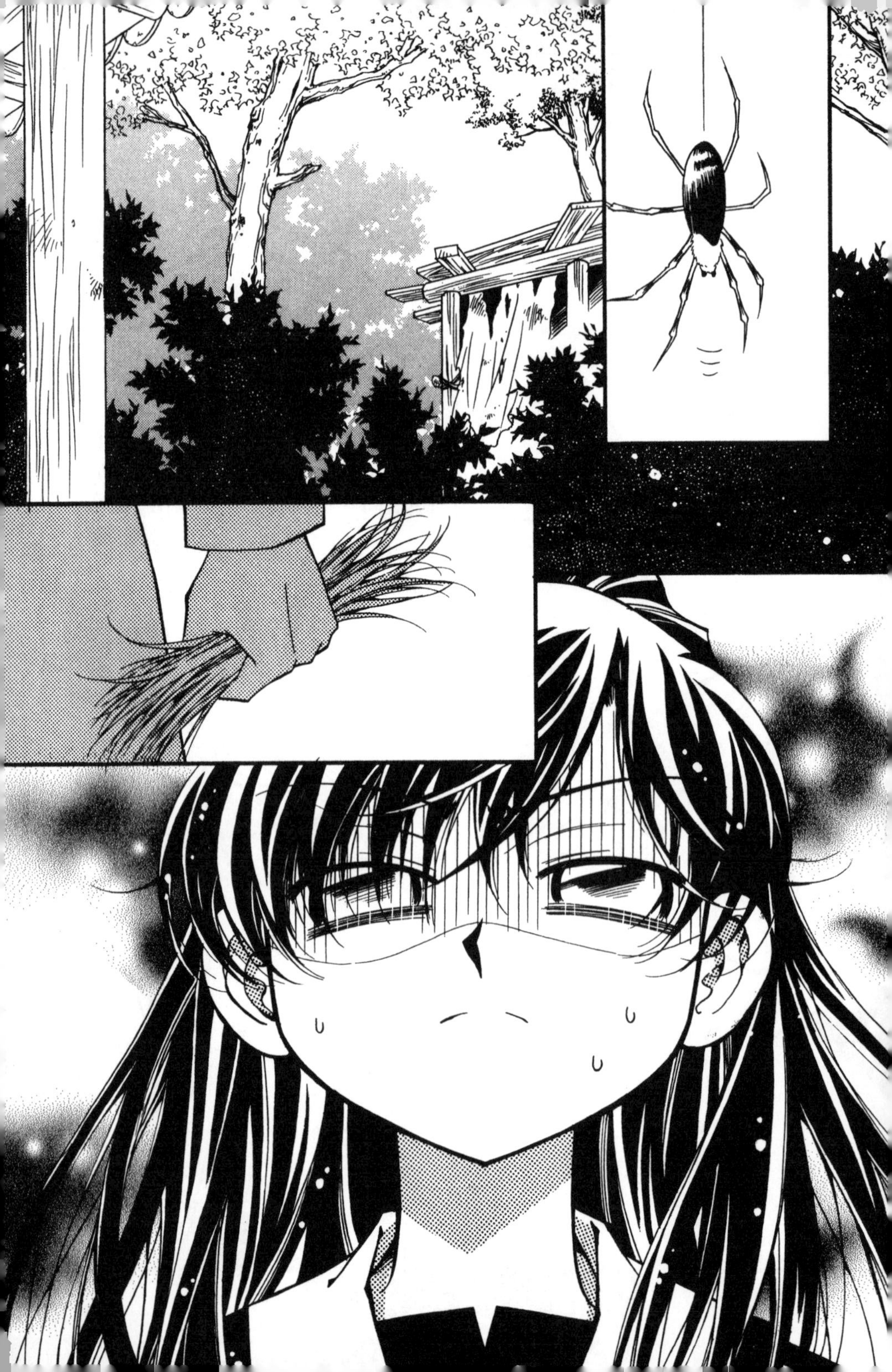

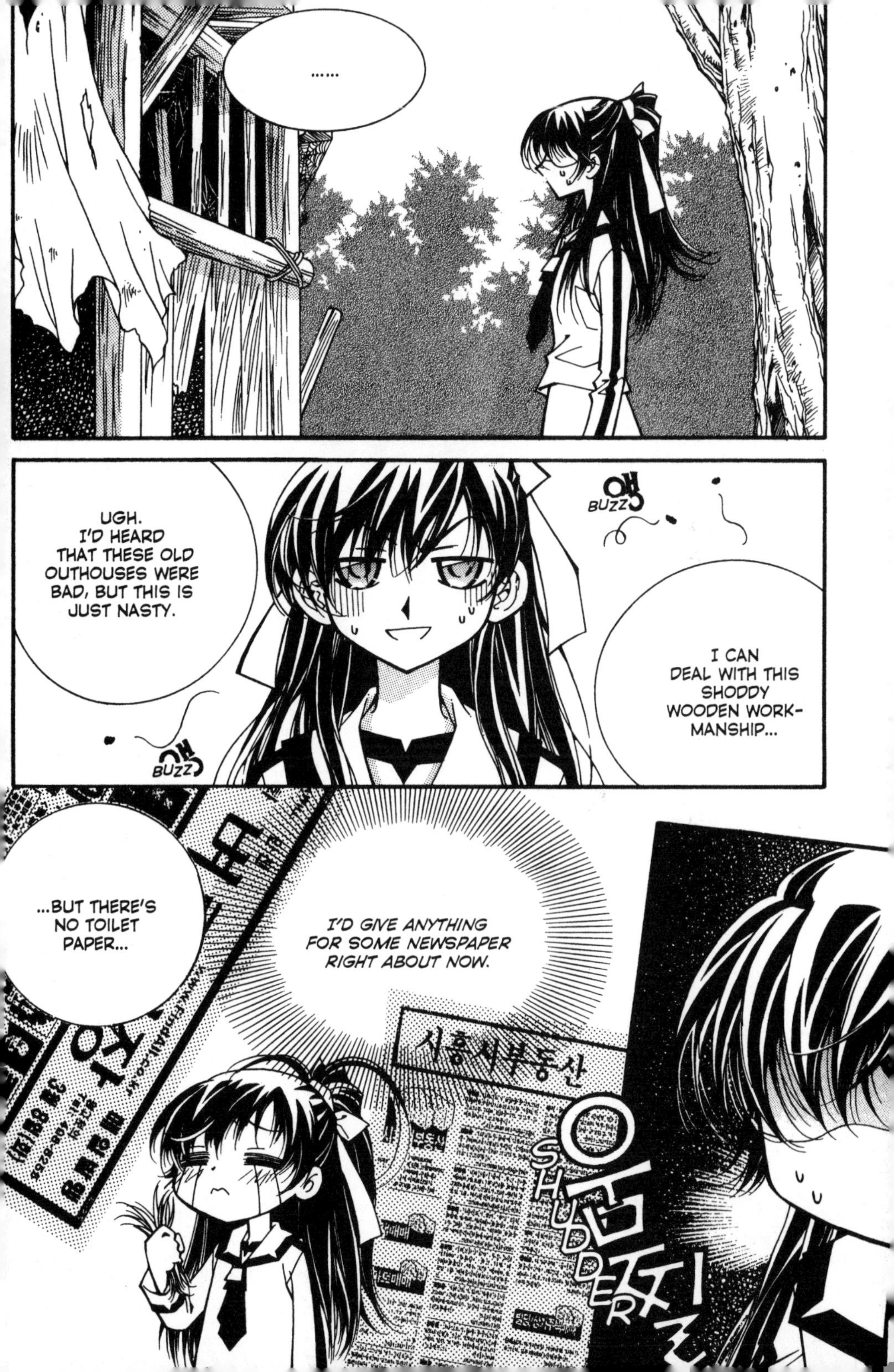
......
BUZZ
UGH. I'D HEARD THAT THESE OLD OUTHOUSES WERE BAD, BUT THIS IS JUST NASTY.
BUZZ
I CAN DEAL WITH THIS SHODDY WOODEN WORK-MANSHIP...
...BUT THERE'S NO TOILET PAPER...
I'D GIVE ANYTHING FOR SOME NEWSPAPER RIGHT ABOUT NOW.
시흥시부동산
SHUDDER

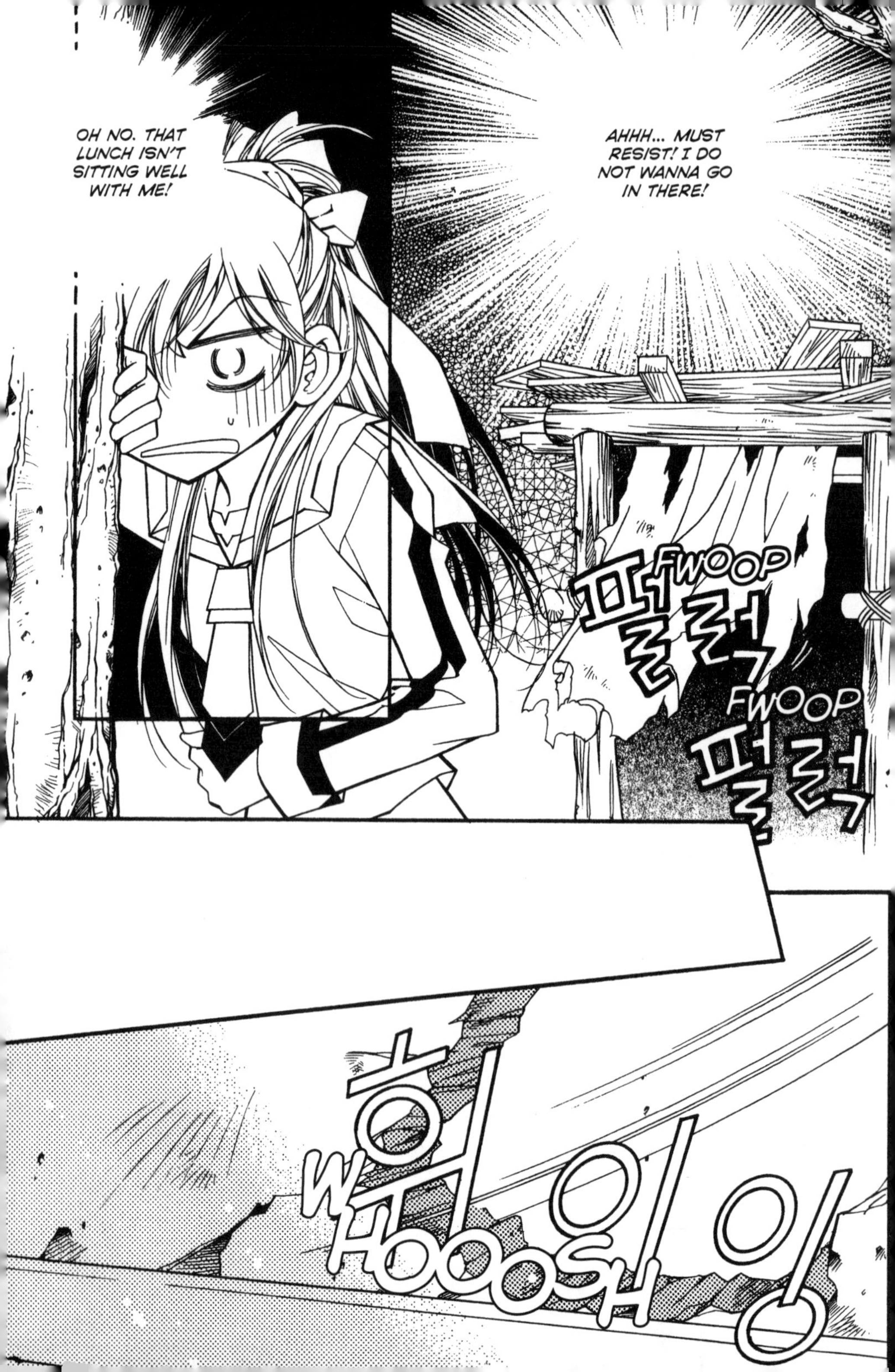
OH NO. THAT LUNCH ISN'T SITTING WELL WITH ME!
AHHH... MUST RESIST! I DO NOT WANNA GO IN THERE!
FWOOP
FWOOP
WHOOOSH

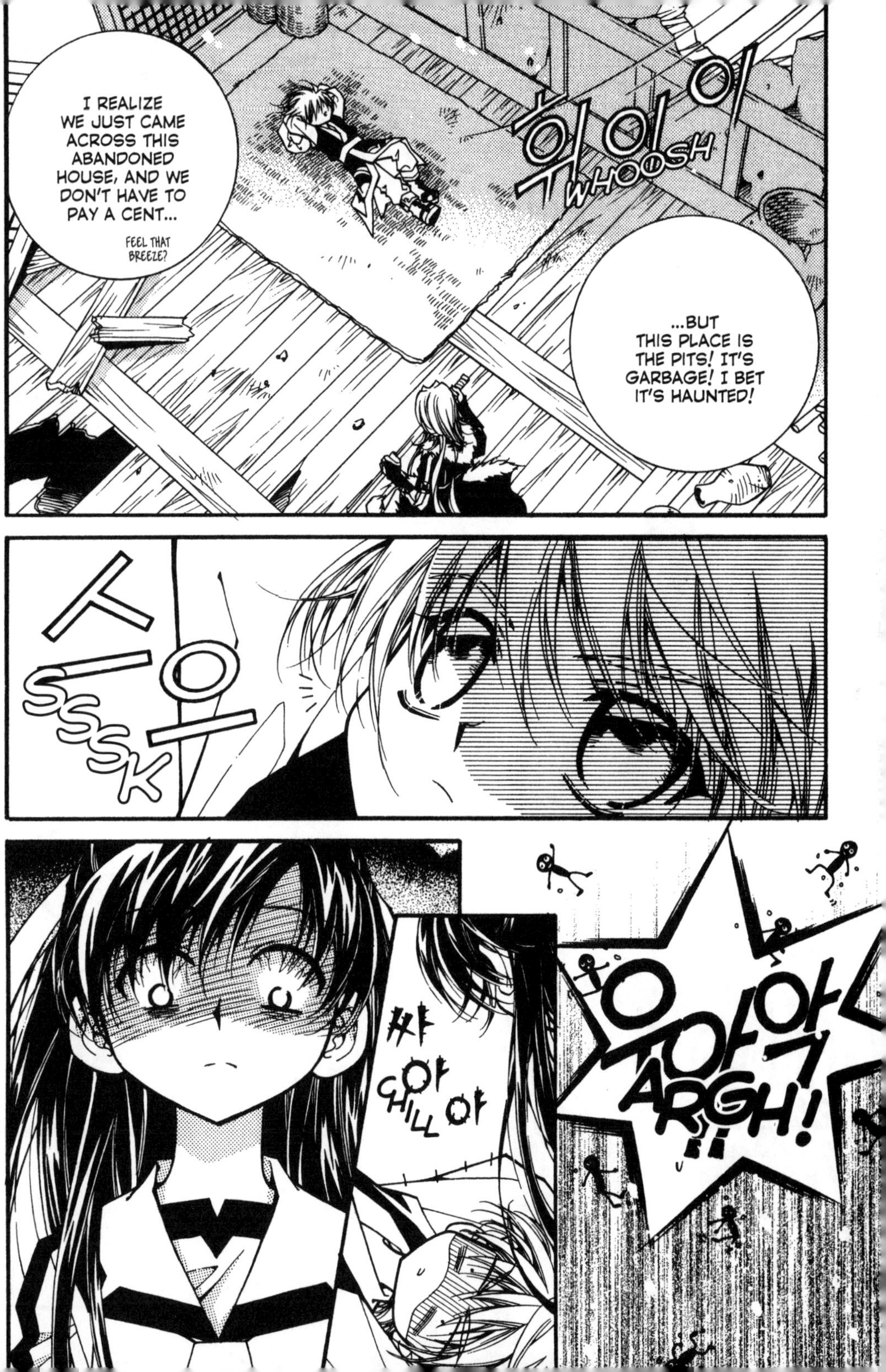
I REALIZE WE JUST CAME ACROSS THIS ABANDONED HOUSE, AND WE DON'T HAVE TO PAY A CENT...
FEEL THAT BREEZE?
WHOOSH
...BUT THIS PLACE IS THE PITS! IT'S GARBAGE! I BET IT'S HAUNTED!
SSSK
CHILL
ARGH!

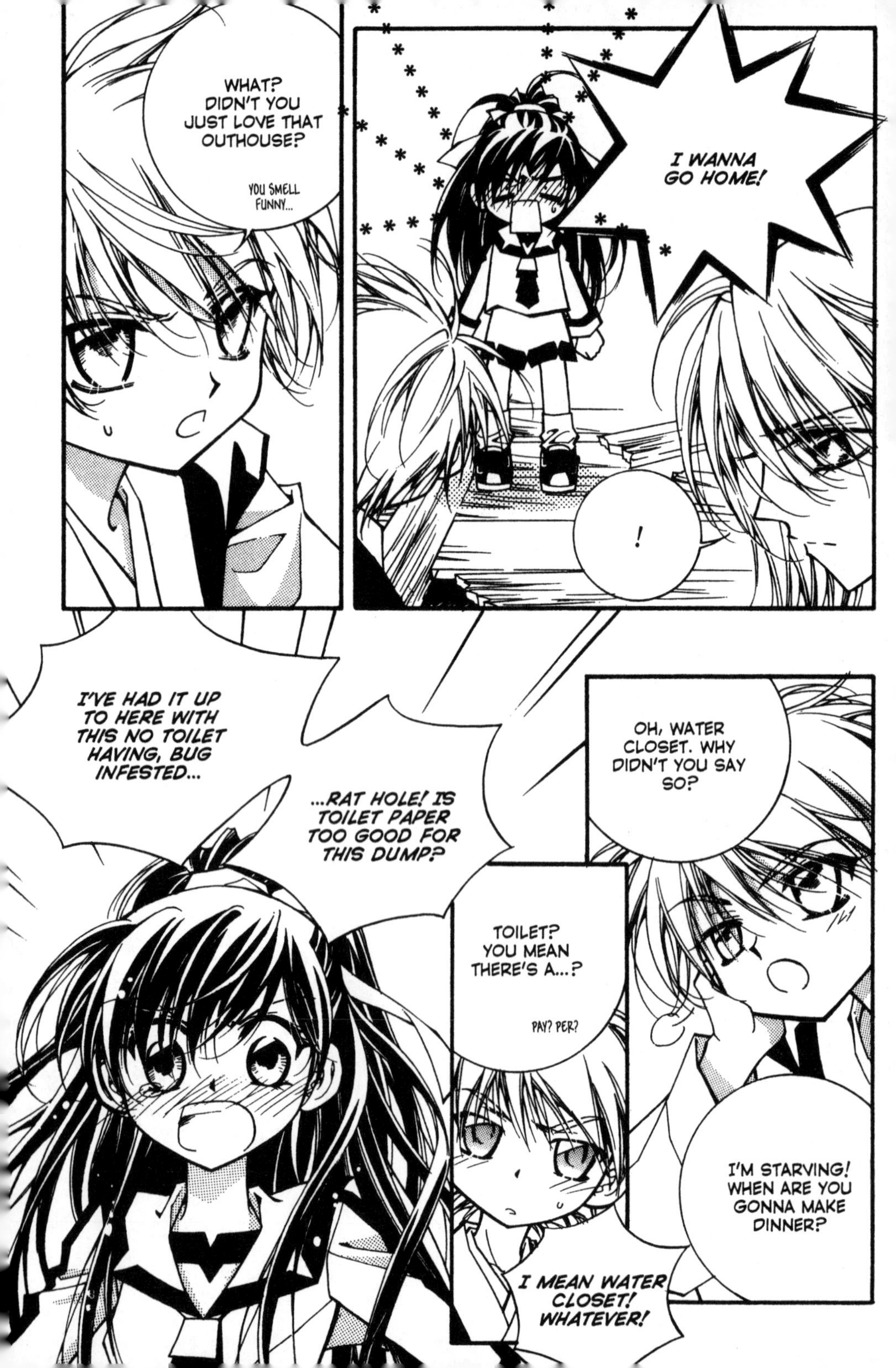
WHAT? DIDN'T YOU JUST LOVE THAT OUTHOUSE?
YOU SMELL FUNNY...
I WANNA GO HOME!
!
I'VE HAD IT UP TO HERE WITH THIS NO TOILET HAVING, BUG INFESTED...
...RAT HOLE! IS TOILET PAPER TOO GOOD FOR THIS DUMP?
TOILET? YOU MEAN THERE'S A...?
PAY? PER?
I MEAN WATER CLOSET! WHATEVER!
OH, WATER CLOSET. WHY DIDN'T YOU SAY SO?
I'M STARVING! WHEN ARE YOU GONNA MAKE DINNER?

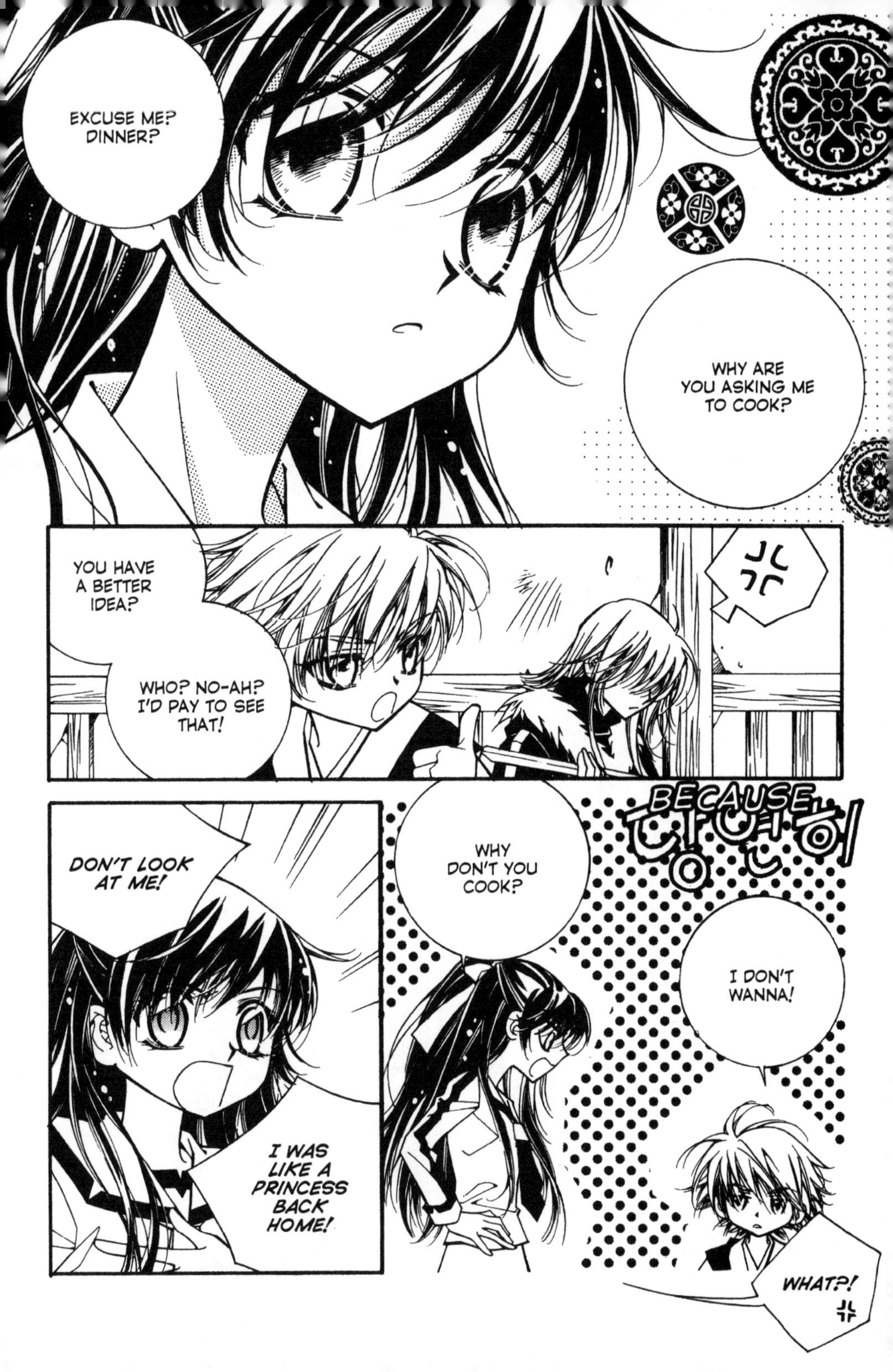

EXCUSE ME? DINNER?
WHY ARE YOU ASKING ME TO COOK?
YOU HAVE A BETTER IDEA?
WHO? NO-AH? I'D PAY TO SEE THAT!
DON'T LOOK AT ME!
I WAS LIKE A PRINCESS BACK HOME!
WHY DON'T YOU COOK?
BECAUSE
당연히
I DON'T WANNA!
WHAT?!

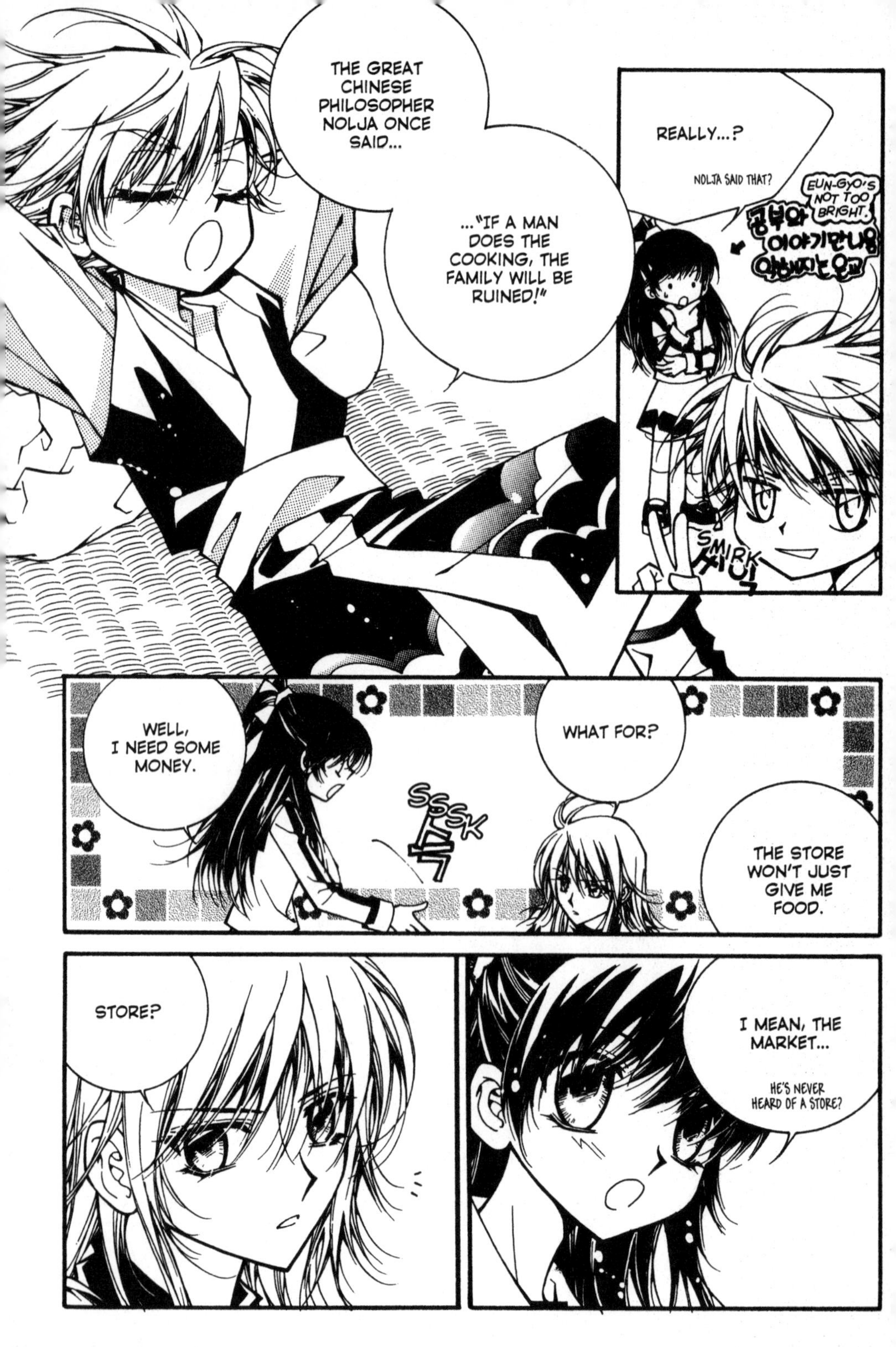
THE GREAT CHINESE PHILOSOPHER NOLJA ONCE SAID...
..."IF A MAN DOES THE COOKING, THE FAMILY WILL BE RUINED!"
REALLY...?
NOLJA SAID THAT?
EUN-GYO'S NOT TOO BRIGHT.
SMIRK
WELL, I NEED SOME MONEY.
SSSK
WHAT FOR?
THE STORE WON'T JUST GIVE ME FOOD.
STORE?
I MEAN, THE MARKET...
HE'S NEVER HEARD OF A STORE?

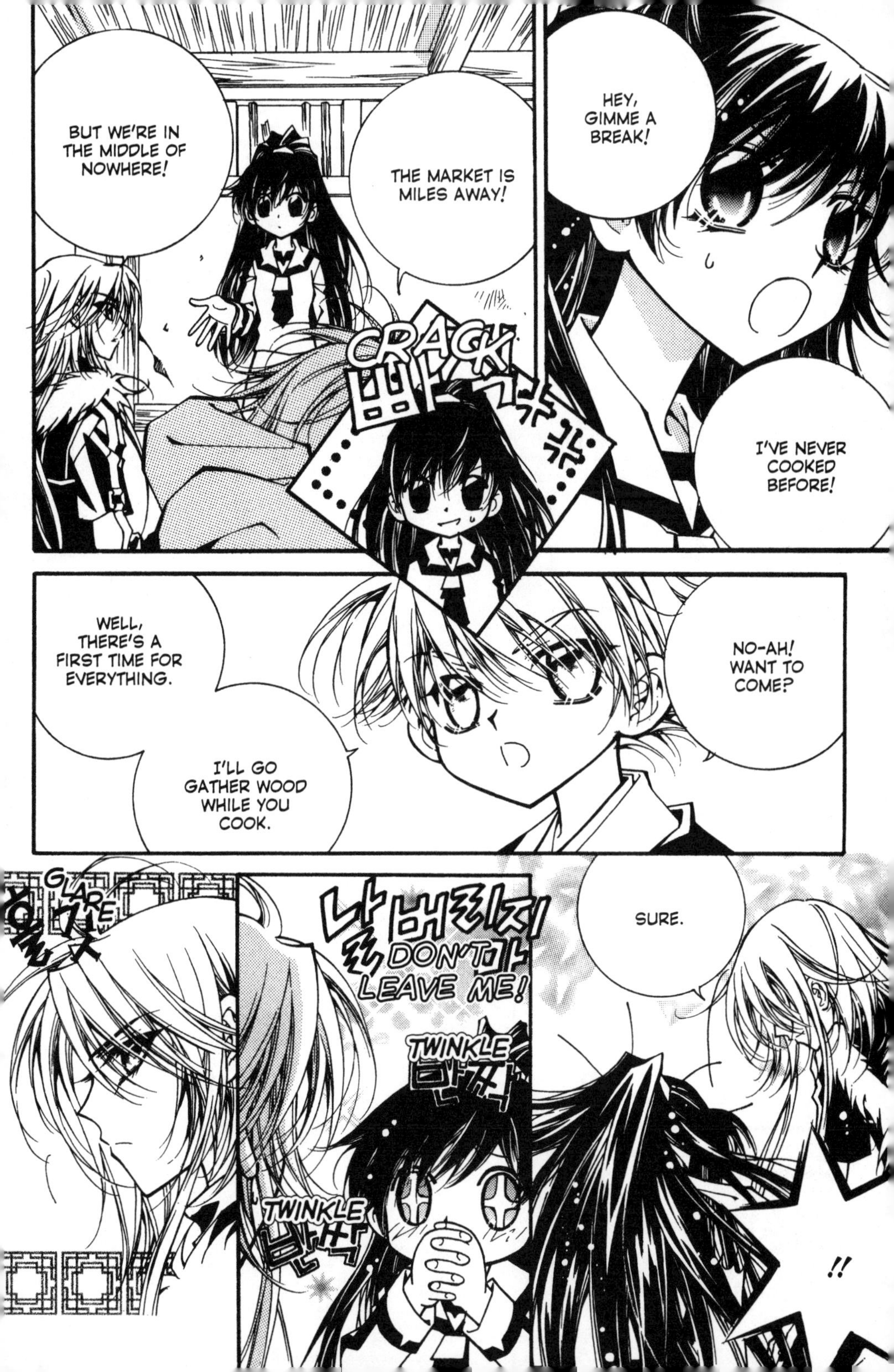
BUT WE'RE IN THE MIDDLE OF NOWHERE!
THE MARKET IS MILES AWAY!
CRACK
HEY, GIMME A BREAK!
I'VE NEVER COOKED BEFORE!
WELL, THERE'S A FIRST TIME FOR EVERYTHING.
I'LL GO GATHER WOOD WHILE YOU COOK.
NO-AH! WANT TO COME?
GLARE
DON'T LEAVE ME!
TWINKLE
TWINKLE
SURE.
!!

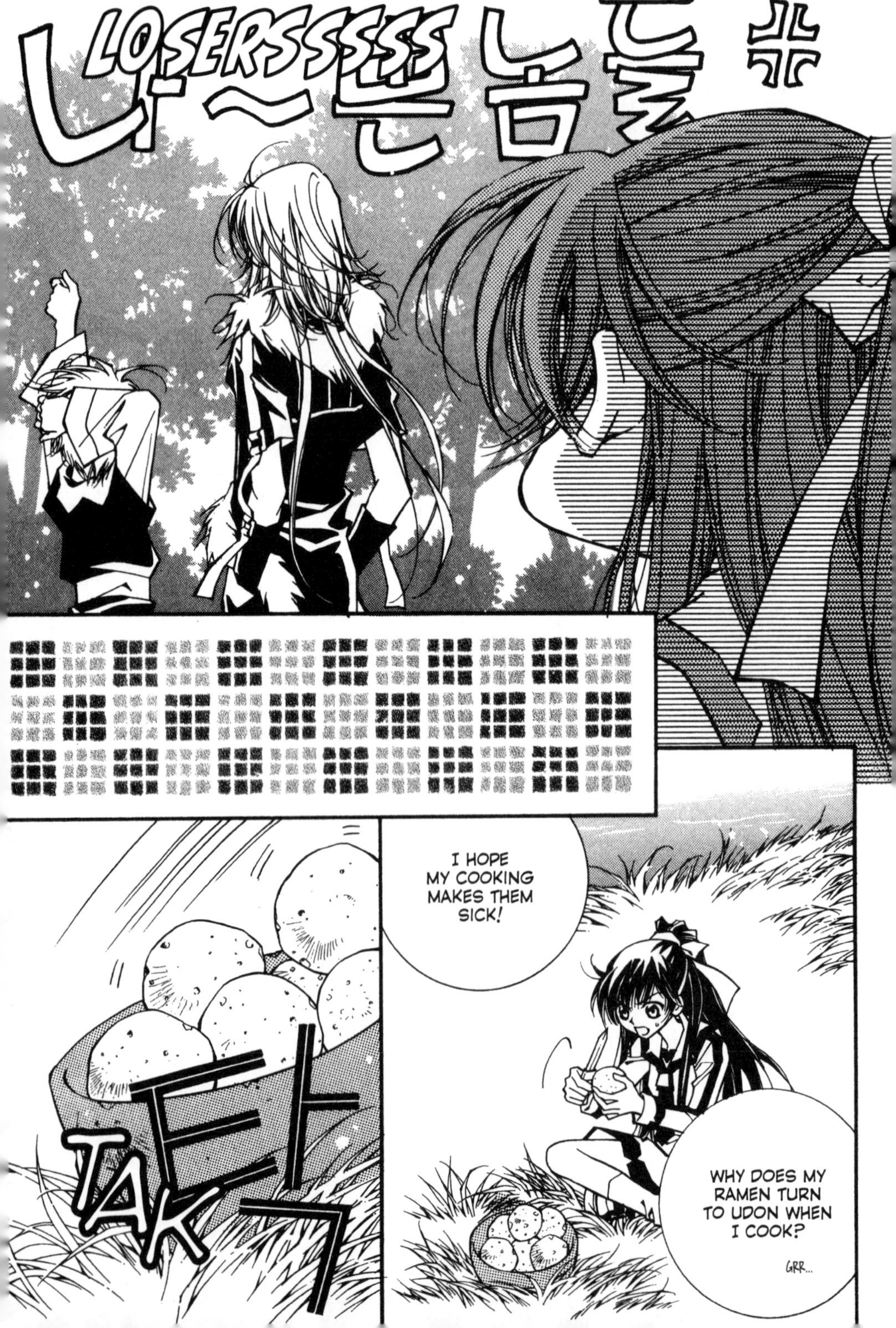
LOSERSSSSS
I HOPE MY COOKING MAKES THEM SICK!
TAK
WHY DOES MY RAMEN TURN TO UDON WHEN I COOK?
GRR...

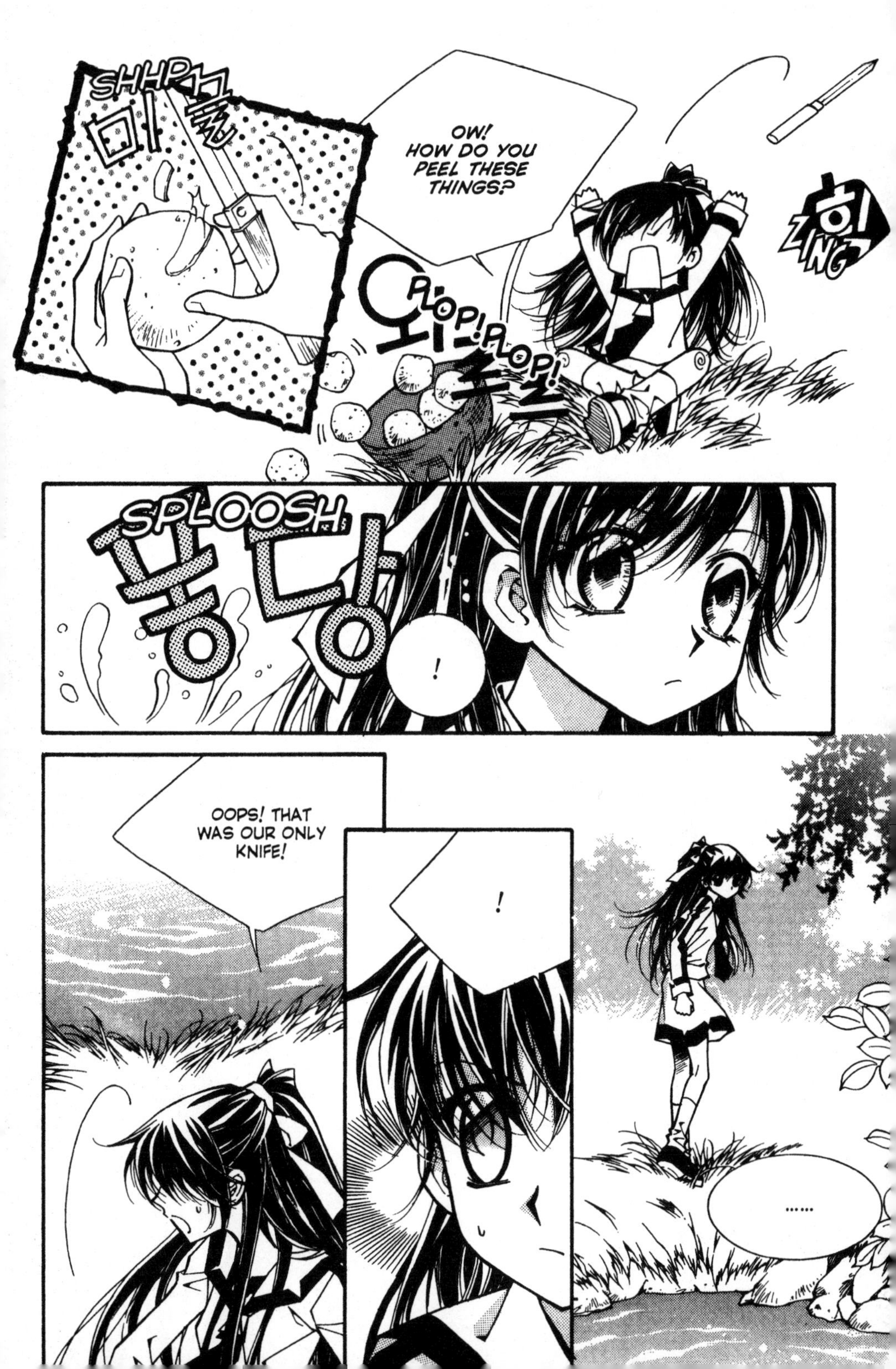
SHHP
OW!
HOW DO YOU
PEEL THESE
THINGS?
PLOP! PLOP!
ZING
SPLOOSH
풍덩
!
OOPS! THAT
WAS OUR ONLY
KNIFE!
!
......

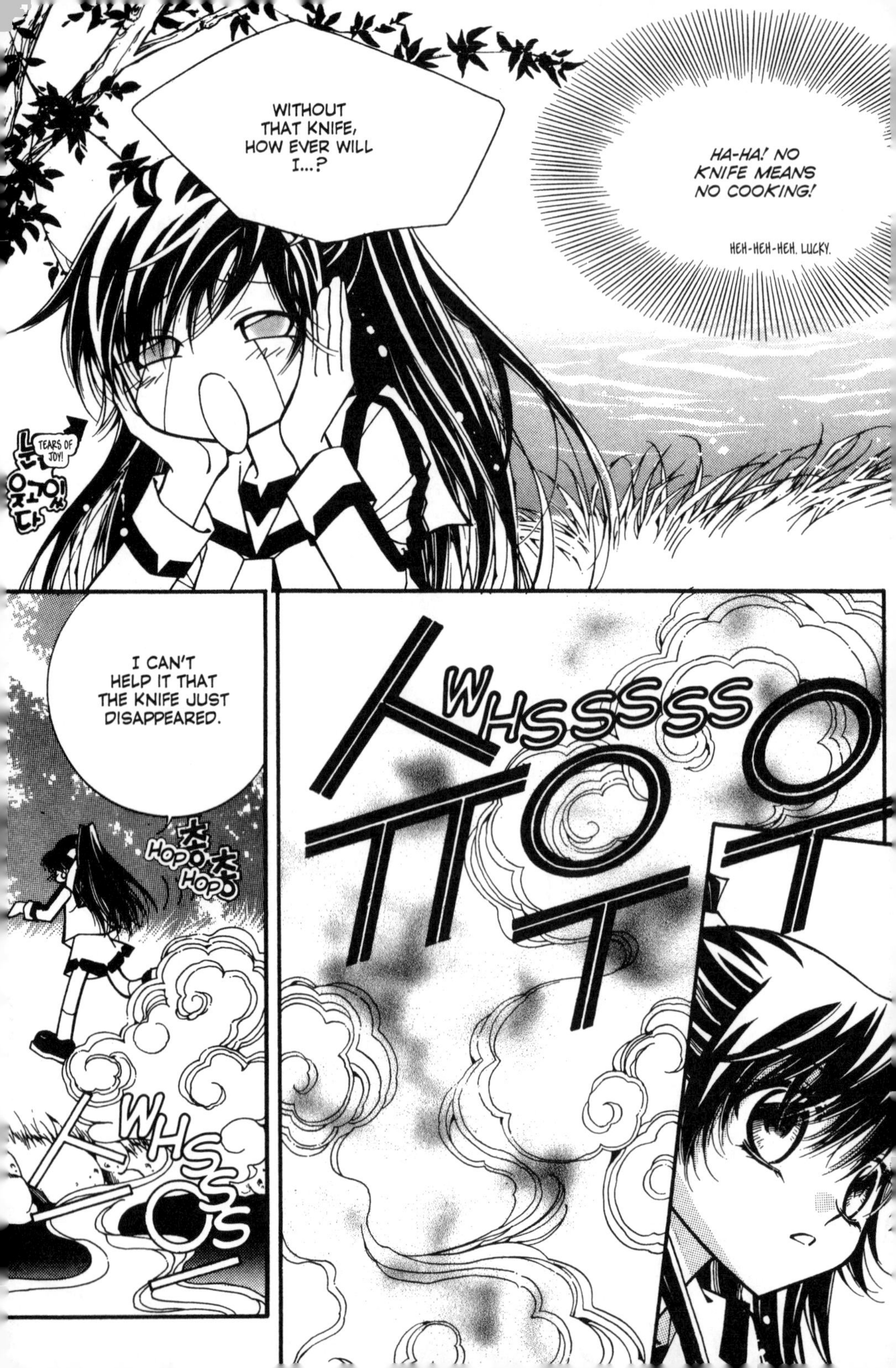
WITHOUT THAT KNIFE, HOW EVER WILL I...?
HA-HA! NO KNIFE MEANS NO COOKING!
HEH-HEH-HEH. LUCKY.
TEARS OF JOY!
I CAN'T HELP IT THAT THE KNIFE JUST DISAPPEARED.
HOP HOP

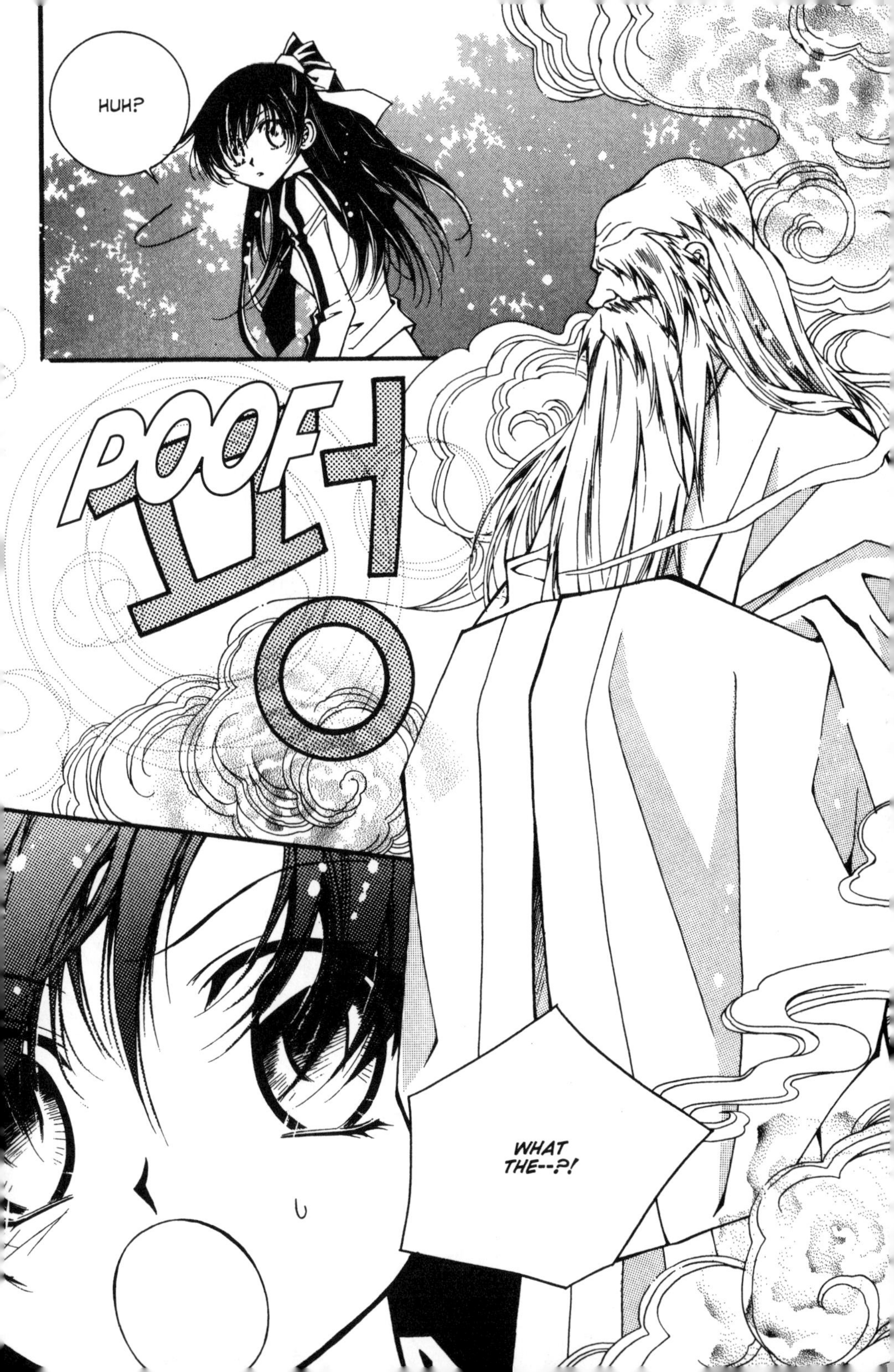
HUH?
POOF
퐁
WHAT THE--?!

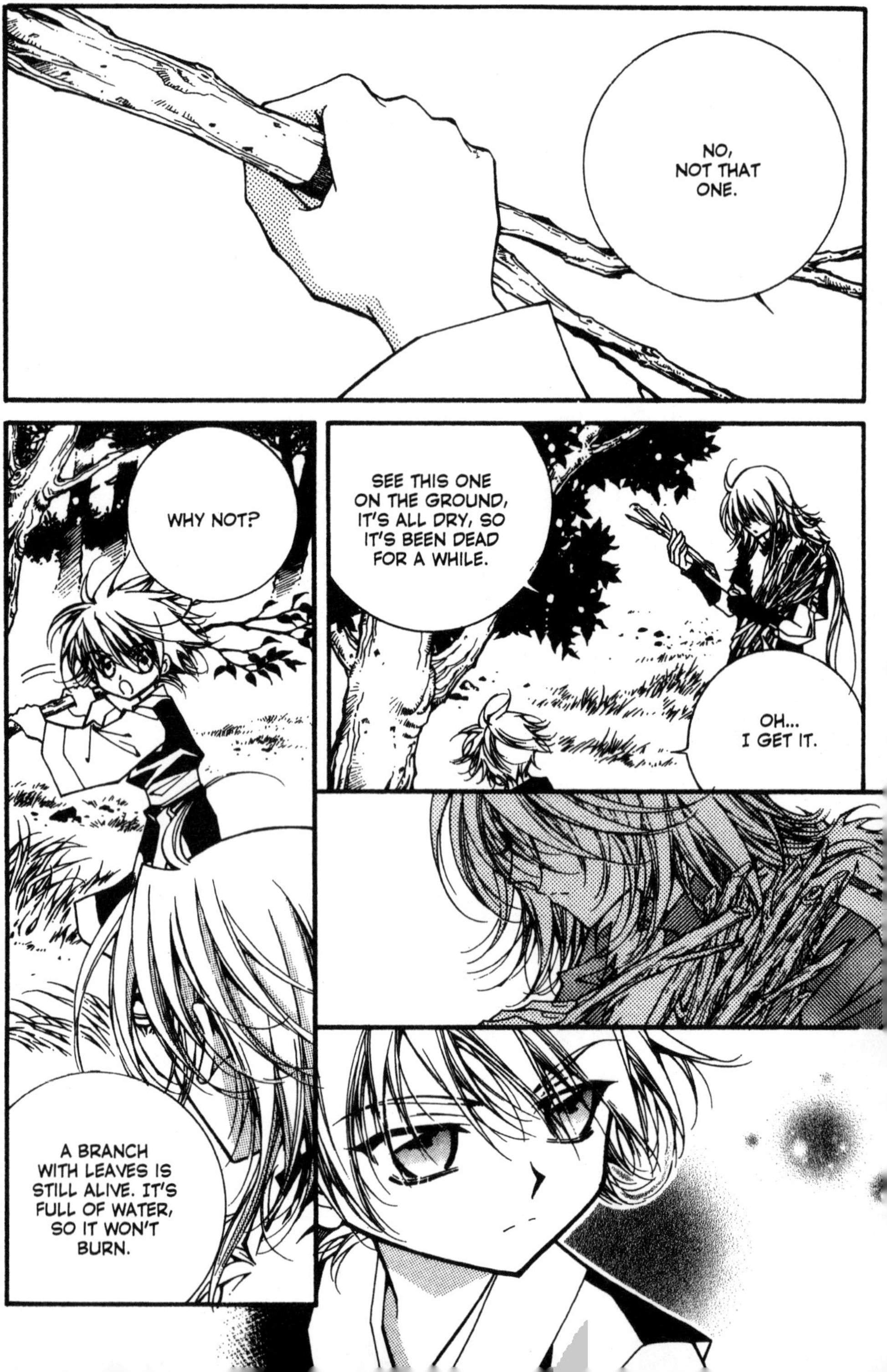
NO, NOT THAT ONE.
WHY NOT?
A BRANCH WITH LEAVES IS STILL ALIVE. IT'S FULL OF WATER, SO IT WON'T BURN.
SEE THIS ONE ON THE GROUND, IT'S ALL DRY, SO IT'S BEEN DEAD FOR A WHILE.
OH... I GET IT.

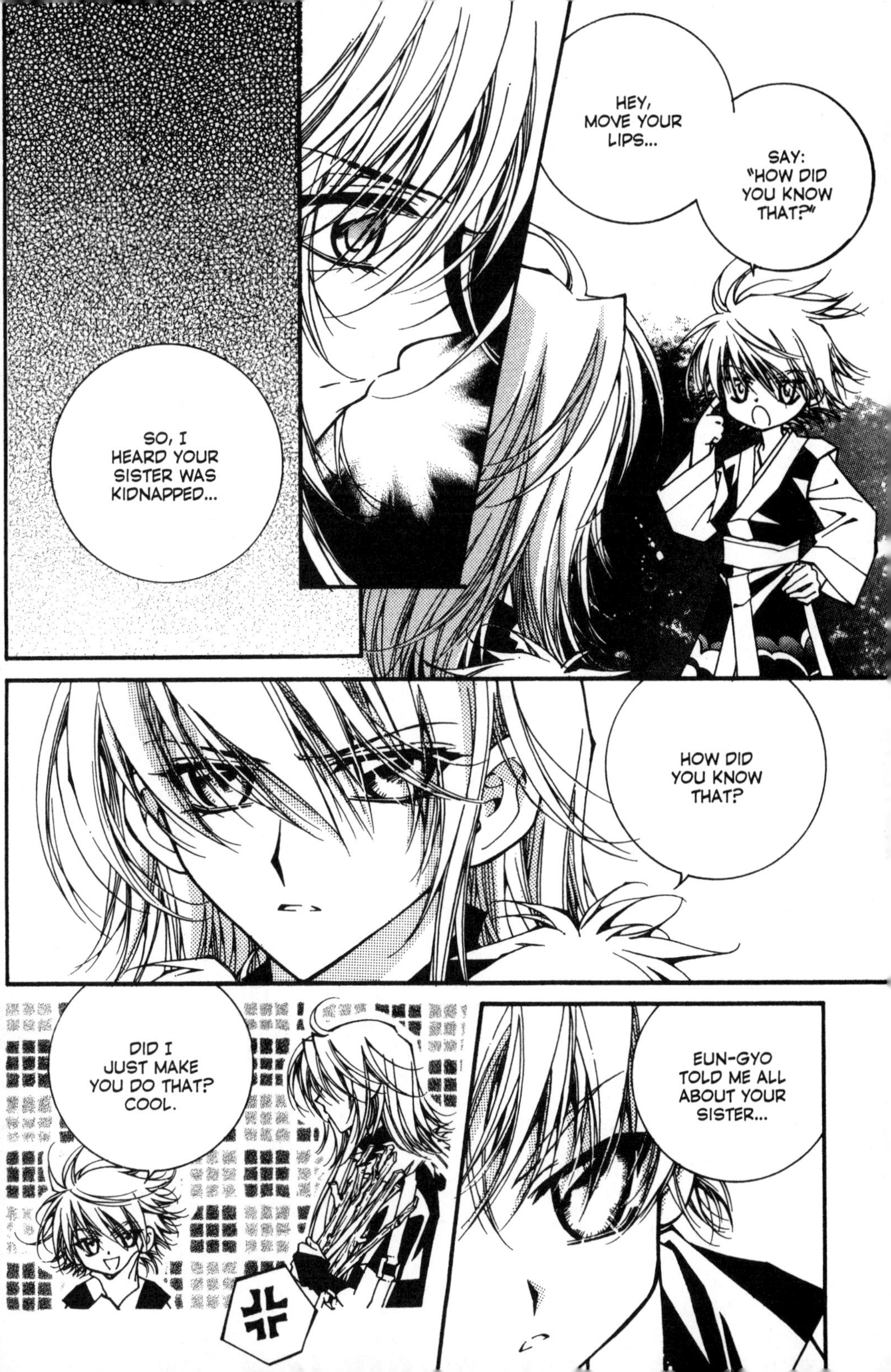
SO, I HEARD YOUR SISTER WAS KIDNAPPED...
HEY, MOVE YOUR LIPS...
SAY: "HOW DID YOU KNOW THAT?"
HOW DID YOU KNOW THAT?
DID I JUST MAKE YOU DO THAT? COOL.
EUN-GYO TOLD ME ALL ABOUT YOUR SISTER...

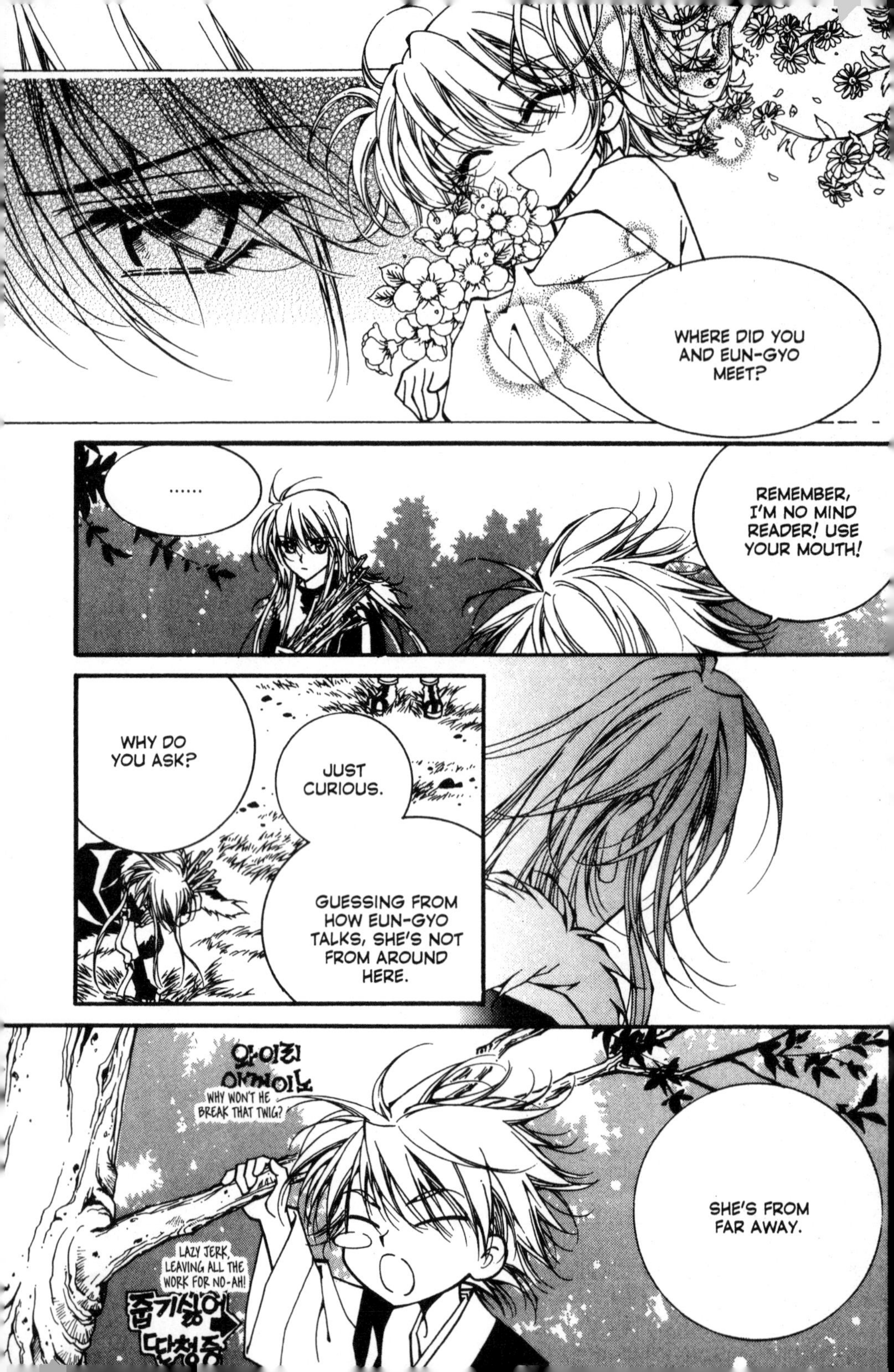
WHERE DID YOU AND EUN-GYO MEET?
......
REMEMBER, I'M NO MIND READER! USE YOUR MOUTH!
WHY DO YOU ASK?
JUST CURIOUS.
GUESSING FROM HOW EUN-GYO TALKS, SHE'S NOT FROM AROUND HERE.
와이리 아끼이노
WHY WON'T HE BREAK THAT TWIG?
LAZY JERK, LEAVING ALL THE WORK FOR NO-AH!
줍기싫어 → 딴청중
SHE'S FROM FAR AWAY.

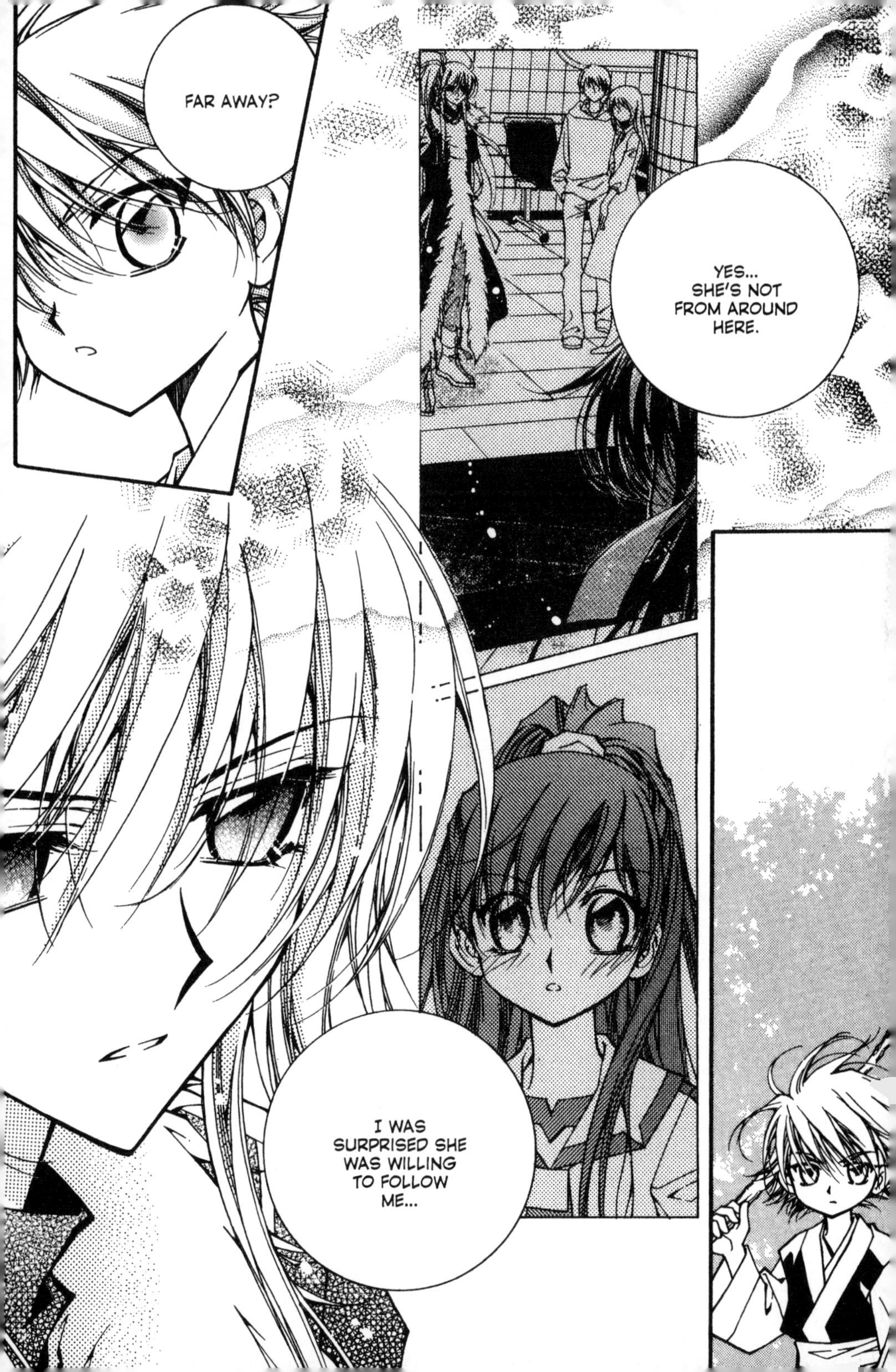
FAR AWAY?
YES... SHE'S NOT FROM AROUND HERE.
I WAS SURPRISED SHE WAS WILLING TO FOLLOW ME...

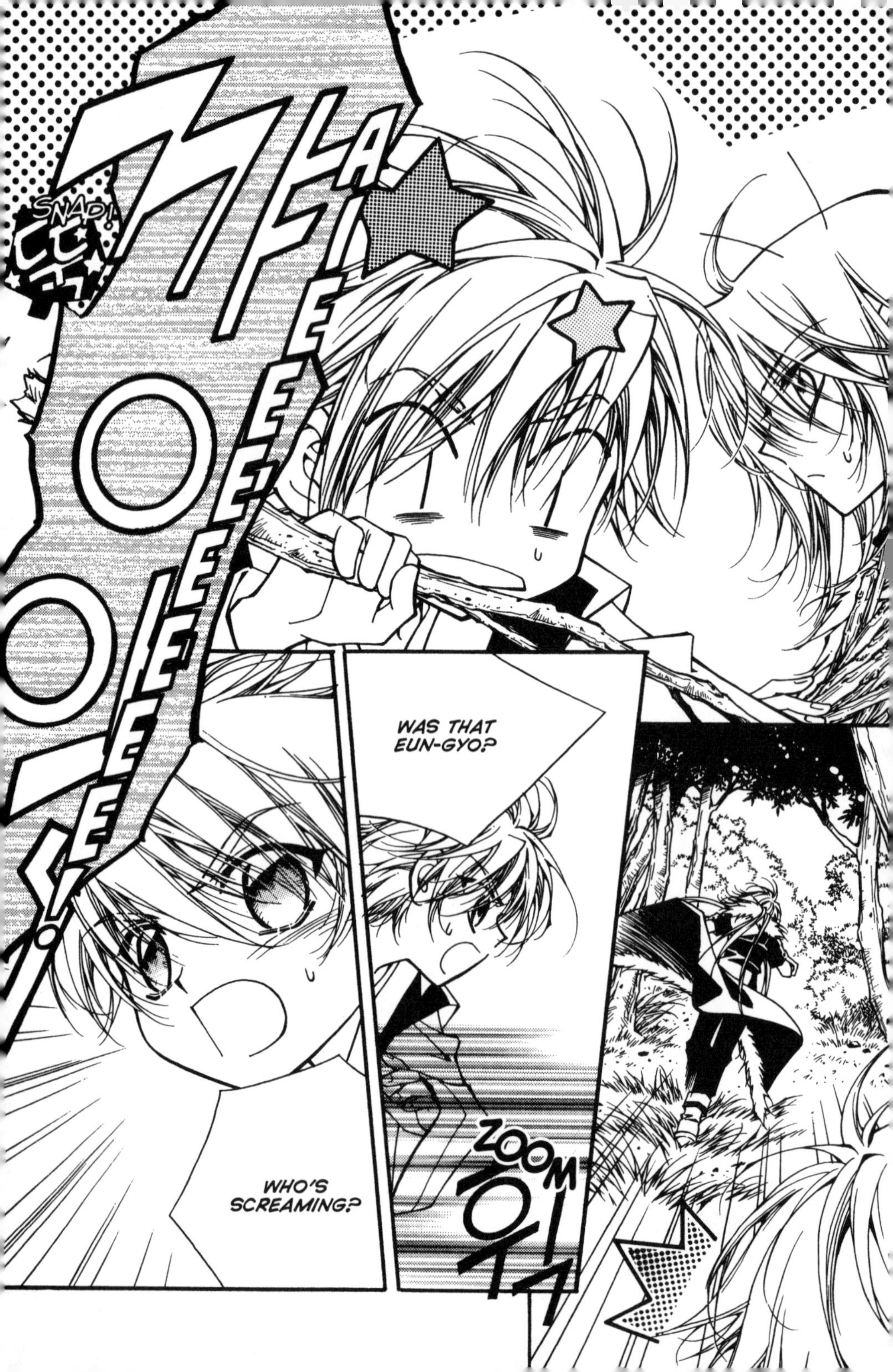
SNAP!
LAIEEEEEEEEEEEE!?
WHO'S SCREAMING?
WAS THAT EUN-GYO?
ZOOM

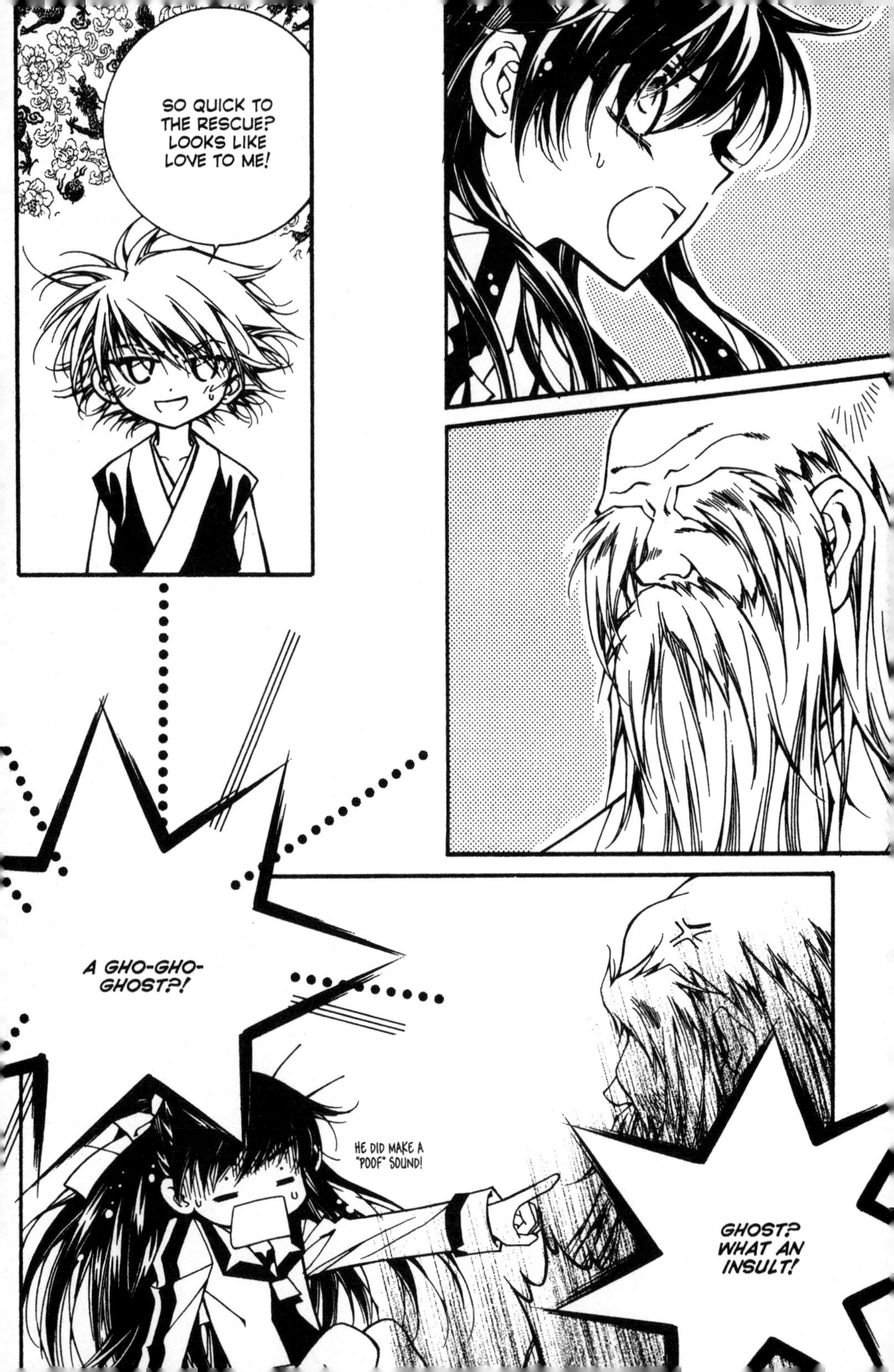
SO QUICK TO THE RESCUE? LOOKS LIKE LOVE TO ME!
A GHO-GHO-GHOST?!
HE DID MAKE A "POOF" SOUND!
GHOST? WHAT AN INSULT!

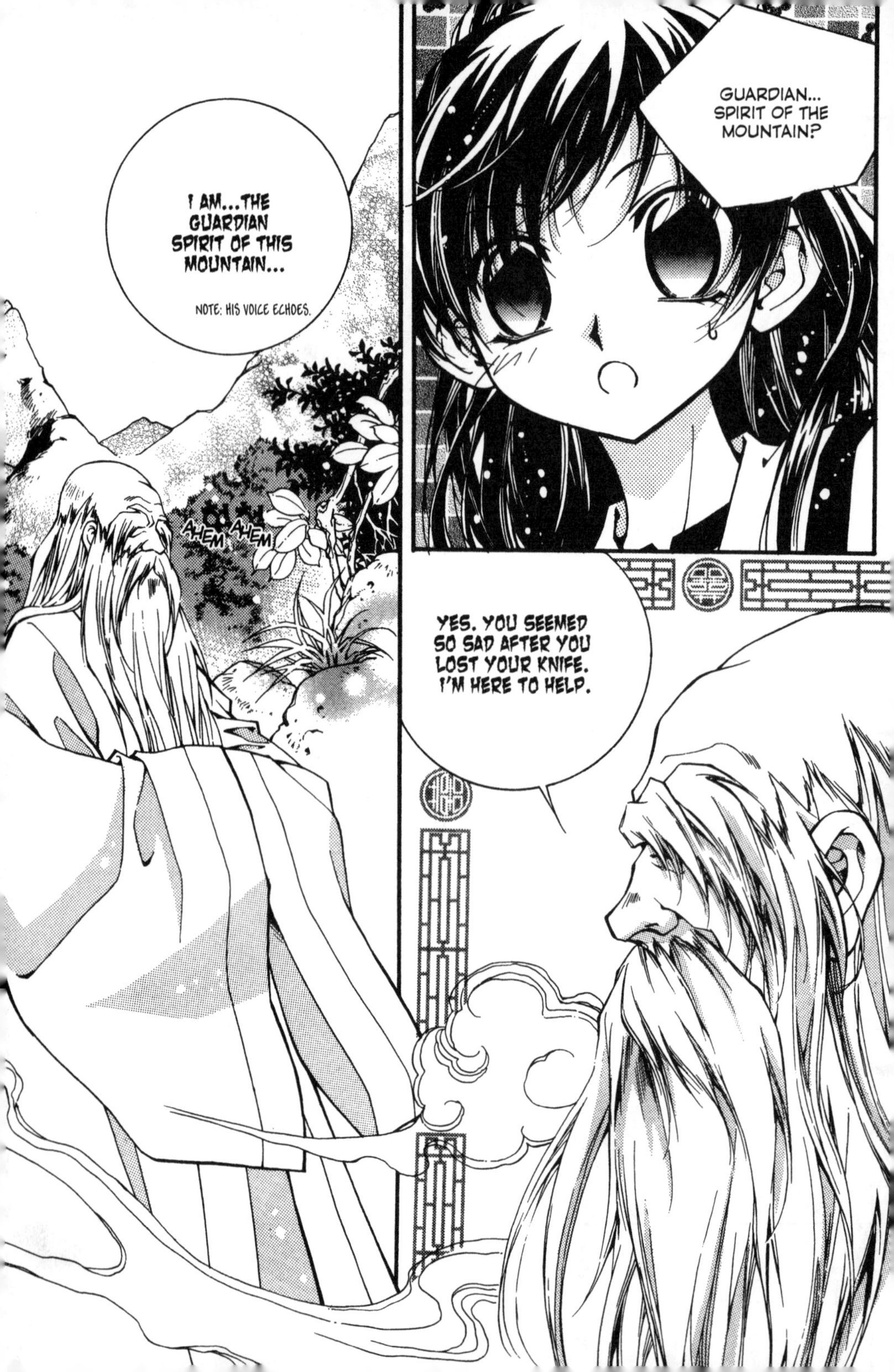
I AM...THE GUARDIAN SPIRIT OF THIS MOUNTAIN...
NOTE: HIS VOICE ECHOES.
AHEM AHEM
GUARDIAN... SPIRIT OF THE MOUNTAIN?
YES. YOU SEEMED SO SAD AFTER YOU LOST YOUR KNIFE. I'M HERE TO HELP.

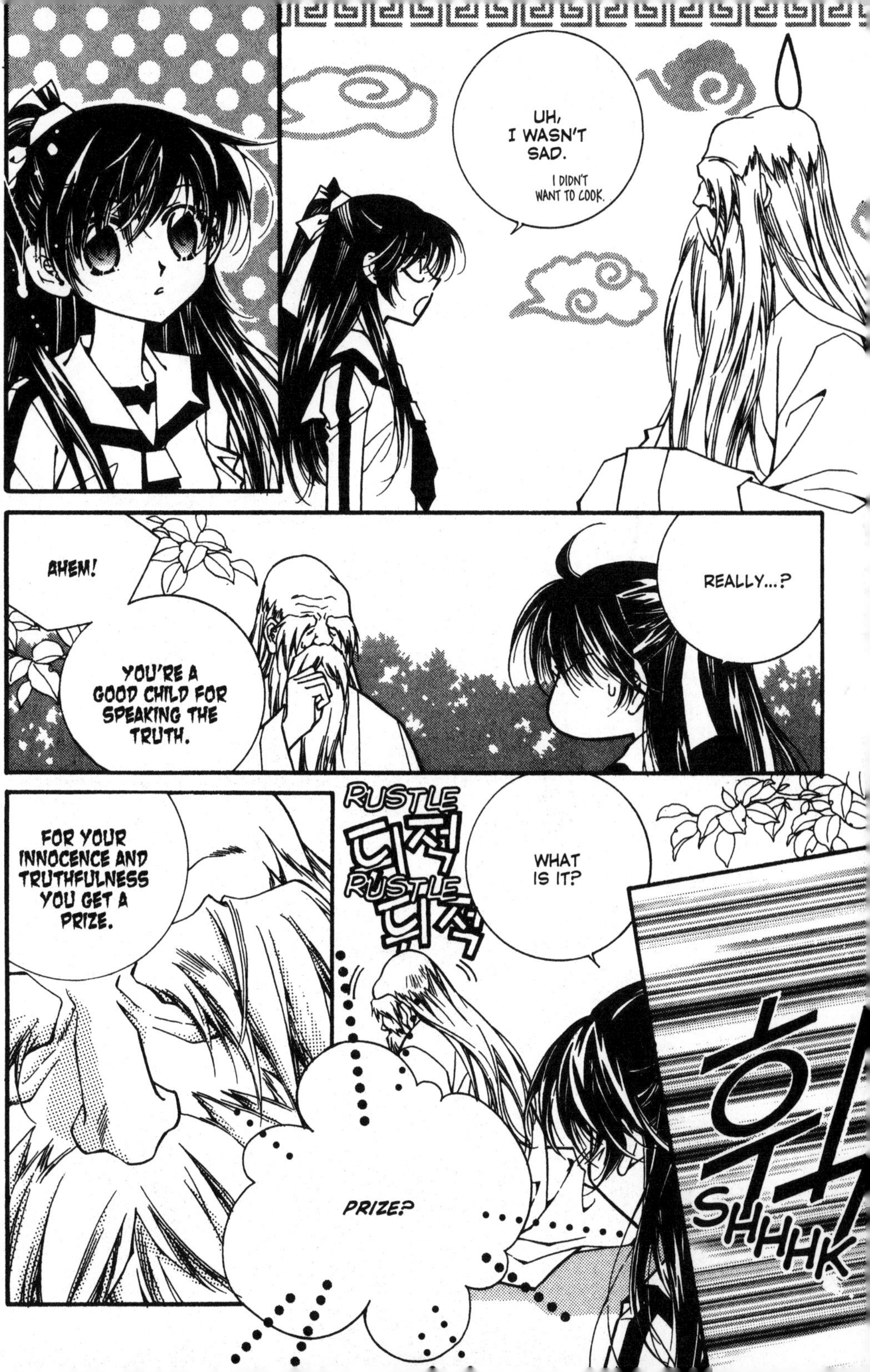
UH, I WASN'T SAD.
I DIDN'T WANT TO COOK.
AHEM!
YOU'RE A GOOD CHILD FOR SPEAKING THE TRUTH.
REALLY...?
FOR YOUR INNOCENCE AND TRUTHFULNESS YOU GET A PRIZE.
RUSTLE
RUSTLE
WHAT IS IT?
PRIZE?
SHHHK

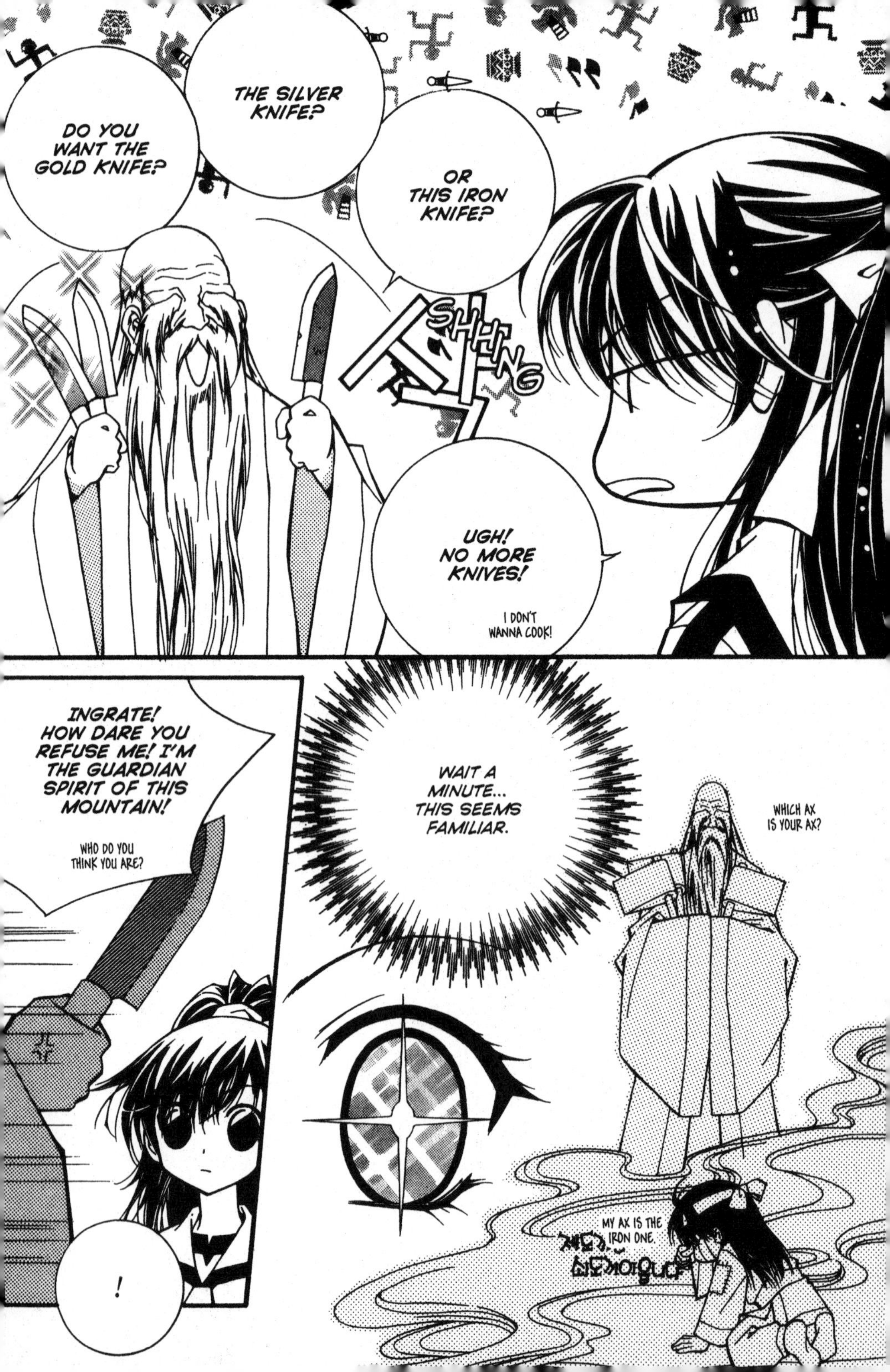
DO YOU WANT THE GOLD KNIFE?
THE SILVER KNIFE?
OR THIS IRON KNIFE?
SHHING
UGH! NO MORE KNIVES!
I DON'T WANNA COOK!
INGRATE! HOW DARE YOU REFUSE ME! I'M THE GUARDIAN SPIRIT OF THIS MOUNTAIN!
WHO DO YOU THINK YOU ARE?
!
WAIT A MINUTE... THIS SEEMS FAMILIAR.
WHICH AX IS YOUR AX?
MY AX IS THE IRON ONE.

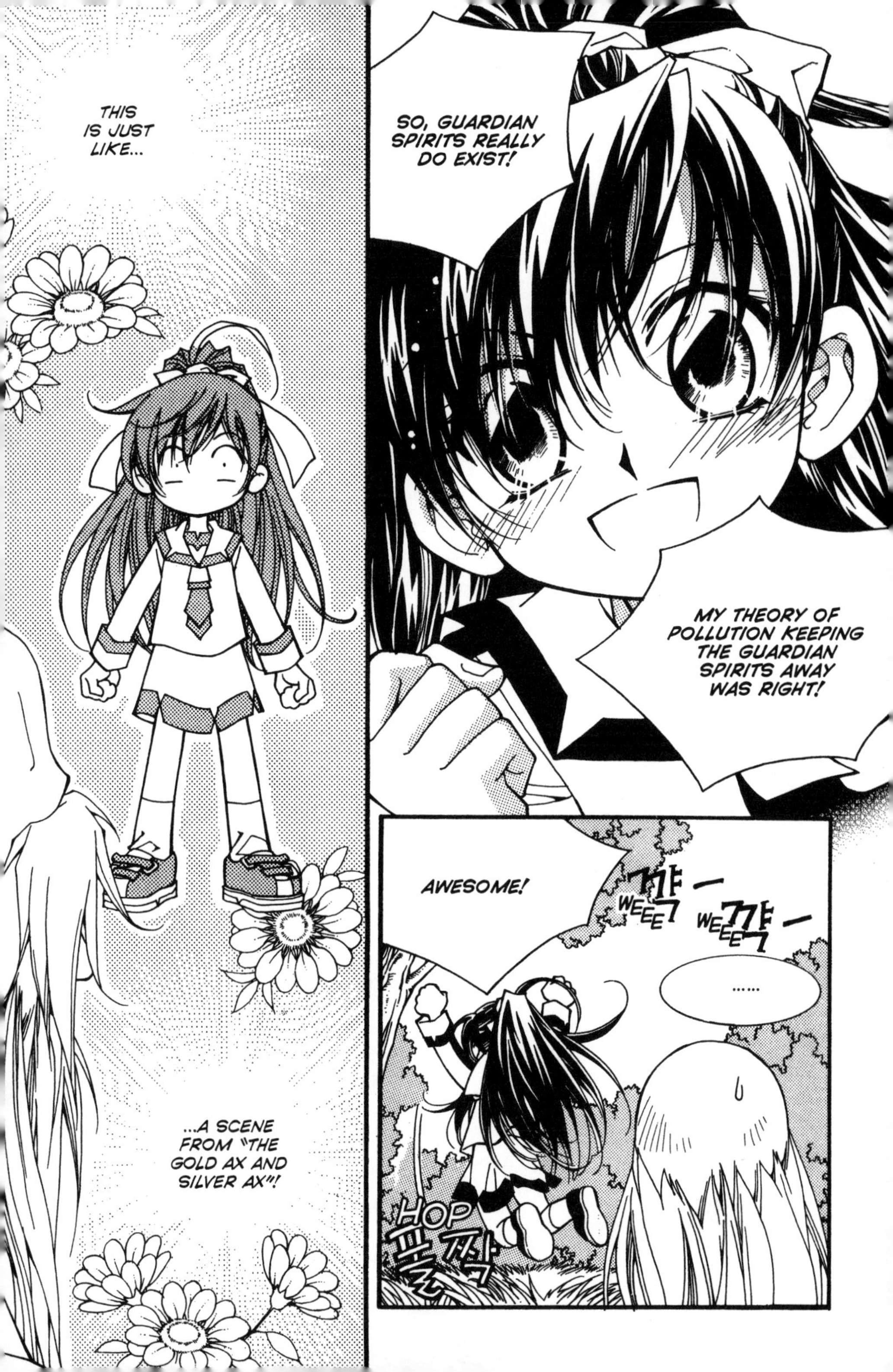
THIS IS JUST LIKE...
...A SCENE FROM "THE GOLD AX AND SILVER AX"!
SO, GUARDIAN SPIRITS REALLY DO EXIST!
MY THEORY OF POLLUTION KEEPING THE GUARDIAN SPIRITS AWAY WAS RIGHT!
AWESOME!
WEEE
WEEE
......
HOP

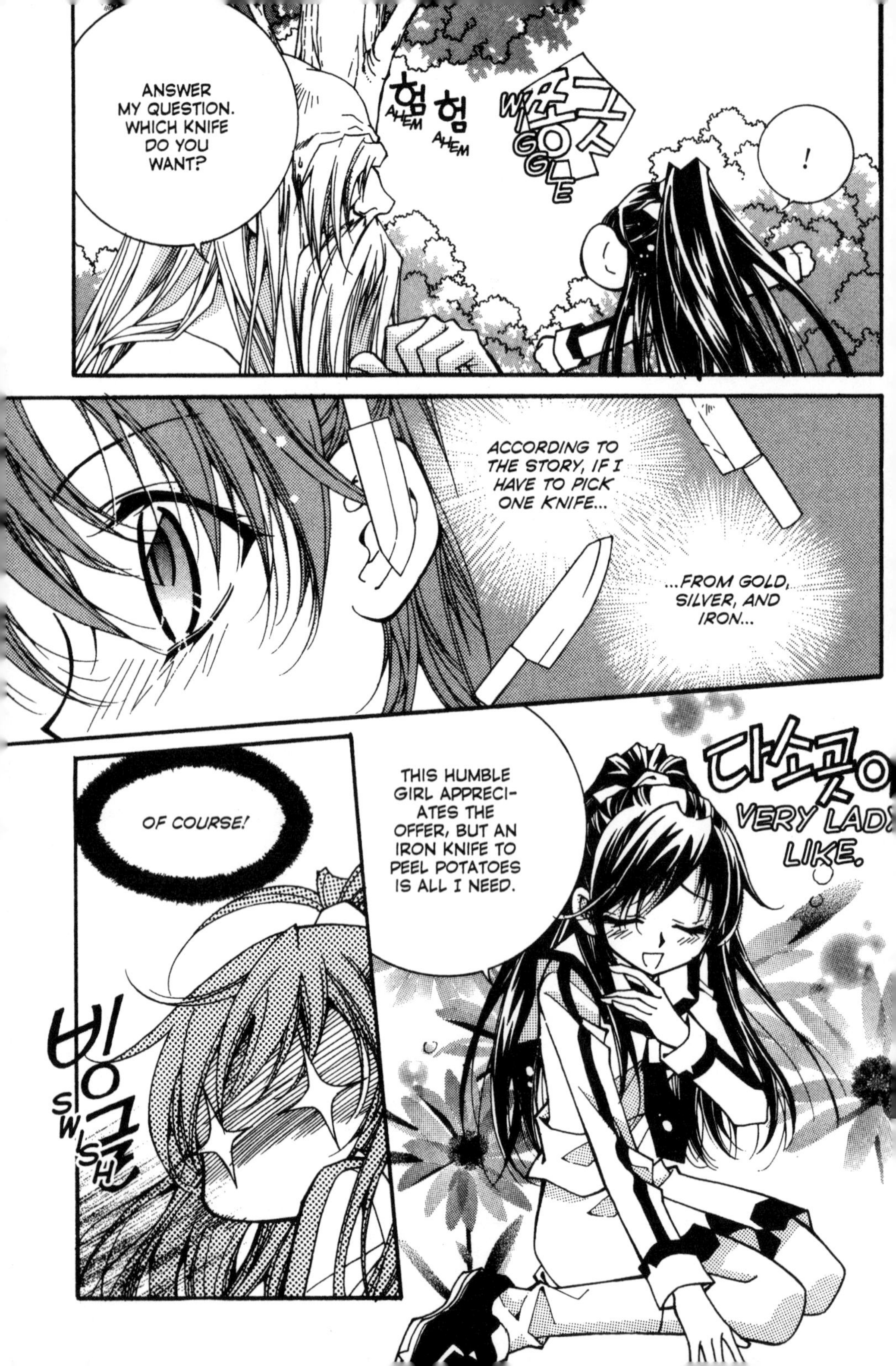
ANSWER MY QUESTION. WHICH KNIFE DO YOU WANT?
험 AHEM
험 AHEM
WIGGLE
!
ACCORDING TO THE STORY, IF I HAVE TO PICK ONE KNIFE...
...FROM GOLD, SILVER, AND IRON...
OF COURSE!
빙글 SWISH
THIS HUMBLE GIRL APPRECIATES THE OFFER, BUT AN IRON KNIFE TO PEEL POTATOES IS ALL I NEED.
다소곳 VERY LADY LIKE.

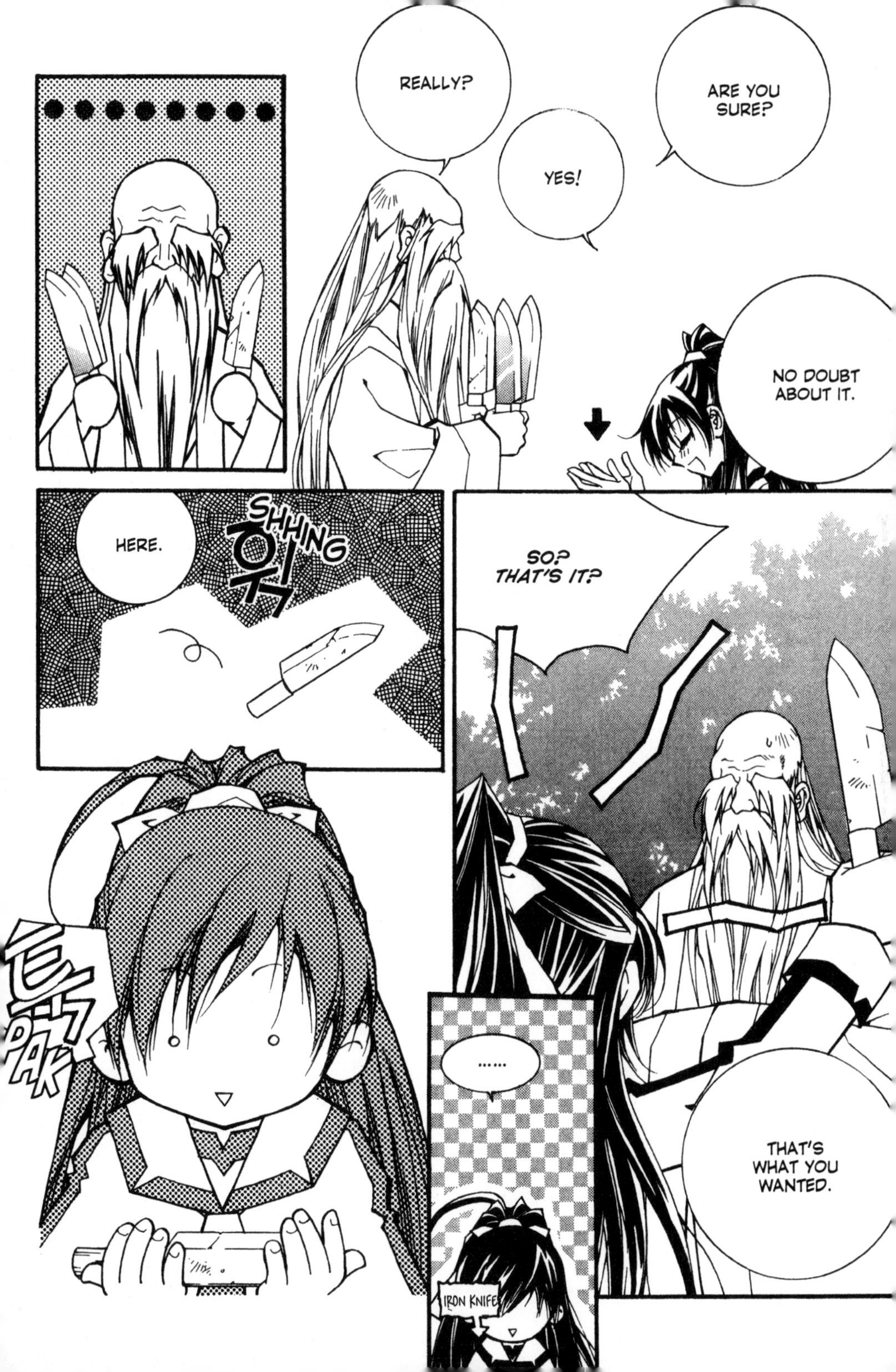
REALLY?
YES!
ARE YOU SURE?
NO DOUBT ABOUT IT.
HERE.
SHHING
PAK
SO? THAT'S IT?
......
IRON KNIFE
THAT'S WHAT YOU WANTED.

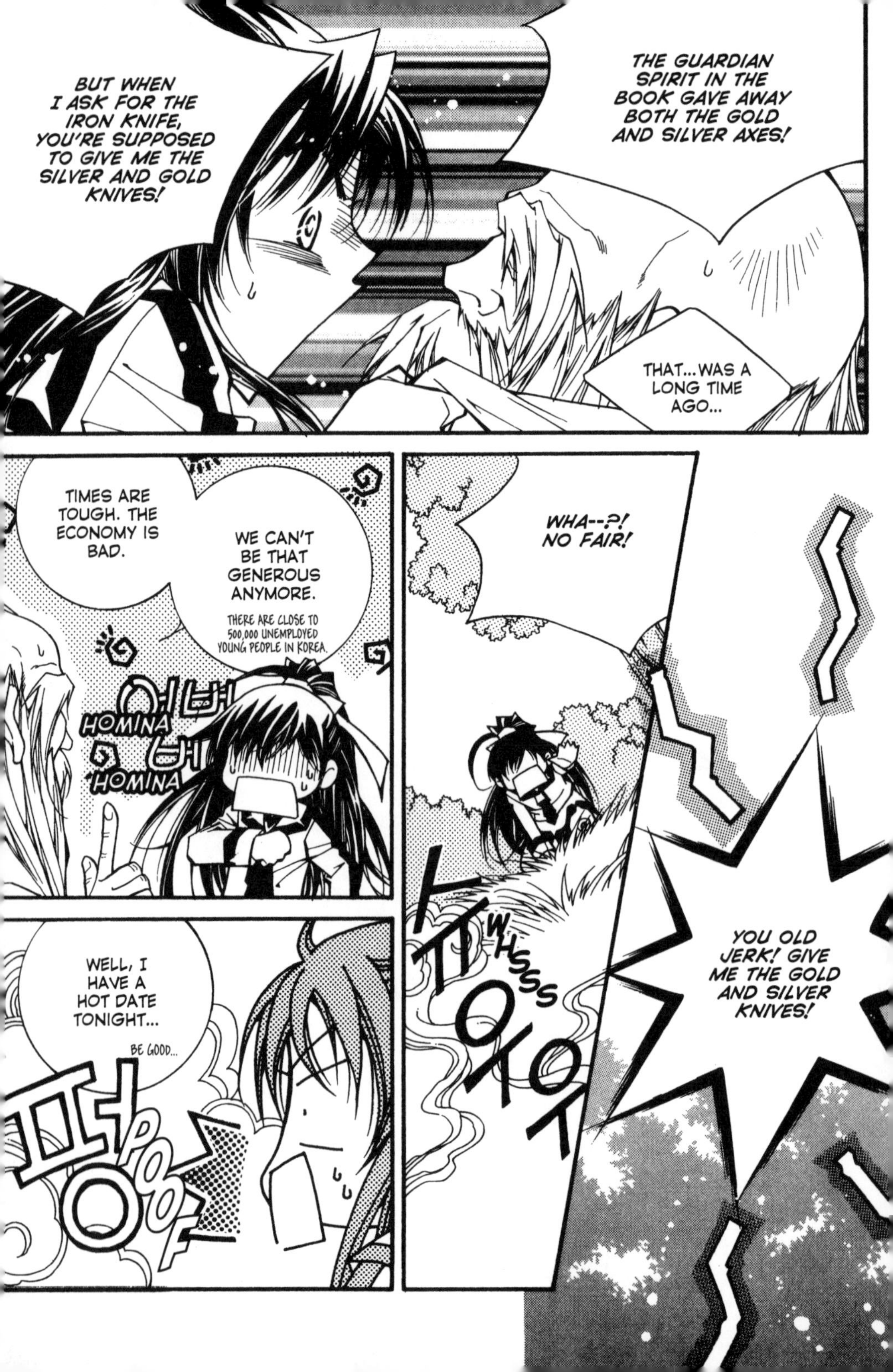
BUT WHEN I ASK FOR THE IRON KNIFE, YOU'RE SUPPOSED TO GIVE ME THE SILVER AND GOLD KNIVES!
THE GUARDIAN SPIRIT IN THE BOOK GAVE AWAY BOTH THE GOLD AND SILVER AXES!
THAT...WAS A LONG TIME AGO...
TIMES ARE TOUGH. THE ECONOMY IS BAD.
WE CAN'T BE THAT GENEROUS ANYMORE.
THERE ARE CLOSE TO 500,000 UNEMPLOYED YOUNG PEOPLE IN KOREA.
HOMINA
HOMINA
WELL, I HAVE A HOT DATE TONIGHT...
BE GOOD...
POOF
WHA--?! NO FAIR!
WHSSS
YOU OLD JERK! GIVE ME THE GOLD AND SILVER KNIVES!

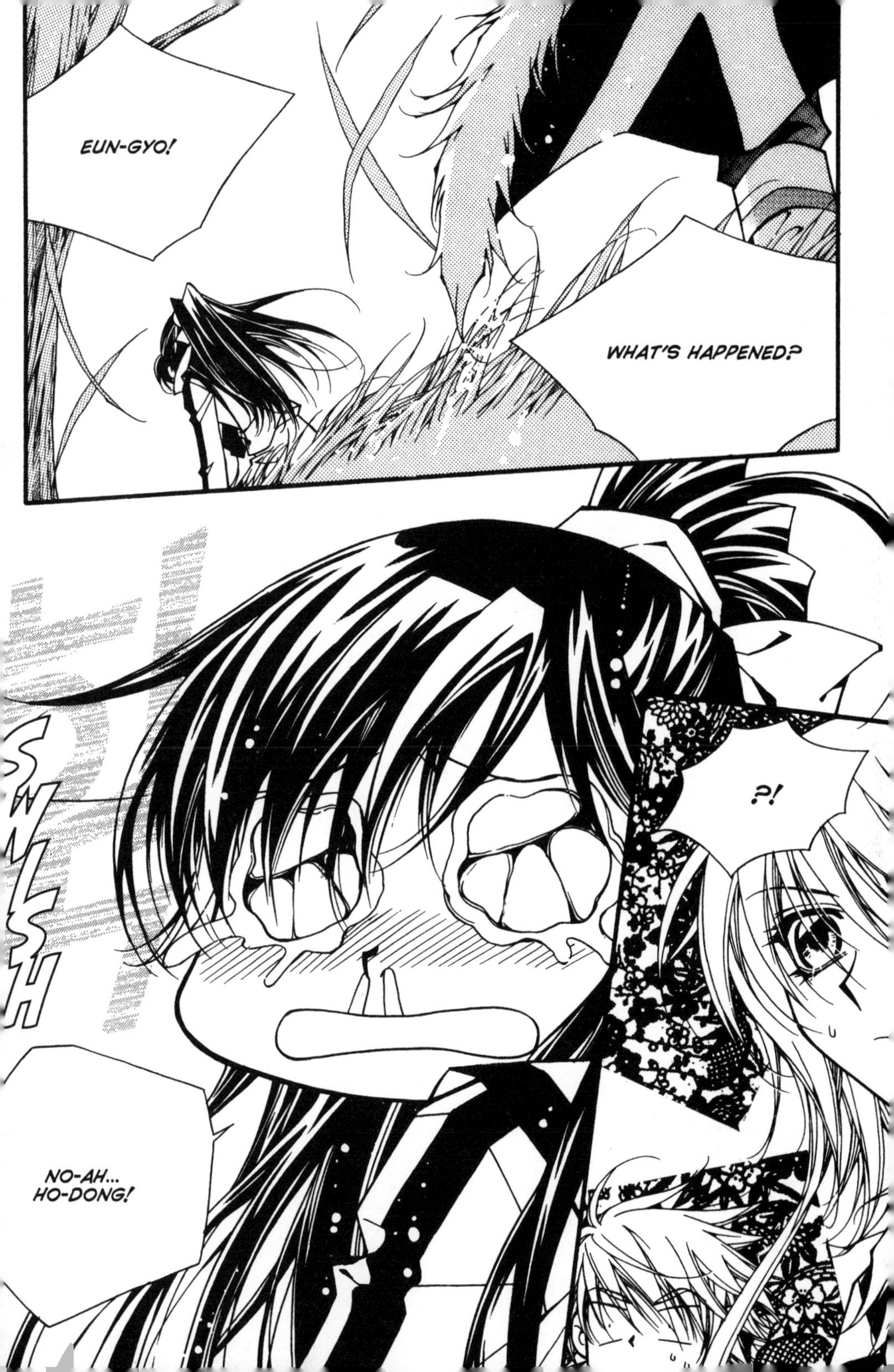
EUN-GYO!
WHAT'S HAPPENED?
SWISH
?!
NO-AH...
HO-DONG!

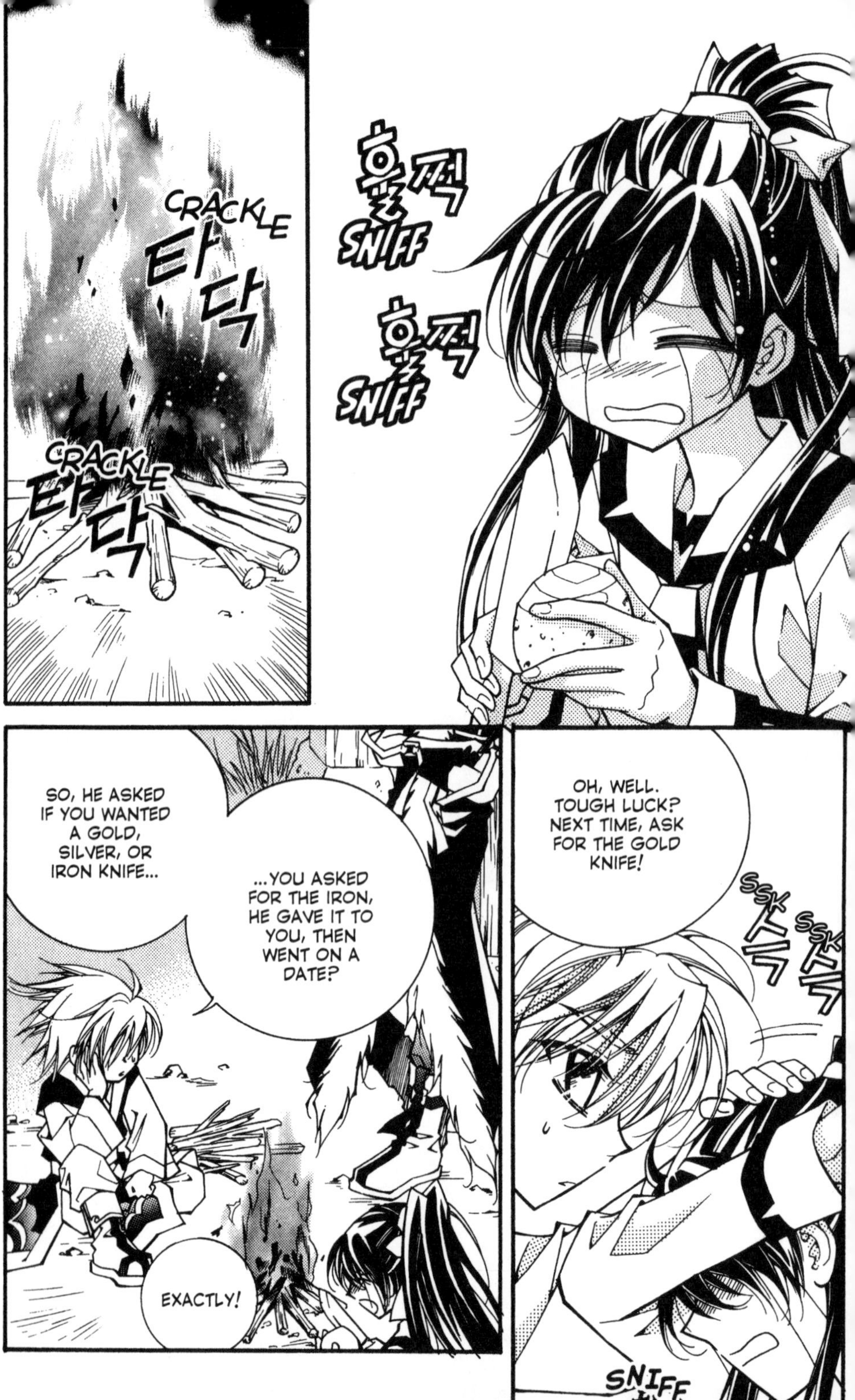
CRACKLE
타닥
CRACKLE
타닥
훌쩍
SNIFF
훌쩍
SNIFF
SO, HE ASKED IF YOU WANTED A GOLD, SILVER, OR IRON KNIFE...
...YOU ASKED FOR THE IRON, HE GAVE IT TO YOU, THEN WENT ON A DATE?
EXACTLY!
OH, WELL. TOUGH LUCK? NEXT TIME, ASK FOR THE GOLD KNIFE!
SSK
SSK
SNIFF

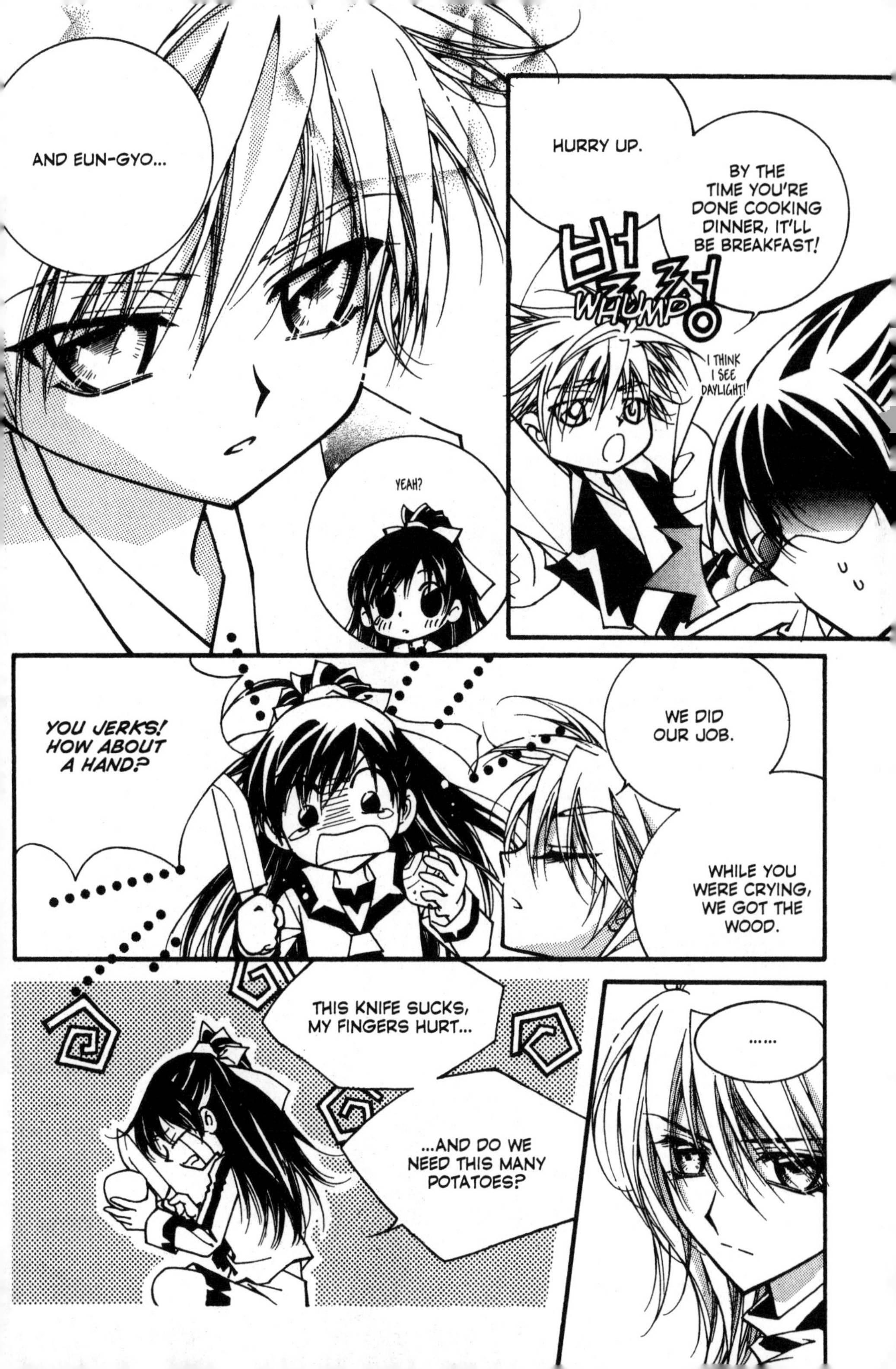
AND EUN-GYO...
YEAH?
HURRY UP.
BY THE TIME YOU'RE DONE COOKING DINNER, IT'LL BE BREAKFAST!
WHUMP
I THINK I SEE DAYLIGHT!
YOU JERKS! HOW ABOUT A HAND?
WE DID OUR JOB.
WHILE YOU WERE CRYING, WE GOT THE WOOD.
THIS KNIFE SUCKS, MY FINGERS HURT...
...AND DO WE NEED THIS MANY POTATOES?
......

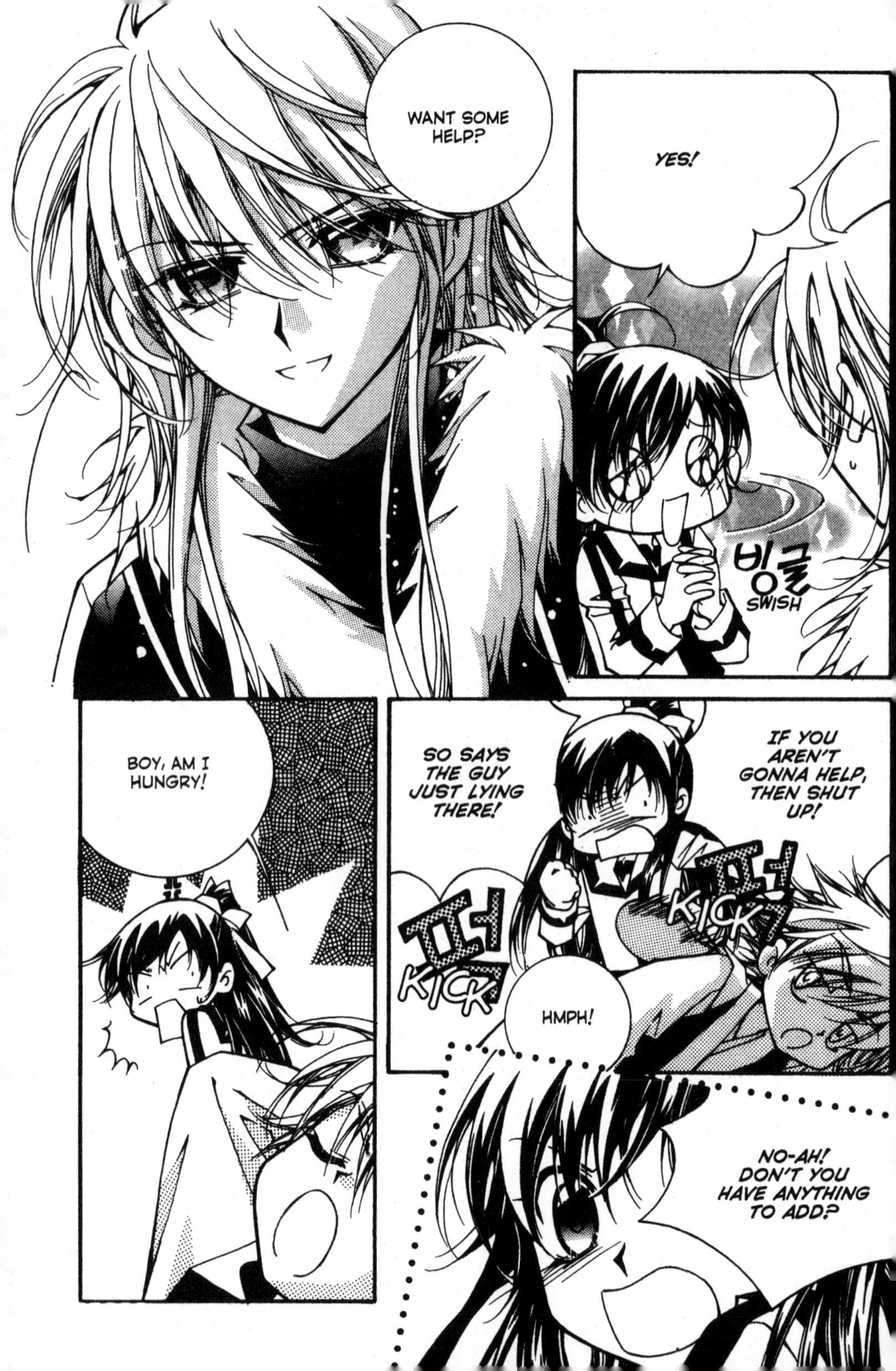
WANT SOME HELP?
YES!
빙글
SWISH
BOY, AM I HUNGRY!
SO SAYS THE GUY JUST LYING THERE!
IF YOU AREN'T GONNA HELP, THEN SHUT UP!
퍽
KICK
퍽
KICK
HMPH!
NO-AH! DON'T YOU HAVE ANYTHING TO ADD?

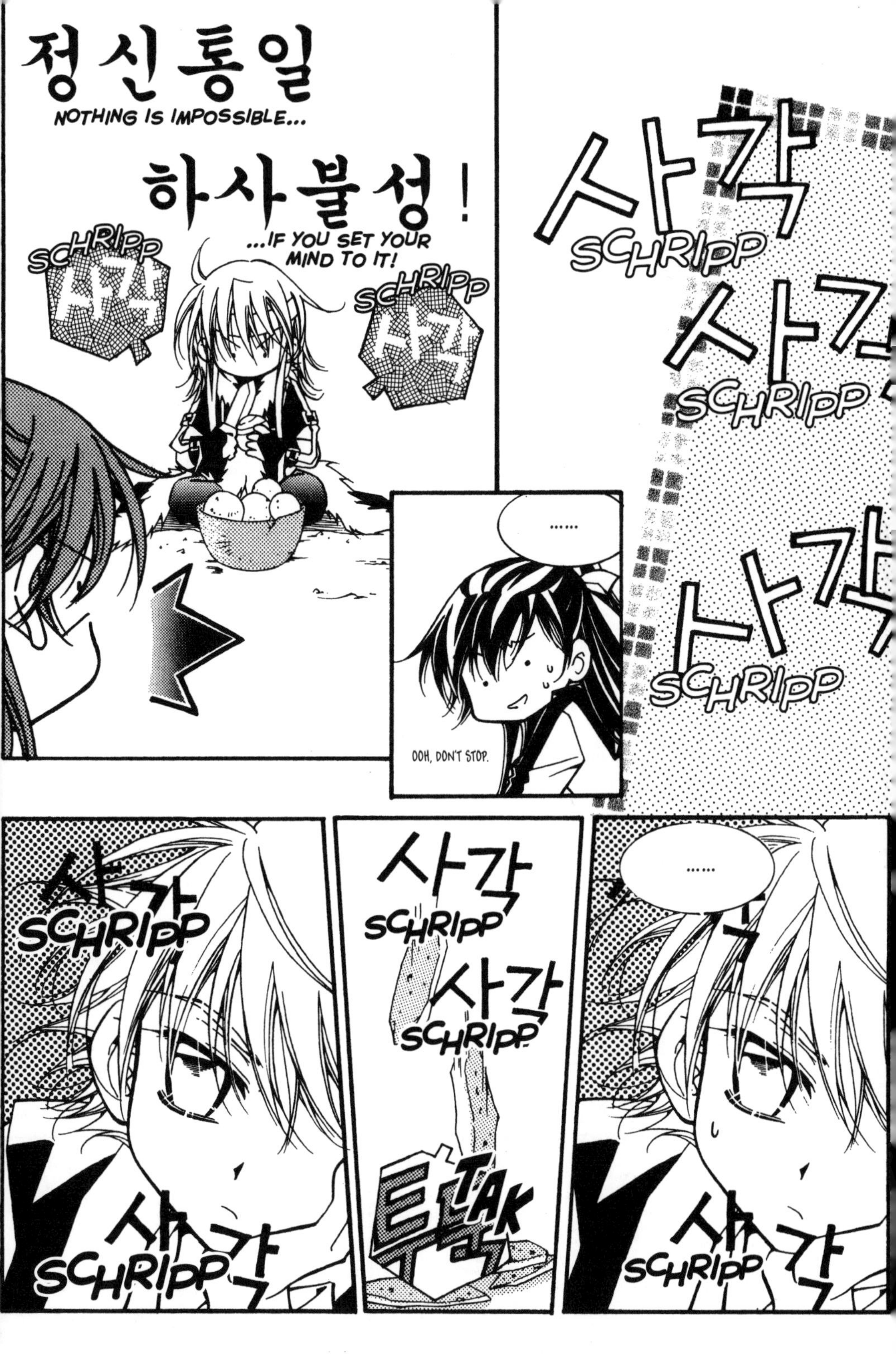
정신통일
NOTHING IS IMPOSSIBLE...
하사불성!
...IF YOU SET YOUR MIND TO IT!
사각
SCHRIPP
사각
SCHRIPP
......
OOH, DON'T STOP.
사각
SCHRIPP
사각
SCHRIPP
사각
SCHRIPP
사각
SCHRIPP
사각
SCHRIPP
사각
SCHRIPP
사각
SCHRIPP
툭
TAK
......
사각
SCHRIPP

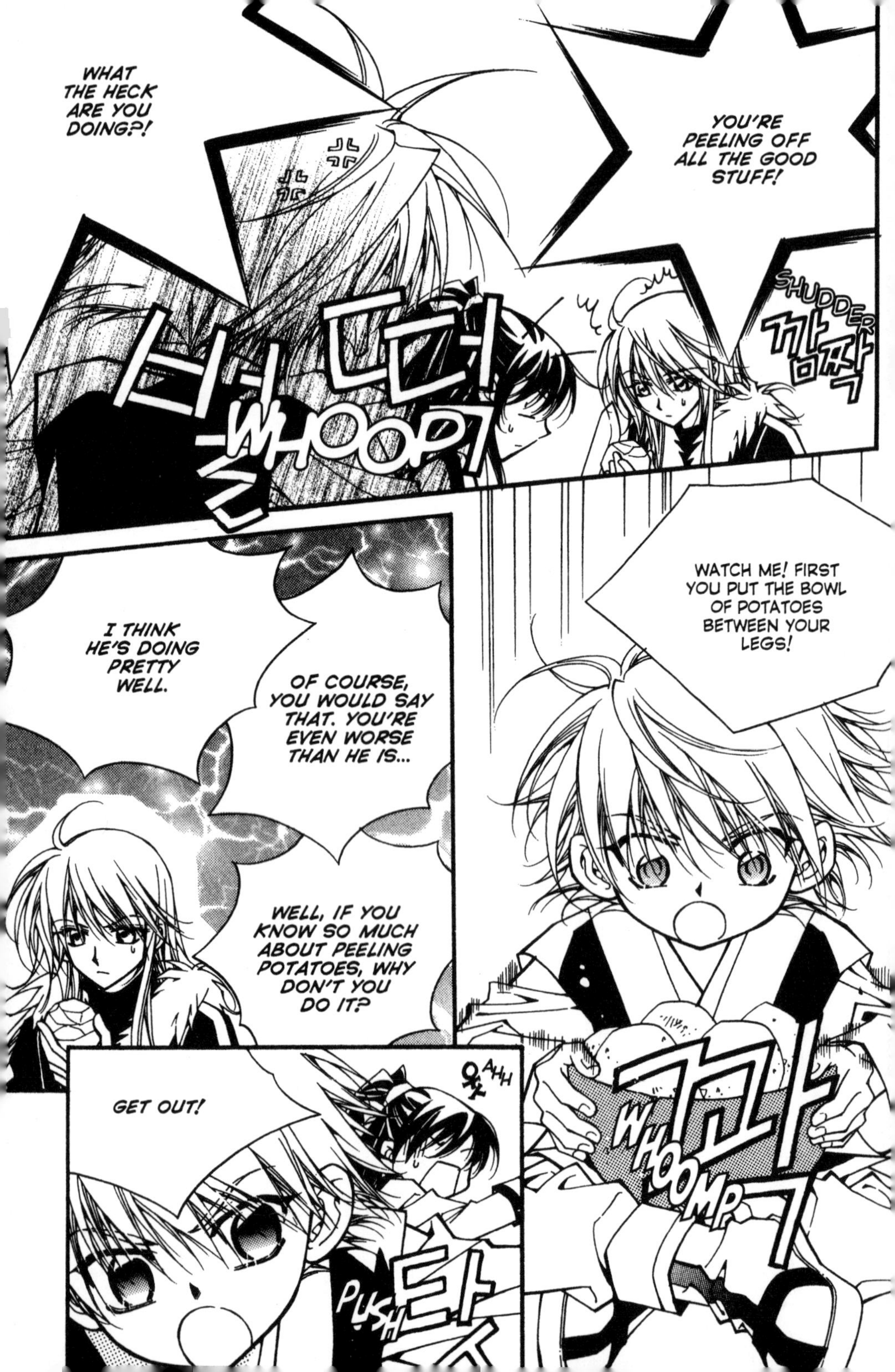
WHAT THE HECK ARE YOU DOING?!
WHOOP
YOU'RE PEELING OFF ALL THE GOOD STUFF!
SHUDDER
I THINK HE'S DOING PRETTY WELL.
OF COURSE, YOU WOULD SAY THAT. YOU'RE EVEN WORSE THAN HE IS...
WELL, IF YOU KNOW SO MUCH ABOUT PEELING POTATOES, WHY DON'T YOU DO IT?
GET OUT!
AHH
PUSH
WATCH ME! FIRST YOU PUT THE BOWL OF POTATOES BETWEEN YOUR LEGS!
WHOOMP

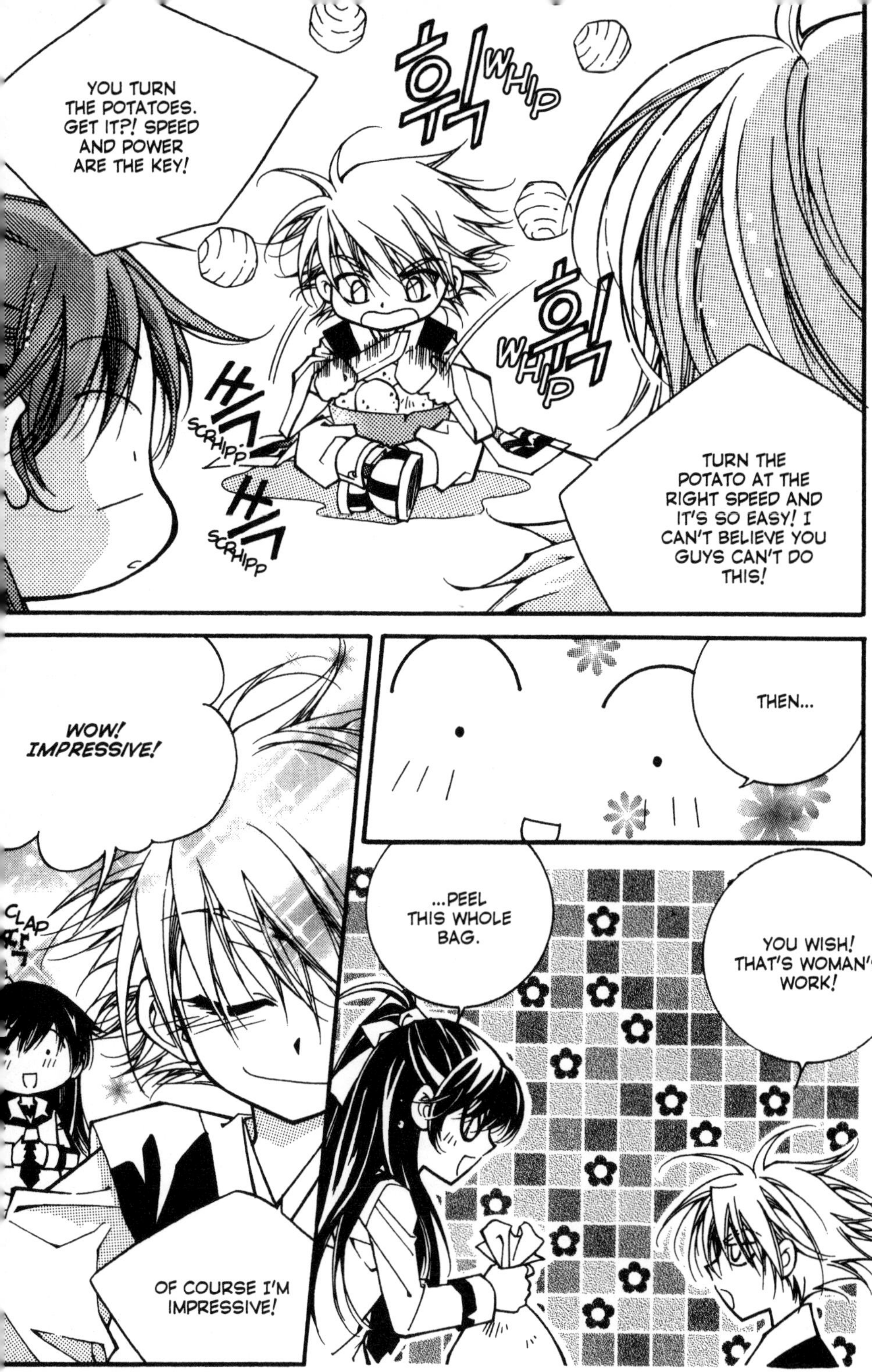
YOU TURN THE POTATOES. GET IT?! SPEED AND POWER ARE THE KEY!
WHIP
WHIP
SCRHIPP
SCRHIPP
TURN THE POTATO AT THE RIGHT SPEED AND IT'S SO EASY! I CAN'T BELIEVE YOU GUYS CAN'T DO THIS!
WOW! IMPRESSIVE!
CLAP
OF COURSE I'M IMPRESSIVE!
THEN...
...PEEL THIS WHOLE BAG.
YOU WISH! THAT'S WOMAN'S WORK!

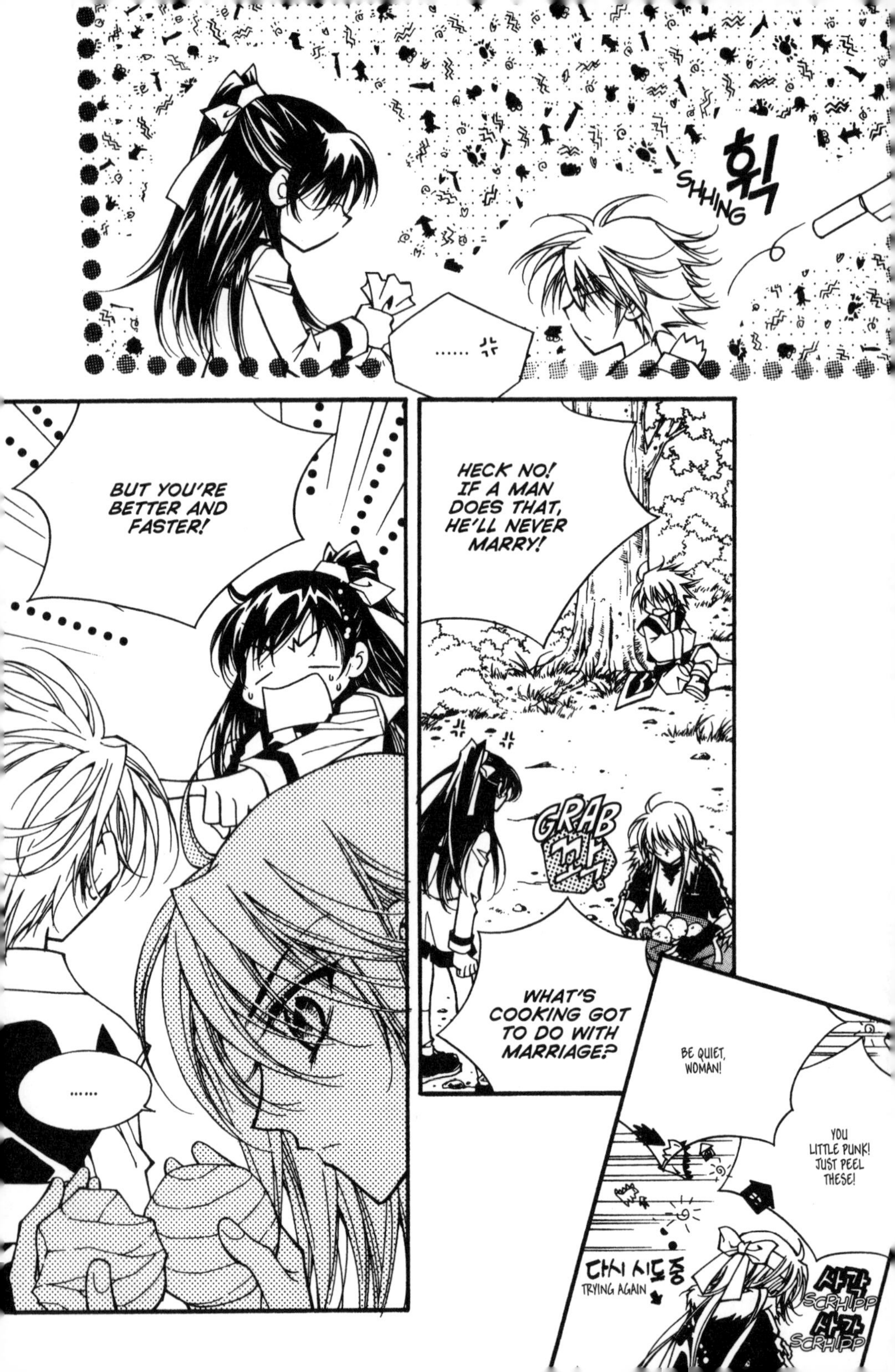
휙
SHHING
......
BUT YOU'RE BETTER AND FASTER!
......
HECK NO! IF A MAN DOES THAT, HE'LL NEVER MARRY!
GRAB
꽉
WHAT'S COOKING GOT TO DO WITH MARRIAGE?
BE QUIET, WOMAN!
YOU LITTLE PUNK! JUST PEEL THESE!
다시 시도중
TRYING AGAIN
사각
SCRHIPP
사각
SCRHIPP

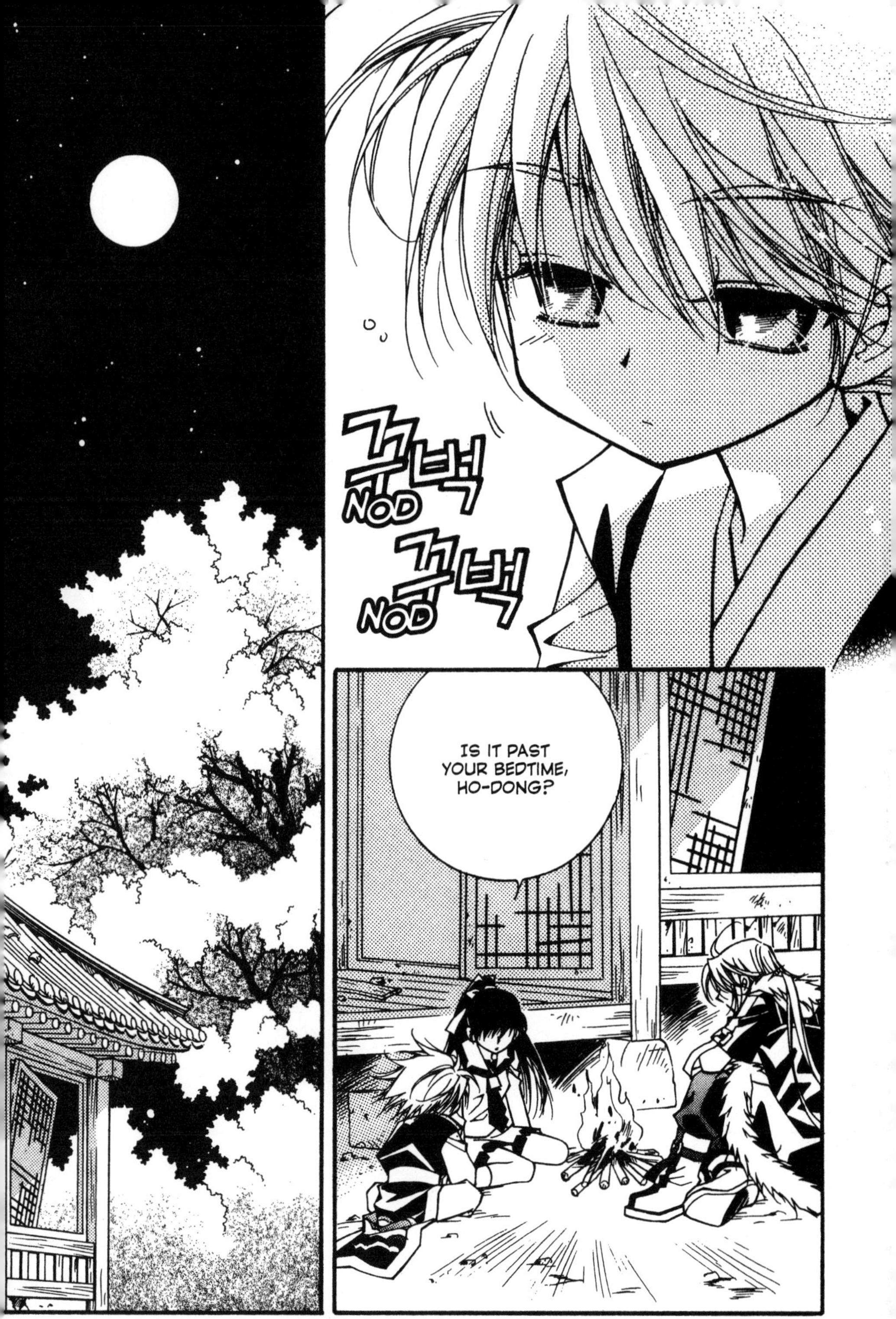
꾸벅 NOD
꾸벅 NOD
IS IT PAST YOUR BEDTIME, HO-DONG?

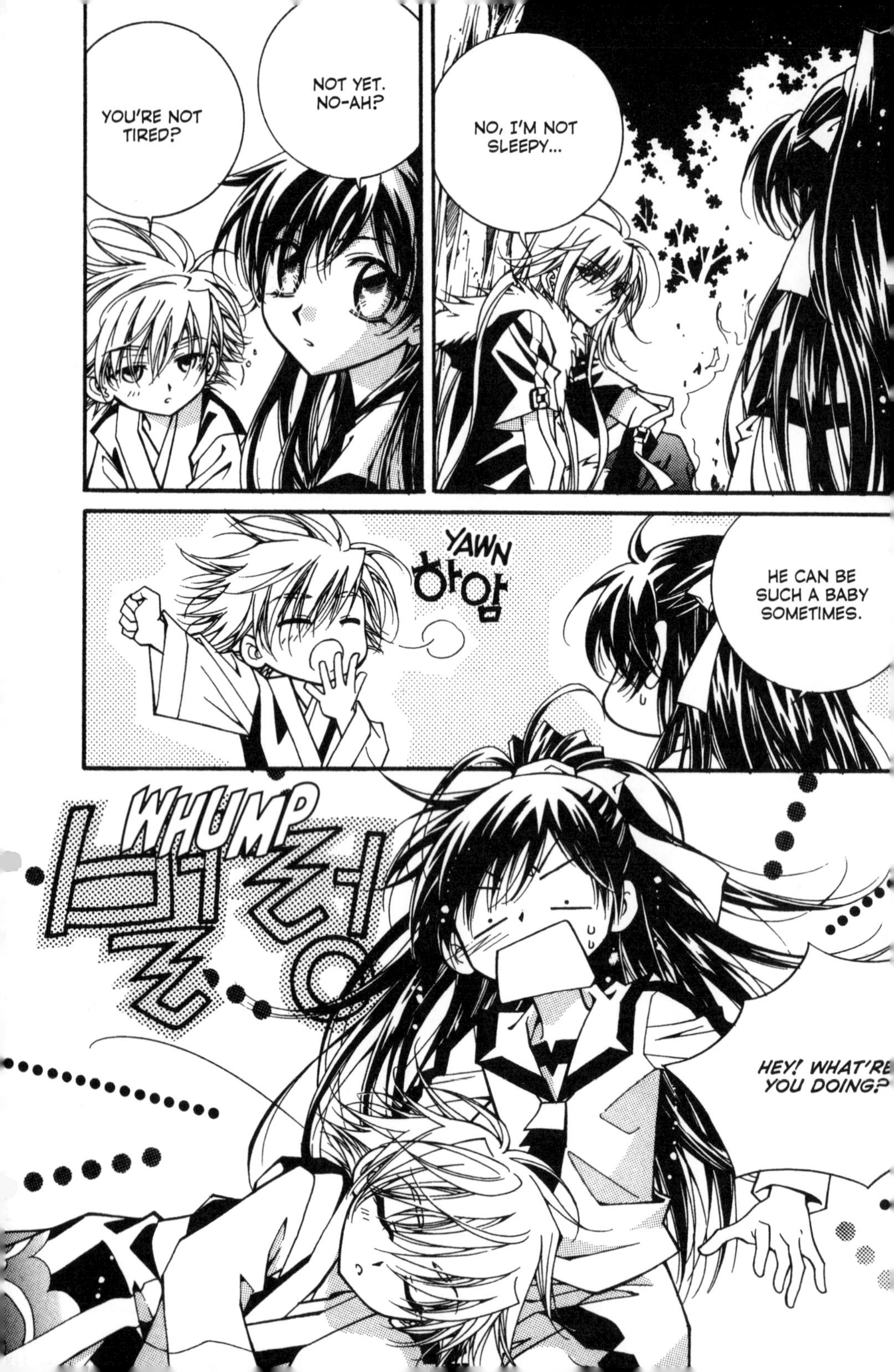
YOU'RE NOT TIRED?
NOT YET. NO-AH?
NO, I'M NOT SLEEPY...
YAWN
하암
HE CAN BE SUCH A BABY SOMETIMES.
WHUMP
털썩
HEY! WHAT'RE YOU DOING?

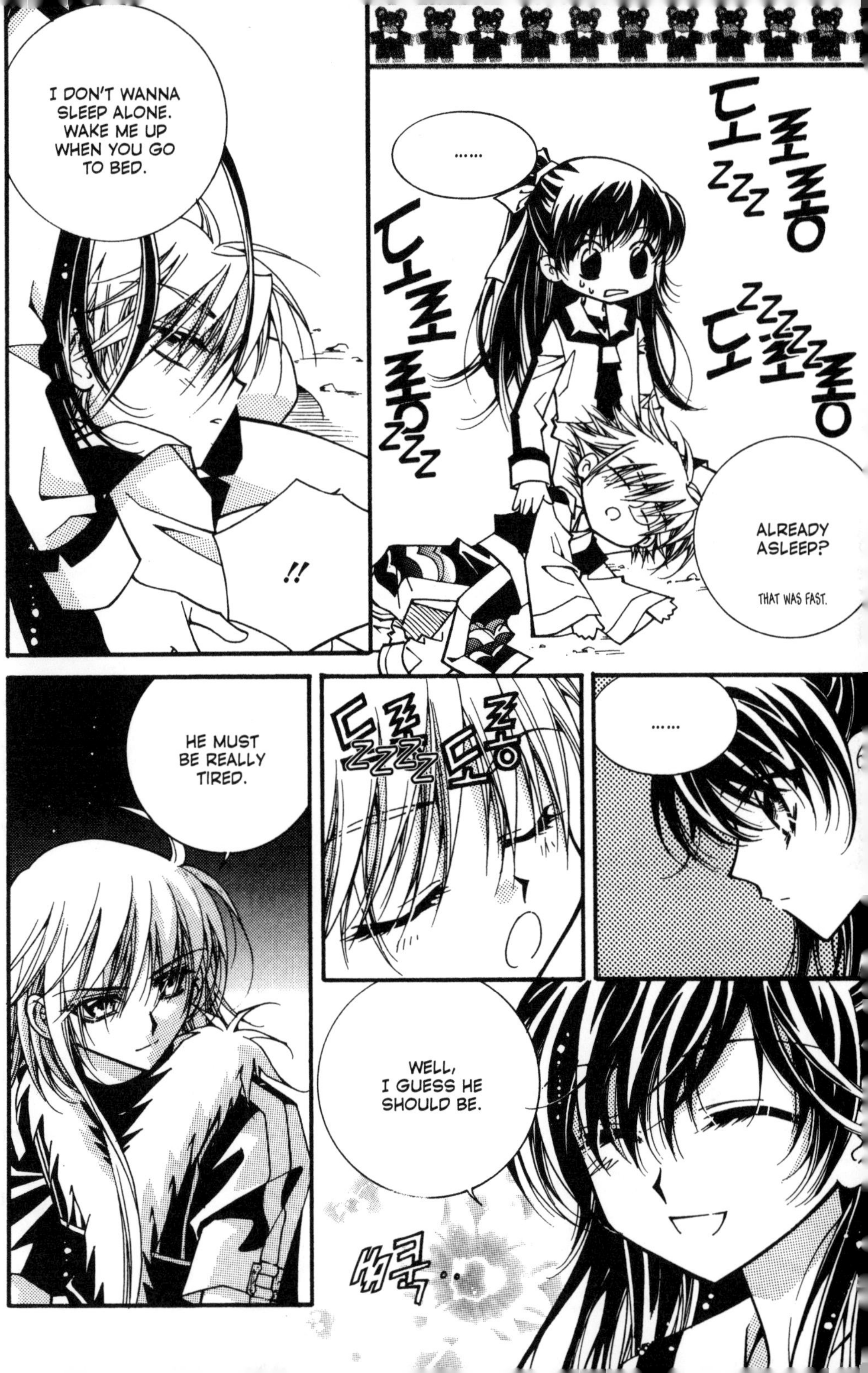
I DON'T WANNA SLEEP ALONE. WAKE ME UP WHEN YOU GO TO BED.
!!
......
도로롱 ZZZ
ALREADY ASLEEP?
THAT WAS FAST.
HE MUST BE REALLY TIRED.
......
WELL, I GUESS HE SHOULD BE.

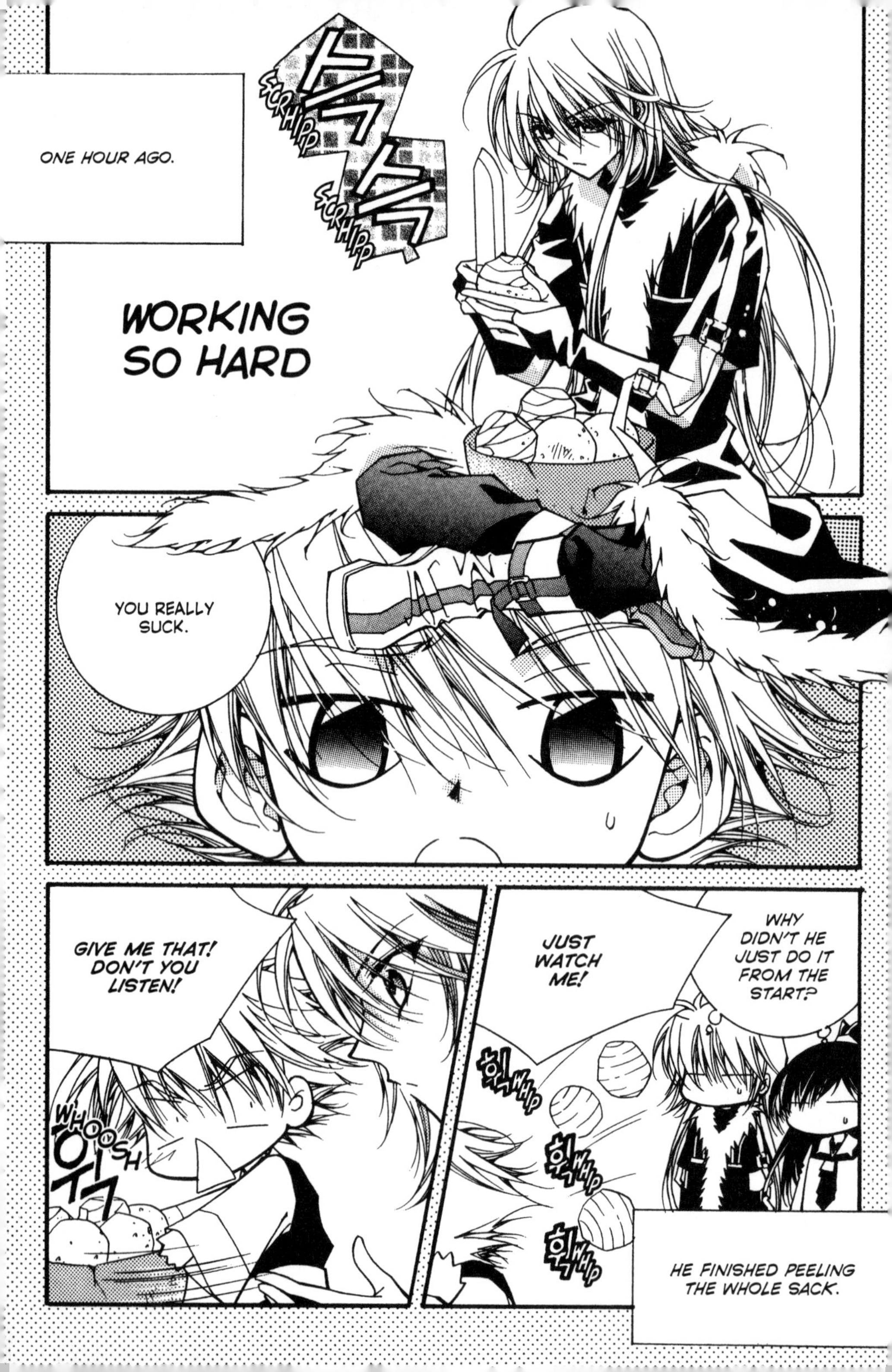
ONE HOUR AGO.
SCRHIPP
SCRHIPP
WORKING SO HARD
YOU REALLY SUCK.
GIVE ME THAT! DON'T YOU LISTEN!
WHOOSH
JUST WATCH ME!
WHIP
WHIP
WHIP
WHY DIDN'T HE JUST DO IT FROM THE START?
HE FINISHED PEELING THE WHOLE SACK.

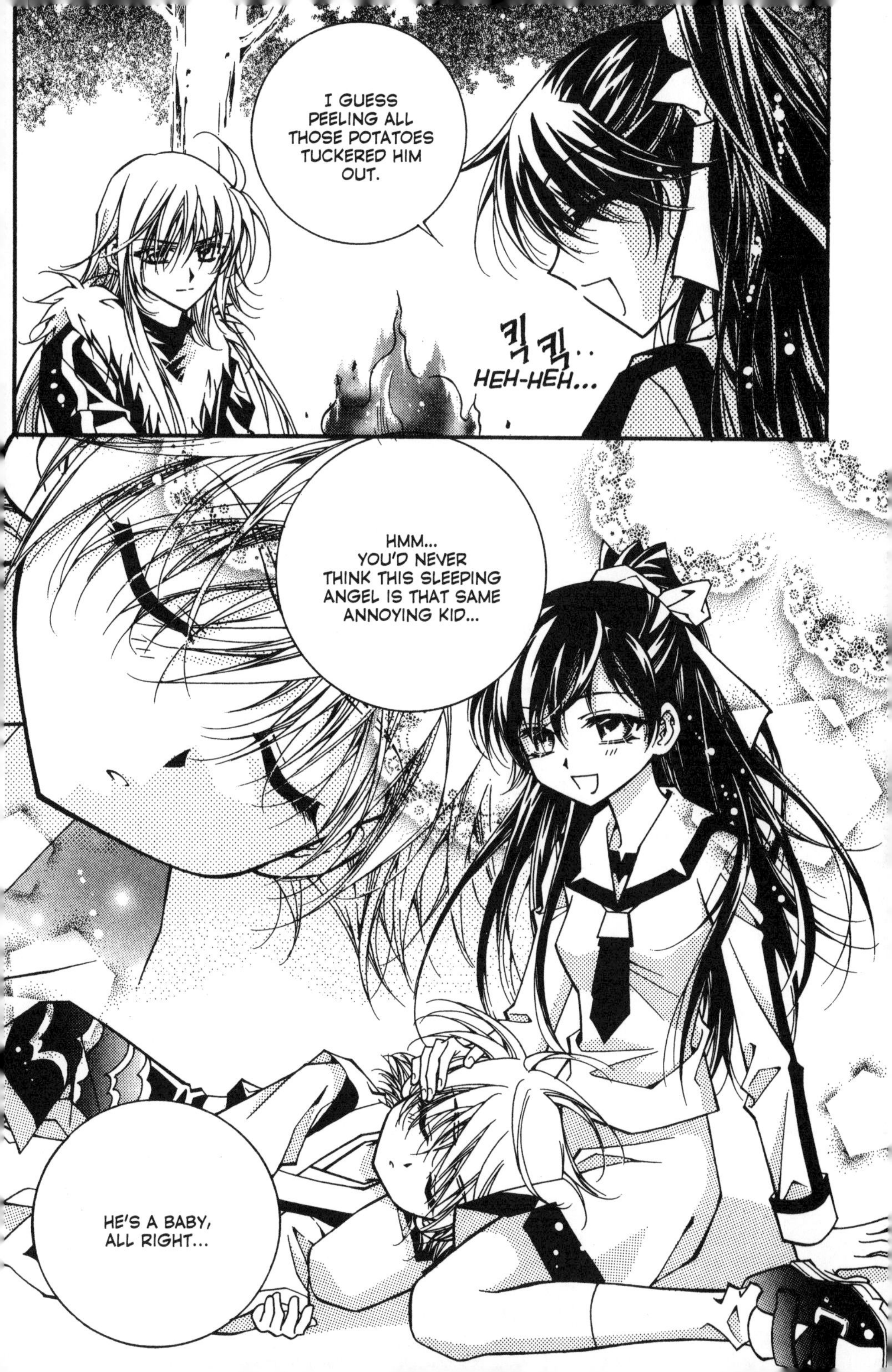
I GUESS PEELING ALL THOSE POTATOES TUCKERED HIM OUT.
킥킥..
HEH-HEH...
HMM... YOU'D NEVER THINK THIS SLEEPING ANGEL IS THAT SAME ANNOYING KID...
HE'S A BABY, ALL RIGHT...

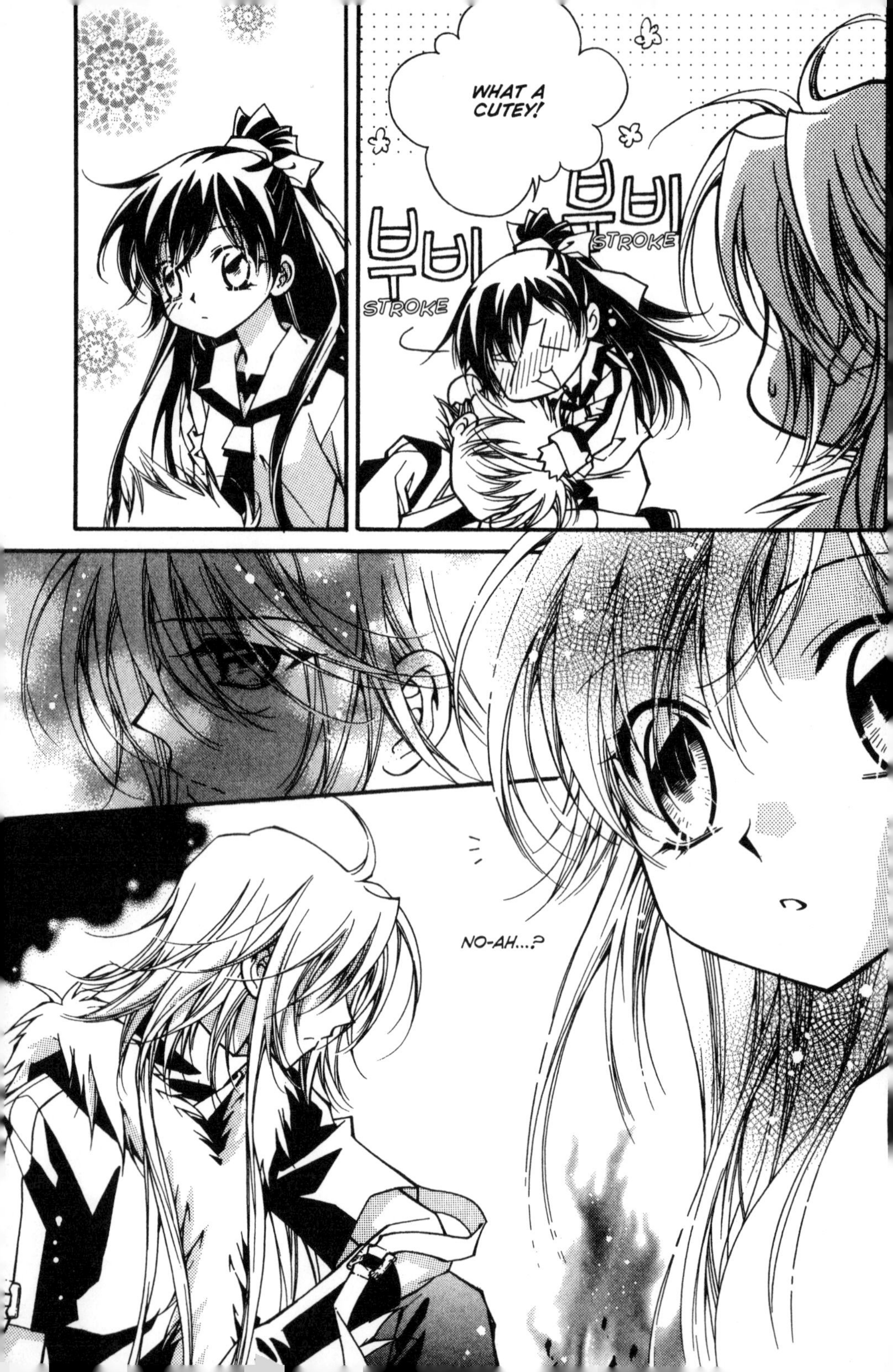
WHAT A CUTEY!
부비
STROKE
부비
STROKE
NO-AH...?

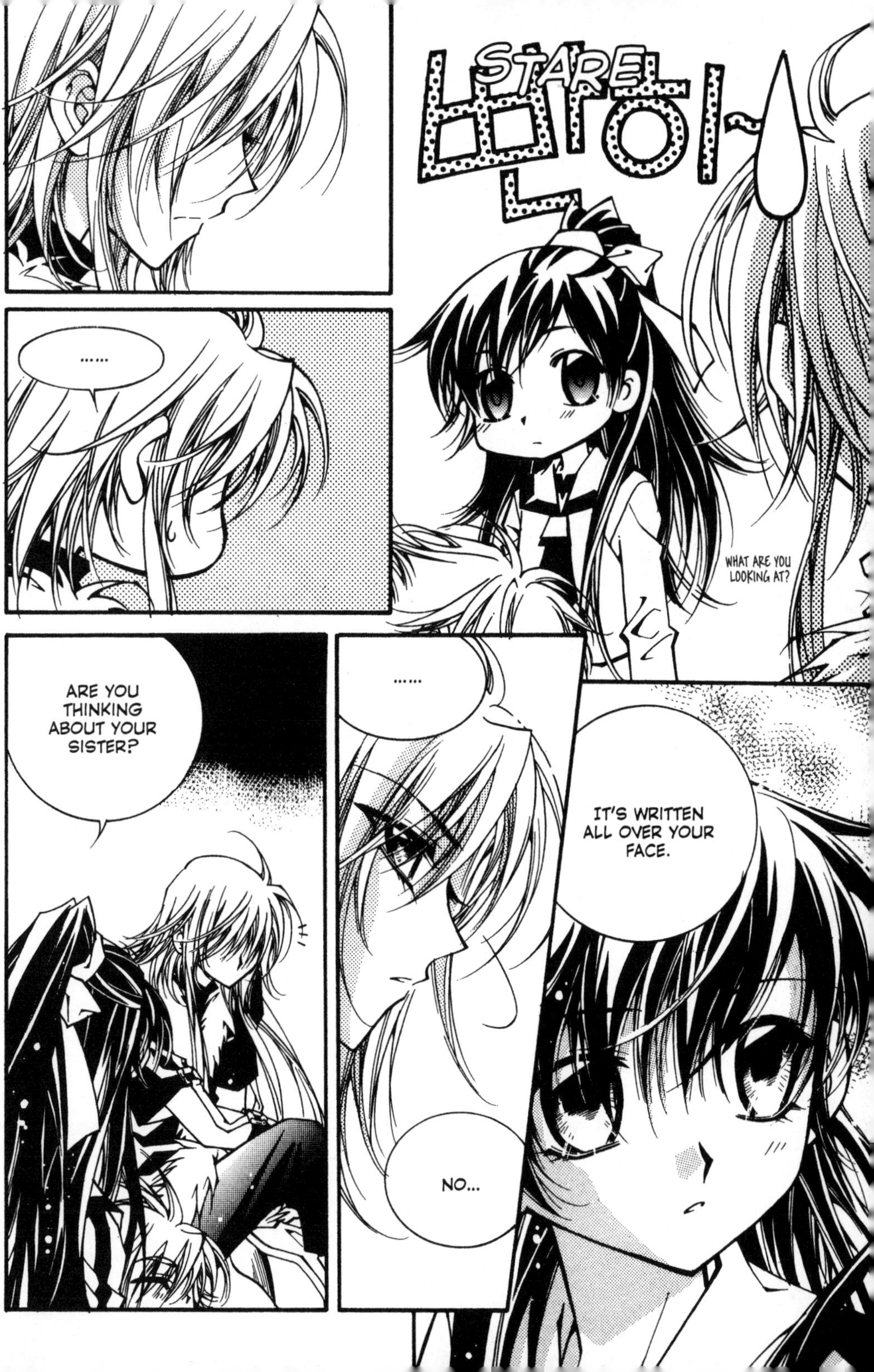
......
STARE
빤이~
WHAT ARE YOU LOOKING AT?
ARE YOU THINKING ABOUT YOUR SISTER?
......
NO...
IT'S WRITTEN ALL OVER YOUR FACE.

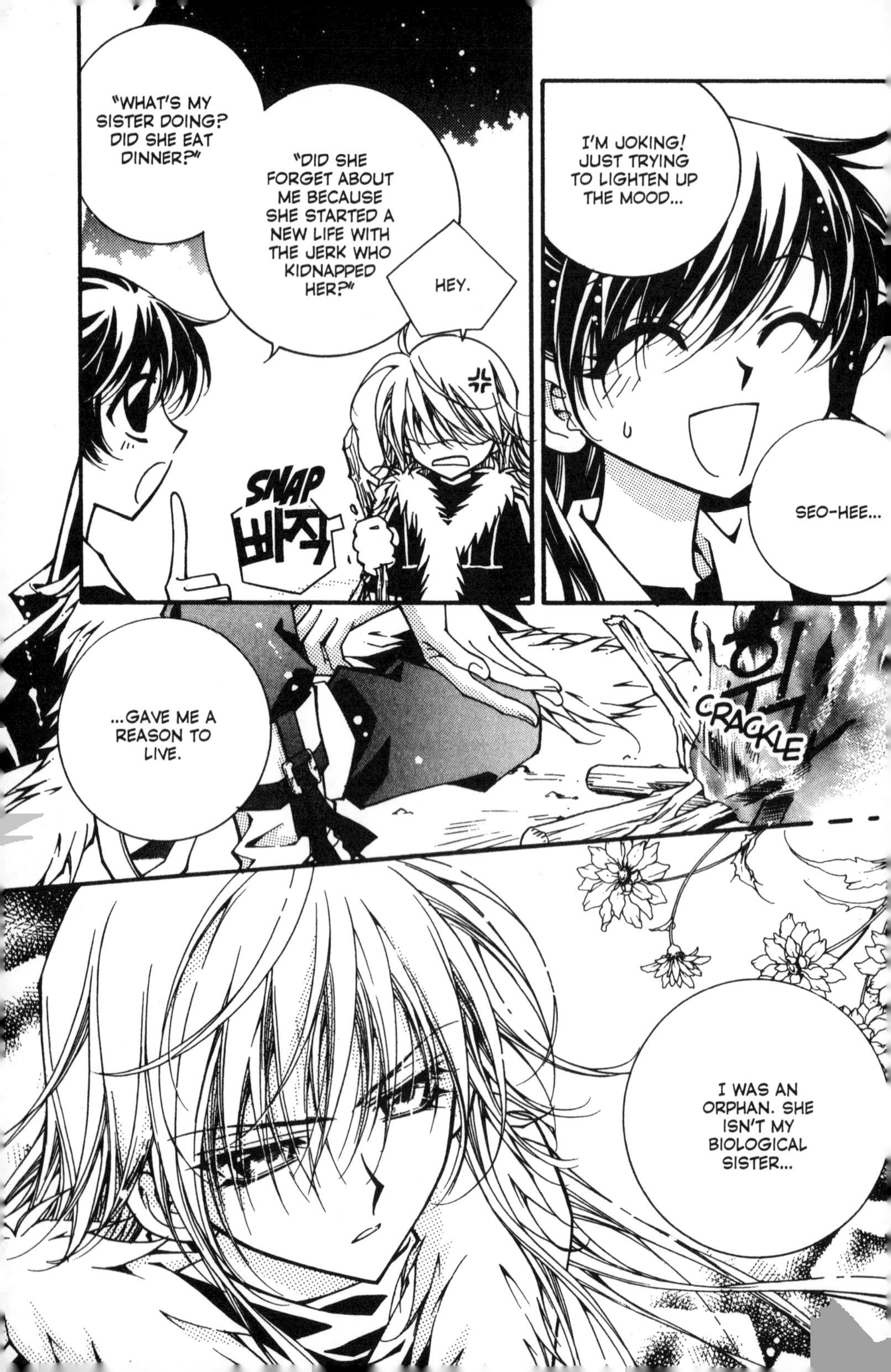
"WHAT'S MY SISTER DOING? DID SHE EAT DINNER?"
"DID SHE FORGET ABOUT ME BECAUSE SHE STARTED A NEW LIFE WITH THE JERK WHO KIDNAPPED HER?"
HEY.
SNAP
빠직
I'M JOKING! JUST TRYING TO LIGHTEN UP THE MOOD...
SEO-HEE...
...GAVE ME A REASON TO LIVE.
CRACKLE
I WAS AN ORPHAN. SHE ISN'T MY BIOLOGICAL SISTER...

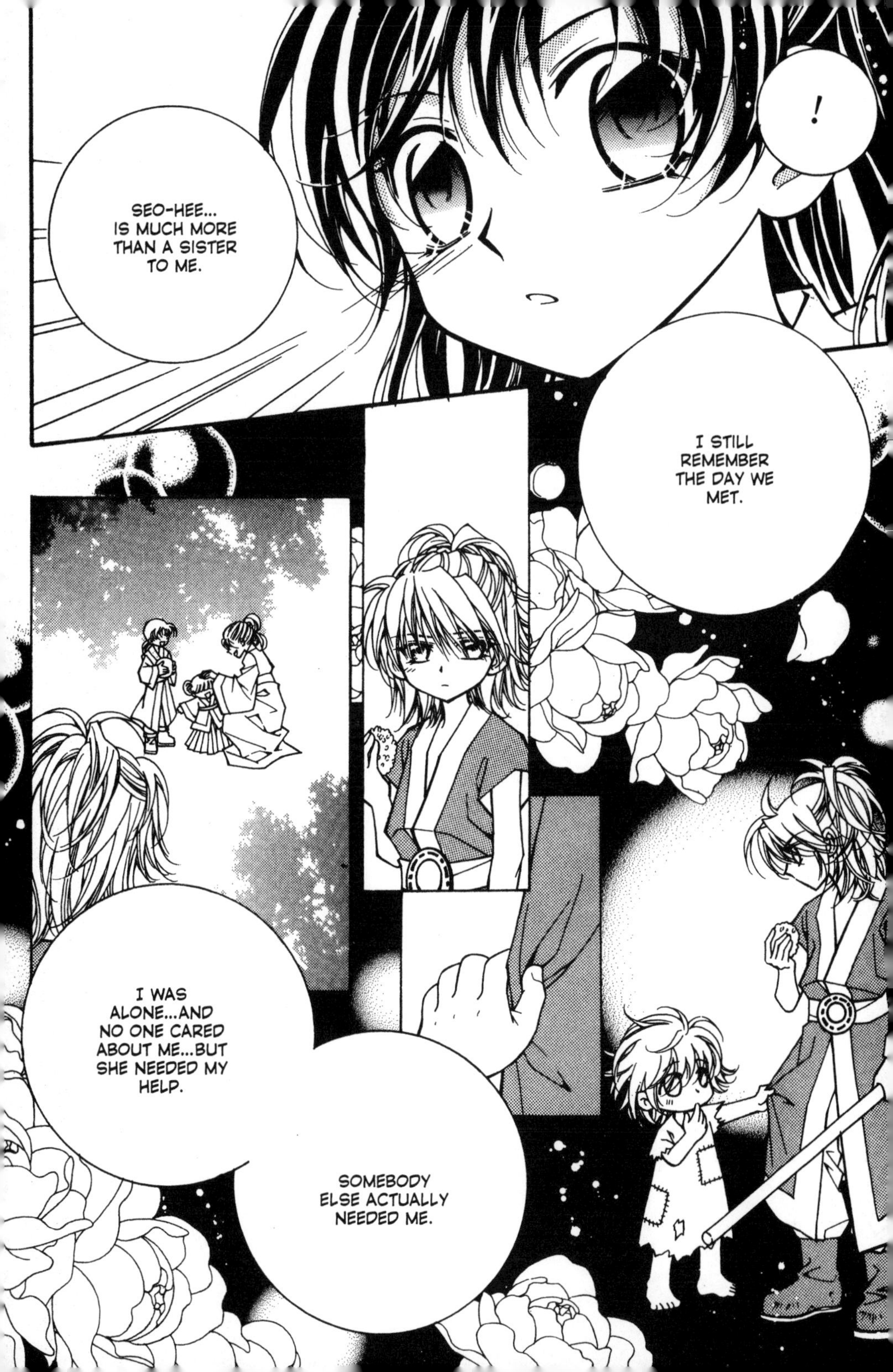
SEO-HEE... IS MUCH MORE THAN A SISTER TO ME.
!
I STILL REMEMBER THE DAY WE MET.
I WAS ALONE...AND NO ONE CARED ABOUT ME...BUT SHE NEEDED MY HELP.
SOMEBODY ELSE ACTUALLY NEEDED ME.

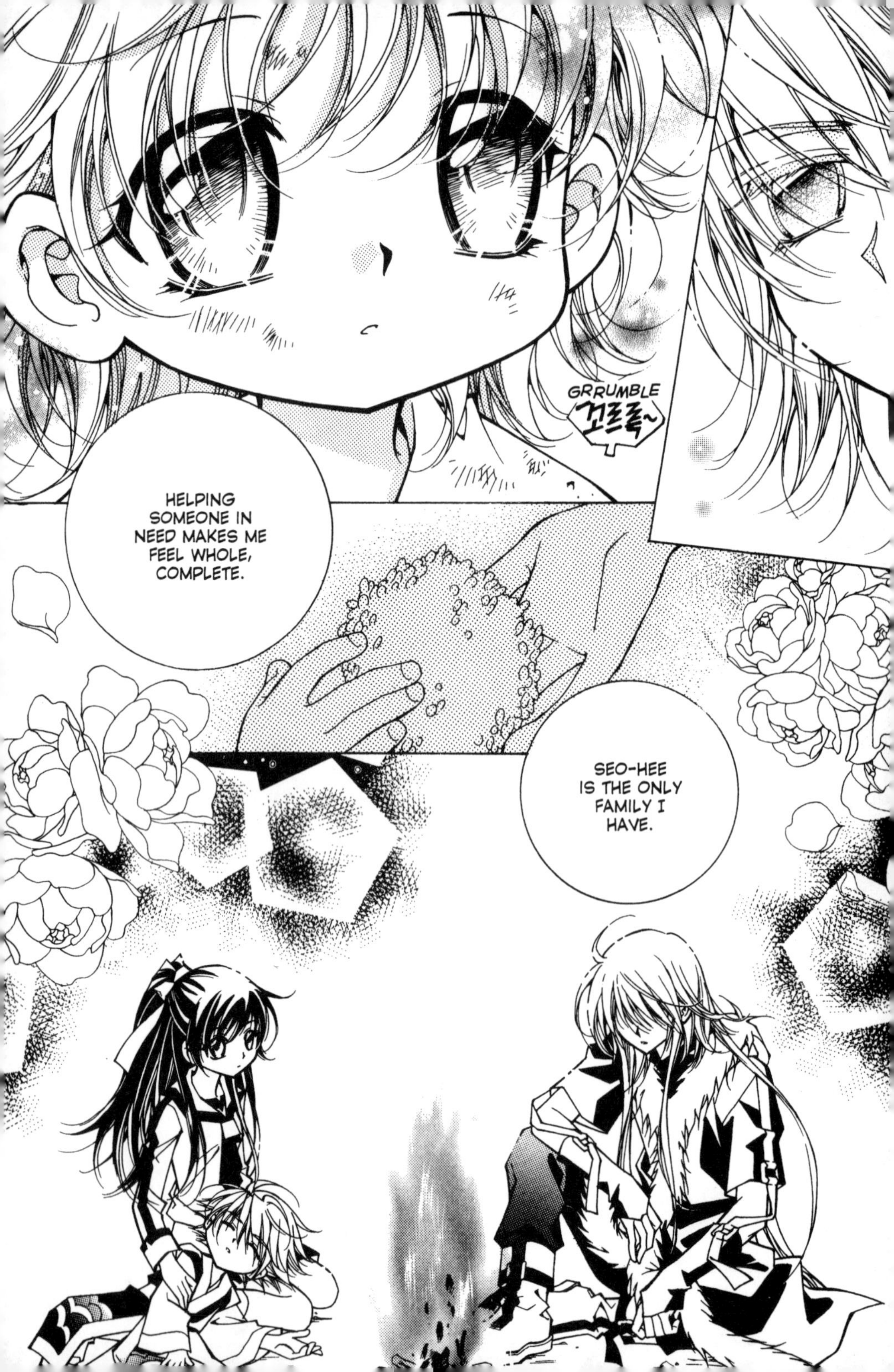
GRRUMBLE
꼬르륵~
HELPING SOMEONE IN NEED MAKES ME FEEL WHOLE, COMPLETE.
SEO-HEE IS THE ONLY FAMILY I HAVE.

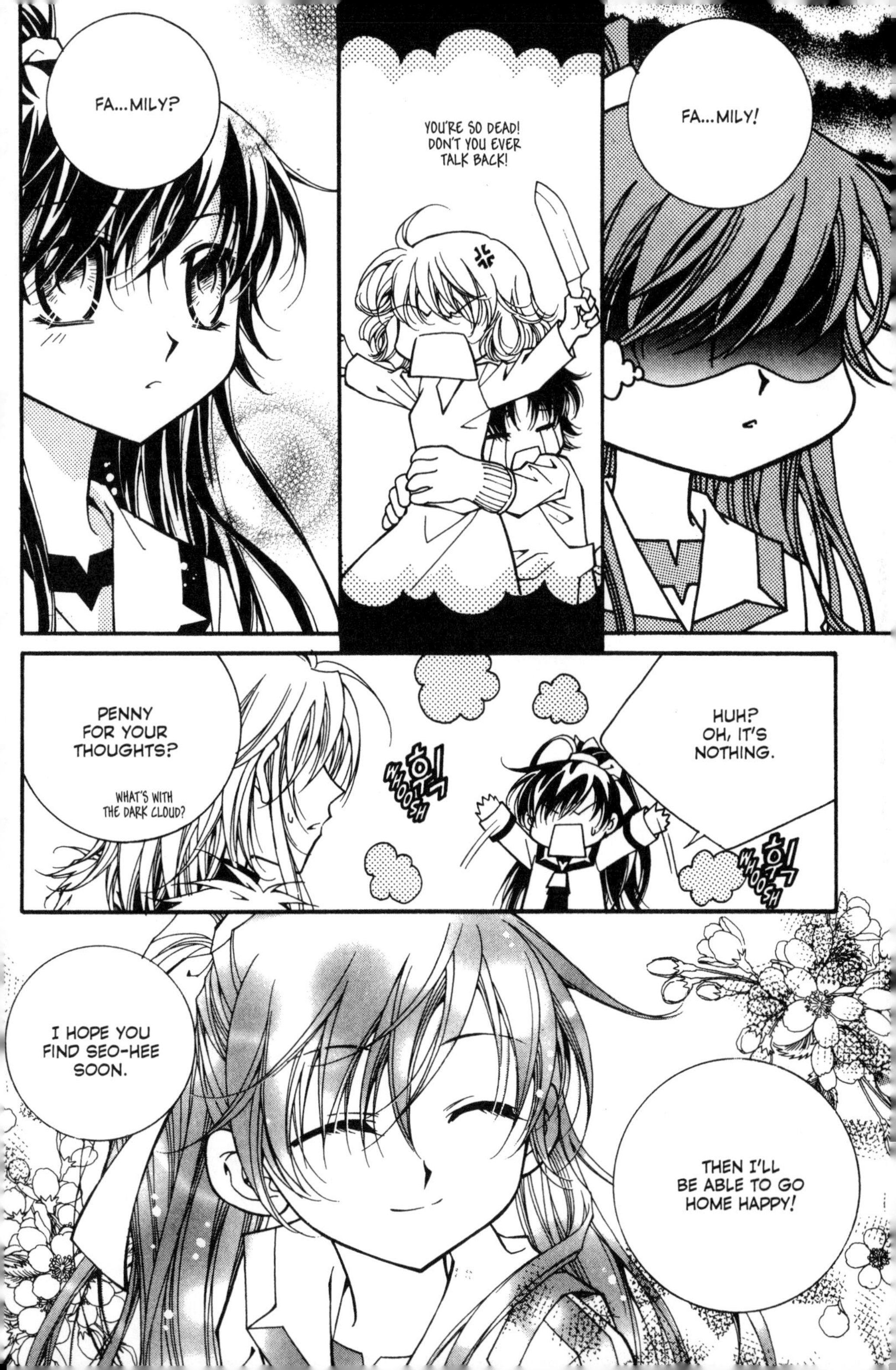
FA...MILY?
YOU'RE SO DEAD! DON'T YOU EVER TALK BACK!
FA...MILY!
PENNY FOR YOUR THOUGHTS?
WHAT'S WITH THE DARK CLOUD?
WHOOSH
HUH? OH, IT'S NOTHING.
WHOOSH
I HOPE YOU FIND SEO-HEE SOON.
THEN I'LL BE ABLE TO GO HOME HAPPY!

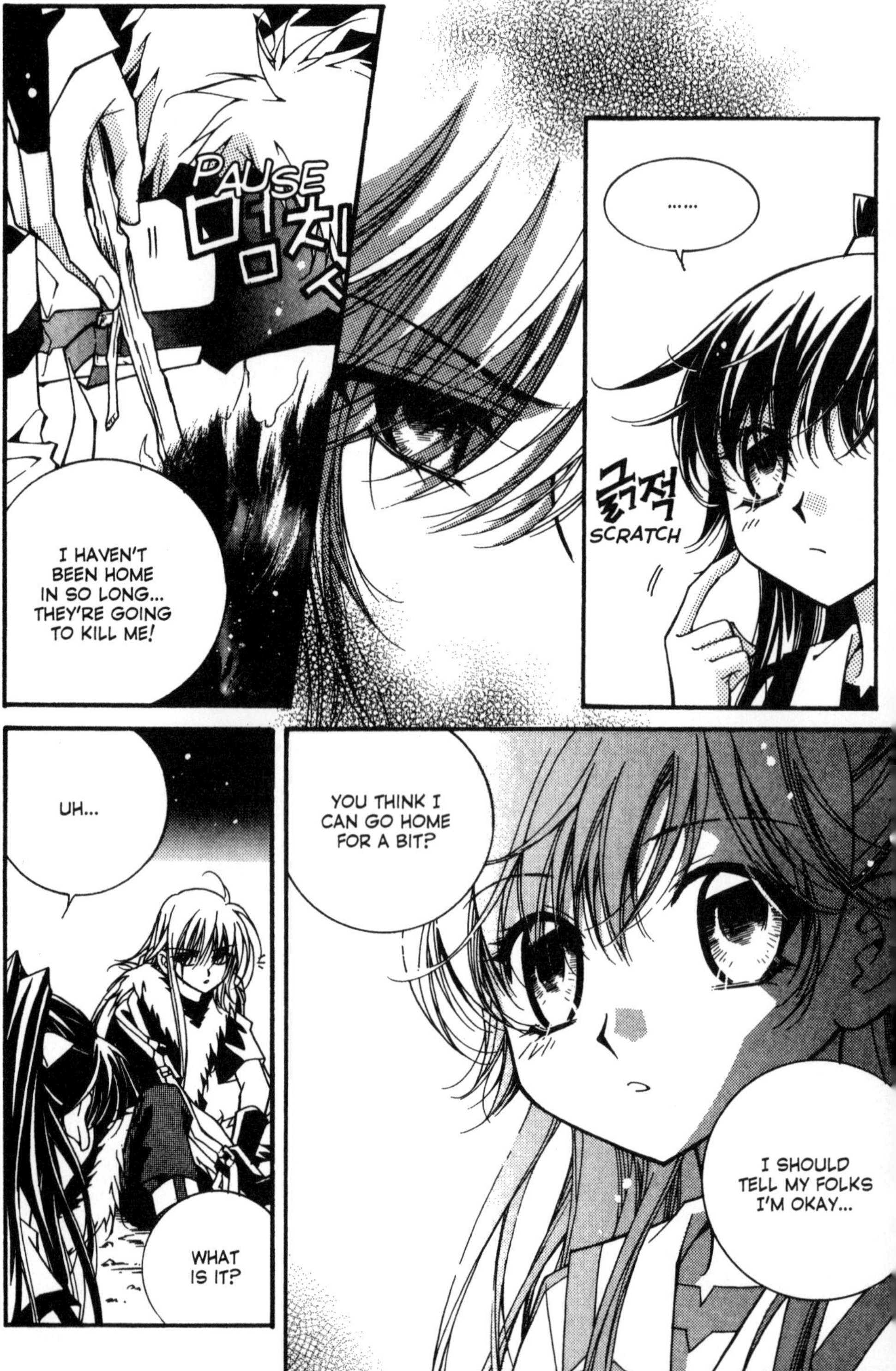
PAUSE
멈칫
I HAVEN'T BEEN HOME IN SO LONG... THEY'RE GOING TO KILL ME!
......
긁적
SCRATCH
UH...
WHAT IS IT?
YOU THINK I CAN GO HOME FOR A BIT?
I SHOULD TELL MY FOLKS I'M OKAY...

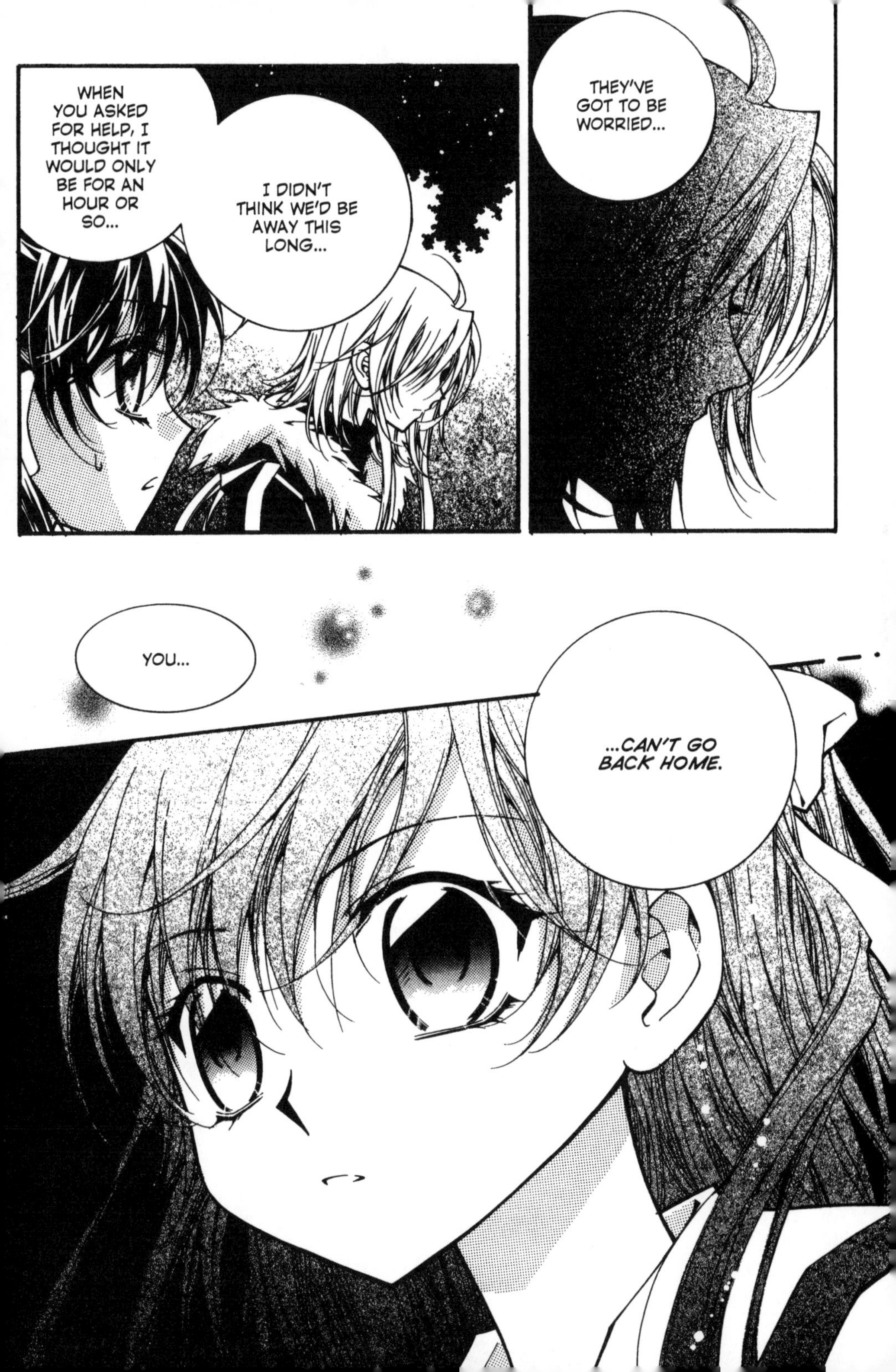
WHEN YOU ASKED FOR HELP, I THOUGHT IT WOULD ONLY BE FOR AN HOUR OR SO...
I DIDN'T THINK WE'D BE AWAY THIS LONG...
THEY'VE GOT TO BE WORRIED...
YOU...
...CAN'T GO BACK HOME.

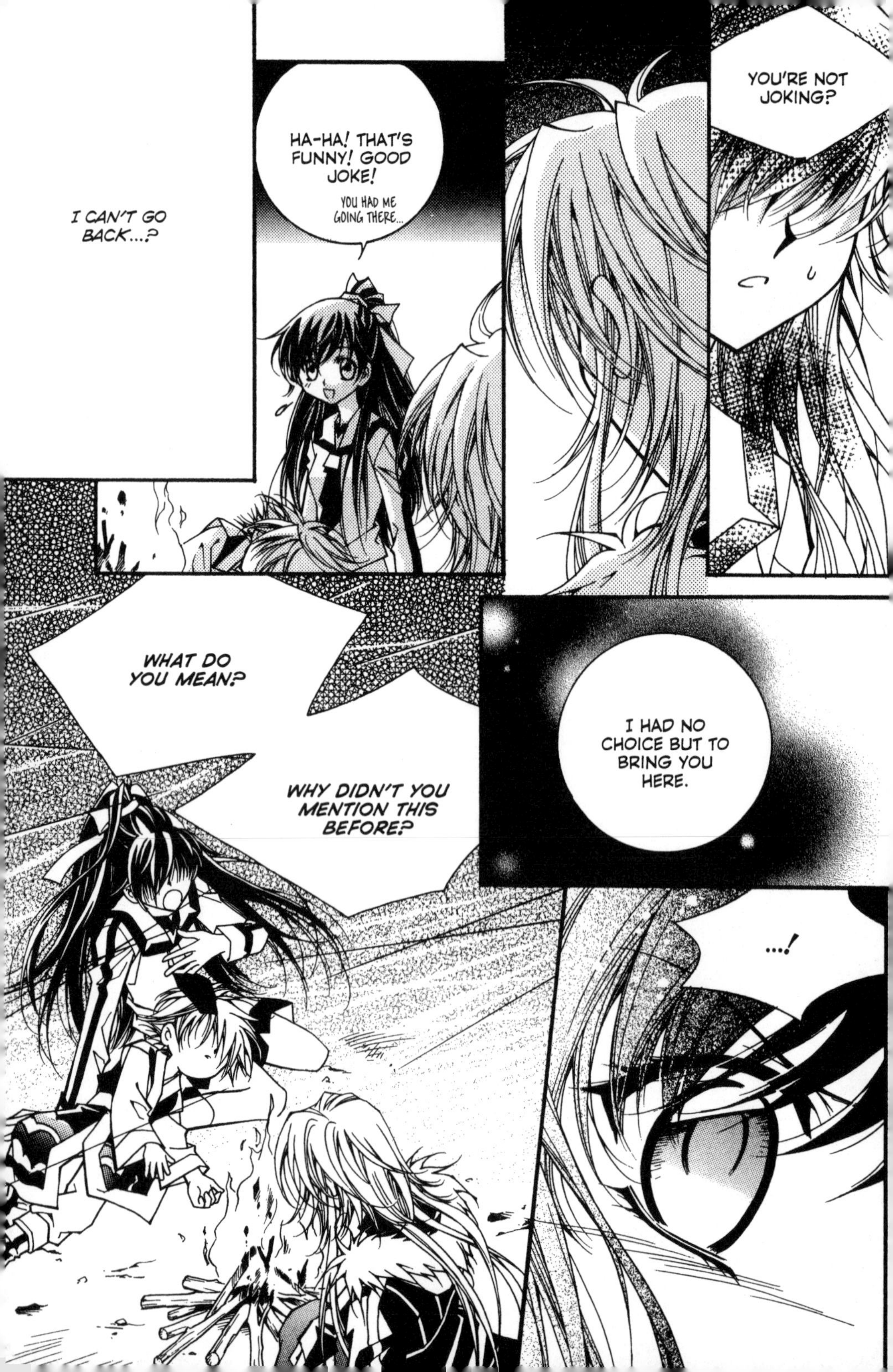
I CAN'T GO BACK...?
HA-HA! THAT'S FUNNY! GOOD JOKE!
YOU HAD ME GOING THERE...
YOU'RE NOT JOKING?
WHAT DO YOU MEAN?
WHY DIDN'T YOU MENTION THIS BEFORE?
I HAD NO CHOICE BUT TO BRING YOU HERE.
...!

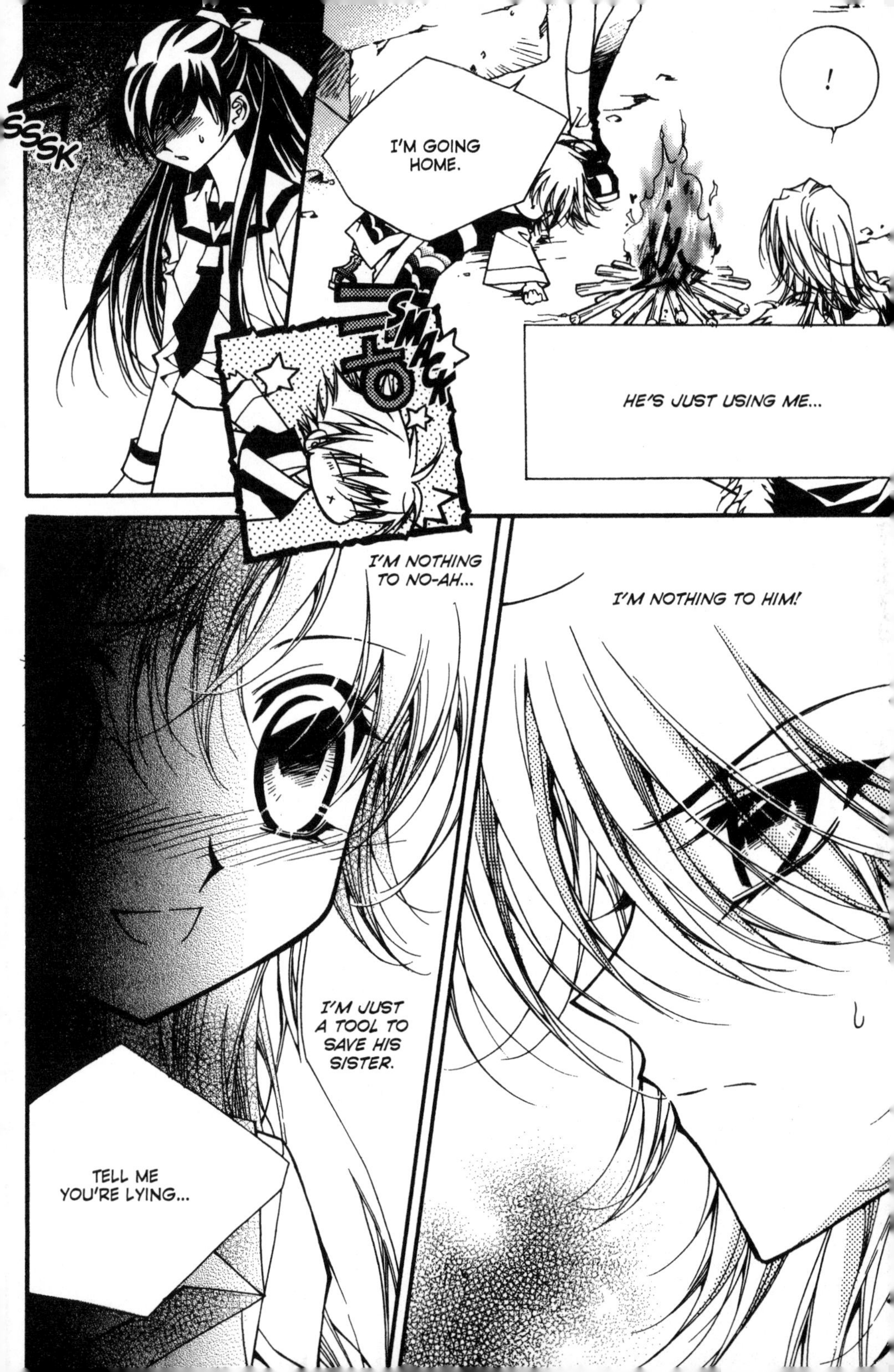
SSSSK
I'M GOING HOME.
SMACK
!
HE'S JUST USING ME...
I'M NOTHING TO NO-AH...
I'M JUST A TOOL TO SAVE HIS SISTER.
TELL ME YOU'RE LYING...
I'M NOTHING TO HIM!

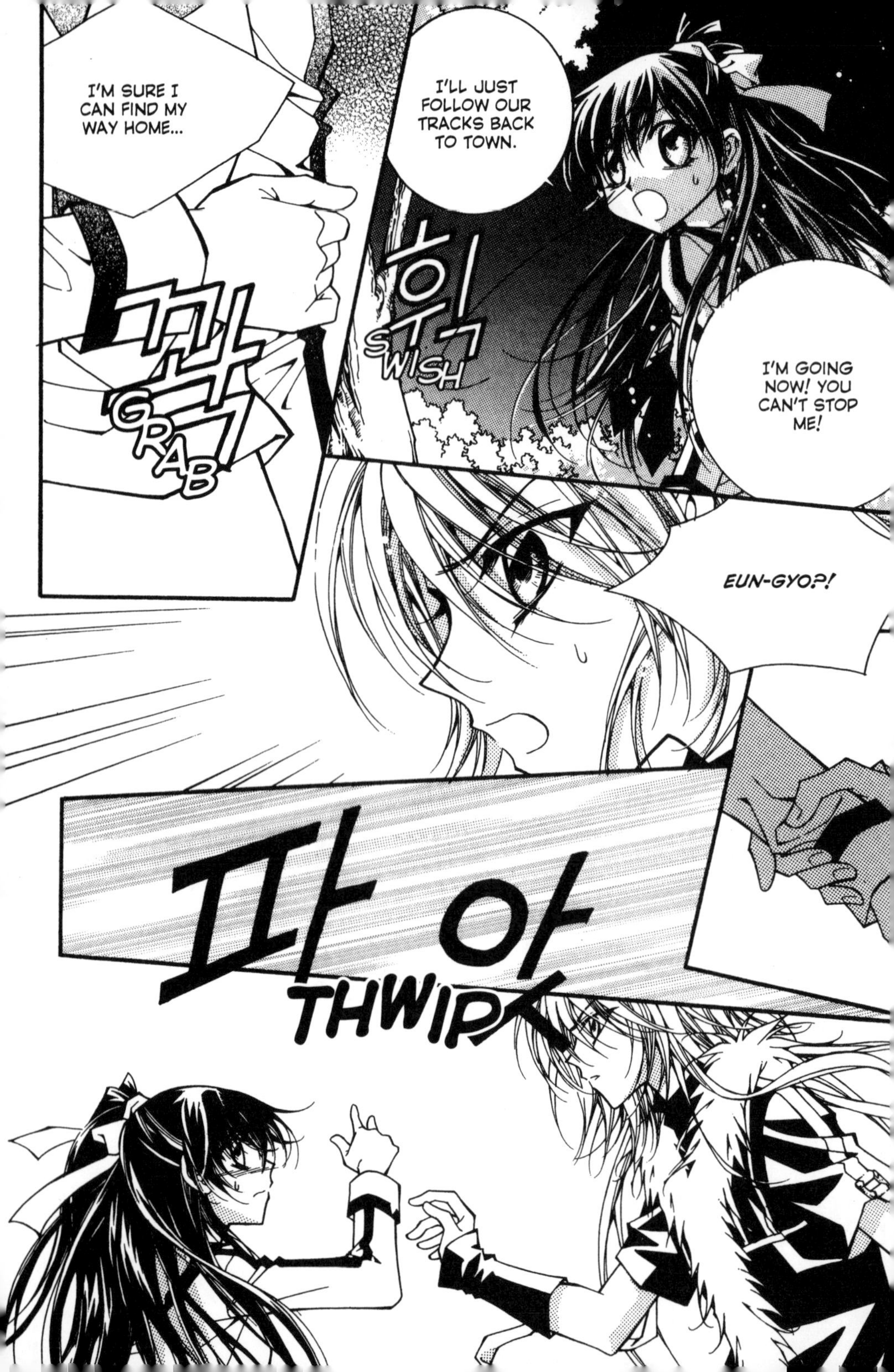
I'M SURE I CAN FIND MY WAY HOME...
꽉
GRAB
I'LL JUST FOLLOW OUR TRACKS BACK TO TOWN.
휙
SWISH
I'M GOING NOW! YOU CAN'T STOP ME!
EUN-GYO?!
파앗
THWIP

I'M SORRY...

ㅎ!
SSK

LEMME GO!
YOU LIAR! YOU
JERK!

I COULDN'T
HATE YOU MORE
RIGHT NOW!
YOU...

$@#*-$#%@!!

↑
HEY, KID! DON'T
USE THIS LANGUAGE
AT HOME! -_-;;

YOU'RE...
YOU'RE
RIGHT.

WHATEVER!
DON'T TRY
SWEET-
TALKING
ME!

I...I SWEAR.

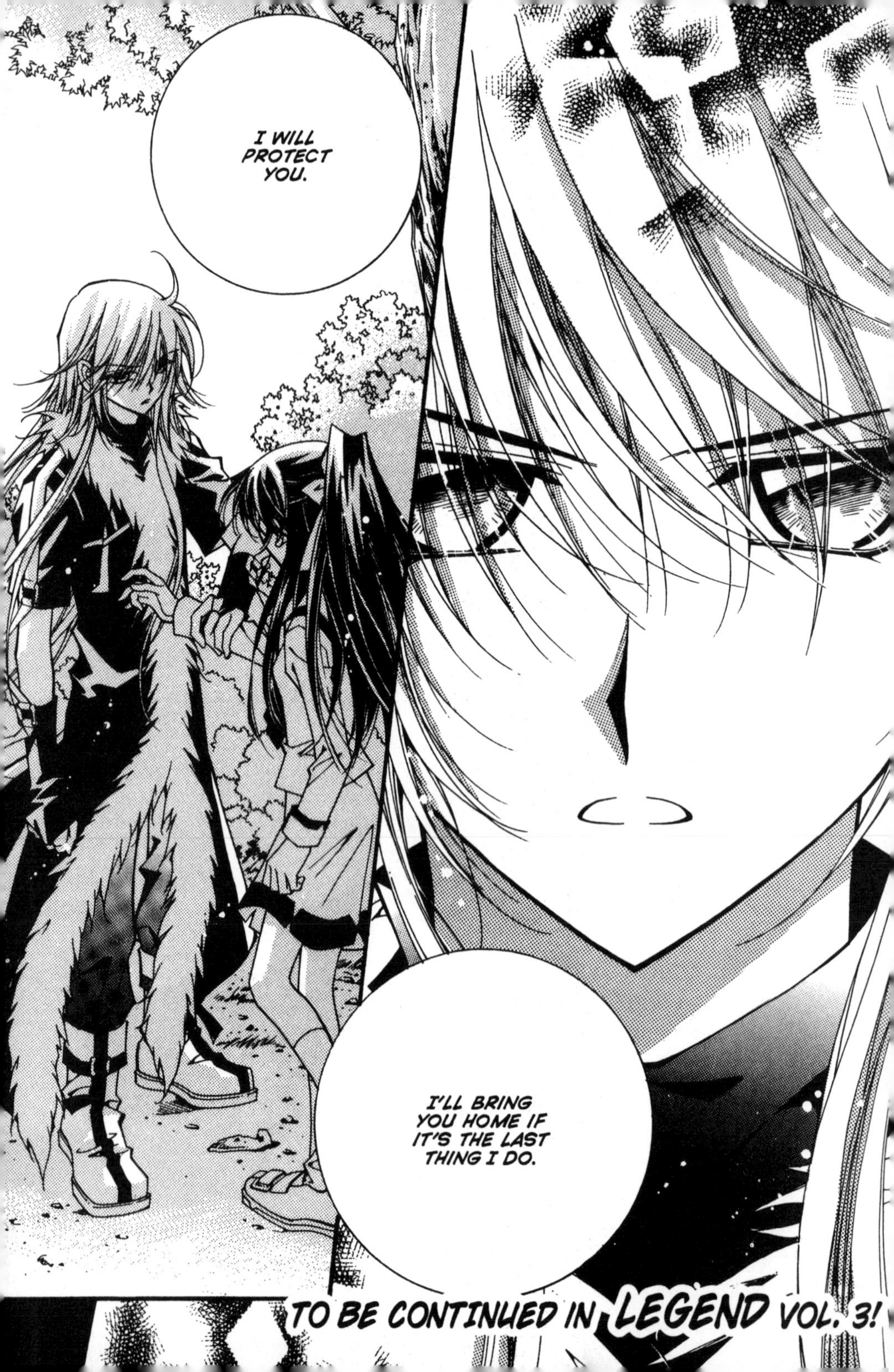
I WILL PROTECT YOU.
I'LL BRING YOU HOME IF IT'S THE LAST THING I DO.
TO BE CONTINUED IN LEGEND VOL. 3!

MINI INTERVIEW

NAME: HO-DONG
AGE: OLD
BLOOD TYPE: B
HEIGHT: 4 FT. 7 IN.
WEIGHT: 71 LB.

PERSONALITY:
PEOPLE SAY I'M HOT HEADED.
I TOTALLY REGRET THE THINGS
I DO BECAUSE OF MY TEMPER.

HOBBY OR SPECIALTY:
SLEEPING. AND DOING NOTHING.

IDEAL GIRL:
SHE'S GOT TO BE SMART AND
QUIET. BEING PRETTY DOESN'T
HURT.

WHEN I'M SAD:
I DON'T HAVE A PROBLEM
EXPRESSING MY EMOTIONS.
EVERYONE SHOULD BE TRUE TO
THEIR FEELINGS.

**WHEN I'M HAVING A HARD
TIME:**
WHEN I HAVE A HARD TIME,
EVERYONE HAS A HARD TIME.

WHAT'S HAPPINESS?
FORGET RIGHT OR WRONG.
HAPPINESS IS WHAT MATTERS
THE MOST!

You're So Cool

vol.1

YoungHee Lee

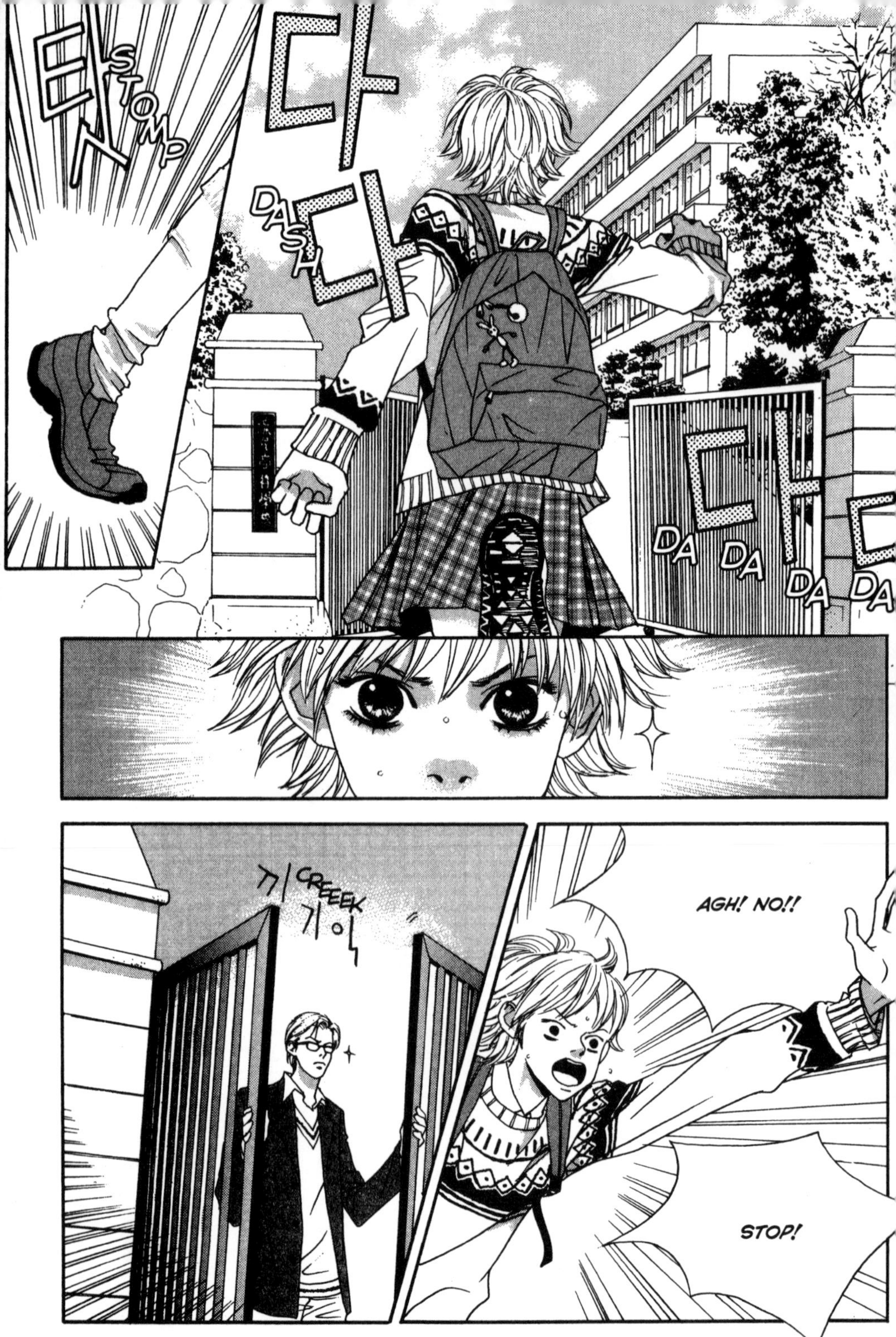
STOMP
DASH
DA DA DA DA
CREEEK
AGH! NO!!
STOP!

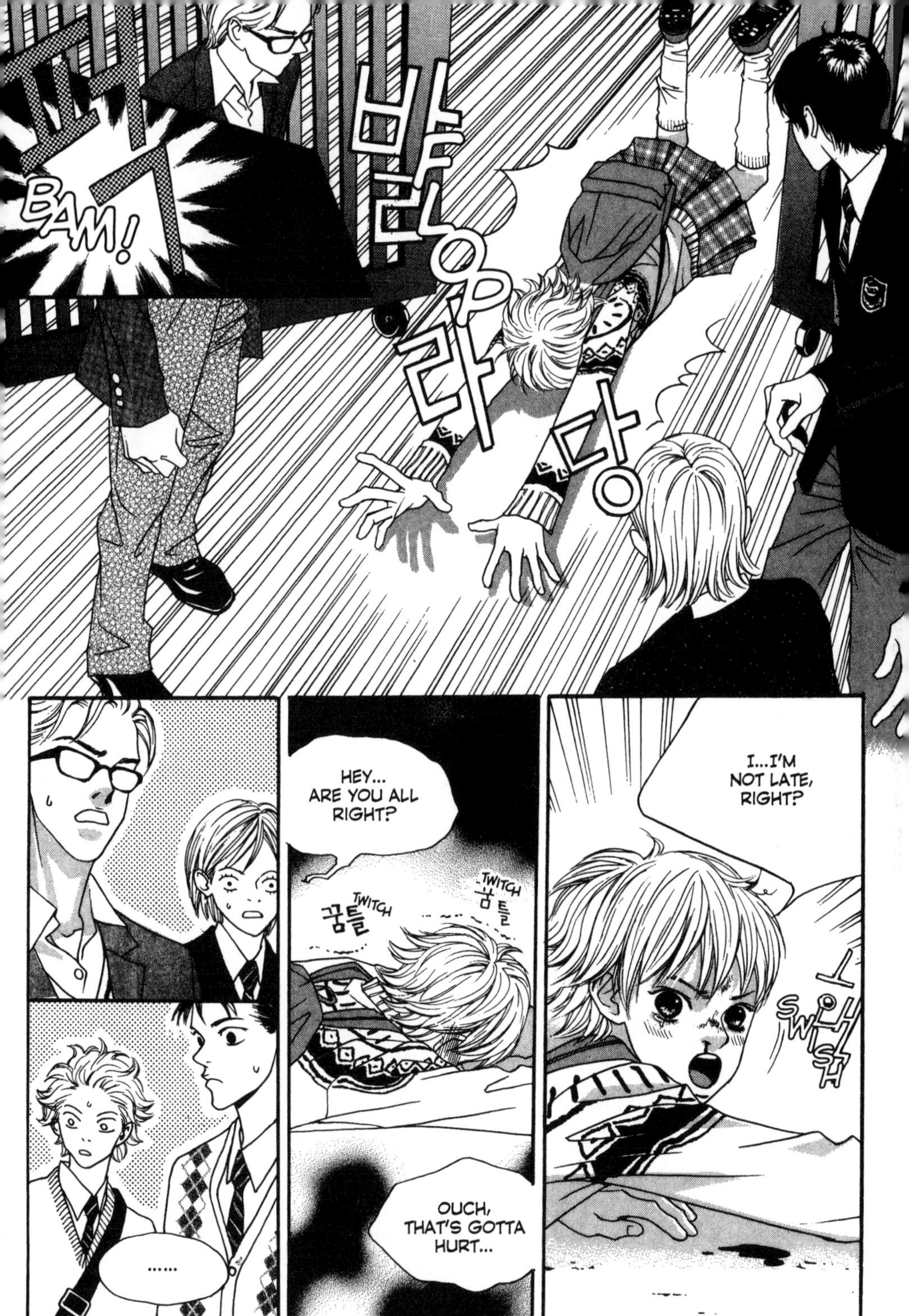
BAM!
HEY... ARE YOU ALL RIGHT?
꿈틀 TWITCH
꿈틀 TWITCH
OUCH, THAT'S GOTTA HURT...
......
I...I'M NOT LATE, RIGHT?
SWISH

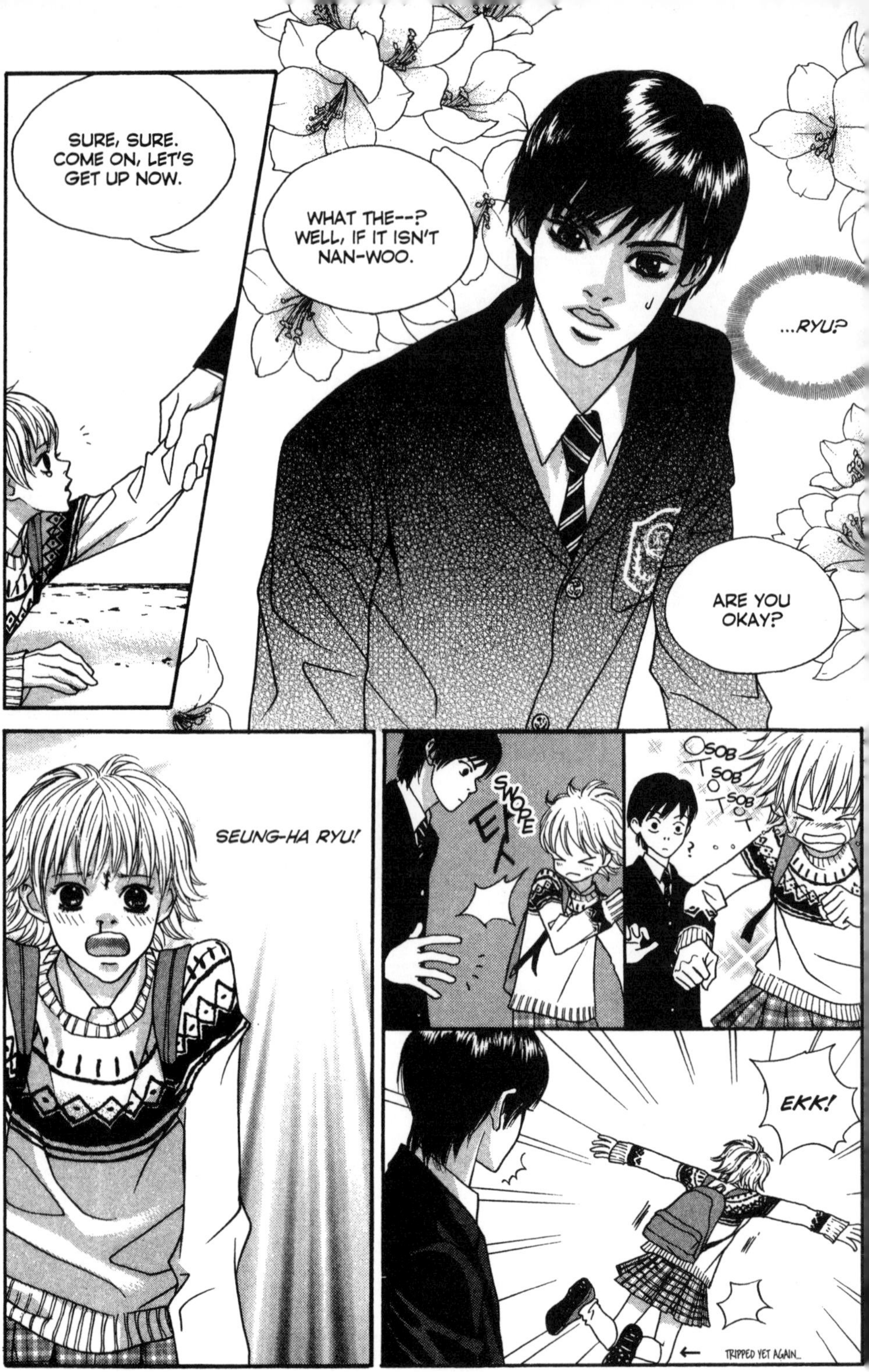
SURE, SURE. COME ON, LET'S GET UP NOW.
WHAT THE--? WELL, IF IT ISN'T NAN-WOO.
...RYU?
ARE YOU OKAY?
SEUNG-HA RYU!
SWOPE
SOB
SOB
SOB
EKK!
TRIPPED YET AGAIN...

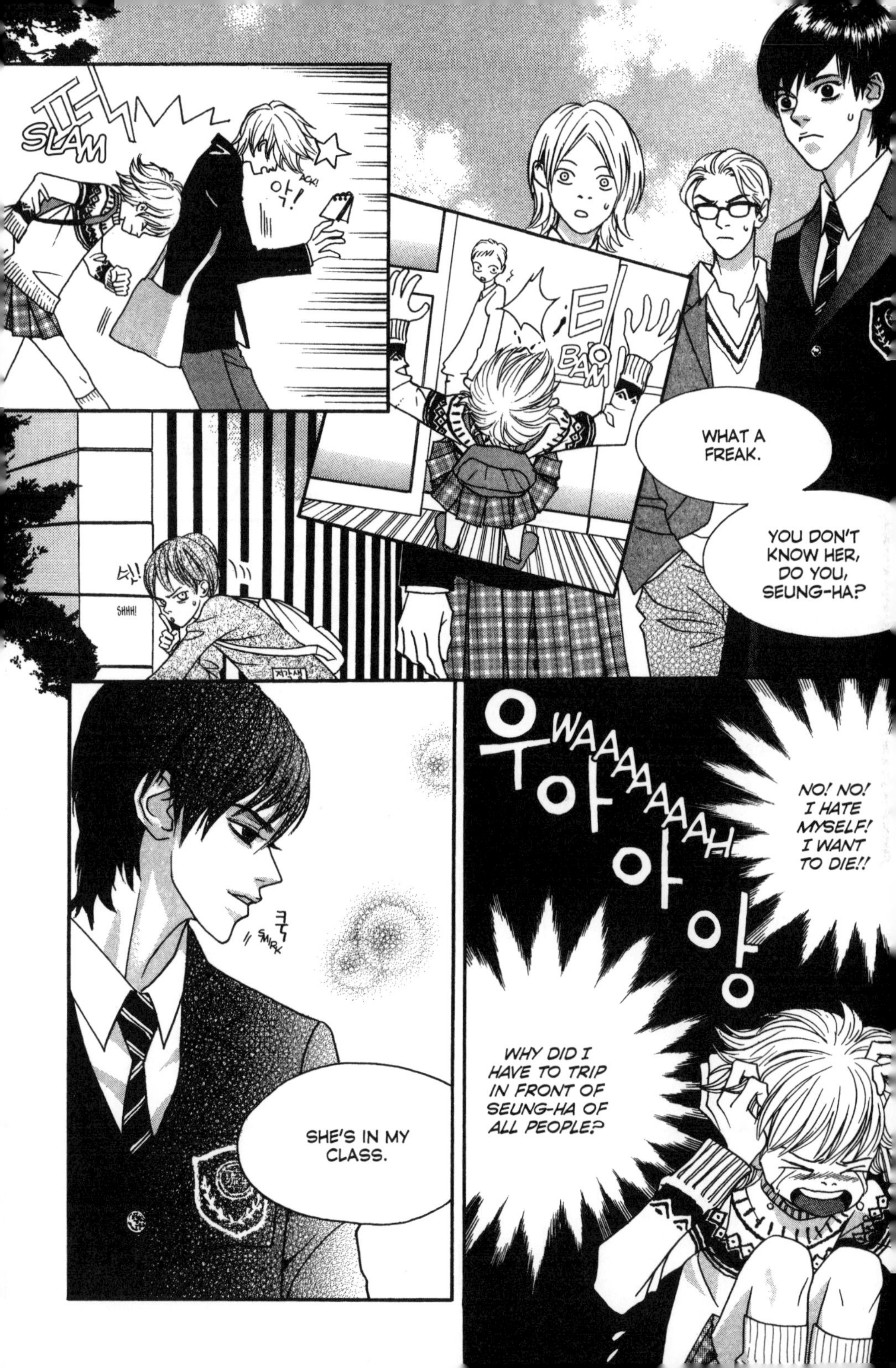
SLAM
악!
ACK!
BAM
쉿!
SHHH!
WHAT A FREAK.
YOU DON'T KNOW HER, DO YOU, SEUNG-HA?
큭
SMIRK
SHE'S IN MY CLASS.
우아아앙
WAAAAAAAAAH
NO! NO! I HATE MYSELF! I WANT TO DIE!!
WHY DID I HAVE TO TRIP IN FRONT OF SEUNG-HA OF ALL PEOPLE?

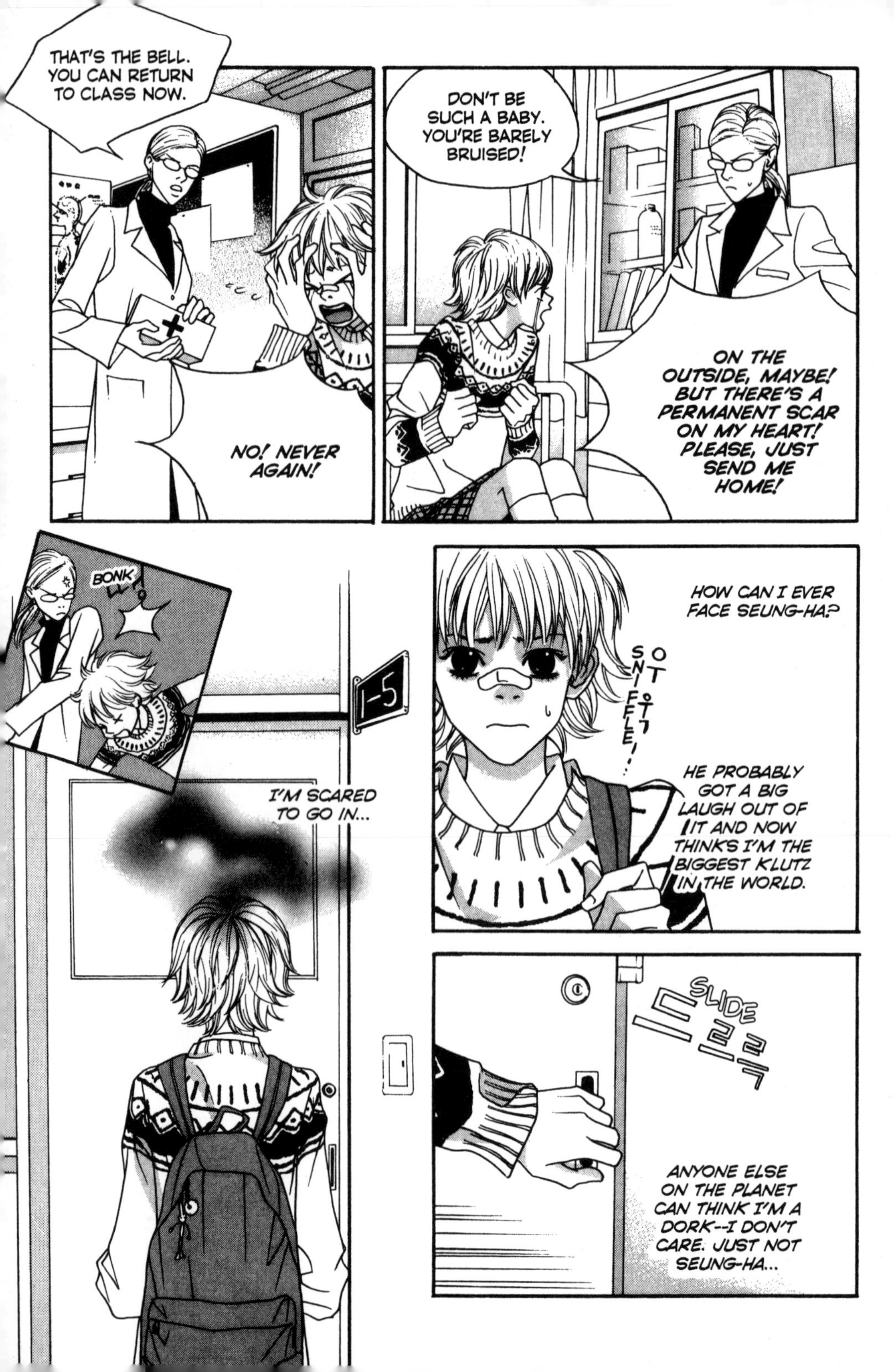
THAT'S THE BELL. YOU CAN RETURN TO CLASS NOW.
NO! NEVER AGAIN!
DON'T BE SUCH A BABY. YOU'RE BARELY BRUISED!
ON THE OUTSIDE, MAYBE! BUT THERE'S A PERMANENT SCAR ON MY HEART! PLEASE, JUST SEND ME HOME!
BONK
I'M SCARED TO GO IN...
1-5
HOW CAN I EVER FACE SEUNG-HA?
SNIFFLE!
HE PROBABLY GOT A BIG LAUGH OUT OF IT AND NOW THINKS I'M THE BIGGEST KLUTZ IN THE WORLD.
SLIDE
ANYONE ELSE ON THE PLANET CAN THINK I'M A DORK--I DON'T CARE. JUST NOT SEUNG-HA...

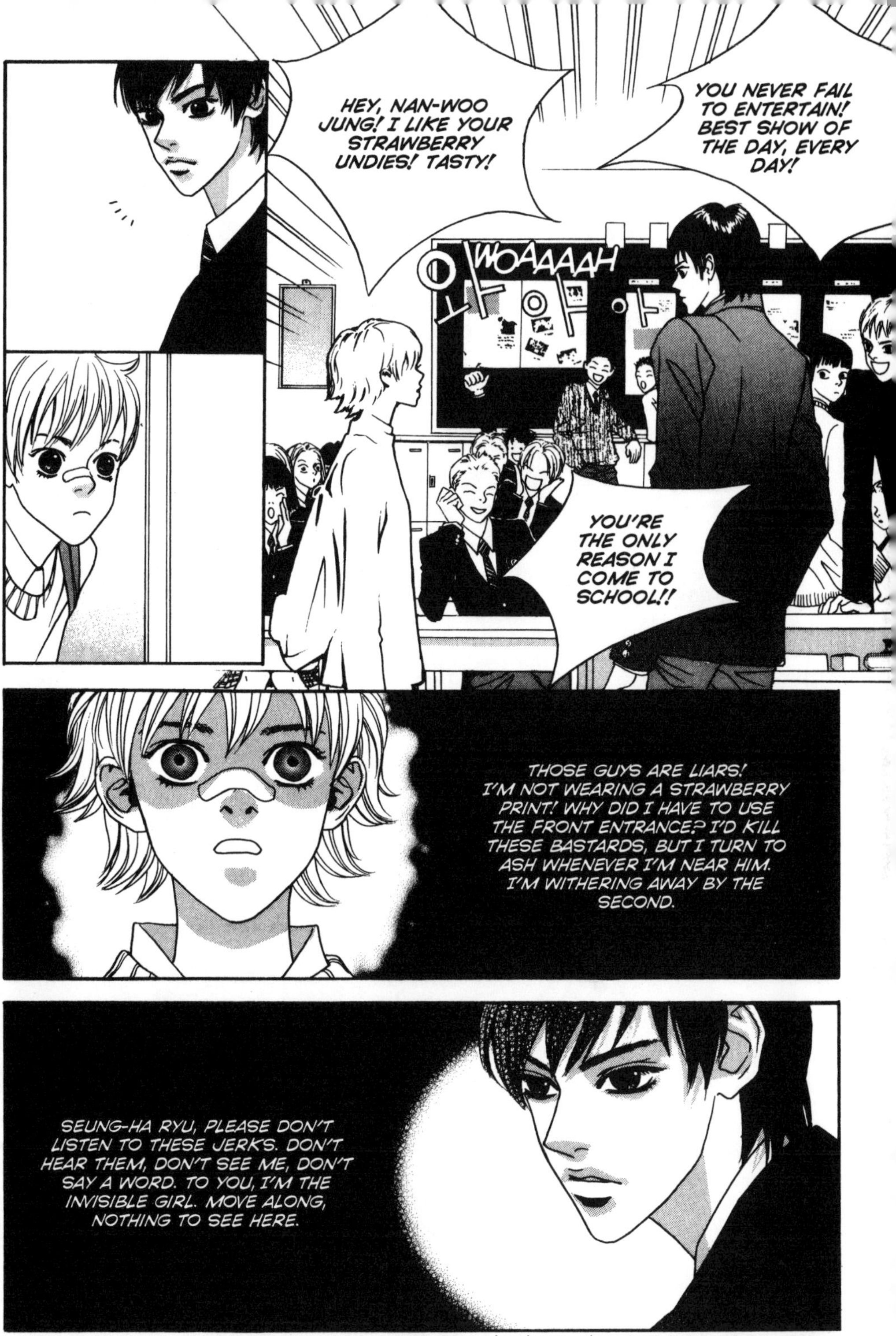
HEY, NAN-WOO JUNG! I LIKE YOUR STRAWBERRY UNDIES! TASTY!
YOU NEVER FAIL TO ENTERTAIN! BEST SHOW OF THE DAY, EVERY DAY!
WOAAAAH
YOU'RE THE ONLY REASON I COME TO SCHOOL!!
THOSE GUYS ARE LIARS! I'M NOT WEARING A STRAWBERRY PRINT! WHY DID I HAVE TO USE THE FRONT ENTRANCE? I'D KILL THESE BASTARDS, BUT I TURN TO ASH WHENEVER I'M NEAR HIM. I'M WITHERING AWAY BY THE SECOND.
SEUNG-HA RYU, PLEASE DON'T LISTEN TO THESE JERKS. DON'T HEAR THEM, DON'T SEE ME, DON'T SAY A WORD. TO YOU, I'M THE INVISIBLE GIRL. MOVE ALONG, NOTHING TO SEE HERE.

TO BE CONTINUED IN YOU'RE SO COOL VOL. 1

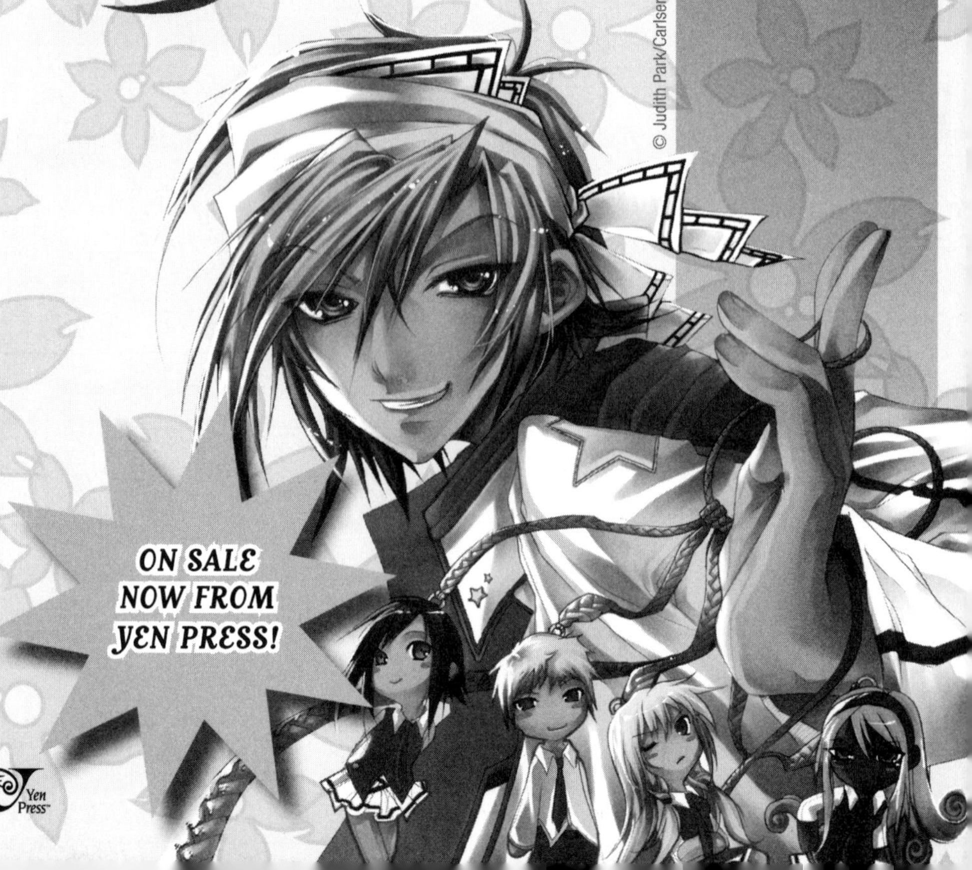
ON SALE
NOW FROM
YEN PRESS!

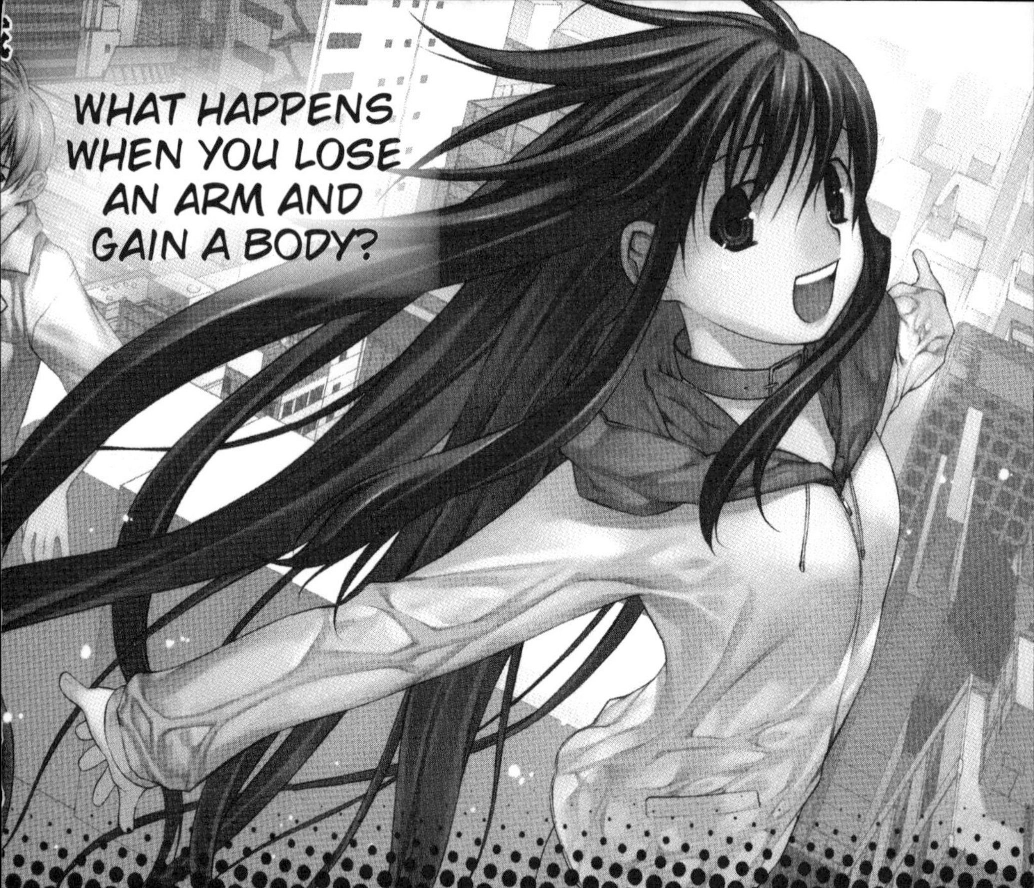
WHAT HAPPENS WHEN YOU LOSE AN ARM AND GAIN A BODY?

Legend vol. 2

Story by SooJung Woo
Art by Kara

Translation: HyeYoung Im
English Adaptation: J. Torres
Lettering: Terri Delgado · Marshall Dillon

Legend, Vol. 2 © 2005 Kara · SooJung Woo. All rights reserved. First published in Korea in 2005 by Seoul Cultural Publishers, Inc. English translation rights arranged by Seoul Cultural Publishers, Inc.

English edition © 2008 Hachette Book Group USA, Inc.

The characters and events in this book are fictitious. Any similarity to real persons, living or dead, is coincidental and not intended by the author.

Yen Press
Hachette Book Group USA
237 Park Avenue, New York, NY 10017

Visit our Web sites at www.HachetteBookGroupUSA.com and www.YenPress.com.

Yen Press is an imprint of Hachette Book Group USA, Inc. The Yen Press name and logo are trademarks of Hachette Book Group USA, Inc.

First Yen Press Edition: May 2008

ISBN-10: 0-7595-2868-3
ISBN-13: 978-0-7595-2868-0

10 9 8 7 6 5 4 3 2 1

BVG

Printed in the United States of America